PRAISE FOR *UNDER THE*

"Acclaimed inequality essayist and comm
White America: Letter to a New Minority, 2012, etc.) reports on the damage being incurred in America whereby "the have-nots and have-lessers are dehumanized while the elite are venerated." In describing how modern society has become a "culture of cruelty," as past attempts to sympathize and support those less fortunate have collapsed beneath the weight of classism and racism, the author explores the framework and the consequences of the nation's economic crisis. He lucidly ponders its genesis as well as the ramifications of wealth inequality, including the rampant demonization of the poor and the valorization of the rich by way of what he refers to as "Scroogism." Wise's extensive experience as an anti-racism activist and a longtime member of the radical left greatly informs his text, which demonstrates, through facts and case histories, that America's enduring racial divide continues to be directly tied to its economic problems. His well-rounded scholarly discussion benefits from the varying intellectual perspectives he offers, including opinions on the damaging effects of blind corporate obeisance to the "myth of meritocracy." What is apparent, he believes, is the need for solutions to achieve the kind of "culture of compassion" necessary for true redemption and a dismantling of social stratification. Wise recognizes that this achievement is a tall order to fill, particularly in the presence of the current elite economic oligarchy possessing the capital and the influence to trounce equalization efforts. Sharp and provocative...the book concludes with hope that his analysis and those like it will spur a counter-narrative outwardly challenging the false notion that both the wealthy and the poor "deserve" their places within our culture's economic stratum. An impassioned, intellectual, and vigorously dense report on the repercussions of severe socioeconomic imbalance in the United States."

—*Kirkus Reviews*

"Tim Wise is one of the great public moralists in America today. In his bracing new book, *Under the Affluence*, he brilliantly engages the roots and ramifications of radical inequality in our nation, carefully detailing the heartless war against the poor and the swooning addiction to the rich that exposes the moral sickness at the heart of our culture. Wise's stirring analysis of our predicament is more than a disinterested social scientific treatise; this book is a valiant call to arms against the vicious practices that undermine the best of the American ideals we claim to cherish. *Under the Affluence* is vintage Tim Wise: smart, sophisticated, conscientious, and righteously indignant at the betrayal of millions of citizens upon whose backs the American Dream rests. This searing testimony for the most vulnerable in our nation is also a courageous cry for justice that we must all heed."

—Michael Eric Dyson, author of *The Black Presidency: Barack Obama and the Politics of Race in America*

"Tim Wise has produced an eloquent, meticulously researched book that could make economic inequality a central issue in the 2016 presidential election. The book I can best compare it to is Michael Harrington's *The Other America* which helped inspire 'The War On Poverty.' Written in passionate prose, invoking honored American traditions, it has the power to change minds and melt hearts. I look forward to sharing it with my students, and with anyone else concerned with justice and equity."

—Mark Naison, author of *White Boy: A Memoir* and *Badass Teachers Unite!*

"America 'under the affluence' is a cruel and heartless place. By word and by deed, we turn against the poor and feast on a diet of resentment and myths. If anyone can unpack the racist and patriarchal lies that undergird our current culture of cruelty, Tim Wise can. In clear, simple language, product of a lifetime of research, he describes how we got here and how we might build a more compassionate place. We need his voice."

—Laura Flanders, author of *Blue Grit*

"A single image—watching the Super Bowl under conditions like our distribution of wealth—is worth the price of *Under the Affluence*. Most of us are dying, crushed because we're stacked 50 in a seat, while the 1% ... But read it for yourself. Wise has spent many hours reading what the Right has written to dehumanize poor people, so you don't have to! He humanizes them back, using real evidence."

—James Loewen, author of *Lies My Teacher Told Me*

PRAISE FOR TIM WISE

"What Tim Wise has brilliantly done is to challenge white folks... to see that they have a responsibility to do more than sit back and watch, but to recognize their own role in co-creating what is either a fair, inclusive, truly democratic society or a society that is predicated on indifference towards those who are labeled as 'others'..."

—Michelle Alexander, author of *The New Jim Crow: Mass Incarceration in an Age of Colorblindness*

"Tim Wise is a truth-teller and long distance freedom-fighter. He is my vanilla brother whose fight against White Supremacy is exemplary and inspiring!"

—Cornel West

"(Wise's) work is revolutionary, and those who react negatively are simply afraid of hearing the truth."

—Robin D.G. Kelley, author of *Yo' Mama's Disfunktional !: Fighting the Culture Wars in Urban America*

"The fate of this country depends on whites like yourself speaking the truth to those who don't want to hear it. In this, you are as one with the Biblical prophets. You are more likely to be condemned than lauded, and yet your words are no less important. So, keep speaking out. At the very least, some future archeologists sifting through the ashes of this civilization may be able to find evidence that there were some who offered truth as a cure for the disease that destroyed us."

—Derrick Bell, author of *Silent Covenants: Brown v. Board of Education and the Unfulfilled Hopes for Racial Reform*

"Tim Wise is a spellbinding herald of anti-racism. His voice resonates especially with young people of all races who represent a generational shift away from the racial toxins and taboos that have been a blot on American democracy."

—Stephen Steinberg, Distinguished Professor of Urban Studies, Queens College & the Graduate Center, CUNY

"Tim Wise is one of the few people, along with perhaps Frederick Douglass, who has ever really spoken honestly and forcefully to white people about themselves. . . ."

—Charles Ogletree, Professor of Law, Harvard Law School; Director, Charles Hamilton Houston Institute for Race and Justice

UNDER THE AFFLUENCE

Shaming the Poor, Praising the Rich and Sacrificing the Future of America

Tim Wise

Open Media Series | City Lights Books

Cover design: Herb Thornby

Open Media Series Editor: Greg Ruggiero

Library of Congress Cataloging-in-Publication Data
Wise, Tim J.
Under the affluence : shaming the poor, praising the rich and sacrificing the future of America / Tim Wise.
pages cm. — (City Lights open media)
ISBN 978-0-87286-693-5 (paperback)
ISBN 978-0-87286-695-9 (ebook)
1. Equality—United States. 2. Social classes—United States. 3. Poverty—United States. 4. Wealth—United States. 5. Racism—United States. 6. Discrimination—United States. 7. United States—Economic conditions—2009- 8. United States—Social conditions—1980- I. Title.

HN90.S6W57 2015
305.0973—dc23

2015022986

City Lights Books are published at the City Lights Bookstore
261 Columbus Avenue, San Francisco, CA 94133
www.citylights.com

Contents

Any city, however small, is in fact divided into two, one the city of the poor, the other of the rich; these are at war with one another.

—Plato

INTRODUCTION

When Charles Dickens began *A Tale of Two Cities* with the famous line "It was the best of times, it was the worst of times," he was referring to conditions in eighteenth-century London and Paris, prior to the French Revolution: a time during which the splendor of great wealth and power rested uncomfortably aside the rising discontent of the masses. Pointing out the grotesque economic, social and moral contradictions of feudal Europe was Dickens's purpose, accomplished by the author in a style and to an extent rarely matched before or since. And yet, although it was a very different time and a very different place than that in which (and from which) I write these words today, much of modern life in the United States calls to mind this opening literary salvo, for here too we can see a tale of two cities, or rather, two nations, increasingly in conflict.

On the one hand, millionaires and even billionaires are being minted at a dizzying pace. McMansions, high-end real estate developments and gated communities are popping up all over the country, barely slowed for even a moment by the economic crisis that struck in the first few months of 2008. The high-end luxury market for everything from cars to private planes to vacation packages to fashion is steaming ahead full bore, with those able to access said markets earning more than ever, able to create for themselves a secure, private and cloistered world. This is an America that regularly pampers its pets at luxurious day spas, adds to its already impressive wine cellars bottles that will never be drunk but are merely to be possessed, and takes regular weekend trips to places most Americans will never see except by way of a

Google search.[1] This is an America willing and able to pay $1 million for a guaranteed parking spot in New York's SoHo,[2] or $9,000 a year to have their own private Facebook rip-off called Netropolitan,[3] which allows them to avoid having their feed cluttered with pictures of middle-class people's cats. This is an America where the thirteen-year-old children of the nation's wealthy help their parents pick out multimillion-dollar condos for the family,[4] and where twenty-two-year-olds to whom the *New York Times* refers as "creative souls" wince at the prospects of finding decent places to live in the city for a mere $3,700 per month.[5] It's an America that throws $50,000 birthday parties for its children because you're only seven once, and it's an America whose richest college students hire "concierge" services to help them do everything: "decorate apartments, get academic tutoring, snag coveted restaurant reservations and handle a litany of other bothersome chores," not to mention assisting them when it comes to getting bidets installed in their fancy bathrooms.[6]

On the other hand, and in stark contrast to this America of ostentatious wealth, there is another, very different, country. Although housed within the borders of the nation itself, it looks nothing like the one previously mentioned; it exists almost as a parallel universe, in which the inhabitants technically share the same galaxy as their better-off cousins and yet experience life entirely differently. It is a world in which millions of households continue to struggle, irrespective of the loudly trumpeted assurances from financial elites that economic recovery is upon us. It's a world in which families continue to face the loss of their homes to foreclosure, and where a serious health emergency can still bankrupt families; where the cost of higher education remains prohibitive for millions; where hundreds of thousands each night face homelessness and food insecurity; where the food pantries and shelters meant to care for such persons as these are short on supplies and space,[7] and where long-term unemployment—jobless spells lasting twenty-six, fifty-two, even ninety-nine weeks or more—are increasingly common. Millions who lost their jobs during the Great Recession are only now beginning to crawl out of the financial hole into which their families fell; and for many, if they have found new work, it is for lower pay, fewer benefits, and less real security than they enjoyed in their previous positions.

These two Americas pass each other occasionally on the street, in the line at a fast-food restaurant or coffee shop, at the grocery, at a sporting event, or in the park on a sunny day. Members of each America may listen to much of the same music, go to the same movies, and watch many of the same television shows; and yet their occasional proximity to one another does little to bridge the experiential gap between them. They may be watching the same game, so to speak, but some are watching it from increasingly remote skyboxes while others are nestled down in the worst possible general admission seats, and still others are having to watch from home on a barely functioning television set. It is not merely that two Americas exist, but that they are pulling farther and farther apart. In some particularly disturbing cases, these two Americas live right next door to one another, in apartment buildings in New York, for instance—but those with lower incomes are being asked to use separate entrances to the same buildings,[8] are prevented from using various building amenities,[9] or have their balcony space limited by a wire fence, behind which they must remain, unlike their more affluent neighbors.[10] In places like San Francisco, where the tech boom has produced staggering amounts of new wealth, tens of thousands of others are struggling to survive in a city where the gap between rich and poor is now actually higher than in Rwanda and only slightly less extreme than it is in Guatemala.[11]

That said, this book is not about those disparities per se. Plenty of writers have tackled that subject, documenting in painstaking detail the ways that inequality is deepening. Although I too will recite some of the woeful evidence of this increasing economic divide, my task here is less to describe the existence of two Americas than to provide some analytical framework for understanding how we got here and why it matters. For our problem is not merely a material one: it is not simply that we are becoming more unjust in terms of income and wealth distribution; we are also becoming a place where the way we *speak* about matters of inequality and economic injustice is increasingly disturbing. As the title of this book suggests, we are a nation increasingly "under the affluence," meaning not only the power of those with excess wealth, but also subordinated to a mentality and ideology of affluence, the effect of which is to rationalize and normalize inequities, no matter how vast and how deep. The end result of all this has been to deepen a culture of cruelty, in which the conditions of the impoverished, the underemployed and the struggling are justified as the inevitable result of inadequate effort on their part, or of cultural flaws, while the wealth and success of the rich are likewise rationalized as owing to their superior talent or value systems.

With all due respect to those who have raised the issue of inequality in the past several years, including activists in the Occupy movement, the broader trends in terms of how we talk about economic disparity are not promising. Increasingly, the right-wing media, politicians and their followers demonize the poor, the unemployed, those lacking health care or those in need of public assistance. The have-nots and have-lessers are dehumanized while the rich are venerated. The political narrative of the "makers and the takers"—those who create wealth and those who are presumably dependent on others—has become not merely a passing political meme, as with the 2012 presidential election; indeed, it has become an almost routine ideological construct, parroted by talk-show hosts and talking heads, and believed by millions who follow their every word. Although most Republicans running for president in 2016 have avoided the polarizing rhetoric that damaged Mitt Romney in the last race, there have been exceptions, as with Donald Trump's vicious attacks on Mexican people. And with the conservative narrative tethered to the notion that the rich create value and the poor live off the rest of us, it is unlikely that top-down class warfare will remain in abeyance for long.

The purpose of this volume is to document the increasingly vituperative narrative of cruelty as regards those at the bottom of the nation's class structure, and to understand why the United States, virtually alone among modern democracies, seems so hostile toward the poor and those in need. What separates us in this regard from the nations with which we like to compare ourselves, nearly all of which have far more generous programs of social uplift, from guaranteed national health care to paid maternity (and even paternity) leave to more extensive unemployment insurance? And why has the national mood about such government efforts on behalf of those in need turned increasingly sour in recent decades?

After all, it wasn't always like this: there was a period from roughly the 1930s until the early 1970s during which large numbers of Americans embraced a more robust and proactive role for government in fighting inequality and ensuring opportunity. Aware of the cruelties of the Gilded Age and the era of the corporate robber barons, Americans had become increasingly skeptical of great fortunes and those who possessed them. The idea that the state had a role to play in the fulfillment of the so-called American Dream was one that was largely accepted by the nation's people. Although the commitment to this ideal was highly selective—so that, as we'll discuss, the programs of the New Deal that were instrumental in creating the white middle class were made largely off-limits to persons of color—there was still a general consensus in the land that the nation had an obligation to help those who were unemployed, poor or hungry (at least so long as they were white). Today, even that race-bound consensus has largely been obliterated. So when and why did the public mood in this regard shift, and what does that tell us about the challenges that lie ahead? It is this question that drives much of the discussion in this book. That, and then the obvious follow-up: How do we move from a growing culture of cruelty to a culture of compassion where we not only perceive and relate to our fellow Americans with a sense of solidarity, but in which public policy reflects community, mutual kindness and concern, and where the idea of the common good is revived so as to replace the alienating, disconnected individualism that threatens to destroy us?

For those familiar with my work, this may seem like a strange departure for me. For someone whose writing and activism have centered mostly on matters of race and racism, a book concerning the nation's class divide and its dangers may appear to be an odd detour. But actually, this volume is a logical extension of that previous work and is much informed by it. The class system in the United States has a very different provenance than class systems in other societies, and much of that difference concerns the unique role of racism and white supremacy in the development of America's economic hierarchy. It is this unique history and the centrality of racism to the development of America's class system that undergirds the culture of cruelty about which this book is concerned. The intersections of race and class have made addressing inequalities here more complicated than in many other modern democracies with more monocultural populations. Unless we understand that, attempts to rectify the current situation will likely fail. It is precisely the lack of a racial analysis among many progressives who focus on economic matters, which makes this volume necessary.

Far from a radical departure, this is a book that has been a long time coming for me. As a young activist I often found myself discussing the ways in which impoverished communities were scapegoated by the political right. My first job out of college was as a youth coordinator and then assistant director of the main group charged with derailing the political campaigns of neo-Nazi and lifelong white supremacist David Duke. Duke, the former Ku Klux Klan leader, had been elected to the Louisiana legislature in 1989, largely by bashing social welfare programs and those receiving benefits from them. By 1990 and 1991 he was seeking to turn resentment toward the poor and those on public assistance, especially blacks, to his advantage as he ran for the United States Senate and then governor of Louisiana. By accusing so-called "welfare mothers" of fraud, laziness and an insatiable desire to birth children out of wedlock, Duke ramped up a narrative that was not his alone—it had become by then a staple of conservative politics going back at least a quarter-century—but which in many ways he had honed to unique and disturbing effect. Much of my time in those campaigns was spent organizing in communities where fending off these racist and classist narratives became the primary job description.

My time in New Orleans has everything to do with why I decided to write this book. I lived there from 1986 to 1996, and my understanding of matters both racial and economic largely owes to that experience. It was from community activists as much as my professors at Tulane that I learned about inequality in America. Since I left, their lessons have only become clearer, especially in the wake of Hurricane Katrina in 2005, and its aftermath. I've traveled to New Orleans many times since, and have witnessed both the ongoing problems of poverty and racial inequity, as well as the way city leaders have put on a polished patina for tourists as if the tragedy had never happened. Developers have swooped in and redesigned entire neighborhoods for more affluent residents, while landlords have hiked rents from a third to seventy-five percent above pre-storm averages. Meanwhile, most of the city's public housing stock has been destroyed, with the residents displaced but rarely relocated in comparable and affordable private housing. New Orleans is a city of distinct haves and have-nots, even more so than before, with the second-largest gap between the rich and the poor of any city in the United States[12]—a tale of two cities, indeed.

Having worked in several public housing developments in New Orleans during the mid-1990s, after the work against David Duke, I came to know hundreds of the folks who called those communities home. There I learned—far more so than I could have from academic books or scholarly research—that the perceptions we often have of people in public housing (and of the poor more generally) are little more than vile caricatures. It was during that time that I came to know Donna Johnigan, a resident of public housing and a colleague at Agenda for Children, the community-based group for which I did my organizing. One weekend her son was murdered, one of more than three hundred young black men killed that year in the city; yet, come Monday, she was at work, insisting that she had a job to do and was determined to do it. I remember thinking how often throughout my life, and even at that particular job, I had called in sick for no better reason than being tired or because I had been out too late the night before; but here was a mother who had just buried her son and who was nonetheless rolling up her sleeves and getting back to the work at hand. This, in a society that too often deems as lazy those who live in public housing or receive other forms of public assistance. America has never met Donna Johnigan, either literally or figuratively; most Americans do not even know that persons such as she exist.

Several years after I had left New Orleans, I stumbled upon a news item in the online version of the *Times Picayune*, the city's main newspaper, that prompted me to pen this volume. It was late July 2012 when I came across the piece, featuring a photo of a young black child on the steps outside an apartment in the Iberville housing development, which sits to the side of the French Quarter and slightly up from Canal Street—the main artery of the Central Business District.[13] The photo bore little relationship to the article it accompanied (which concerned the pending implosion of a nearby office building and fears that dust produced by its destruction might pose a health risk), but in all likelihood attracted more attention than the story itself, seeing as how it pictured that child sitting on a project stoop holding what appeared to be an iPad.

It shouldn't be too difficult to envision the outrage that greeted the site's comment boards and streamed into the personal email of the author of the article that accompanied the photo.[14] Some asked, with only the most thinly veiled hostility: How could someone in the projects afford an iPad? It just goes to show the ubiquity of welfare fraud, suggested others. There were resentments too, as some indicated that they couldn't afford an iPad for their own children but here was someone in the projects who had one. The general tenor of the reaction was swift, furious and disturbing. Later revelations that the child's parents had bought him the iPad with their own money, and that he had only been visiting relatives in the neighborhood, helped stanch the anger among some, but even then, merely reinforced the larger point: namely, if he *had* been a project resident, he surely would not have deserved the luxury of technology that proved out of reach to so many others. If he *had* been a resident of the so-called ghetto, he would clearly be of such inferior stock as to barely merit compassion at all, or so the logic seemed to suggest.

It's the kind of narrative that has long been typical in this country. When I worked in the city's public housing developments and would tell people what I did, they would almost always express their disdain for those I was working with, none of whom they had ever met. The poor and those in public housing were lazy fraudsters in their estimation, gaming the system, and of course, they all needed to take "personal responsibility" for their lives rather than expecting the government to take care of them. It didn't matter to these folks that most of their beliefs about low-income communities were wrong, as we'll see. They knew what they knew. Facts could hardly dislodge the fervently held fictions to which they seemed so indissolubly wedded.

It was a narrative that reemerged with a vengeance after Katrina, at which point conservative commentators rapidly retreated to blame-the-victim mode, bashing the poor of the city for not having the wherewithal to evacuate before the flooding due to a well-entrenched dependence on government bred by the welfare state.[15] This they insisted upon, even though census data indicated there had only been 4,600 households in New Orleans receiving cash welfare at the time of the flooding—4,600 households out of a citywide total of 225,000 households.[16] With a typical household size of two to three persons, this means that even if *all* 120,000 people stuck in New Orleans during Katrina had been poor, and even if no one receiving public assistance had managed to escape before the flooding, no more than ten percent of those stuck during the flooding would have been welfare recipients, let alone persons rendered dependent on benefits for long periods. Indeed, the notion of dependence on such benefits was laughable: at the time of Katrina, the average cash benefit for New Orleans households receiving aid under the Temporary Assistance for Needy Families program (TANF) came to only about $2,800 *per year*.[17] Even food stamps (now known as SNAP, or the Supplemental Nutrition Assistance Program)—a program with more lenient terms allowing even the near-poor to qualify for minimal benefits—were only received by eleven percent of New Orleans households as of Katrina. Clearly, such minimal coverage was hardly indicative of a general mindset of welfare entitlement in the city.[18]

Even in the poorest communities of New Orleans, like the Iberville or Lafitte housing developments or parts of Central City, at least one-third and often a majority of households reported income from paid employment before Katrina.[19] By the time of the aforementioned article on Iberville and the photo that accompanied it, the residents of the community bore little resemblance to the stereotype. Among households in Iberville, two out of three were *not* headed by a single mother with children, roughly three in four adults had at least a high school diploma or GED, and nearly half of all resident income was being earned from employment. Another thirty-six percent of resident income came from Social Security payments to elderly residents and the disabled,[20] who together comprised nearly a third of all heads of household in the community.[21] Only 7.5 percent of income there was represented by TANF benefits, or what most call "welfare." In other words, residents of Iberville were far more likely to receive income from work (either past or present) or from disability payments than from cash assistance.

Upon seeing the photo and again being exposed to the vitriol regularly aimed at some of the nation's most vulnerable, I began thinking about what such a display might mean. What might it say about the times we live in and the culture we share? What might such hostility, such resentment, such contempt for the poor say about where we're headed as a nation? Since bashing the poor has been so common in recent decades, some might say there was nothing particularly remarkable about the response to that photograph. But something about it struck me as deeply indicative of a broader national trend, something even angrier and uglier than much of the rhetoric many of us remember hearing during the 1980s, when Ronald Reagan had come to power criticizing "welfare queens" and promising to pare back public assistance.

As we'll see, it is not just that attitudes toward the poor seem more vicious than ever; there is also an increasing and parallel valorization of the rich, and a concerted effort on the part of some to justify the growing gaps in income and wealth between the nation's haves and have-nots. As the Occupy movement—which emerged in 2011 and sought to challenge inequality between the nation's wealthiest one percent and the bottom ninety-nine percent—gained steam, America's wealthy began working overtime to rationalize their status. During the 2012 presidential campaign, Republican candidate Mitt Romney suggested that there were forty-seven percent of Americans whom he could never reach because they didn't want to work and were comfortable living on government handouts. Meanwhile, his Republican running mate, Congressman Paul Ryan, has claimed that as many as six in ten Americans are "takers" rather than "makers" because they receive one or another form of government assistance. It's a familiar tune repeated regularly by *Fox News* commentators and the nation's most prominent talk show hosts.

This seems different to me. While the Reaganites supported tax cuts for the wealthy and seemed to believe the poor suffered a plethora of character flaws that explained their condition, I never really felt that Reagan and his ilk *hated* the poor. In those days, conservative support for policies intended to benefit the rich was always couched in rhetoric that suggested such efforts would directly benefit low-income persons. No matter the evidence, they really seemed to sincerely believe that the benefits of tax cuts for the wealthy would "trickle down" to the rest of us. If nothing else, they had felt compelled, either morally or politically, to at least *make* that case. It was Ronald Reagan, along with congressional liberals, who supported expanding the Earned Income Tax Credit for the working poor. It was Jack Kemp, the late Republican congressman and vice-presidential candidate in 1996, who campaigned in public housing and stumped for programs that would help public housing residents own their own units.

These days, commentators and politicians don't even bother pretending that their ideas are about benefiting the working class or poor. Those at the bottom are increasingly an afterthought, just as removed from the minds of the aristocracy as they are separated from them physically, thanks to the gated communities in which so many of the nation's affluent live. One would have to be given to particularly bizarre hallucinations to imagine a world in which Mitt Romney or Sarah Palin might campaign in public housing projects as Kemp did, or indeed to imagine a Republican Party in which the likes of Jack Kemp would even be welcomed today. While the Reagan years brought plenty of policy changes that amounted to institutional cruelty, now those same kinds of policies (this time on steroids) are being proposed alongside a much more vicious and dehumanizing rhetoric. That rhetoric, by undermining the compassion that might otherwise lead folks to reject proposals to slash-and-burn antipoverty budgets, makes the current moment more dangerous than the bad old days of the 1980s—especially given 24-hour news and talk radio, which allow the proponents of such cruelty to reach larger audiences than ever before.

Since beginning work on this volume, evidence for the culture of cruelty has only become clearer. In both rhetoric and policy, things are getting uglier by the week. Republican governors have refused to expand Medicaid in their states, leaving millions without the health care guarantees that would otherwise have applied to them as part of the Affordable Care Act (so-called Obamacare), while conservative congresspersons fight any increase in the federal minimum wage despite its inadequacy at the current level, to support the many families who rely on it. For his part, President Obama has proven largely unwilling to resist austerity measures favored by the political right and Wall Street so as to tame budget deficits, even though the deficit recently fell to its lowest point since he took office and half the level it was when George W. Bush left the White House.[22]

Indeed, President Obama was so desirous of being seen as a deficit hawk himself, he moved to deficit reduction as a "bipartisan" goal immediately after pushing through a stimulus bill that most economists agreed was too small to reverse the economy's slide. The pivot to deficits forced an agreement on spending that ultimately guaranteed the government sequester of 2013 and the resulting spending limits in place since then.[23] Although he briefly railed against rising inequality in late 2013, the president has since moved away from such arguments, returning to the safer but less specific trope of "providing opportunity to all." While no doubt a safer political narrative, the wording of the switch glosses over the uncomfortable truth that inequality itself is what currently impedes opportunity for millions. Despite sounding recent populist notes—calling for expanded public spending and higher taxes on the wealthy to pay for it—these efforts are likely too little, too late, given the Republican takeover of both houses of Congress in the 2014 mid-terms. Already, the GOP leadership has announced it will seek more tax cuts for corporations, while holding the line on significant new spending and even cutting spending in several key areas if possible.[24] Meanwhile, many on the right continue to push for the repeal of the Affordable Care Act—a move that would roll back health care coverage for millions—even as the Supreme Court has repeatedly upheld its constitutionality and rebuffed efforts to overturn it via lawsuits. Despite signs that the economy is beginning to improve for some—though far too slowly for most Americans, and only to an extent that will make up for some of their losses in the past decade—Republican plans to slash spending as well as taxes on the nation's wealthy could send the country back into a fiscal tailspin. There are likely to be some very dim days ahead, especially considering how reluctant most mainstream Democrats are to focus on chronic economic injustice as a central campaign issue. Worried about the large sums of money needed by presidential candidates in the modern era, and aware of how much of that money resides with the financier class in the wealthiest fraction of the population, the Democratic Party has largely downplayed the matter of class warfare from above, even as that warfare is waged relentlessly on the American public.

As for this volume, in the first chapter I will examine the ongoing economic crisis and its effects on the nation's most vulnerable, and contrast their experiences with those of the affluent, who in many ways have never done better. I will place current inequality in historical context and explore the various explanations for it. This chapter will examine persistent poverty and unemployment, as well as income and wealth inequality. I will also explore the myth of upward mobility and demonstrate that counter to aristocratic narratives, which insist that America remains a place where people can easily move from rags to riches, we are actually becoming less and less mobile, both in relation to our own past and when compared to other nations.

In the second chapter, I will document the extent to which growing inequality has been met with an increasingly hostile rhetoric in which the poor and needy are demonized while the wealthy are venerated, and inequality is rationalized and justified as merely reflecting differences between productive and unproductive people. I will offer factual and analytical rebuttals to common critiques of Americans who are impoverished, underemployed and eligible for public assistance, and explore what this often hateful and entirely incorrect rhetoric portends in terms of national policy. Likewise, I will examine common narratives of praise for the rich and similarly rebut the arguments made to justify that praise: that the rich shoulder a disproportionate share of the nation's tax burden; that they have "earned" their fortunes and position; and that they, unlike the poor, don't rely on help from the government. Importantly, I will demonstrate that contrary to the popular "culture of poverty" theory, which holds that the impoverished find themselves in such a position due to pathological and dysfunctional cultural attributes, it is actually a small group of economic minorities—those who hoard wealth and harm the overall well-being of most Americans in the process—who actually demonstrate the most destructive behaviors, values and cultural tendencies.[25] The problem is not a culture of poverty; rather, it is a culture of predatory affluence.

In the third chapter, I will discuss how we might rebuild a culture of compassion and equity, and defeat the culture of cruelty documented in the previous two sections. Central to this process is having a clear understanding of what we're up against. If we don't understand how the right has established cruelty as a national rhetorical and policy norm, we can't possibly build a counter-narrative, let alone a political movement to challenge and defeat it. It is my contention that there are two primary forces operating in concert to push a culture of cruelty forward, both of which have long blunted class-conscious organizing among those at the bottom of the nation's economic structure, and as a result have strengthened the hand of the wealthiest among us.

The first factor is the nation's core ideology itself: meritocracy and rugged individualism. It is this notion—the idea that anyone can make it in America if they try—that has long bedeviled attempts to create a more equitable society. If one believes in this fundamental ideology of Americanism, it becomes easy to look at those who don't succeed in life and conclude that they have no one but themselves to blame. Likewise, it becomes easy to view the successful as exemplars of hard work and inherent talent. Even though Americans are expressing concerns about rampant inequality in ways they haven't for many years, there is evidence that the vast majority continue to adhere to a stubborn faith in meritocracy, which makes combatting the culture of cruelty more difficult. With the mass media daily presenting images of wealth and celebrity as "normal," faith in meritocracy becomes harder to shake. Unfortunately, too often liberals fail to challenge the notion of American exceptionalism and meritocracy—or even feed these ideas directly by their rhetoric—and in so doing, undermine support for economic equity and justice for all.

The second critical factor—in some ways as central to the development of America as the notion of meritocracy—is the role of white racial bias in dividing the nation's working class and, over the last several decades, shaping hostility to those in need and the programs designed to support persons who are struggling. As I will demonstrate in this chapter, the rich have regularly sought to play white workers off against people of color, sowing racial hostility against black, Asian and Latino labor as a way to divert attention from their own exploitation of white workers. Sadly, the relative elevation of whites over people of color, combined with the rhetoric of racial supremacy meant to justify racial division, has proven effective over the years. It has created both a "psychological wage" of whiteness, as W.E.B. Du Bois first termed it, and also a real material stake in the perpetuation of white supremacy. But this stake, though real, is also fraught with danger. By cleaving to whiteness, even at the expense of their overall economic interests—which would frankly be better served by solidarity with the black and brown—white workers have fallen into a trap. From colonial times to the present era, racism has divided working people, strengthened the hand of capital relative to labor, and thereby helped further the inequalities that are the material engine of the culture of cruelty.

Likewise, racism and the manipulation of white racial resentment have been critical to stoking opposition to government programs to help those in need. Widespread public support for government programs to address unemployment and poverty, which was normative in the wake of the Depression and for several decades after it, began to dissipate rapidly as soon as the public face of those things came to be black and brown. As persons of color gained access to government programs that had previously been largely if not exclusively the purview of whites, narratives about fraud, abuse and the "undeserving poor" gained traction. Because welfare programs are now so linked in the white imagination with blacks and Latinos, millions of whites who would benefit from a more generous safety net go without, all because racial scapegoating by political aristocrats has stigmatized such efforts and prompted lean budgets with little forbearance for those who are struggling. There is even some evidence that racial bias against black folks is the factor that most directly explains the inadequacy of the nation's welfare efforts when compared to those of other industrialized democracies. Unfortunately, many liberal and left voices on the larger issue of inequality give little attention to the centrality of racial bias in the perpetuation of America's class structure, and thus make altering it infinitely more difficult.

After establishing the persistent obstacles to building a more just and equitable society, I will then examine some of the rhetorical and movement-building strategies we might use to break through those obstacles. The good news is that there are ways to build an effective counter-narrative to the culture of cruelty and to emerge intact from under the affluence, a counter-narrative rooted in a deeply ethical vision that can speak to the desire of most Americans to live out the best aspect of our national creed—the non-negotiable promise of freedom, equality and justice for all.

I realize that for many—and especially those of us on the political left—paeans to the national creed might seem horribly regressive, even nationalistic in a way we normally spurn. This is especially true considering that other aspects of American ideology, which some might also consider creedal notions—like rugged individualism, about which I'll have more to say later, and little of it positive—contribute so heavily to the very inequalities this volume seeks to critique. And yet to accept that the national creed as a whole, or that American ideals per se are so inherently reactionary and intrinsically flawed that they must be avoided and even openly spurned is unwise for two reasons. First, as a strategy for building social movements in the United States it is the height of dogmatic ignorance. Most Americans feel a strong pull from the concept of Americanism, however much that notion has been historically misused, and however much certain aspects of it, like the myth of meritocracy, actually serve to undermine its more laudable aspects, like the quest for equality and justice. As such, to suggest that those who take inspiration from the national creed are little more than brainwashed, hyper-patriotic fools is to ensure that our movements for a more equitable society will fail. No revolution in the history of the world has developed from beneath a soil watered with contempt for the people one hopes to organize. Quite the contrary, revolutionaries always start with a love for the people and a love for the nation they seek to change. It is by appealing to the national principles—and by showing how the forces of repression and injustice regularly violate those principles, trampling on them in the name of expedience and domination by the wealthy—that revolutions are won. We can and we must tease out of the national creed those parts that serve the common good, while strenuously critiquing those parts that run counter to such a purpose.

Second, and equally important, to avoid appealing to the national creed simply because reactionary and autocratic forces have so often used such an appeal in the name of repression is to forever cede the notion of Americanism to those on the right; it is to grant them the patent on the country and the culture, to invest them with the rhetorical copyright, and to make believable their insistence that we are the ones bent on violating the country's principles, that *we* are the ones whose beliefs are un-American. Progressive forces must reframe the debate and demonstrate how inequality and elitism—though longstanding parts of the American practice—fundamentally strike at the heart of the American *ideal*; refusing to appeal to those ideals will leave those on the left increasingly vulnerable and isolated. Rather than making *them* defend inequality and the culture of cruelty as the highest calling of the nation, refusing to appeal to the American ideal will force *us* to prove how equity and compassion fit with those concepts in the face of the other side's isolated individualism. That such a choice would make our job far harder should be readily apparent.

And the simple fact is, the right does not own the national creed, however much they profess to be its natural guardians. Individualism, though surely a part of the national self-concept, has long existed side by side with a countervailing focus on the collective good and the concept of community well-being. From the colonial period to the Revolution itself to the Civil War, Great Depression, World War II and even the aftermath of 9/11, the national narrative has always held up the concept that the United States was, is, and can continue to be an ideational place, and that the idea of America has been one of *E Pluribus Unum* ("Out of Many, One"). That the motto and ideal have been regularly and consistently violated by the evil of white supremacy and a vicious system of class division, among other things, hardly alters the fact that such concepts are embedded in the conceptual framework of the culture. They are deeply felt symbols resonant with meaning for Americans, however much they have been routinely sacrificed on the altar of elitism and the interests of the few.

It is with this in mind that we who seek to build a more just and equitable society can do so without having to go outside the contours of the American framework. While we can and should be willing to borrow liberally from the lessons of other nations and from international human rights standards and treaties, we can also look inward to the best of our own tradition in order to create a new and better nation. The notion of collective uplift and a common good is not counter to our tradition but part of it, at least in theory; it is not some exotic notion from a galaxy beyond our own, but a concept that has lived at the heart of the national framework from the beginning; and it is every bit as central to that framework as the commitment to individualism.

In the modern era, to whatever extent individualism has been a central component of the so-called American dream it was always linked to a broader notion of collective uplift. In fact, the very phrase "American Dream" was not popularized until the early 1930s, and at the time was understood to be a concept inherently linked to the ideal of a more equitable national community—one that was being damaged greatly by rampant individualism and materialism. As literary scholar Sarah Churchwell explained recently, discussing the cultural importance of F. Scott Fitzgerald's *The Great Gatsby*:

> As a catchphrase, the American dream did not explode into popular culture until the 1931 publication of a book called *The Epic of America* by James Truslow Adams, which spoke of "the American dream of a better, richer and happier life for all our citizens of every rank, which is the greatest contribution we have made to the thought and welfare of the world. That dream or hope has been present from the start. Ever since we became an independent nation, each generation has seen an uprising of ordinary Americans to save that dream from the forces that appear to be overwhelming it. . . . " In the early years of the great depression Adams's book sparked a great national debate about the promise of America as a place that fosters "the genuine worth of each man or woman. . . ." Two years later, a *New York Times* article noted: "Get-rich-quick and gambling was the bane of our life before the smash"; they were also what caused the "smash" itself in 1929. By 1933, Adams was writing in the *New York Times* of the way the American dream had been hijacked: "Throughout our history, the pure gold of this vision has been heavily alloyed with the dross of materialistic aims . . . the making of money and the enjoying of what money could buy too often became our ideal of a full and satisfying life. The struggle of each against all for the dazzling prizes destroyed in

> some measure both our private ideals and our sense of social obligation. . . ."

Importantly, as Churchwell points out, "The phrase the American dream was first invented, in other words, to describe a failure, not a promise: or rather, a broken promise, a dream that was continually faltering beneath the rampant monopoly capitalism that set each struggling against all; and it is no coincidence that it was first popularized during the early years of the Great Depression."[26]

In short, to whatever extent the American Dream is endangered, it is not by movements for more equality—not by the left—but by the current reality of economic oligarchy and those right-wing and neoliberal voices who defend said oligarchy against the tides of change. It is my firm belief that by engaging this discussion honestly and openly it may yet be possible to develop a truly radical Americanism, which would usher in a very different and more compassionate consciousness than the one that holds sway at present. By openly challenging the nation's secular gospel—the myth of meritocracy and the sufficiency of rugged individualism to foster success—we can produce a counter-narrative to the culture of cruelty. By telling our own stories of how we personally have benefited from government interventions in the economy, or from friends, connections and even simple luck, we can chip away at the idea that the wealthy have "earned" all they have while the poor similarly deserve their station. To confront the creation myth of a culture is never a simple task, but in this case it is a necessary one, and in the final chapter I will explore ways we might begin to craft such a confrontation.

I would like to thank those who have been central to my understanding of the dynamics of inequality over the years and are therefore implicated in this work. Especially the late Shelly Coverman, Ron King, Lance Hill, Larry Powell, Ron Chisom, Barbara Major, Donna Johnigan, David Billings, Diana Dunn, Marjorie Freeman, William Ryan, Angela Y. Davis, bell hooks,

Randall Robinson, Kimberlé Crenshaw, Melvin Oliver and Thomas Shapiro, Michelle Alexander, Sut Jhally, Eduardo Bonilla-Silva, Charles Ogletree, Howard Zinn, Doug Henwood, Ishmael Reed, Noel Ignatiev, Paul Marcus, Felicia Gustin, Jean Caiani, Michael Eric Dyson, Joe Feagin, Anne Braden, Derrick Jensen, James Baldwin, Ted Allen, Mab Segrest, Thandeka, Sharon Martinas, Stuart Hall, Michael Benitez, Chris Crass, Alicia Garza, Patrisse Cullors, Opal Tometi and John Bracey. To all my friends and colleagues with whom I have worked and laughed and cried and struggled throughout the years, and who have stuck with me through good times and bad, thank you. To my editor, Greg Ruggiero, and to all the folks at City Lights, thanks for your patience as I slowly went through the process of birthing this, our fourth book together. To Jamie Lynn Moeller, who provided substantial and critical research assistance throughout this process, there is no way to thank you enough. To my best friend, Albert Jones, as always, thank you for advice, insight and camaraderie these past forty years. To my wife Kristy, and our children, Ashton and Rachel: you make my life more complete than I could have ever imagined was possible. I am honored to be in your lives and I hope I bring honor and fullness to yours.

Finally, to A.R. Ward: Remember that email debate we were having a while back about antipoverty efforts, the size of government and racial inequality? Remember how we went back and forth for two rounds and then I dropped the ball and never got back to you on your final rebuttal? Yeah, well—*this*. (Drops the mic, walks away.)

Nashville, Tennessee
July 2015

CHAPTER I

PULLING APART: THE STATE OF DISUNITED AMERICA

Though many things change with time, some truths appear to be largely unaltered by the turning of the hands on a clock or the progression of a calendar. It has been more than two millennia, after all, since the Greek philosopher Plato gave voice to a social reality easily recognizable in each generation from his time to the present:

> Any city, however small, is in fact divided into two, one the city of the poor, the other of the rich; these are at war with one another.[1]

As with Plato, philosophers, novelists and poets down through the ages have made note of inequality. While the work of Dickens, mentioned previously, is perhaps the obvious referent here—and indeed we will come back to him—many others have written and spoken just as descriptively about the reality of class division. At the turn of the twentieth century, Theodore Dreiser described the divide with regard to New York City, in his novel *Sister Carrie*:

> Along Broadway men picked their way in ulsters and umbrellas. Along the Bowery, men slouched through it with collars and hats pulled over their ears. In the former thoroughfare businessmen and travelers were mak-

ing for comfortable hotels. In the latter, crowds in cold errands shifted past dingy stores.[2]

Seventy-five years ago, in *The Grapes of Wrath*, novelist John Steinbeck described in visceral prose the way that economic division so often plays out, with the rich unaware of the strain and suffering felt by those struggling to survive:

> The fields were fruitful, and starving men moved on the roads. The granaries were full and the children of the poor grew up rachitic, and the pustules of pellagra swelled on their sides. The great companies did not know that the line between hunger and anger is a thin line. . . . On the highways the people moved like ants and searched for work, for food. And the anger began to ferment.[3]

James Baldwin, whose graphic depictions of America's racial divide were among the most searing ever produced, famously discussed the difference between Park Avenue uptown, in Harlem, and Park Avenue midtown, where the affluent and white caroused in a universe quite their own: one city but two worlds, separated by gulfs of race and class, as foreign to one another as persons living in lands divided by vast oceans:

> I still remember my first sight of New York. It was really another city when I was born—where I was born. We looked down over the Park Avenue streetcar tracks. It was Park Avenue, but I didn't know what Park Avenue meant downtown. The Park Avenue I grew up on, which is still standing, is dark and dirty. No one would dream of opening a Tiffany's on that Park Avenue, and when you go downtown you discover that you are literally in the white world. It is rich—or at least it looks rich. It is clean—because they collect garbage downtown. There

> are doormen. People walk about as though they owned where they are—and indeed they do. And it's a great shock. It's very hard to relate yourself to this. . . . You know—you know instinctively—that none of this is for you. You know this before you are told.[4]

Far from seeking to inspire the reader to rediscover great literature, my purpose here is to establish the way in which scholars, artists and public intellectuals have long recognized inequity as a serious social problem; and just as in their respective times, so too today the economic inequities to which these authors gave voice are as real as ever, and in some ways more deeply entrenched than before. This is not because such vast inequities are natural or inevitable—the commonly believed but altogether false assumption made by many—but because of decisions we have made within political and civil society, decisions that can be just as readily undone through collective action once we recognize the source of the trouble.

Don't misunderstand: a certain degree of inequality between persons is to be expected. We all have different talents and interests, after all; some can sing, some cannot; some are artists, some are not; some simply work harder than others. But the extremes between rich and poor to which we are being exposed today are unlike anything that can be written off to the normal distribution of abilities. It is not the simple fact of inequalities that concerns us, but the extremity of the gap, the shape of those disparities, and their increasing impermeability that should give us pause. There is nothing normal or acceptable about those things, however much we may allow for a reasonable range of talents and rewards based upon them. Not to mention the fact that what we have chosen to value in society—which work, for instance, is most amply rewarded in the market—has been the result of *choices* we've made, rather than some natural process. As such, the inequities we can readily see all around us reflect little about the individual worth of people at the top or bottom of the scale; rather, they reflect social power relationships that have elevated the work product of some above others, even when (as we'll see) many of those "others" perform work generally acknowledged to be more socially valuable than the work performed by the wealthy economic minority. So even if a certain degree of inequality is inevitable in any remotely free society, we should not extrapolate from that fact the notion that those inequities that currently exist are preordained.

To get a sense of the "two cities" nature of modern American life, consider the following: As of 2014, the stock market reached an all-time high.[5] Corporate profits as a share of the overall economy have risen to a level unseen since the late 1920s,[6] and as a share of all national income those profits are higher than at any point in recorded history.[7] For the wealthiest one percent of Americans (roughly three million people), incomes rose by about a third from 2009 to 2013, largely making up for whatever stock market–related losses they suffered during the recent Great Recession.[8] And yet, while corporate profits are at their highest level in the past eighty-five years, worker compensation as a share of the economy remains at its *lowest* point in the past sixty-five. For millions of average working people the recession never really ended, and far from a one-third increase in average wages, income for the bottom ninety-nine percent of us only rose four-tenths of one percent (0.4) from 2009 to 2013.[9] In other words, virtually all the income gains during the first few years of the recovery flowed to the nation's top one percent.[10]

Even those gains for persons who weren't one-percenters were received exclusively by the next nine percent. From 2009 to 2012, the bottom nine-tenths of the wage-earning population saw their incomes actually fall, meaning that a statistically improbable but nonetheless true *116 percent of all income gains* in the first years of the recovery went to the highest-earning tenth of Americans.[11] In 2013, hourly wages grew at only one-fifth the rate of corporate profits, barely staying ahead of inflation, suggesting that the economy is producing far higher returns at the top than in the middle and bottom of the distribution.[12] Although economists have pointed to recent Labor Department data to suggest that things are getting better—so, for instance, as of January 2015, wages seemed to be finally ticking upward—it remains to be seen whether this trend will last, and whether the wage gains will extend to the lowest rungs of the job ladder.[13] Despite claims of recovery, from January through April wage growth has bounced around from 0.5 percent down to 0.1 percent,[14] back to 0.3 percent[15] and finally to virtually no growth at all by late spring.[16] But even if higher gains manage to return, such that the annual growth of wages might reach as much as 2.2 percent per year, this would remain well below normal economic recovery targets,[17] and after inflation would only come to about one percent annually in real terms, hardly sufficient to reverse the slide of the past decade.[18]

Even more disturbing, there is good reason to believe that the job and wage recovery of the last few months (as of this writing) won't last long, if current rumblings from the Federal Reserve—the nation's central bank—are to be believed. Although the Fed has been holding interest rates down for years in the hopes of spurring businesses and consumers to borrow so as to boost consumption, production and economic growth, now that things are beginning to look up, the Fed seems concerned that more jobs and rising wages might push up prices. Recently, Fed chair Janet Yellen signaled the bank's intention to begin raising interest rates so as to keep inflation low by putting the brakes on borrowing a bit, and thus on economic growth. The thinking here is that if the labor markets tighten too much and employee pay grows "too fast" (a concept that must seem laughable to workers given the last two decades of wage stagnation), people will spend their increased earnings and inflation will spiral out of control, thereby damaging the economy. And this is feared, even as wage-related inflation has been largely nonexistent for several decades. Ultimately, if the Fed hikes interest rates (and this appears a certainty as of this writing), the result could be the loss of hundreds of thousands of jobs that would otherwise have been created, as borrowing for the purpose of new job creation and business expansion becomes too expensive.[19] Such a move could easily choke off the job and wage recovery, long before it has time to filter throughout the ranks of the working class. In short, despite recent signs that things may be getting better for American workers, the long-term prospects for fundamental gains in wages and living conditions remain sketchy at best.

Joblessness and Underemployment in Post-Recession America

While the rich ride high, there are still millions of Americans whose economic situation is grim. As of April 2015, there were still about 8.5 million people who were officially unemployed (which means jobless and actively seeking employment), and several million more who say they want a job but have given up looking for one at present. On top of these there are about 6.6 million additional workers who say they desire full-time employment but are having to settle for part-time jobs.[20] So although the official unemployment rate is only 5.4 percent—a definite improvement since early 2013 when it was still hovering around eight percent, and far superior to the ten percent rate in 2010[21]—once we consider the plight of involuntary part-timers and discouraged workers, the true rate of joblessness and underemployment is likely to be nearly twice as high.

And even though recent reports suggest that jobs are beginning to come back to the private sector, it is worth noting how these jobs differ from those lost during the slowdown. Although jobs in lower-wage industries (paying less than $13.33 per hour) represented only twenty-two percent of job losses during the recession, they have accounted for forty-four percent of new jobs since 2010. Today, lower-wage industries are employing nearly two million more workers than they were in 2008. As for mid-range-paying jobs (paying as high as $20 per hour), these have actually slipped in the recovery, and now account for nearly a million fewer jobs than at the outset of the recession. And while higher-paying jobs (paying up to $32 per hour on average) represented more than forty percent of job losses in the recession, they have only accounted for thirty percent of recent job growth. As a result, there are nearly a million fewer higher-paying jobs now than in 2008 when the recession began.[22] In other words, even when people are finding work it is often at income levels well below that which they had been earning prior to the economic collapse. In the most recent jobs report as of this writing, there were only 1,000 new jobs created in manufacturing, out of 225,000 new jobs in all (this, after an actual decline in manufacturing positions during the previous month). Meanwhile, some of the biggest gains were in areas such as retail sales, low-paid health care jobs like physician's assistants and home health care aides, temporary services, and jobs in restaurants and bars. Indeed, more than half of all jobs created in the most recent month were in these categories.[23] On average, during 2014, new jobs created paid about twenty-three percent less than the jobs lost during the recession.[24] Unless the recent bump in wages and employment continues and accelerates, the hollowing out of the middle class will not likely be arrested, nor are we likely to see a diminution of rising income inequality.

Although the job picture has been bleak for Americans of all races and ethnicities, communities of color are having an especially difficult time. Latinos are about sixty percent more likely than whites to be unemployed (so much for the often heard refrain that they're "taking all the good jobs") and African Americans are almost two and a half times as likely as whites to be out of work: nearly ten percent unemployment for blacks as opposed to just a bit more than four percent for whites.[25] Even when only comparing whites and persons of color possessing the same degree of education, racial gaps persist. Latinos and Latinas with a diploma have an unemployment rate more than twenty percent higher than that of similar whites, while Latino/a college graduates are fifty percent more likely than comparable white graduates to be out of work. Meanwhile, black high school graduates are twice as likely as comparable whites to be unemployed, and even black folks with college degrees are seventy percent more likely than white college graduates to be out of work.[26] Things are especially troubling for recent black college graduates. Despite persistent cries about "reverse discrimination" from whites who seem to feel they are being bumped from jobs by less qualified African Americans, recent black college grads are more than twice as likely as comparable whites to be unemployed. For graduates between the ages of twenty-two and twenty-seven, unemployment rates for blacks are 12.4 percent, compared to only 4.9 percent, for comparable whites—a *quintupling* of the jobless gap between white and black recent college graduates just since 2007.[27] This pattern holds true for graduates in every possible category of academic study, regardless of their majors. Even black folks who obtained engineering degrees are nearly twice as likely as white engineering grads to be out of work.[28] Among millennials (ages eighteen to thirty-four), racial disparities remain stark: white, male, high school dropouts have the same chance of finding work as black males with two years of college.[29]

For many, their stint on the unemployment line is no brief interlude between jobs. Millions find themselves out of work for half a year, a full year, even two full years, no matter how hard they look for a job. As of April 2015, nearly thirty percent of the unemployed—about 2.5 million people in all—had been out of work more than twenty-six weeks, despite actively looking for a job the entire time, and forty-two percent had been out of work for at least fifteen weeks. Indeed, unemployed persons are just as likely to be out of work for twenty-seven weeks or more as they are to be unemployed for less than five weeks, meaning that long-term unemployment is now just as prevalent as short-term joblessness.[30] And while unemployment is always stressful, long-term unemployment is especially crushing. Those who suffer this fate will typically experience impaired emotional and physical well-being, significantly elevated rates of suicide, and substantial family dysfunction because of their job situations.[31] Even when the long-term unemployed finally do find work, it is usually at wages well below what they were earning previously, and often without the benefits available in their old jobs.[32]

Poverty, Wage Stagnation and Deprivation Amid "Recovery"

By the end of 2013, there were forty-five million Americans officially living below the poverty line—about one in every seven persons in the country.[33] To understand what this means in practical terms, consider that to be officially poor that year a single individual would have to have made less than $11,188; the threshold for a two-person household averaged $15,142; for three persons $18,552, and for a family of four $23,834.[34] In other words, if you made even $12,000 in 2013 as a single individual, you would not be considered poor in America despite how incredibly difficult it would be to live on such an income. Likewise, if you and your partner had one child and your combined income reached even $19,000, you would no longer be considered poor, despite your precarious economic station; so too in a family of four earning even $24,000 a year. So when we speak of poverty, we are talking about substantial financial insecurity. Worse still, a growing number of Americans are not simply poor but are living in extreme poverty, defined as income less than *half* the poverty lines above. As of 2013, nearly twenty million people lived in this state of destitution,[35] which is an increase of about eight million since 2000.[36]

While the national poverty figures are disturbing enough, the picture is even more distressing for persons of color. Although whites make up the largest group of people living in poverty at nineteen million, or forty-one percent of the total,[37] the rate of poverty is far higher for Americans of color. According to the Census Bureau, African Americans are nearly three times as likely as whites to be poor, and Latinos are 2.5 times as likely as whites to live in poverty. Approximately one in four Latinos and twenty-seven percent of blacks officially live below the poverty line.[38] Among American Indians and Alaska Natives, between twenty-five and thirty percent are poor, and in some indigenous communities—particularly reservation lands on which about a third of the nation's Indian peoples live—nearly half of the community lives in poverty.[39]

Although some have pointed to Asian American income as proof of equal opportunity in America—and to suggest that there is something wrong with blacks, Latinos and Indian folks who lag behind—the data marshaled for this purpose is misleading. To begin, as mostly voluntary migrants, Asian Americans are a more self-selected group than blacks, Latinos or indigenous persons. They include more persons who came to the country with middle-class status, had college degrees, or were in the process of obtaining those degrees upon arrival. So naturally, we would expect Asian Americans in the aggregate to therefore appear more "successful" than groups whose members represent more of a cross-section of class status and experience. That said, when we actually examine Asian American status relative to white status, we discover persistent evidence that Asian folk too, despite claims of their "success," are struggling and lag behind the dominant group. For instance, according to the most recent data on earnings, when we compare whites and Asians of the same age and with the same degree of education, whites routinely earn more than their Asian American counterparts. For those with high school diplomas only, white males between the ages of thirty-five and thirty-nine earn twenty-three percent more than comparable Asians—a gap that grows to a nearly fifty percent advantage between the ages of forty and forty-four. For those with undergraduate degrees, white males between thirty and thirty-four earn twenty-two percent more than comparable Asian Americans, and by the time those white men are in their mid-forties they are earning forty-six percent more than their Asian American counterparts—almost $30,000 more each year, on average.[40]

Additionally, claims that Asian American households are doing as well or better than even white households—because they have higher aggregate income than white households nationwide and poverty rates that are only slightly higher than whites'—rely on data that masks substantial disparities at the state and local level.[41] About half of all Asian Americans live in the higher-income (and higher-cost-of-living) West, with roughly sixty percent residing in just six states: California, Hawaii, New York, New Jersey, Illinois and Washington. As a result, they will tend to have higher incomes and lower poverty rates than members of other groups who are more geographically dispersed in much lower-income and lower-cost areas.[42] However, if we examine income and poverty data in the places where so many Asian Americans actually live, thereby comparing them to others who live in those same higher-income areas, things change dramatically. In cities with heavy Asian American presence like Los Angeles, San Francisco and New York, Asian American poverty rates are roughly double the rates for whites.[43] In other words, despite claims of Asian "success" and the attempts of some to cast them as a "model minority" to be emulated by other more presumably problematic ones, Asian Americans too are struggling relative to whites.

As with poverty in general, extreme poverty is a particular concern for people of color. In fact, blacks and Hispanics are more likely to live in *extreme* poverty than whites are to be poor at all: one in eight African Americans are extremely poor and one in eleven Latinos are living at half the poverty line or below, compared to only about one in twenty-five whites who are that impoverished.[44] Among the impoverished, people of color are also far more likely to live in high-poverty neighborhoods than are whites, further deepening the severity of their economic condition and limiting their ability to escape impoverishment. Impoverished African Americans are more than seven times as likely as poor whites to live in high-poverty neighborhoods, while poor Latinos are nearly six times as likely to do so.[45] Although deprivation is always stressful for those experiencing it, living in communities of heavily concentrated poverty magnifies those stresses many times over. Such communities have fewer hospitals per capita than other communities, are less likely to have access to healthy food, and are less likely to have adequately resourced schools, in part because school funding is so over-reliant on property taxes in most places. Residents in concentrated-poverty neighborhoods are also cut off from the job and opportunity networks that exist for middle-class families, and even for lower-income families who live in communities where middle-class families are still largely present. Additionally, impoverished urban communities are far more likely to be places where there are waste facilities that directly compromise the health of residents, particularly children and the elderly.[46]

An especially disturbing number of the nation's poor are children. About fifteen million children, or nearly one in five kids in the U.S., live in poverty,[47] and since 2013, slightly more than half of all children in the nation's public schools live in poverty.[48] Far from an abstract concept, poverty has long-term impact on child development. Research has found that children in poverty are significantly more likely than their middle-class and affluent peers to show signs of impaired brain development in the prefrontal cortex, which is critical for problem-solving and analytical skills.[49] Independent of other factors known to impact neural development, poverty appears to have a uniquely debilitating impact on kids, due to the stresses of life in a low-income family and the subsequent lack of opportunities to which such children are exposed. Additional research finds that growing up in poverty can result in an unhealthy level of stress hormones being released into the bloodstream, which can impair neural development and contribute to a number of health problems, including heart disease, hypertension and stroke.[50] The poor, and especially the extremely poor, are in many cases subjected to environments that produce a form of Post-Traumatic Stress Disorder (PTSD) similar to that experienced by combat veterans.[51]

Even those who aren't "poor" are struggling to keep their heads above water. According to one recent survey, roughly three in four Americans live paycheck to paycheck, meaning they either have no savings or so little in savings that they could not withstand a layoff or medical emergency. Only one in four have sufficient savings to cover six months of expenses, half could only survive a three-month loss of income, and about twenty-seven percent have no savings at all.[52] When we include those who are no more than fifty percent above the poverty line, and are therefore intensely vulnerable to a layoff or economic downturn, more than seventy-six million Americans, or nearly one in four, are poor or near poor.[53]

Meanwhile, even as local papers across the country herald the beginnings of a new boom in housing construction and a rejuvenated real estate market, at least fourteen million Americans continue to face the real prospect of losing their homes, equity, and access to credit due to foreclosure.[54] They are unable to make their mortgage payments and have received little or no relief from the government, even as that government bailed out the very bankers whose actions helped to precipitate so much of the pain felt by homeowners. Additionally, rents in many areas have soared past the point of affordability,[55] and in other cases tenants are being evicted from apartments under cover of local nuisance laws, solely for calling police "too many times"—a practice that is forcing poor women facing domestic violence to live with their abusers rather than face being put on the street.[56] Having lost their homes to foreclosure, tens of thousands in the past several years have spent some portion of time without a place to live or in makeshift tent cities reminiscent of those that sprouted up with regularity during the 1930s,[57] and on any given night, more than 600,000 Americans are homeless.[58] Even as the nation's wealthiest often have the option of luxuriating in one of many homes, Americans without housing security are quite literally dying on the street from exposure to the winter cold.[59] As of 2013, 2.5 million children (an all-time record) were experiencing homelessness at some point in the year—approximately one of every thirty children in America.[60]

Despite assurances by billionaire investor Peter Schiff that "people don't go hungry in a capitalist economy"—this from the same guy who says "mentally retarded" people should be paid $2 per hour—food insecurity and inadequate nutrition persist for far too many Americans.[61] In the last few years there have been as many as seventeen million households composed of more than forty-five million people who faced real difficulties affordably meeting their nutritional needs.[62] As of 2013, there were about five million people living in households with such low food security that they had to substantially reduce their food intake, skip meals altogether on certain days, or in some cases even go several days at a time without eating, all because of the financial condition of their families.[63] Meanwhile, homeless Americans who rummage through garbage cans in search of food are subjected to arrest, as happened to homeless veteran James Kelly in Houston last year,[64] while McDonald's is counseling their employees to break food into smaller pieces so as to "keep them full," rather than paying them enough of a wage to allow them to buy more food.[65] As for health care, although the Affordable Care Act has removed millions from the ranks of the uninsured—with about ten million people added to the health care rolls just since 2013[66]—there remain millions more who are falling through the cracks of the system due to the refusal of mostly conservative governors to extend Medicaid in more than twenty states.[67] In a country where most personal bankruptcies are caused by a medical emergency for which patients have insufficient funds, to not ensure comprehensive and affordable care for all is to force too many of the ill into destitution.[68]

Still more worry about how, or if, they'll be able to send their children to college, especially as higher education continues its three-decades-long drift toward loan-based financing and away from grants, thereby burdening students with a crushing debt. Today's typical college graduates finish college with nearly four times the debt of their counterparts from the early 1990s—about $35,000 as compared to a bit more than $9,000.[69] In 1987, tax dollars covered more than three-fourths of the cost of operating public colleges and universities, but by 2012, states had slashed their support for higher education to such an extent that only fifty-three percent of such costs were covered by taxpayers, while the rest have been made up by tuition and fee hikes.[70] Average tuition and fees for both public and private colleges have more than doubled since the early 1980s, increasing the gap between the share of affluent kids and poor kids who are able to attend.[71]

Some of the problems that we can see so clearly in today's economy—especially wage stagnation—have been a long time coming. Ever since the early 1970s, real wages for average American workers have been largely flat.[72] This has been true, even as average worker productivity has roughly doubled in that period.[73] If workers' wages had kept pace with productivity and continued to grow along with wages at the top, as they had for the previous several decades, incomes for middle-class Americans would be about $18,000 higher than they are today.[74] While standard economic theory holds that wages and productivity should rise together as workers earn a commensurate share of the value they produce, this relationship between pay levels and productivity has been shredded over the past few decades. Likewise, wages have remained flat even as employees are working more hours today than ever before. From the early 1970s until 2007, the average annual number of hours worked rose by seventeen percent.[75] Workers are working harder than before and being more productive than ever, but they are making very little if any real gains in financial well-being.

Things have only gotten worse since the most recent recession. From 2007 to 2012, wages fell for the bottom seventy percent of the wage distribution despite productivity growth of 7.7 percent. When these data are combined with the wage stagnation that had already occurred since 2000, it is no exaggeration to say that for most workers, the first ten years of the new millennium was a lost decade for wages.[76] Median income today is $3,600 lower than it was in 2001, adjusted for inflation, and has fallen $2,100 just since 2009.[77] Things have been especially grim in terms of income stagnation for American men. In 1972, the median income for men between the ages of thirty-five and forty-four was equivalent to more than $54,000 today. But now, in large part because of the decline in manufacturing employment (a subject to which we'll return), the median for such men stands at just above $45,000.[78] The only reason that median income has been able to nudge up slightly for American families on the whole has been the entry of more women into the workforce; there are more two-earner families today than in the early 1970s. On the one hand, expanded opportunities for American women are obviously a positive and needed development. But on the other, if families today need two incomes to remain at the same level they enjoyed forty years ago with only one income-earner, something is clearly wrong with the larger economy.

Income and Wealth Inequality: Long-Term Trends and Current Realities

Among the things most Americans have long seemed to believe about our country is the idea that in some sense, we're all part of one big team. Nods to national unity are common, and surely it isn't hard to recall how, in the days following the terrorist attacks of 9/11, millions of Americans slapped bumper stickers on their cars sporting the slogan UNITED WE STAND. One part nationalistic and militaristic hubris, one part a genuine expression of emotional empathy with the victims and their families, the slogan and the concept behind it spoke to a deep-seated component of the nation's ideology: the notion of reciprocity, or, more simply put, the idea that "we're all in this together."

Of course, in the wake of the 9/11 tragedy not all Americans shared this sentiment equally, and there was a marked gap between the willingness of white Americans to adorn their vehicles in such a manner and that of people of color. Non-whites, more viscerally aware of the ongoing inequities between their own life conditions and those of most in the white majority, were not as likely to sport such stickers or engage in the flag-waving that became so commonplace in the aftermath of the attacks. Unity, after all, is not something that can be wished into existence, or something that manifests simply because a tragedy has transpired. For many African Americans and other people of color there had been many 9/11s, so to speak, throughout their history on this continent, none of which had brought real unity or equity of experience.

That said, and with exceptions duly noted, the notion of unity, togetherness and reciprocity is something to which we have all been exposed and to varying degrees have likely internalized. While the ideology of unity and reciprocity hardly fits with the lived reality of those belonging to marginalized groups, the aspirational if not existential lure of the dominant narrative remains strong, so much so that many of our most recognizable national slogans over the years conjure this notion, from "What's good for General Motors is good for America" to "A rising tide lifts all boats."

Yet, in recent years, the idea that America is one big team has been increasingly difficult to accept, because of the rapidity with which disparities of income and wealth have been growing, opening up a vast chasm between the nation's wealthiest and everyone else. Between late 2007 and 2009, the economy imploded, doubling unemployment rates and destroying more than a third of the nation's housing value (particularly among the middle and working class), and yet *Wall Street profits rose by 720 percent.*[79] When the majority of the American people can be thrown into the worst economic situation of the past seventy-five years, even as a small economic minority can enjoy massive profits due to their deliberate and predatory actions, the idea of America being one big unified homeland becomes almost impossible to swallow.

Economic injustice, though increasingly exposed since the onset of the Great Recession, has been emerging as a serious and intractable national problem for several decades. Whereas incomes of those in all income quintiles grew together from the late 1940s until the late 1970s, after that period, incomes for all but those at the top began to stagnate.[80] By 2007, right before the collapse of the economy, the richest one percent of Americans was already receiving twenty-three percent of national income. This nearly one-quarter share of national income was the highest percentage received by the top one percent since immediately prior to the onset of the Great Depression,[81] and nearly three times the share that was being received by this wealthy group just thirty-one years earlier in 1976.[82] From 1979 to 2007, the richest one percent of Americans (2.5 to 2.8 million people during that time) nearly *quadrupled* their average incomes. Meanwhile, the middle three-fifths of Americans only saw a forty percent gain in average incomes over that time—less than 1.5 percent income growth per year.[83] From 1993 to 2012, adjusted for inflation, real incomes for the bottom ninety-nine percent of American families grew by less than seven percent while incomes for the wealthiest one percent nearly doubled.[84]

To put income inequality in graphic terms, consider that in 2013, 165,000 Wall Street bankers took home average bonuses of $162,000 each, resulting in an overall bonus bonanza of nearly $27 billion: that's nearly *double* the amount taken home annually by all 1.1 million Americans working full-time at the minimum wage *combined*.[85] Even more disturbing, the most successful hedge fund managers—a group that manages investment portfolios for the super-rich, and about whom there will be more to say later—quite typically can make in *one single hour of work* what the average American family earns in twenty-one years.[86]

Sadly, income inequality is only the tip of the iceberg when it comes to understanding the depths of disparity that plague modern America. Much more substantial is the vast inequity in tangible assets from which families derive long-term financial security. Wealth disparities, in other words, represent the much larger portion of the iceberg—the part that remains under the metaphorical water, often unseen. Even before the economy cratered, disparities in wealth—from housing value to stocks and bonds to commercial real estate—were already significant. Once the housing bubble burst, taking with it about $6 trillion in lost assets (and often the only assets held by middle-class and working-class Americans), that gulf grew even wider.[87] As of 2010, the bottom half of the American population owned only about one percent of all national wealth, while the wealthiest one percent possessed *more than a third* of all wealth in the nation.[88] As for those assets most likely to generate substantial income, meaning investment assets like stocks, financial securities, and business equity and trusts, the wealthiest one percent of Americans own just over *half* of all such assets in the nation.[89] Today, wealth inequality in America stands at a level double that of the Roman Empire, where the top one percent owned about sixteen percent of all assets.[90]

However significant this level of disparity may sound, it actually understates the problem. Within the top one percent of wealth holders there is a big difference between those who barely make it into this group, and those at the pinnacle who reside in the top one-tenth (0.1) or top one-hundredth (0.01) of one percent. As of 2012, the top one-tenth of one percent (roughly 160,000 families) owned about twenty-two percent of the nation's assets, which is equal to the share of national wealth possessed by the poorest ninety percent of Americans. Meanwhile, the richest one-hundredth of a percent (about 16,000 families) owned 11.2 percent of all national assets.[91]

To visualize what this means, we can analogize the distribution of wealth to the distribution of seats in a football stadium. Let's imagine we were going to the Super Bowl in a stadium that seats 65,000 people. If the seats in the stadium were distributed the way that wealth is in America, just sixty-five fans would get to share 14,300 of the seats in the stadium. In fact, forget sharing seats: they could knock out the seats entirely and bring in big lounge chairs, umbrellas, Jacuzzis and their own personal cabanas instead. They would have so much space they could play Frisbee during commercial breaks or time-outs if they felt like it, never worrying about bumping up against the rest of us. Six or seven of these people would actually be able to cordon off 7,280 of these seats for themselves. This would leave the other fifty-seven or fifty-eight fans within the top 0.1 percent to fight over the remaining 7,020 seats (tough, but I suppose they'd manage). Meanwhile, the poorest half of the fans, or roughly 32,500 of them, would be struggling to fit into only 650 seats, representing the one percent of the seats they own. Think of it as the absolute worst musical chairs game ever. People would have to sit on top of each other, more than fifty deep, just to make the math work. This is the extent of wealth inequality in America today; only in the real world, the disparities obviously have more consequence than the distribution of stadium seats.

For a few more examples to illustrate the astounding depths of wealth inequality in modern America, consider:

- As of 2014, the four hundred wealthiest Americans were worth $2.3 trillion. This is more than double what the same group was worth a decade ago, $300 billion more than what they were worth just *one year earlier*,[92] and $600 billion more than in 2012.[93] The average member of the Forbes 400 now has 70,000 times the wealth of the typical American family, no doubt because they have worked *exactly* 70,000 times harder or are *exactly* 70,000 times smarter.[94]
- As of 2013, the wealthiest thirty people in the United States owned $792 billion worth of assets, which was the same amount owned by the poorest half of Americans: about 157 million people in all.[95]
- From 2011 to 2014, nine of the wealthiest people in America—Bill Gates, Warren Buffet, Mark Zuckerberg, the two Koch brothers and the four principal Walton heirs—gained an average of over $13 billion from capital gains on pre-existing assets. These gains did not flow from new work on their part, nor an increase in their personal productivity or particular genius. They weren't working more hours, and they didn't come up with some new and innovative technological breakthrough in

that time. They simply owned a bunch of stuff, and over a three-year period that stuff became more valuable because of gains in the stock market. Considering that the median income for American workers was $51,000 in 2013, it would take a quarter of a million years—which is about 50,000 more years than humans have even existed—for the typical American to earn as much as the average capital gain earned by these nine people just since 2011.[96]

- For a visual understanding of what all that means, consider that if the typical American stretched his or her annual income out, in one-dollar bills, from end to end, it would stretch roughly 25,500 feet, which is about 4.8 miles. Over three years at the same income, those bills would now stretch about 14.5 miles. Meanwhile, if we took the median amount of money gained by those nine super-rich Americans mentioned above over that same three-year period, and stretched it out, in one-dollar bills, from end to end, the money chain would stretch 1.2 million miles—a money chain long enough to circle the earth forty-eight times,[97] or alternately, to stretch from the earth to the moon and back twice, and then stretch around the globe a few more times for good measure.[98]
- In all, the six heirs to the Walmart fortune are worth as much as the bottom forty percent of the American population, or roughly 120 million people.[99] In fact, the Walton heirs, who are rich simply because of the family into which they were born (or in the case of Christy Walton, the one into which she married), have so much wealth at their disposal that they could buy every house, condo and townhome in Seattle or Dallas or Miami and still have $40 billion to spare, with which they could buy all the homes in Anaheim, California (if they love Disneyland), or Napa (if they really like wine). Just to put

the Walton's wealth in perspective, while the six heirs could purchase every home in these major U.S. cities, someone like Oprah Winfrey (whom most people think of as fabulously rich) could only afford to buy up all the homes in Mokena, Illinois, wherever that is.[100] In fact, the combined wealth of Oprah, Steven Spielberg, Donald Trump, Ted Turner, Howard Schultz (the founder of Starbucks), Mark Cuban (owner of the Dallas Mavericks), Jerry Jones (owner of the Dallas Cowboys), Phil Knight (founder of Nike), and Mark Zuckerberg (founder of Facebook)—a total of about $77.5 billion as of 2015—does not equal even *half* the wealth held by the Walton heirs. Even if we added the wealth of Bill Gates to the mix—the world's wealthiest individual—the combined wealth of these ten would still fall about $15 billion short of Walton money.[101] Meanwhile, most Walmart employees work for wages that leave them near the poverty line if not below it, forcing many of them to rely on food stamps to supplement their meager incomes, as we'll explore later.

Wealth disparities are especially stark when examined racially. Because of the nation's history of enslavement, lynching, segregation and overt racial discrimination, families of color did not have the same opportunity as whites to accumulate land and other tangible assets. Although civil rights laws were passed in the 1960s to prohibit formal discrimination in employment and housing, the head start afforded to whites over many generations obviously did not evaporate simply because anti-discrimination laws were passed. Due to a history of unequal opportunity to accumulate assets,[102] and the racially disproportionate impact of the recession on the real estate values of people of color,[103] the median net worth of white American households as of 2011 stood at a level *15.7 times* greater than the median for blacks and 13.3 times the median for Latinos.[104] As for financial assets such as stocks and investments other than home equity, the ratio is nearly *two hundred to one* in favor of whites, with the median financial wealth for whites standing at about $36,000 and the median for blacks a virtually non-existent $200, which in most cases represents merely the money in their bank accounts.[105] Even when black households are comparable to white households in terms of income, vast wealth discrepancies remain due to a history of unequal opportunity to accumulate and pass down assets. Comparing households that are middle class in terms of income, whites still have three times as much wealth as blacks, and among those in the top ten percent of income earners, white households have a nearly five-to-one advantage over black households.[106] Most disturbing, white families with a high school dropout as the head of household have median net worth of $51,300, while the median for black families with *college-educated* heads of household is only $25,900.[107] In other words, black households with heads who have a college degree have *half* the net worth of white households whose head finished tenth grade.

But it's not only the weight of past racism that explains current wealth gaps. In recent years, wealth disparities between whites and blacks have been intensified because of blatant discrimination in mortgage lending. During the run-up to the housing collapse, even African American borrowers with solid credit were given subprime, high-interest loans, often by lenders who were deliberately targeting them for these purposes, such as Wells Fargo. While only about six percent of white borrowers with credit scores above 660 were given subprime loans, over twenty-one percent of blacks with comparable credit received these higher-cost mortgages.[108] Most recently, discrimination testing conducted by the Fair Housing Justice Center in New York uncovered strong evidence of racial bias against potential homebuyers of color. According to a recent lawsuit against M&T Bank, prompted by the testing:

> [The bank] sent out trained actors to explore whether white and non-white homebuyers would be treated differently when trying to prequalify for a mortgage. All

> followed a similar script, telling bank officers they were married with no children and were first-time home-buyers. The black, Latino and Asian testers presented slightly better qualifications when it came to income, credit and additional financial assets. In nine separate interactions recorded either with a camera or an audio device, employees at M&T Bank's New York City loan office can be seen or heard treating the white applicants differently than the others, according to the suit. In one instance, a black candidate was told she did not have enough savings to buy a home. A white applicant with slightly lower income and credit scores and $9,000 less in savings was pre-approved for a loan. In another case, a Latina candidate was told she would qualify for a mortgage $125,000 less than the test's white candidate with lower income, poorer credit and less cash.[109]

Although the type of disparate treatment evident in the M&T case may not be as egregious as that of Wells Fargo, which a few years ago had been deliberately steering low-income African Americans (whom they called "mud people") into so-called "ghetto loans," it nonetheless suggests ongoing obstacles to equal housing opportunity.[110] As such, a significant portion of disparities in home ownership and net worth must be laid at the feet of discrimination in the present, and not seen merely as the residue of the past. The combined effects of past and present racial bias on the financial position of persons of color should not be underestimated as we examine why so few black and brown folks sit atop the nation's economic structure. Of all persons in the top one percent of national wealth holders, ninety-six percent are white.[111] Indeed, the four hundred wealthiest white people in America were worth approximately $2 trillion as of 2014: approximately the same amount as all forty million African Americans *put together*—no doubt because those four hundred white people have worked *just as hard* as all black people combined.[112]

Despite the evidence just examined, however, many continue to insist that America is a land of opportunity, and uniquely so, compared to the rest of the world. Such persons claim that even the poorest here are better off than virtually anyone else in the world, and that inequities between the haves and have-nots are smaller than they are elsewhere. But there is growing reason to doubt this rosy image. As for poverty, among industrialized nations, the United States has the third-largest percentage of citizens living at half or less of the national median income—the international standard for determining poverty. Only Mexico and Turkey rate worse among thirty-four modern, industrial democracies in terms of poverty rates.[113] While conservatives claim that even the poor in America live better than the middle class elsewhere—a subject to which we'll return in the next chapter—this argument simply isn't true. Compared to those industrialized nations with which the United States likes to compare itself, not only are the poor here doing worse than the middle class elsewhere, they are also doing worse than the *poor* elsewhere, in large measure because of less complete safety nets in America. For instance, before the effect of taxes and various welfare benefits are considered, twenty-seven percent of Swedes are poor, which is slightly more than the twenty-six percent of Americans who are; but *after* the effects of taxes and transfers are considered, the poverty rate in Sweden plummets to only five percent, while safety nets in the United States only bring our poverty rate down to seventeen percent. Likewise, thirty-four percent of Germans are poor prior to the effects of social safety net efforts, but only eleven percent remain poor after them. In the U.K., where the poverty rate is the same as in the United States, safety nets cut poverty by more than two-thirds to only eight percent, which is twice as big a cut as that afforded by such programs in the United States.[114]

As for inequality compared to other nations, here too America's contemporary record is not enviable. Among industrialized countries, the United States ranks fourth worst in income inequality between top earners and those at the bottom, and inequality here is actually growing much faster than in those other nations.[115] At present, the poorest half of Americans own less of our nation's wealth than the poorest half on the continents of Asia and Africa, and less than the poorest half in India, the U.K. and China. In other words, inequality is actually more severe in America than elsewhere.[116] Importantly, it isn't just the gap between the rich and poor in America that signifies our nation's greater inequality relative to other countries; we also have the greatest wealth gaps between the *middle* class and the wealthy of any industrialized nation.[117] Recent evidence suggests that this gap between the wealthy and the middle class is only getting larger, in fact; since 2010, middle-class wealth has remained flat, while wealth at the top has continued to grow, producing the largest gap between the affluent and the middle class in recorded U.S. history.[118]

But What About Mobility? Aren't the Poor Just Temporarily Embarrassed Millionaires?

There is a long-disputed (and likely inaccurate) quote attributed to John Steinbeck to the effect that the reason socialism never took root in the United States was because workers didn't consider themselves an exploited class, but rather, simply "temporarily embarrassed millionaires." In other words, the poor and struggling may be poor and struggling today, but since America is a land of opportunity where one can climb from rags to riches with the right combination of effort and skill, there is no reason to fight for major social change or equality—just work harder so that you can be the one on top next time. Putting aside the inaccurate provenance of the sentiment itself, it is hard to dispute that a faith in upward mobility has always been strong in America; so too, it is hard to doubt that such faith could have the effect of dampening concern over inequality, even the incredibly deep divisions documented thus far, and the poverty, unemployment and wage stagnation that have marked the last several years. If one believes that a little extra effort will allow one to move up the ladder, after all, then one is free to view inequality and poverty as temporary way stations on the road to prosperity. Certainly, this is the mindset encouraged by Florida senator and presidential candidate Marco Rubio, when he says (echoing the phony quote from Steinbeck) in language all too real:

> We have never been a nation of haves and have-nots. We are a nation of haves and soon-to-haves, of people who have made it and people who will make it.[119]

Yet, putting aside the sincerely held faith in American upward mobility, just how often do people rise in the economic hierarchy? Although the idea of upward mobility as a unique and central feature of the American experiment is long-standing, the sad truth is that such mobility seems to be less common in the United States today than elsewhere. According to the *Global Wealth Databook* for 2013, the likelihood of persons moving up in the wealth distribution is actually lower in the United States than in any other industrialized nation.[120] Indeed, chronic inequality appears to be a central cause of limited mobility here. The available evidence suggests that in nations with greater inequality, intergenerational mobility is far *less* common than it is in more egalitarian societies. In more equitable nations such as Finland, Denmark, Sweden and Norway, the correlation between your parents' income when you were a child and your own income as an adult is less than half as strong as in the United States and United Kingdom, both of which have far greater levels of inequality between the top and bottom.[121]

Although most kids born into the poorest fifth of American families will make it to a greater income level as adults, nearly four in ten will not. Even those who manage to improve their status economically don't improve it by much: sixty percent of persons born into the poorest fifth will remain in the lower two-fifths as adults, meaning that at most they will move from poor or near-poor to lower middle class. Only one in ten will make it into the top fifth of earners. On the other end of the spectrum, nearly a third of all persons born into the top quintile will remain there, and about six in ten will remain in the top two quintiles—in other words, the upper middle class at least—while only one in nine will fall from the top to the bottom.[122] For those in the bottom fifth of the income distribution, only 0.2 percent will climb into the top one percent of earners, while about eighty-three percent of those who started in the top one percent will manage to remain at least in the top ten percent as adults.[123] So while some will go from rags to riches or riches to rags, the influence of parental status on one's own status is strong. Poor families are ten times more likely to remain poor than to move into the highest income quintile, and those who start out rich are five times more likely to remain there as to fall into either of the lower two quintiles of earners.[124] As for wealth, research that examined families from the 1980s through 2003, discovered that about three-fourths of the responsiblity for where an individual ends up in terms of wealth is explained by the wealth of one's parents.[125]

Intergenerational mobility is especially limited for persons of color. For instance, half of black children born into families in the bottom fifth of income earners will remain there as an adult, compared to only twenty-three percent of white children. Nearly eight in ten African Americans born poor will remain in the bottom two-fifths of income earners (poor or lower-middle-class) as adults, compared to only forty-two percent of whites. Only an anemic three percent of blacks born poor will ultimately make it to the top quintile, and only one in ten will make it into the upper middle class or better. Although most whites born to impoverished families won't gain access to the upper middle class or the ranks of the affluent either, they are five times as likely as blacks to go from the bottom to the top, and more than a third will attain upper-middle-class status at the very least.[126]

Mobility also plays out differently by race among those in the middle class. For whites born middle-class, forty-four percent will move up and only a third will fall backward, while for middle-class blacks, only one in seven will move up and a stunning *sixty-nine percent* will fall backward. In short, upward mobility is more than three times as likely for middle-class whites as for blacks, while downward mobility is more than twice as likely for middle-class blacks as for whites.[127] When it comes to wealth, the ability to retain high status also differs by race: according to research that followed persons over a fifteen-to-twenty-year period, sixty percent of whites who were in the top fourth of wealth holders at the beginning of that period remained there by the end, compared to only twenty-two percent of African Americans.[128]

As for why mobility levels differ so markedly by race, it appears that the biggest culprit is the effect of concentrated poverty and disadvantage within the geographic spaces where most African Americans live. For whites born between 1955 and 1970, only five percent were raised in high-disadvantage neighborhoods (places with high poverty rates, lower school quality, less social capital, etc.), compared to eighty-four percent of blacks raised in such spaces. In contrast, only two percent of blacks born in that period were raised in low-disadvantage communities, compared to nearly half of whites.[129] If blacks are seventeen times as likely to have been raised in high-disadvantage neighborhoods, while whites are twenty-two times as likely to have been raised in low-disadvantage neighborhoods, it isn't hard to figure out why the opportunity structure remains skewed from year to year and generation to generation. Although rates of concentrated poverty have fallen somewhat, as noted previously, the ratio of concentrated poverty for blacks relative to whites remains high, ensuring ongoing inequity into the future.

Whodunit? Exploring the Causes of Growing American Inequality

But all of this begs the obvious question: *Why?* Why does America appear to be pulling apart, with ever-increasing levels of inequality in terms of both income and wealth? Why does the position of American workers seem to be declining while the position of the affluent is rising ever higher? There are several explanations for the economic maladies thus far discussed, some of which are better understood and recognized than others. Among the most commonly discussed, and certainly important, are the decline of manufacturing employment since the early 1970s—spurred in large measure by trade policies that opened up American markets to lower-cost goods from abroad—as well as the decline in the real value of the minimum wage, the weakening of the power of labor unions, and the preferential treatment afforded in the tax code to income from capital gains as opposed to labor. Less appreciated, but perhaps even more critical to the process of growing inequality, is the long-term economic trend away from a production-based economy toward an economy focused on financial services. This trend, which amounts to a casino-ization of the American economy, puts a premium on rampant speculation in stocks and various investment instruments and thereby disproportionately benefits that relatively small sliver of the population who make their living on Wall Street. Let's examine these each in turn.

Looking first at the role of trade: Increased trade with poorer nations can exacerbate inequalities in richer countries for two reasons. First, increased trade results in an influx of low-cost goods from abroad, which undermines high-paying employment at home; and second, offshoring of production undermines the job status of workers in wealthier nations as corporations use low-wage employees abroad for work that would previously have been done by higher-paid persons in the richer nation. Far from a theoretical abstraction, this appears to have been the concrete reality in America since the 1980s, at which point trade barriers were lowered for both U.S. goods abroad and other nations' goods here. Due to a spate of free trade agreements, inequality in the United States has increased, with as much as forty percent of the growing gap between the haves and have-nots due to trade policy and its impact on certain job sectors.[130]

It is estimated that trade policy accounts for about one-fifth of the decline in manufacturing employment during the 1990s, and another third of the decline that continued from 2000 to 2007. As a result of the loss of higher-paying manufacturing jobs and their replacement with lower-paying service-sector jobs, wages have stagnated at the bottom and middle of the income pyramid, contributing to the overall growth in income disparity.[131] While increased trade and offshoring of production has been lucrative for corporate America and those with significant stockholdings in companies engaged in global trade, the impact on most has been quite the opposite. The ability to buy goods more cheaply—the supposed benefit of trade liberalization, which we're told makes up for the decline in manufacturing employment in America—seems weak compensation for wage stagnation and little or no job security. After all, being able to buy things for less doesn't matter much if the service-sector job you managed to get only pays a fraction of your previous position.

In addition to the effects of increased trade, the decline in the value of the minimum wage has contributed to growing economic injustice and chronic poverty. When the minimum wage was first created in the 1930s, it was set at a level that came to about half of the nation's average wage. By 2010, at $7.25 per hour, the minimum pay level came to only thirty-nine percent of the average national wage. Five years later, it has continued to decline in real value. Today, the value of the minimum wage has fallen by more than a fifth since the late 1970s.[132] Economists at Princeton and the University of California estimate that at least twenty percent of the recent rise in wage inequality can be traced to the falling real value of the minimum wage.[133] Refusals by conservatives to support a proposed hike to just over $10 per hour (still less than what the minimum wage would be if it had kept pace with productivity), is literally keeping people poor. Although conservative talking heads like Bill O'Reilly claim that a boost in the minimum wage would have little impact on the well-being of workers (since relatively few earn it),[134] such hikes in the wage floor would raise the pay of more than just the lowest-paid workers themselves. Those workers who earn slightly above the minimum would also see wage pressure push upward as their employers scrambled to keep ahead of the rising minimum. The Congressional Budget Office estimates that a higher minimum wage (somewhere in the $10-per-hour range) would boost pay levels for about 16.5 million workers and lift about a million people from the ranks of the poor,[135] while the Economic Policy Institute predicts that the overall effect of such a minimum wage hike would be to lift the wages of nearly twenty-eight million workers: those currently receiving the minimum wage, those whose earnings are between the current minimum and $10 per hour, and even many whose current earnings are slightly above $10 per hour.[136]

Contrary to claims that such a boost might have a negative impact on overall employment—principally by raising labor costs for employers—evidence from sixty-four separate studies suggests the impact of minimum wage hikes on employment and unemployment levels is negligible at best, and certainly offset by the boost in income to those who are dependent on such wages for survival.[137] In fact, the most recent evidence clearly debunks the notion that higher minimum wages destroy jobs. At the beginning of 2014, thirteen states increased their minimum wages, four because of new legislation and nine others because their minimums are pegged to the inflation rate automatically. After evaluating the impact of minimum wage increases in these states, economists found that states where the minimum wage went up actually had *faster* employment growth than states where it did not.

Perhaps the strongest rebuttal to the claim that a hike in minimum wage will harm the economy comes from Seattle. The city, which will be phasing in a $15-per-hour minimum wage over the next several years—and has been pilloried in the business press as signing its economic death warrant for doing so—already had a much higher minimum wage than the national average, even before the recent hike. But had that fact harmed the city? Hardly. As billionaire investor Nick Hanauer—an admitted and proud member of the nation's one percent—explained it to his fellow plutocrats recently:

> Most of you probably think that the $15 minimum wage in Seattle is an insane departure from rational policy that puts our economy at great risk. But in Seattle, our current minimum wage of $9.32 is already nearly 30 percent higher than the federal minimum wage. And has it ruined our economy yet? Well, trickle-downers, look at the data here: The two cities in the nation with the highest rate of job growth by small businesses are San Francisco and Seattle. Guess which cities have the highest minimum wage? San Francisco and Seattle. The fastest-growing big city in America? Seattle. Fifteen dollars isn't a risky untried policy for us. It's doubling down on the strategy that's already allowing our city to kick your city's ass.

Hanauer then went on to explain the economic logic behind a higher, rather than lower and stagnant minimum wage. Putting it in terms that even the most jaded of corporate executives should be able to comprehend, he notes:

> If a worker earns $7.25 an hour, which is now the national minimum wage, what proportion of that person's income do you think ends up in the cash registers of local small businesses? Hardly any. That person is paying rent, ideally going out to get subsistence groceries at Safeway, and, if really lucky, has a bus pass. But she's not going out to eat at restaurants. Not browsing for new clothes. . . . Please stop insisting that if we pay low-wage workers more, unemployment will skyrocket and it will destroy the economy. It's utter nonsense. The most insidious thing about trickle-down economics isn't believing that if the rich get richer, it's good for the economy.

> It's believing that if the poor get richer, it's bad for the economy.[138]

Although conservatives recently latched on to an article in *Seattle Magazine*, which suggested restaurants were closing their doors because of the wage hike there (and that restaurant owners were "panicked" at the new policy), an investigation by the *Seattle Times* debunked the claim. Indeed, the very restaurant owners whose decision to close certain locations had been chalked up by conservatives to the increase in the minimum wage, told the *Times* exactly the opposite. They support the wage increase and were in the process of opening entirely new locations or restaurants elsewhere in the city.[139] If anything, both logic and experience tell us that policies to reduce inequality by boosting wages at the bottom can be expected to spur job creation and economic growth rather than suppress it.[140] When workers have more they spend more, which in turn allows companies to produce more or provide more services to more people.

As for the importance of unions: their power from the 1940s through the 1960s allowed workers to successfully demand higher pay and ensure that as their productivity rose, so would their income and benefits. Shared prosperity between workers and owners served the nation well, as the economy was strong throughout the period of growing unionization. Indeed, most of the basic measures for human dignity that we now take for granted were the result of union efforts. As Tim Koechlin, director of the International Studies Program at Vassar explains:

> A hundred years ago, U.S. workers—including millions of children—worked long hours for low wages in unsafe workplaces. Because of organized labor, the prospects for working Americans improved dramatically over the course of the twentieth century. Because of unions, millions of U.S. workers were able to achieve a middle-class life—economic security, home ownership, health insur-

> ance, vacation time and, perhaps, a college education for their children. From 1948 to 1973, the incomes of working-class families in the U.S. nearly doubled. In addition to higher wages, the struggles of organized labor have delivered virtually every protection and benefit enjoyed by U.S. workers. Unions have brought working Americans the forty-hour week, paid vacation, Social Security, Medicare and Medicaid, overtime pay, child labor laws, the Occupational Safety and Health Act, whistleblower protection laws, sexual harassment laws, lunch breaks and coffee breaks, wrongful termination protection, sick leave, the Americans with Disabilities Act, the weekend and much more. These rights, benefits and norms were not gifts from employers. They are the result of relentless organized struggle by working Americans.[141]

Unfortunately, union membership has declined, in large part due to deliberate efforts by corporations to break organizing drives by their employees, leaving workers vulnerable to stagnant wages, benefit give-backs, longer hours and less job security than in the past. Beginning in the 1970s, corporate America began a concerted campaign to blame unions for a loss of competitiveness in American industry. They also regularly threatened to move plants overseas if workers formed unions in places where they didn't yet exist. Even though the evidence suggested mismanagement at the top was to blame for the slide in the domestic auto industry, for instance, blaming the United Auto Workers for the loss of domestic car sales became a dominant narrative and fed anti-union efforts.[142] Although many of the resulting tactics of intimidation and union busting have been illegal, there has been little enforcement of labor law from either the Justice Department or National Labor Relations Board, both of which have been largely starved of funds for the purpose, and which are populated mostly by corporate attorneys who are disinclined to side with workers over management.[143]

The effects of anti-union efforts by corporate America have been substantial. While unions represented almost a third of the nation's workforce in the late 1940s, by 2010, fewer than twelve percent of all workers were unionized. Even this number exaggerates union strength, because it encompasses both private sector unions and public unions, like those for municipal workers, teachers, police and firefighters. Looking only at private sector workers, membership in unions has fallen from about one in four in the early 1970s to less than seven percent today.[144] As rates of union membership have declined, wages for most workers have stagnated, in part because the relative strength of labor and its ability to obtain a fair share of their increased productivity has been diminished.

As for taxes, over the last several decades the nation's tax burden has shifted off the backs of wealthy individuals and corporations and onto those of average workers and families, thereby contributing to overall income inequality. Income taxes were steeply progressive for most of the mid-century period, with the top marginal rate reaching ninety-one percent in 1957 on all income over $300,000 for an individual and $400,000 for a married couple.[145] But by the 1970s, conservatives were pushing for drastic cuts in income taxes for those at the top, as well as cuts in corporate income taxes and the creation of loopholes to allow companies to avoid taxes they would otherwise owe. Among the most important policies contributing to rising inequality, the preferential treatment of capital gains income ranks at the very top. A recent analysis of rising inequality of incomes since the early 1990s, for instance, found that capital gains income, along with the preferential tax treatment such income receives, has been the largest single contributor to growing income disparities during that time.[146]

The wealthy have long argued that income from capital gains—that is, income derived from increases in the value of investments—should be taxed either not at all, or at a lower rate than regular labor income. According to those who advocate such policies, low or no taxes on capital gains will spur the wealthy to invest more of their resources, thereby creating jobs and boosting the economy. In actuality, there is no evidence that lower capital gains tax rates spur investment or economic growth and quite a bit of evidence to negate the theory. Indeed, the economy has generally performed better when capital gains and labor income have been taxed at the same rate (and higher) as opposed to years when taxes on capital gains have been lower.[147] Nevertheless, policymakers have been taken in by the argument for years—lobbied by the business class to create such a two-tiered tax structure—and so today, capital gains are taxed at a maximum rate of twenty percent (and most often as low as fifteen percent), as opposed to a 39.6 percent maximum for all regular labor income above roughly $407,000.

The effect of preferential treatment for capital gains income has been to treat the wealthy minority far better than the rest of the country's people when it comes to taxation. Although middle-income families occasionally possess assets that produce capital gains, the overall distribution of financial assets remains incredibly unequal. Due to the far greater likelihood that the wealthy will own stocks, pooled investment funds or other income-producing assets, the median value of financial assets for the middle fifth of income earners is only about $17,000, while the median value of such assets held by the wealthiest tenth of earners is about $551,000.[148] The top tenth of income earners are four times as likely as middle income earners to own stock, and more than twelve times as likely as persons in the bottom fifth of income earners to do so.[149] So economic policies that favor income derived in the stock market will produce a disproportionate benefit for the wealthiest Americans, while meaning little in practical terms to the rest of us.

Because capital gains income receives such preferential treatment, America's wealthiest families—a group whose incomes average more than $345 million annually and stem mostly from rents, interest and dividends, rather than active labor—actually pay taxes at a lower rate than households with average incomes as low as $75,000. In fact, the nation's wealthiest four hundred families have a total effective tax rate averaging about 16.6 percent of their income, essentially the same as the 16.3 percent average paid by households with annual earnings as low as $50,000.[150] Fully ninety percent of all benefits from the preferential treatment of capital gains income accrue to taxpayers with more than $200,000 in annual income, with seventy-eight percent of benefits received by those earning more than a half-million dollars per year. By 2015, it is estimated that the typical taxpayer with more than $1 million in income will save more than $131,000 in taxes each year on average, all because of this provision in the tax code that treats investment income more favorably than income earned from work.[151] Currently, the wealthiest one percent of Americans make more annually from capital gains—not from actual work, but from interest, dividends and rents on things they already possess, even if they didn't work one hour of the year—than the entire cost of all safety net program payouts in the United States *combined*, including Social Security, Medicare and Medicaid.[152] And yet this income, received by about three million people, is taxed at a lower rate than the income earned by construction workers, physicians, food inspectors or law enforcement officials.

Other tax policies, including corporate tax loopholes that shelter offshore profits from taxation, or allow for accelerated depreciation write-offs, or permit deductions for the cost of advertising, have lowered the tax burden on American companies relative to average American families and individuals. Companies can avoid taxes in the U.S. by claiming huge losses at home while declaring massive profits abroad. Even though eighty-two percent of Bank of America's revenue is earned in the United States, the company was recently allowed to claim that *all* of its profit was made overseas, where it is untouched by U.S. taxes, while it supposedly suffered $7 billion in losses stateside. By rigging its balance sheets this way—a practice that is entirely legal under existing law—BoA was able to avoid billions in tax liability, as did other large corporations. Pfizer, for instance, made more than forty percent of its revenue domestically and had $31 billion in profits overseas in 2011–2012, but declared $7 billion in American losses so as to avoid taxes.[153] In all, according to the *Wall Street Journal*, sixty of the largest corporations in the United States "parked a total of $166 billion offshore" in 2012, thereby protecting more than forty percent of their profits from domestic taxation.[154]

No doubt it is programs and policies like this that help explain why corporate taxes as a share of overall taxes, as a share of national income, and as a share of corporate profits have all declined dramatically. Although financial aristocrats and their media defenders often complain about U.S. corporate taxes being too high—since the thirty-five percent statutory rate is higher than the rate in other industrialized nations—few companies actually pay anywhere near that percentage of their income in taxes, due to generous loopholes, shelters and gimmicks that allow them to substantially reduce their burdens. For instance, the 288 corporations in the Fortune 500 that were consistently profitable from 2008 to 2012 ultimately paid taxes at a rate that was only 19.4 percent of their income over that period, with one-third of these paying less than a ten percent rate. Twenty-six companies, including Boeing, General Electric and Verizon, paid *no federal income tax at all* over that five-year period, and roughly forty percent of the companies that remained profitable from 2008 to 2012 had at least one year during which they paid no taxes.[155]

No matter how one examines the data, there is simply no doubt that the tax picture for U.S. corporations is an increasingly rosy one. Whether examined as a share of the economy,[156] as a share of all income taxes,[157] or as a share of all federal tax revenue, corporate taxes are at historic lows. Today, corporations are contributing only about one-fifth as much of overall federal revenue as they did in the mid-1940s.[158] Finally, in 2012 corporate taxes fell to only 12.1 percent of profits, the lowest level since 1972, and about half the norm that held from the late 1980s until the economic collapse in 2008.[159]

Indeed, while America's wealthy minority complains about corporate taxes, many American companies actually pay less in taxes to the government than they pay to their chief executives each year. In 2013, for instance, seven of the nation's largest firms, despite earning more than $74 billion in pre-tax profits in the United States, received nearly $2 billion in federal tax *refunds*, while paying their CEOs over $17 million in average compensation. Of the one hundred highest-paid CEOs in the U.S., twenty-nine of them were paid more in 2013 than their companies paid in federal income taxes. Their companies made average pre-tax profits of $24 billion that year, while raking in, on average, $238 million in tax refunds. In other words, these mega-wealthy corporations had effective tax rates of *negative one percent.*[160] No wonder inequality is increasing in a tax environment such as this.

Finally, the increased financialization of the American economy has dramatically skewed economic returns to the rich relative to the rest of us. By financialization I mean the move away from productive economic activity—the manufacture of tangible goods for sale or the provision of basic services used by broad swaths of the public—and towards speculative investment, the buying and selling of companies to pump up stock values and, in particular, the increasingly popular practice of company stock buy-backs, in which companies use their profits not to increase production or hire new workers but to repurchase their own stock, thereby driving up stock prices by artificially inflating company value relative to what it would be if those shares remained in the open market. This stock overvaluation then pays substantial dividends to executives and shareholders while doing absolutely nothing for average Americans.

In the 1960s, forty percent of company earnings and borrowing went to investments in new production, equipment and company growth. By the 1980s, only ten percent of earnings was going back into investment, thanks to the growing power of shareholders demanding dividend payouts and higher stock values, which could be procured via stock buy-backs. Today, companies are literally borrowing money so as to pay shareholders and buy back their own stock, rather than invest in new production.[161] According to economist William Lazonic, co-director of the Center for Industrial Competitiveness at the University of Massachusetts–Lowell, the 449 publicly traded companies in the S&P 500 Index used more than half of their profits—nearly $2.5 trillion in earnings—from 2003 to 2012 simply to repurchase their own stock shares, and thirty-seven percent more to pay dividends to shareholders. Less than one dollar in ten earned by these firms was put back into production, expansion, hiring, research or development. And some companies were actually spending more to repurchase stock than what their firms were making in net income in a given year.[162]

But as disturbing as those numbers may sound, 2014 was even worse. Last year, the same companies spent *ninety-five percent of profits* on stock repurchases and dividend payouts.[163] Obviously, when earnings are used to buy up stock or pay shareholders, rather than expand a company or produce goods (which would require more workers or raises for those already working), the result will be increasing inequality between those at the top who make their money from things like stock value and the masses who make their money from labor income. Although the strategy works well for companies in the short term—by inflating stock values, share buy-backs help firms meet quarterly "earnings-per-share" prices—but in the long run can undermine their financial health by diverting resources from growth and development into activity that benefits only a very narrow stratum. Because the practice of open-market stock buy-backs has been largely unregulated since 1982, companies are increasingly using the practice less to help stabilize undervalued shares (one of the arguments made in favor of the practice) than to manipulate stock prices for the benefit of executives and short-term stockholders,[164] contributing significantly to rising incomes and wealth at the top and stagnant income growth for everyone else.

Ultimately, the post–World War II consensus—a social contract of sorts—which held that working class persons should have access to a growing piece of the economic pie, and safety net protections for when they fell through the cracks, has been largely abandoned. Throughout the mid-twentieth century there was widespread and largely shared agreement from members of both main political parties in America as to the importance and value of strong unions, rising minimum wages, Social Security, government housing and jobs initiatives, and even progressive taxation. Far from left-wing concepts, these were seen as fully *American* concepts. However hard this may be to believe, the evidence is right there, embedded in the 1956 Republican Party platform, which included the following line:

> We are proud of and shall continue our far-reaching and sound advances in matters of basic human needs—expansion of social security—broadened coverage in unemployment insurance—improved housing—and better health protection for all our people. We are determined that our government remain warmly responsive to the urgent social and economic problems of our people.

Later in the platform, the GOP bragged about the fact that under the leadership of President Eisenhower, "the Federal minimum wage has been raised for more than 2 million workers. Social Security has been extended to an additional 10 million workers and the benefits raised for 6½ million. The protection of unemployment insurance has been brought to 4 million additional workers," and there had been "wage increases and improved welfare and pension plans for federal employees." Not content to stop there, Republicans trumpeted the fact that union membership was up by two million since 1952. Later, the platform called for "equal pay for equal work regardless of sex," maintaining prevailing union wages for employment on public contracts, extending minimum wage laws even further, and providing "assistance to improve the economic conditions of areas faced with persistent and substantial unemployment." It also called for revisions to existing labor law that would protect the "rights of workers to organize into unions and to bargain collectively,"[165] and actually called for an *Equal Rights Amendment* so as to essentially illegalize institutional sexism in the labor market.

Of course today, the Republican Party leadership would reject their 1956 platform, and those conservative commentators who hold sway on talk radio would roundly condemn it. It is hard to imagine such a pro-union platform, for instance, surviving amid the likes of reactionary talking heads such as Ann Coulter, who says the nation's largest labor federation represents "useless" workers—including kindergarten teachers—rather than "men who have actual jobs,"[166] or the even more influential Rush Limbaugh, who insists that unionized workers are "freeloaders," as opposed to "real, working, non-unionized people."[167] But conservative hostility to unions and those who belong to them is not limited to the merely rhetorical; indeed, lawmakers in New Jersey, Wisconsin and Illinois have been leading an active assault on the rights of unionized workers, raiding pension funds for teachers and child welfare caseworkers (among others), and seeking to break unions altogether by allowing workers who are covered by a union contract to avoid paying dues even as they reap the benefits of collective bargaining. Additionally, the requirement that workers who choose not to join a union should still have to pay their "fair share" portion of collective bargaining costs—given that they benefit from bargaining on their behalf—is under attack. If successful, such an attack on union funding would functionally destroy organized labor by giving workers the benefits of unionization without asking them to shoulder any of the expense.[168]

Opposition to organized labor is so intense, in fact, that a conservative state senator in Tennessee recently complained about a plan by Volkswagen to bring over 200,000 jobs to the state, precisely because the German company is supportive of labor unions. As lawmaker Bo Watson put it, the VW plant would be a "magnet for unionized labor," which might alter the "culture" of Tennessee—yes, apparently by creating jobs and boosting wages and benefits for its autoworkers, thereby undermining the "culture" of low-wage employment preferred by reactionaries like Watson.[169] This is how far to the right the Republicans have moved in a half-century or so, and how glaringly "under the affluence" the nation's mindset toward working people has become in the same period.

The longstanding and relatively liberal post-war consensus had been developed in large measure to co-opt the rising militancy of the working class in the wake of the Depression—in other words, to limit the threat of class warfare from below—but by the mid-1970s and 1980s, the rich had opted to abandon the consensus and wage their own brand of class warfare from above. Today, rather than supporting previously settled matters like the value of the minimum wage, politicians and commentators on the right often openly question the very existence of a minimum earnings floor—a position that was historically associated only with the most extreme and marginal libertarians.[170] Even basic protections against the use of child labor are no longer considered sacred, with Maine's far-right Governor Paul LePage proposing changes in labor law that would allow twelve-year-olds to work up to fifteen hours weekly.[171] It is almost as if—as several other commentators have put it—conservatives are seeking to repeal the twentieth century in the interests of the affluent minority and with no concern for the well-being of the masses, who increasingly suffer the consequences of rising inequality and economic insecurity. Though such a charge may sound hyperbolic, it's hard to avoid such a conclusion when Eric Bolling of FOX can say, as he did recently, that rather than emulating European nations that are seeking to cut back on hours in the workweek—a step that has been shown to boost productivity—we should emulate China by repealing all labor laws, including minimum wage protections, child labor laws and any upper limits on how many hours an employee can be made to work.[172]

Distressingly, as the social contract between the business class and working class has been torn up—at least insofar as aristocratic obligations to the public are concerned—that same public is still expected to do *for* the wealthy, as with the $800 billion no-strings-attached taxpayer-bailout of the very financial institutions that were responsible for the economic crisis in the first place. While defenders of the bailout insist it was necessary and that every dollar has been paid back, or is being paid back with interest, such an argument misses the larger point: namely, if America can bail out the wealthiest individuals and institutions on the face of the earth as a way to prevent financial catastrophe, why can't that same nation bail out homeowners facing foreclosure? Why can't we bail out the long-term unemployed, or those working at minimum wage? The rich may well pay back all the bailout money and then some—they surely should, and hardly deserve thanks when they do, as if they had done *us* some great favor—but it must mean something that so many policymakers think nothing of forking over hundreds of billions of dollars to institutions already noted for their illegal, unethical and irresponsible behaviors, while resisting the same for the poor and struggling. After all, such a bailout for the rest of us would also likely "pay the country back" in economic stimulus, consumer spending, greater tax revenues, reduced reliance on safety net programs, reduced health care costs and a host of other benefits. But in a society with an increasingly tattered social contract, it is apparent that sacrifice is only expected to run in one direction.

Some Final Words About Race and the Economic Crisis

Before concluding this chapter, it is important to note that for millions of Americans the downturn of the past several years and its effects in terms of wage stagnation, persistent unemployment, and struggles with affordable health care, housing and higher education, are nothing particularly new. For millions of people of color, such economic insecurity has been distressingly normal, generation in and generation out, for all of American history. Regardless of the health of the economy, it is virtually a truism that

African American unemployment and poverty levels continually hover around or beyond recession levels.

In fact, it could be argued that part of why so many have taken notice of the crisis in recent years, and why it has become such a topic of concern, is precisely due to the way that normatively black and brown economic conditions have bled over into the white community. So long as economic pain was localized in subgroups with less power and influence—especially when those subgroups have long faced a history of discrimination and stigma—it failed to register on the radar screens of the larger citizenry. But once the insecurity began to be shared a bit—even then not equitably, but more so than white Americans had been used to—the magnitude of the problem suddenly appeared more obvious. Double-digit unemployment in the white community, even for a brief time, was truly new for many. White Americans on the whole had not experienced that kind of insecurity in the job market for three generations, since the Great Depression.

While people of color fared far worse during the recent collapse than whites—they were still the first to lose their jobs and the last to be hired back, and saw the vast majority of their already minimal wealth levels wiped out, particularly in terms of home value—the downturn seems to have had a greater *psychological* impact on whites. Precisely because of the relative advantage most white Americans have long taken for granted, we were less prepared for the kind of setback to which we were subjected in recent years. This is no doubt part of the reason why recent surveys have found that despite ongoing relative advantages over persons of color in the job market, housing market, educational system and elsewhere—about which I have written extensively in my previous books, and which I further document herein—white Americans are more pessimistic about the future than ever, and whites are far more pessimistic than members of other racial groups who are doing quite a bit worse.[173]

For a graphic and telling consideration of just how distressing the downturn seems to have been, especially for whites, one need look no further than the lead story in *Newsweek* from mid-April 2011 concerning what the cover referred to as "Beached White Males." Therein, the author suggested that *now* the economic meltdown was really a crisis, because whites—even whites in the managerial class—were feeling the pinch, with some even experiencing the long-term unemployment that had previously been seen as the purview of only the lesser classes.[174] There is a distressing and even heart-breaking irony to the article once one sifts through the self-loathing of corporate executives who can't seem to cope with having to pound the pavement looking for work like mere mortals. Reading the piece, it becomes obvious just how dangerous it can be to have blind faith in the system, as apparently many of the men in the article long had. Once they came to realize that hard work and playing by the rules was not enough—something people of color and even poor whites have long understood—they were ill prepared for it.

None of this is to dismiss the real stresses faced by white Americans because of current economic conditions; rather, it is to say that part of our current predicament may indeed be worse precisely because we paid so little attention to the crisis when it was only affecting those *other* people. In fact, not only did we pay insufficient attention, but in many cases, the government helped facilitate the crisis directly by way of its actions. So, for instance, in 1999 North Carolina passed a law prohibiting banks from offering predatory and deceptive loans to homeowners, in large measure because lenders were targeting the poor and people of color with these instruments. Rather than applaud the ruling and seek to extend it nationwide or with comparable national legislation, the federal government overrode the new law, paving the way for several more years of these kinds of loans, which ultimately became the fulcrum of the economic meltdown.[175] Had we cared more, attended to the warning signs, and resisted the growing culture of cruelty with regard to the needy, perhaps we wouldn't be in the predicament we're in at all. It is that culture of cruelty to which I now turn.

CHAPTER II

RESURRECTING SCROOGE: RHETORIC AND POLICY IN A CULTURE OF CRUELTY

In 1843, Charles Dickens visited Cornwall, in Southwest England. There he encountered children laboring in the tin mines that were the centerpiece of local economic production. The deplorable conditions he witnessed, along with a recently released Parliamentary report that exposed the nationwide scandal of child labor, led him to begin work on a political pamphlet, the title of which was to be "An Appeal to the People of England, on Behalf of the Poor Man's Child." Dickens hoped that such a treatise might stir the conscience of the British and move the nation to end such practices as had by then become all too common.[1] While at work on the pamphlet, however, Dickens ultimately concluded that his point might best be made within the boundaries of a fictional story. Upon making the switch from political screed to novella, Dickens wrote to one of the Parliamentary commissioners who had issued the child labor report, exclaiming that the story he had in mind would "come down with twenty times the force—twenty thousand times the force—I could exert by following out my first idea."[2]

And so began the process by which Dickens's *A Christmas Carol* would come to be: as a call to charity and compassion in a nation turned hard and cold by the vicissitudes of Victorian working conditions and Poor Laws, intended to wring out every last drop of labor from those at the bottom of England's class struc-

hile greatly enriching those at the top of it. Beginning in ober, Dickens's frenzied creative pace allowed him to finish e book in a mere six weeks. He self-published its first run in time for the Christmas holidays, shortly after which it became a literary sensation. To this day, it has never been out of print.

If you are familiar with it, you will doubtless recall one of the story's early scenes, in which two men enter the business of Ebenezer Scrooge and his former (and recently deceased) partner, Jacob Marley, hoping to procure alms for the poor at Christmas time. It is worth excerpting Dickens here, at some length.

> "At this festive season of the year, Mr. Scrooge," said the gentleman, taking up a pen, "it is more than usually desirable that we should make some slight provision for the Poor and Destitute, who suffer greatly at the present time. Many thousands are in want of common necessaries; hundreds of thousands are in want of common comforts, sir."
>
> "Are there no prisons?" asked Scrooge.
>
> "Plenty of prisons," said the gentleman, laying down the pen again.
>
> "And the Union workhouses?" demanded Scrooge. "Are they still in operation?"
>
> "They are. Still," returned the gentleman, "I wish I could say they were not."
>
> "The Treadmill and the Poor Law are in full vigour, then?" said Scrooge.
>
> "Both very busy, sir."
>
> "Oh! I was afraid, from what you said at first, that something had occurred to stop them in their useful course," said Scrooge. "I'm very glad to hear it."
>
> "Under the impression that they scarcely furnish Christian cheer of mind or body to the multitude," returned the gentleman, "a few of us are endeavouring to raise a fund to buy the Poor some meat and drink and

means of warmth. We choose this time, because it is a time, of all others, when Want is keenly felt, and Abundance rejoices. What shall I put you down for?"

"Nothing!" Scrooge replied.

"You wish to be anonymous?"

"I wish to be left alone," said Scrooge. "Since you ask me what I wish, gentlemen, that is my answer. I don't make merry myself at Christmas and I can't afford to make idle people merry. I help to support the establishments I have mentioned — they cost enough; and those who are badly off must go there."

"Many can't go there; and many would rather die."

"If they would rather die," said Scrooge, "they had better do it, and decrease the surplus population. "[3]

For Scrooge, the answer to the problems of the poor and destitute was simple: ship them off to workhouses established during that time to allow the wretched of England to labor away their unpaid debts, imprison them if they would not work; but by no means should one extend to such human refuse compassion or charity of any kind. To Scrooge, the poor had it coming. In his estimation, their economic failings merely reflected their far greater moral ones; beggars were beggars for want of industriousness, or acumen, or drive and determination. They were, in the parlance of the modern era, "takers" not "makers," and as such should be left to their own devices. And if they died, well then, such passing would merely reduce the "surplus population" of persons greedily thieving all that oxygen from their betters, and especially from men such as Ebenezer Scrooge.

Of course, as Dickens unfolds the story, Scrooge learns the true importance not merely of Christmas but of compassion and kindness more generally. He is visited by Marley's ghost, who seeks to warn him of the moral error of his ways—ways that Marley himself had all too gladly practiced while alive—and then by three additional ghosts (of Christmas past, present and future) who provide him with visions that cause him to rethink his miserly and caustic manner, and to understand not only the plight and struggle of others but even the sources of his own cold and bitter heart. He is transformed.

Which brings us to the present, 172 years after Dickens. For if Scrooge were merely a fictional character, like so many others typically overdrawn and caricatured, we could perhaps leave him within the pages of his book, only to be dusted off during the holiday season along with other characters of Dickens's creation, like Tiny Tim. But sadly, the relevance of Scrooge goes beyond the confines of *A Christmas Carol.* Just as Dickens saw Scrooge, in part, as a representation of his own cruel father, and more broadly of the era's contemptible attitudes toward the poor held by so many among the affluent, so too must we interpret his more comprehensive meaning for a new era. Unfortunately, many of the calumnies heaped upon the Victorian poor and working class are not unknown in our time. In many ways they are making something of a comeback. And while Dickens himself was clear that Scrooge was the heel, the villain and the bad guy, it appears that in modern America there are some who have missed that small detail, and are essentially seeking to resurrect Scrooge as some great moral philosopher. Even worse, there are many who have institutionalized "Scroogism" as a predatory financial system that both disadvantages the poor and needy and aims to eliminate any real safety net to assist them when the money runs out.

Whereas Dickens intended for readers to be appalled by the cruel and callous soliloquies of Scrooge (and rest assured, they were), we can hear many of the same kinds of things being said in the United States today, which, although updated for modern times, signal a contempt for the poor no less certain than that which animated Dickens's famous character. And the judgmentalism on display regarding the have-nots goes hand in hand with a valorization of the wealthy, with which Scrooge would have been all too familiar. It is the new "Scroogism" and its historical antecedents to which I now turn.

Past as Prologue: The Origins of Class and Cruelty in America

In some ways, it might actually be too forgiving to America to suggest that Scrooge has been resurrected. After all, to resurrect someone it is necessary for the object of reanimation to have first died. Yet, if anything, Scroogism has been the norm for most of American history, interrupted by occasional bouts of compassionate reform, but never fully discarded. If we think of various historical moments—from the social gospel movement of the early 1900s to the New Deal in the 1930s and Great Society of the 1960s—as the social policy equivalents of religious reformations, let us be clear that most of the nation's history has been marked by the social policy equivalent of the Inquisition.

Indeed, blaming the poor for their condition has been a long-standing tradition. As Georgetown professor of law Peter Edelman notes:

> Beginning with the Bible and continuing through the Elizabethan poor laws, throughout history there has been an instinctive belief among some that the poor have no one to blame but themselves. A special version of this illusion exists in the United States, the Horatio Alger mythology that one makes it (or doesn't) on his or her own. The pioneer spirit and rugged individualism—values to be admired on the whole—contribute to the American version of the "blame the poor" story.[4]

Frankly, the poor were always especially troubling to Protestant zealots, and never more so than when engaged in public begging. As Max Weber notes in *The Protestant Ethic and the Spirit of Capitalism*, "Begging on the part of one able to work, is not only the sin of slothfulness, but a violation of the duty of brotherly love."[5] Protestant leaders like John Calvin and Martin Luther believed that poverty was evidence of sin and that the poor deserved neither charity nor public forbearance; and this they insisted upon even as the proliferation of the poor in Europe stemmed directly from the private and forcible enclosure of public lands, which drove previously self-sufficient farmers from their livelihoods. In other words, even when systemic factors beyond the control of the poor were responsible for rising destitution, church leaders found fault with those in need. Throughout the middle of the last millennium, Europe increasingly developed means of punishment and public degradation for the poor, from whippings to debtors' prisons, all of which were thought to help cure the character deficiencies from which the destitute were believed to suffer. Central to England's harsh treatment of the poor was a belief that it was only the threat of crushing destitution that could possibly encourage them to work. As British physician and clergyman Joseph Townsend put it in 1786:

> The poor know little of the motives which stimulate the higher ranks to action—pride, honour and ambition. In general it is only hunger which can spur and goad them on to labour.[6]

Once in the colonies, political and religious elites continued their harsh rhetoric and treatment of the needy and impoverished. Preachers like Cotton Mather insisted that when it came to the unemployed, the proper policy was to "let them starve."[7] In the eighteenth century, workhouses for the poor, as well as what were called "bettering" houses (in which not only hard work but moral instruction was prescribed) spread throughout the colonies. As with their European counterparts, these institutions were designed to be misery-inducing places, so undesirable as to convince even the laziest of the poor to take any job, no matter how lowly, so as to avoid them.[8] Any forms of actual monetary relief for the poor—of which there were few, either in Europe or the colonies—were set at such a level as to be well below the lowest wage available in the workforce. In this way, it was thought, the poor would take jobs no matter how miserable, as doing so would still ensure they were better off than if they relied on cash relief.

By the nineteenth century, behavioral pathologies such as laziness or alcohol abuse were the presumed culprits for poverty. Armed with such presumptions about the poor, policymakers established little in the way of safety nets to catch those in need.[9] Regular moralizing about the vice of poverty and the virtue of wealth was commonplace. In the years after the Civil War, Russell Conwell—who was a minister, author, graduate of Yale Law School, and a founder of Temple University—became famous for a lecture he would deliver thousands of times nationwide. Called the "Acres of Diamonds" speech, its message was simple: anyone can get rich if they try. As Conwell put it:

> I say that you ought to get rich, and it is your duty to get rich . . . The men who get rich may be the most honest men you find in the community . . . That is why they are rich . . . I sympathize with the poor, but the number of poor who are to be sympathized with is very small. To sympathize with a man whom God has punished for his sins . . . is to do wrong . . . Let us remember there is not a poor person in the United States who was not made poor by his own shortcomings. . . .[10]

In keeping with the notion that the poor were to blame for their plight, "outdoor relief"—basically, public assistance outside the confines of a workhouse—was eliminated in most all major cities of the United States in the 1870s, due to a growing belief that "indiscriminate charity" indulged the bad habits of the poor and rendered them incapable of personal betterment. Even in the aftermath of the greatest economic crisis the nation had seen to that point—the Depression that began in 1873—it was common to hear condemnations of any kind of relief for the poor. In Chicago, a relief organization that had been established in the wake of the great fire two years earlier, refused to disburse the $600,000 in its coffers to persons who were out of work because of the downturn. Its director insisted that unemployed men "loafing around the streets" could find a job easily were they "not too lazy to look for it."[11] This kind of thinking dovetailed directly with the desires and interests of industrial aristocrats. The business class sought to limit or end government support for the poor because they increasingly needed low-wage workers to stoke the engines of their own profitability. If the poor and desperate had alternatives to low-wage and dangerous labor, industrialists feared their business interests would suffer.[12] To make the financial minority richer, it was necessary that others be made and kept destitute.

The Reformation: From Social Gospel to the New Deal and Beyond

By the latter decades of the nineteenth century, however, a kind of reformation was beginning to take hold in the form of the social gospel movement. Although the movement encompassed a broad range of theologians who differed as to their public policy preferences, the uniting strand of the social gospel was the idea that Christians should apply religious morality to social problems and involve the church in addressing many of the pressing issues of the day, including poverty and the exploitation of workers.

Although instrumental to the progressive movement of the late nineteenth and early twentieth centuries, there were still elements of judgmentalism inherent in the new and emerging liberal Christianity. Preachers of the social gospel stressed the need for the poor to live moral and sober lives, and sought to establish institutions that would instruct them as to proper work habits and lifestyles and thereby improve them, much as the workhouses had claimed to do. But whereas the workhouse movement had been rooted in a belief that the poor were solely to blame for their condition, social gospel theologians acknowledged that the institutional forces of industrial capitalism were creating massive social and moral dislocations that required public action, and especially the attention of committed and affluent Christians. In *Progress and Poverty*, economist and social gospel thinker Henry

George criticized wealthy churchgoers for sitting comfortably in finely apportioned pews while exhibiting little concern about "the squalid misery that is festering but a square away."[13] Although it must be noted that George was a vicious racist whose repugnant broadsides against Chinese labor marked him as firmly committed to a whites-only vision of economic justice, he stands as an example of the developing consciousness around the gaps between rich and poor.[14]

Theologian Walter Rauschenbusch penned perhaps the most significant articulation of social gospel thinking in his 1907 book, *Christianity and the Social Crisis*. Therein, he disputed the commonly held notion that "religion is purely personal; or that God is on the side of the rich," and argued that Christian civilization was obligated to fight inequality, poverty and the abuse of workers, among other injustices.[15] By the end of the first decade of the 1900s, most all of the mainline Protestant denominations had adopted the "Social Creed of the Churches," which called for an end to child labor, the creation of disability insurance, and the shortening of the workweek. Speaking for Catholics, Pope Leo XIII's 1891 encyclical, *Rerum Novarum*, postulated the basis for social justice activism among American Catholics by calling for a more humane capitalism, including support for labor unions.[16] Although the Pope opposed government-mandated redistribution of the wealth that had become so concentrated in the hands of a few—he preferred redistribution motivated by Christian compassion and charity—his view of the rich could not have been much less charitable. As he explained it:

> The whole process of production as well as trade in every kind of good has been brought almost entirely under the power of a few, so that a very few rich and exceedingly rich men have laid a yoke almost of slavery on the unnumbered masses of non-owning workers.[17]

During this period, Christian churches helped establish settlement houses intended to Christianize residents as well as to enrich their intellectual, academic and cultural attachments. Others, like Jane Addams, created secular settlements such as Hull House in Chicago, the purpose of which was to enhance opportunities for working-class women to learn literature, history and art, among other subjects. Hull House residents also learned to conduct social science research in the surrounding neighborhood concerning the social dynamics of inequality, especially as it affected recent immigrants.[18] Though even here the politics and philosophy of the settlement houses was complicated—Addams, for instance, believed that women's proper role was in the home, caring for children, rather than working to help support a family—the efforts were yet evidence of a slowly liberalizing attitude toward persons in need.[19]

But despite the efforts of social gospel activists, there were still few government-sponsored programs for the poor and unemployed during the early part of the twentieth century, and those that did exist tended to operate at the state or local level. It was only after the onset of the Great Depression, when millions had been thrown into destitution by the collapse of the American economy, that the federal government began to establish broad-based programs to support those in need. These programs included cash-based income support (originally known as Aid to Dependent Children, or ADC) as well as large-scale public housing initiatives, public works programs like the Civilian Conservation Corps (CCC) and Works Progress Administration (WPA), retirement insurance in the form of Social Security, and other government interventions in the economy, like the minimum wage, all intended to promote economic recovery, lessen the extremes of impoverishment, and generally promote the national welfare.

And the evidence makes clear that such efforts succeeded: government programs to put people back to work on any number of important infrastructure and community improvement projects not only stabilized the economy but also crafted a sense of mutual aid and national purpose. Although the programs of the New

Deal were hardly as inclusive as they should have been—persons of color were discriminated against in public works efforts, home loans and cash assistance, and the programs tended to prioritize the employment needs of men over those of women—the general tenor of the times was that government had a direct role to play in addressing joblessness and improving the economic health of the country. As a 2010 report from the Urban Institute reminds us:

> The WPA (Works Progress Administration) achieved remarkable scale by putting more than 3 million unemployed Americans back to work at its peak in 1938. Its most enduring legacy is found in its contributions to the nation's infrastructure. Under the program, the nation built or reconstructed 617,000 miles of new roads, 124,000 bridges and viaducts, and 35,000 buildings. It also financed a wide array of other labor-intensive work projects, including the construction of sidewalks, street curbs, school athletic fields, parks, playgrounds, and landing fields as well as national landmarks such as the Philadelphia Art Museum and New York City's Central Park Zoo and LaGuardia Airport.[20]

Although the business class opposed virtually every one of these government initiatives, and for the very same reasons one still hears today—they amounted to intrusive interventions in the free market, they raised the cost of doing business, and they elevated tax rates—for the most part, these efforts proved popular. Roosevelt would be elected four times (no longer allowed thanks to the Twenty-Second Amendment to the Constitution), in large measure because of widespread support for his economic policies. In other words, beginning in the early 1930s, American "Scroogism" was on the ropes, discredited by a capitalist economy that had proven incapable of producing acceptable levels of access to opportunity and mobility for the general population.

Additionally, labor militance during this period boosted the number of workers in trade unions as well as support for unions among the American people. The threat of mass strikes and revolutionary organizing was sufficiently frightening to the ruling class that many of their number—despite their dislike of New Deal policy—relented and came to accept the emerging social contract. After all, in the minds of the financial aristocracy, social programs that reformed capitalism were preferable to a revolution that might end it outright.[21] Mindful of the Russian revolution of 1917, and afraid that socialist upheaval in the United States might lead to a similar overturning of the social order here, capitalists embraced a two-pronged program to allow for reform but to ensure their continued hegemony over the nation's economy. First, they backed overt political repression—for instance, crackdowns on socialist and communist organizing, and violence against militant union efforts—and second, they grudgingly accepted the broad contours of the American version of the limited welfare state.

Support for government social programs and state intervention in the economy would remain relatively strong throughout the period following World War II. Bolstered by the concrete benefits such efforts afforded—the low-interest loan program created by the Federal Housing Administration helped produce the white middle class,[22] and the G.I. Bill provided concrete job and educational opportunities to returning (especially white) soldiers[23]—the welfare state enjoyed widespread support. So too, the relatively high taxes levied upon the upper middle class and affluent so as to fund such efforts also remained relatively uncontroversial throughout this period. As mentioned previously, both major political parties generally accepted the notion of an activist state, intervening on behalf of working people and families. There was no "tax revolt" movement, no Tea Party screaming about being "taxed enough already" and no broad-based backlash to "big government," despite the fact that taxes throughout the 1950s were always two to three times higher on most taxpayers than they are today.[24] Except in the minds of certain persons on the far right, those in libertarian circles, or novelists and itinerant pseudo-philosophers like Ayn Rand (who believed that *any* intervention by the state in the workings of the free enterprise system amounted to tyranny), the general notion that government had an obligation to ensure a modicum of opportunity was taken as a given. But soon the reformation would give way to a retrenchment, in which some would seek a restoration of the prior order. This restoration, pushed for by a business class and a conservative movement beholden to it, would begin the resurrection of Scroogism in the modern era.

The Restoration: Backlash, Reaganism and the Liberal Capitulation

By the mid-1960s, during the height of the American civil rights movement, attention began to shift from some of the more basic demands of that struggle—like desegregation of schools, voting rights and anti-discrimination protections in the workplace—to bread-and-butter economic justice matters like jobs, housing and economic development in marginalized communities of color. Not content to accept integration into what even Martin Luther King Jr. came to see as a "burning house," racial justice activists demanded higher wages, community empowerment, fair housing laws and an assault on poverty as the next stage of the freedom struggle.[25] So too, new attention to the mostly white poor of the Appalachian region focused national eyes upon the ongoing problem of communities living in poverty and hunger.

President Lyndon Johnson was forced to address these matters, and the escalating anger in the nation's cities, which spilled over into open rebellions throughout most of his presidency. Ultimately, he succeeded in pushing through a number of programs under the rubric of fighting a "war on poverty." These efforts, part of what became known as the "Great Society" initiative, went beyond merely expanding pre-existing social welfare programs such as food stamps, public housing and cash assistance. In addition to these older efforts, the Johnson years witnessed the establishment of Medicare and Medicaid to ensure some degree of health care security for the poor and elderly, as well as community development initiatives, pre-school education programs, and other efforts intended to tackle persistent urban poverty. Although these efforts proved largely successful in a short time—contrary to popular perception, as we'll discuss below—it was during this time and shortly after that backlash to the so-called welfare state began to flower.

Whereas government initiatives on behalf of the poor and unemployed had remained popular for roughly three decades, by the early 1970s, discontent over such programs was growing. When he ran for the Republican presidential nomination in 1976, former California Governor Ronald Reagan regularly capitalized on that souring public mood toward welfare with various stories of fraud and abuse in government antipoverty programs. Although many of the stories he told were as fictional as the movies in which he had once starred (including a claim about a lavish public housing project with a gym and a swimming pool), they were political dynamite, playing upon growing resentments about supposedly lazy welfare recipients who were collecting handouts while hard-working taxpayers struggled to make ends meet. The racial subtext of these appeals was hard to miss, in part because by then welfare programs had generally been racialized in the white imagination by media representations of the urban poor, but also because Reagan telegraphed that subtext in ways that were hardly subtle. His most notorious story involved a "woman from Chicago," who, according to Reagan:

> . . . used 80 names, 30 addresses, (and) 15 telephone numbers to collect food stamps, Social Security, veterans' benefits for four nonexistent deceased veteran husbands, as well as welfare. Her tax-free cash income alone has been running $150,000 a year.[26]

Later in the campaign, Reagan would boost the presumed profligacy of her fraudulent ways by insisting she had been operating in fourteen states using 127 names and fifty addresses "in Chicago alone." According to Reagan she also had "three new cars [and] a full-length mink coat, and her take is estimated at a million dollars." While the woman in Reagan's story (whom he identified by name in some speeches as Linda Taylor)[27] was not entirely fabricated—Taylor had indeed been charged with welfare fraud a few years prior—he grossly exaggerated the extent to which she had bilked the taxpayers. Ultimately, Taylor would be found guilty of having scammed a total of $8,000 in cash welfare benefits, rather than $1 million; and rather than eighty names (let alone 127) used to defraud the government, she had used four bogus aliases to do so.

But the facts didn't matter to Reagan or to a public predisposed to believe just about any story they were told about persons on public assistance. All the better if those persons were designated as being "from Chicago"—a large urban area with lots of black folks in it—as opposed to a place like Charleston, West Virginia, where there were no doubt also a few folks gaming the system about whom he could have spoken, but whence the story would not have had nearly the same political impact. Importantly, the fact that Taylor had been caught in her deceits suggested that the larger welfare system of which she had been a part was not as broken as Reagan had claimed. It was the way in which her actions stood out from the norm that had made them newsworthy. But to Reagan and those of his mindset, there was nothing wrong with turning someone like Taylor into a stereotype for welfare recipients more broadly, nor was there anything untoward about using her as a prop in his campaign against them.

By the same token, Reagan once told a tale of "strapping young bucks" buying T-bone steaks with food stamps: a phrase calculated to conjure images not only of welfare fraud, but fraud specifically committed by black men, as the term had long been a well-understood Southern euphemism for physically imposing

African American males.[28] Though Reagan and his supporters would deny the racial coding behind the images he crafted, it was hard to escape the conclusion that, at least implicitly, Reagan was hoping to play upon white anxieties about urban blacks in the post civil–rights era, at a time when resentment about the gains of the 1960s were reaching a fever pitch.

After being elected president, Reagan succeeded in slashing spending on public housing initiatives as well as cash welfare and food stamps, and he continued cuts in other Great Society initiatives that had been on the chopping block since the presidency of Richard Nixon.[29] By the time Reagan left office in 1989, most programs had survived, but the real dollar value of benefits had been slashed to the point that they were less capable of boosting the living standards of the poor beyond mere subsistence. Indeed, according to Reagan's first budget director, David Stockman, Reagan's early policies—massive tax cuts on the wealthiest Americans, combined with a huge buildup of the Pentagon budget—were *calculated* to produce such a substantial budget deficit that Congress would be forced to cut safety net programs.[30] The deficit was made to balloon so that those cuts could then be made in the name of a balanced budget rather than the ideological mindset that truly undergirded them.

Reagan succeeded in reducing the size of antipoverty initiatives in part because of his uncanny ability to put forward a cohesive narrative—a story religiously scripted by the conservative movement dating back to the crushing defeat of Barry Goldwater in 1964—which portrayed the poor and those receiving assistance as undeserving, and as persons rendered lazy by an overindulgent federal government. The idea that there was now a "culture of poverty," especially in urban communities of color, became conventional wisdom. Originally conceived by anthropologist Oscar Lewis in his study of poor communities in Mexico,[31] the culture of poverty thesis chipped away at the structuralist theories that had been used to explain inequality, impoverishment and social marginality since the Great Depression. Whereas the previous several generations had largely accepted the notion that families became poor because of circumstances beyond their control, earlier notions that placed the onus of responsibility on the poor themselves had now re-emerged in full force. Books such as George Gilder's *Wealth and Poverty* and Charles Murray's *Losing Ground*, both of which insisted that government antipoverty programs had created dependence and engendered all manner of social ill, became policy bibles for the Reaganites. Invigorated by this traditional "blame-the-victim" mentality (as it was termed in the early 1970s by psychologist William Ryan),[32] conservatives set about to dismantle much of the existing welfare state, emboldened by a public (especially a white public) that had increasingly turned against the very kinds of programs that only a generation before had proved popular.

It is hard to exaggerate how effective the conservative narrative has been in terms of its impact on the national consciousness. First, backlash to the welfare state has persuaded large swaths of the American public that antipoverty programs have been monumental failures and that such programs are to blame for virtually every social problem imaginable, even though the evidence debunks each of these notions. Second, the power of the reactionary narrative has proven so substantial as to force even erstwhile liberals to abandon any focus on fighting poverty as one of their principal concerns. From Bill Clinton to Barack Obama, Democratic Party presidential candidates and the party itself have largely gone silent on the concerns of the poor, rarely mentioning them on the campaign trail, choosing instead to speak of their desire to help the "middle class." For most politicians, the poor are an afterthought—or worse, sacrificial lambs to be offered up for political slaughter.

In 1996, President Clinton signed into law a welfare bill that substantially reduced benefits for millions of families based almost entirely on conservative "culture of poverty" notions.[33] Among the changes: recipients of cash aid were limited to two consecutive years of assistance or five years over the course of their lifetime, regardless of local economic conditions; benefits were slashed for children born after the initial receipt of assistance; and most important, automatic eligibility was terminated. Whereas eligibility for cash aid (then known as AFDC, or Aid to Families with Dependent Children) had been automatic for families below poverty prior to reform, after reform, aid was distributed in block grants to the states based on the amount of funding those states had been disbursing *as of 1996*. Even if more families found themselves in need due to worsening economic conditions, the amount of available cash assistance—now called TANF (Temporary Assistance for Needy Families)—would basically be frozen at 1996 levels, creating an incentive to disallow new cases and to cut the rolls, regardless of whether work opportunities were available. Since that time, cash welfare rolls plummeted from over thirteen million to only 3.6 million today. Although states could have taken the surplus money that was left after cutting so many from the program, and perhaps plowed those funds back into other job or education initiatives intended to address economic inequity, few have done so. Instead, most have taken the savings and diverted them into other, often unrelated programs. Few, if any, of the benefits were passed on to the needy.[34] Although the early years after passage of the reform bill brought praise from many quarters as the number of recipients fell and work rates for single moms increased, once the economy soured, those signs of progress and promise evaporated, much as reform critics had predicted they would.[35]

Despite significant reductions in the number and percentage of Americans receiving assistance after the 1996 reform, the narrative of welfare abuse, dependency and the "culture of poverty" have continued as if nothing had changed. Likewise, harsh judgments about the poor and struggling remained the norm, even as the economy fell apart, leaving millions in conditions over which they hardly had control. Even in the midst of the recession, with millions out of work and wages stagnant, rhetoric aimed at discrediting government intervention to help those in need could be heard regularly. In the middle of the housing crisis, as families were losing their homes by the hundreds of thousands—many after having been roped into financial instruments like adjustable rate mortgages that had blown up—CNBC commentator and recognized "Godfather of the Tea Party movement" Rick Santelli launched his now-famous rant in which he berated the "losers" who wanted the government to come to their rescue.[36] Bail out the banks? Of course. Bail out the homeowners from whom the banks had extracted all that money? Not a chance. The poor and those losing their homes were, to the Rick Santellis of the world, victims not of the economic system or predatory lenders, but of their own cultural and intellectual deficiencies. Radio talk show host Bill Cunningham expressed the typical conservative belief about the poor on his program in 2008 when he claimed: "People are poor in America . . . not because they lack money; they're poor because they lack values, morals, and ethics."[37]

Even President Obama has fed culture-of-poverty notions through his rhetoric and public policy pronouncements. For instance, on more than one occasion he has implored black fathers, and *only* black fathers, to take "personal responsibility" for their children—the presumption being that they are relieved of this duty thanks to government programs.[38] In 2012, he even lectured the black male graduates of Morehouse—one of the nation's finest schools—not to blame others for their shortcomings and to "be responsible."[39] That anyone, least of all the president, would think Morehouse men need to be cajoled into hard work merely suggests how deep conservative thinking about the culture of poverty truly runs—and especially with regard to its racialized component.

In some ways, this liberal capitulation to culture-of-poverty thinking has been a long time coming. Ever since Daniel Patrick Moynihan's 1965 report on the "state of the black family" was released, which suggested there was a culture of deviance in the "urban ghetto" that was perpetuating black poverty, many liberals have been given to viewing impoverished communities, and especially those in urban centers with high concentrations of families of color, through a lens of group defect.[40] Moynihan was a devoted Democrat, an adviser to Lyndon Johnson who helped design many of the Great Society programs for which Johnson would become known; yet, as with many white liberals, Moynihan found it easier, ultimately, to view people struggling with poverty as the problem, rather than the people and system perpetuating their impoverishment. And he certainly found it easier to seek to "fix" those same poor people, rather than attempt to seriously transform or radically alter the economic and social realities that had come to normalize conditions of injustice and poverty.

Bashing the War on Poverty: The Presumption of Failure, The Reality of Success

It is widely believed—to the point of being very nearly a matter of secular political faith—that antipoverty initiatives have been a massive failure. After all, since the 1960s, hundreds of billions (even trillions) of dollars have been spent on such efforts, and yet the poor are still with us, and the percentage of persons in poverty isn't much lower today than it was in the early 1970s. But to claim that we fought a war on poverty "and poverty won," as Reagan often quipped, overlooks the evidence suggesting that safety-net programs lessen hardship for millions. From 1959 to 1973, during which period programs like food stamps and cash assistance were dramatically increased and entirely new programs (including Medicare, Medicaid and President Johnson's urban empowerment initiatives) were developed, the percentage of Americans living in poverty was cut in half, from 22.4 percent to only 11.1 percent.[41] This included a reduction in African American poverty from just over fifty-five percent of all blacks in 1959 to slightly more than thirty-three percent by 1970.[42] Although social programs were not the only factor driving the reduction in poverty during this period—the economy was also undergoing stronger than average growth—such a decline in the poverty rate certainly suggests that safety-net programs played a role and goes far towards debunking the idea that such efforts were counterproductive or kept recipients "locked in poverty." To insist, as some have, that welfare programs have made African Americans worse off than under segregation (or even slavery)[43] is not only to grotesquely diminish the horrors of those systems, but to demonstrate a profound and undiluted ignorance about the actual effects of antipoverty initiatives.[44] It is to suggest that black folks were better off with poverty rates that were far higher, not to mention lower graduation rates, higher rates of hunger, and worse health outcomes—all of which were realities in the years prior to the supposedly horrible government programs about which conservatives have such fits.

Secondly, to claim that antipoverty efforts don't work because poverty rates have barely budged lately, regardless of program spending, ignores the way that poverty rate information is tabulated. When calculating income, government benefits like SNAP and the refundable portion of the Earned Income Tax Credit—both of which boost the income and living status of those who receive them—are not counted as income. This creates the appearance that the programs "don't work," because those receiving benefits from SNAP or the EITC (or housing benefits) will still be poor in official tables, even though they may actually be living at a level equal to those with an above-poverty income. So despite the fact that the programs actually have improved the lives of millions of people, they receive no credit for having done so and come to be seen as failures that should be scrapped or scaled back. If they were included in government tabulations of poverty, these programs would reveal themselves to be quite successful. If SNAP benefits were counted as income, *four to five million fewer people* would have been categorized as poor in 2013—roughly a twelve percent reduction in poverty from just that one program.[45] Likewise, another three million or so would have been removed from the poverty category by the EITC that year. There are also many people who are *not* counted as poor today but who would be if it were not for the existence of antipoverty efforts and forms of income support. For instance, there would have been nearly two million more people in poverty in 2012 had it not been for unemployment insurance benefits, which *are* counted as income for the purpose of tabulating government data on income and poverty rates.[46]

Of course, it's not only the raw financial benefit of safety-net programs that matters. More important, these programs meet the specific needs for which they were created, and far better than most realize. For instance, when evaluating the success or failure of the food stamp (SNAP) program, the primary issue is not whether this program eliminated or even reduced poverty. First, because benefits are not counted as income, it cannot have much effect on the official poverty rate. Second, the program was not intended to end poverty, but rather to improve the food and nutritional security of poor people, thereby blunting the most extreme *conditions* of poverty. So the primary matter is whether the program worked on those terms, and the literature in this regard is quite unambiguous. According to a study for the National Bureau of Economic Research, access to the food stamp program has improved childhood nutrition in particular, thereby contributing to substantial reductions in obesity, high blood pressure and diabetes among recipient households.[47] Access to food stamps has also been correlated with an eighteen percent boost in high school graduation rates, likely due in large part to better nutritional health provided by access to the program, and its corollary effect on academic performance.

Likewise, the Earned Income Tax Credit should be judged not on whether it eliminated poverty—again, because benefits are not counted as income for the calculation of the official poverty rate, by definition, it cannot accomplish this task—but whether it achieved its more limited purpose of "making work pay" by subsidizing low-wage employment, since one can only get the benefits by having a job. A second and related matter is whether or not the EITC helps reduce reliance on other benefits like cash welfare. When it comes to these and related matters, the EITC scores well: EITC expansions are credited with being the most important factor in boosting work by single mothers from 1993 to 1999, as well as the key to reductions in traditional welfare caseloads. In fact, the EITC was a much bigger contributor to employment by low-income single moms *and* substantial reductions in cash welfare rolls than even the strict time limits and other punitive elements of the welfare reform legislation that were passed for those purposes.[48]

And finally, public health care benefits are best judged not by their ability to reduce poverty per se, but by how well they do what they are intended to do: namely, improve the health outcomes of persons who would otherwise go without care. Medicaid expansion in the 1980s and 1990s, for instance, is credited with reducing childhood deaths among poor kids by more than five percent, as well as reducing infant mortality and low birth weight among babies born to poor moms by 8.5 and 7.8 percent respectively.[49] Although those children may still be poor, it is worth noting that they are, importantly, still alive—an outcome that would be considered a victory by most, and yet which prompts no such accolades from those on the right for whom such successes are apparently trivial.

Victim Blaming, Poverty Shaming and Culture Defaming in Modern America

Beyond the all-too-common belief that antipoverty programs don't work, there is a far more pernicious narrative about which compassionate Americans should be concerned. It is a narrative that not only calls into question the practical efficacy of such efforts, but seeks to demonize those who rely on them. Those who craft the rhetoric of modern-day Scroogism do so by way of three principal devices: first, by expressing blatantly dehumanizing views about poor people, the unemployed and those on various forms of public assistance; second, by way of poverty denialism (essentially the idea that the poor and unemployed don't really have it that bad); and finally, by way of the "hammock theory" of government aid, which purports to prove that welfare programs are so generous they create long-term dependence and contribute to a culture of poverty that subsidizes irresponsibility and perpetuates impoverishment. Let's look at these one at a time.

The Rhetoric of Hate: Dehumanizing and Humiliating the Poor

When it comes to the poor and struggling, not only are many on the right hostile to various programs intended to help these groups, they are increasingly hostile to the poor themselves. The aforementioned rant by business journalist Rick Santelli, in which he referred to those who were facing foreclosure due to the implosion of the housing market as "losers" is, sadly, par for the course nowadays. Tea Party activists and political candidates like Nevada's Sharron Angle insist that the unemployed are all "lazy welfare queens"[50] who, according to still others, need to be forcibly placed in labor camps where they will have to work for free and be taught personal hygiene—a proposal seriously floated by Carl Paladino, the Republican candidate for governor of New York in 2010.[51] Rush Limbaugh asks listeners, as if the answers were self-evidently negative, if they "know any low-income people who actually *want* to get a better job?" and wonders, "Do they even *want* to work?"[52] Most recently, Speaker of the House John Boehner (who has said he would commit suicide before voting to increase the minimum wage unless said increase were tied to massive tax cuts for the wealthy and their corporations)[53] suggested that what's been holding back job creation in America is not the lack of employment openings but "this idea that has been born . . . that you know, I really don't have to work . . . I think I'd rather just sit around."[54] According to conservative leaders, many Americans actually enjoy long-term unemployment.

For some on the right, it's not just the unemployed whom we should scorn but also those who work, if they get minimum wage. Conservative commentator Erick Erickson expressed contempt for low-wage workers recently when he claimed: "If you're a 30-something-year-old person and you're making minimum wage, you've probably failed at life."[55] In other words, an adult who works at minimum wage trying to support his or her family, and who no doubt hopes for something better, is really just a loser to whom we should offer nothing but derision. Likewise, even if you work full-time and make a solid middle-class income but happen to work for a nonprofit organization—for instance, the United Way or Habitat for Humanity—you are deserving of repudiation in the eyes of Rush Limbaugh. According to Limbaugh, who apparently believes all "real work" is work that seeks to make a profit, nonprofit employees are "lazy idiots" who are no different from "rapists in terms of finance and economy."[56] Or if you are a government employee making a decent living, paying your taxes and stimulating the economy, you're still a parasite according to FOX's Stuart Varney, who has said of government workers furloughed during the government shutdown of 2013, "I want to punish these people."[57]

As for Americans living in poverty, Limbaugh has likened them to wild animals that become dependent on others and forget how to feed themselves if they receive any form of assistance.[58] He has also compared children living in impoverished families to puppies who will never bond with their owners (or parents) if fed by another, such as a school through a breakfast or lunch program.[59] Yes, because children—none of which, it should be noted, Limbaugh actually has, and with whom he has virtually no experience whatsoever—are exactly like cocker spaniels. Limbaugh has suggested that if poor kids, whom he refers to as "wanton little waifs and serfs dependent on the state,"[60] have trouble finding food at home during the summer break:

> . . . there's always the neighborhood dumpster. Now, you might find competition with homeless people there, but there are videos that have been produced to show you how to healthfully dine and how to dumpster dive and survive until school kicks back up in August.[61]

Fellow talk show host Sean Hannity has said much the same thing, comparing persons on public assistance to animals who will no longer remember how to feed themselves if we continue to support them with programs like SNAP.[62] Likewise, right-wing commentator Ann Coulter insists that welfare programs create "generations of utterly irresponsible animals."[63] And if you're wondering what kind of animal conservatives have in mind when they call the poor and those on public assistance such names, conservative activist, musician and avid hunter Ted Nugent—a man who can make even a pacifist wish that deer could shoot back—will gladly make it plain: according to Nugent, persons who receive benefits from the government are "gluttonous, soulless pigs."[64] Others insist they are essentially swamp-dwelling amphibians, as Republican congressman John Mica put it in 1996 during debate over that year's welfare reform bill, holding up a sign on the House floor that read DON'T FEED THE ALLIGATORS, and insisting that providing assistance to poor women would encourage them to have more children so as to get more "free handouts."[65]

Not to be outdone, conservative author and talk-show host Neal Boortz, who has compared the poor to the "toenail fungus" of America,[66] came up with particularly vicious ways to refer to the poor of New Orleans after Hurricane Katrina. In the wake of that catastrophe, in which more than a thousand people died and tens of thousands were displaced, Boortz referred to the city as a "city of parasites" and those who lived there as "garbage." On one particular episode of his radio program, Boortz referred to those who were displaced as "complete bums, just debris." He then went on an extended rant premised on entirely inaccurate perceptions of the city's poor (as discussed in the introduction), but provided a disturbing window into the soul of modern conservatism. Responding to those who implored us to hear the anguish of those displaced by the flooding, Boortz retorted:

> That wasn't the cries of the downtrodden; that's the cries of the useless, the worthless. New Orleans was a welfare

> city, a city of parasites, a city of people who could not and had no desire to fend for themselves. You have a hurricane descending on them and they sit on their fat asses and wait for somebody else to come rescue them. . . . You had a city of parasites and leeches.[67]

As much as we might hope such vitriol would find little fertile ground in which to take root, the evidence suggests hostility to the poor is easily internalized in a culture where such contempt is so common. Research by Princeton psychologist Susan Fiske has found that when hooked up to brain scan imaging machines and shown pictures of poor people or the homeless, large numbers of subjects react the same as if they had been shown pictures of *things* as opposed to people: a common sign of revulsion and lack of empathy.[68]

The lack of empathy evident in Fiske's lab experiments can also be observed in everyday real-world settings. Consider the results of one disturbing experiment recently conducted by a filmmaker in Austin, Texas. The filmmaker and a homeless man there named Sandy Shook went to a local thrift shop and purchased a blazer, slacks, and dress shoes for Shook. Shook then stood on the street and asked passersby for spare change to help pay for bus fare or, alternately, for his Subway sandwich. Inevitably, people would stop and gladly interact with Shook and give him the change he requested. Then Shook tried the same experiment dressed as he normally is, in an old T-shirt and dirty jeans. The results were the opposite: people routinely passed him by, refused to give him change and in at least one case shouted "No!" at him even before he had asked for money.[69] In other words, giving money to someone who looks as though he wouldn't normally need it is far easier for most than giving to someone who looks like he does. It's as if the decision to give isn't based on need so much as a judgment of the moral deservingness of the person doing the asking.

Elsewhere, evidence of callousness to the homeless is even more blatant. As just one example, Hawaii state representative

Tom Brower proudly goes hunting for homeless people who have filled shopping carts with their meager belongings; upon finding them, Brower, who says he's "disgusted" by the homeless, smashes their carts with a sledgehammer.[70] Even in relatively "liberal" San Francisco, the city's main Catholic Church has installed a sprinkler system to drench homeless folks who occasionally sleep in the doorways.[71] And recently, Alaska Congressman Don Young suggested that if wolves were introduced into communities where they weren't currently to be found, those areas "wouldn't have a homeless problem anymore."[72] It is no doubt this kind of visceral contempt that animates the recent rise in hateful assaults upon the homeless around the nation. Up by more than twenty percent just between 2012 and 2013, such attacks are becoming more brazen, including most recently, the attack on a fifty-eight-year-old man in Ventura, California who was set on fire by three young white men with shaved heads, resulting in second- and third-degree burns over his entire body.[73]

Part of the disgust felt by many toward the poor apparently stems from a sense that those in need lack sufficient humility. Commentator Bill O'Reilly, for instance, has openly advocated shaming the poor as a solution to the problem of poverty. In June 2004 he explained on his radio show that Ronald Reagan was too nice and not willing to be tough and nasty with the poor—especially the black poor. According to O'Reilly:

> Reagan was not a confrontational guy, didn't like confrontation, much rather be your pal . . . doesn't want to get involved with the really nasty stuff, the tough stuff, and that's what racial politics is—nasty and tough . . . you gotta look people in the eye and tell 'em they're irresponsible and lazy. . . . Because that's what poverty is. . . . In this country, you can succeed if you get educated and work hard. . . . You get addicted, you don't know anything, you'll be poor. But Reagan did not want to confront the issue.[74]

Far from an outlier, O'Reilly is par for the course among right-wing commentators. For the right it isn't enough that the poor should be poor; rather, they should be humiliated by their economic condition, essentially ashamed to look at themselves in the mirror. Recently, FOX Business contributor Charles Gasparino lamented that when it comes to income assistance or housing aid, "the stigma is gone about accepting that check,"[75] and Rich Lowry of the nation's most prominent conservative magazine, *National Review*, says it's "a disgrace" that the stigma of "being on the dole" has eroded, as if to suggest that what the poor have too much of is pride, and what they need is more shame to add to their economic deprivation.[76] Evidently, shame has long been known to cure poverty.

Other conservative commentators have pushed for fingerprinting food stamp recipients and suggested that resistance to such a humiliating requirement, which essentially presumes that the poor are criminals, is part of the left wing's unjustified "war on shame."[77] Still others have blamed the switch from stamps to Electronic Benefits Transfer (EBT) cards—which allows beneficiaries to feel less conspicuous since the EBT functions like a debit card—for reducing the stigma of receiving assistance, thereby boosting enrollment.[78] Others self-righteously bray about not accepting EBTs as payment in their establishments and are praised for refusing to do so. As yet another FOX contributor recently put it, "Why can't we make someone feel embarrassed" for receiving public assistance?[79] In each case with rhetoric like this, the implicit assumption is that humiliation, not food, is the commodity of which the poor need more.

Even poor children should not be spared the lash of public humiliation for their condition. In recent years, conservatives from Newt Gingrich to West Virginia lawmaker Ray Canterbury have endorsed putting poor kids to work in their schools so they will learn work habits and earn their free and reduced price meals there.[80] As Canterbury put it, "I think it would be a good idea if perhaps we had the kids work for their lunches: trash to be taken out, hallways to be swept, lawns to be mowed, make them earn it."[81] Naturally, because we wouldn't want children to start thinking they were entitled *to eat*. Of course in many localities, poor children receiving school lunches are already stigmatized by being forced to go through separate lines where they receive prepackaged meals, unlike their non-poor peers who get to choose their own items. Fully a third of school districts operate these separate-and-unequal systems for school lunch recipients, creating such shame that some kids are skipping lunch altogether rather than facing the stigma of going through the separate line. They would rather go hungry.[82] When one principal in Colorado objected to her school's policy of stigmatizing free lunch recipients by stamping their hands and giving them different food than the other students, she was terminated.[83]

So too, economically strapped persons with disabilities are fair game for the hateful mocking of conservatives, as with an infamous confrontation in Columbus, Ohio, in 2010 between Tea Party activists opposed to health care reform, and a disabled counter-protester with Parkinson's disease. Though the man with Parkinson's was simply sitting on the ground making his support for health care reform known, he apparently wasn't sufficiently ashamed of his condition for the right-wingers assembled. The Tea Partiers screamed at him, with one insisting that he was on the "wrong side of town for handouts," and that "you have to work for everything you get." Meanwhile, another Tea Party activist mockingly threw dollar bills at the man while another proclaimed that the disabled man was clearly a communist.[84] More broadly, it is increasingly common for conservatives to attack disability benefits and those who receive them. Even though research suggests that fewer than one percent of disability payments from the Social Security program are received fraudulently, Kentucky Senator and possible presidential candidate Rand Paul suggested recently that most persons receiving such benefits were fakers. According to Paul:

> Over half the people on disability are either anxious or their back hurts. Join the club. Who doesn't get up a little anxious for work every day and their back hurts? Everyone over forty has a back pain.[85]

In the same cruel vein, Tom Sullivan, who is both a FOX News radio host and FOX Business commentator on television, recently told a caller who said she has bipolar disorder that her disease was "something made up," as the "latest fad," and that she had likely been "talked into feeling that way" by someone else.[86] Though he also argued that perhaps there was a financial incentive for over-diagnosing certain illnesses so as to make more money for pharmaceutical companies (a quite possible reality, and one that might not sit well with his business-friendly employer), the tone he struck with the caller was one that well encapsulated the general and growing hostility to those who are struggling with illness and disability.

Whether they are targeting able-bodied adults, kids or those with disabilities, one thing is certain: conservatives long for the days when public assistance carried more stigma. FOX commentator Charles Payne wishes recipients were more embarrassed about needing help. As he puts it:

> I think the real narrative here, though, is that people aren't embarrassed by it. People aren't ashamed by it. In other words, there was a time when people were embarrassed to be on food stamps. There was a time when people were embarrassed to be on unemployment for six months, let alone demanding to be on it for more than two years.[87]

Payne has long been among the most consistently cruel of conservative commentators, trotting out his own story of having grown up poor but having gone on to "make it" as evidence of how poor people have no one but themselves to blame. That Payne speaks in one breath of having grown up on welfare as a child, and then assures us in the next breath that people on assistance used to feel shame, raises obvious questions about the contempt he must feel for his family and himself, and tells us much about the psychological torment that his conservatism is intended to exorcise. According to Payne, poverty in America is "a little (too) comfortable,"[88] and if there were more stigma associated with programs like food stamps, people would be less willing to stay on the program for so long.[89] Of course, this is the kind of thinking one might expect from someone who says, "If you can't pass a test to become a bus driver but you know you're still going to eat, there's a problem,"[90] and that suffering from gout—a disease that is increasingly prominent among those with low income—is no big deal since gout was once considered a "rich man's disease."[91]

According to a conservative blogger at the prominent website *The Daily Caller*, not only should the poor be forced into the "humiliation" of shopping at substandard government-run stores rather than being able to shop where the rest of us do, they should also lose voting privileges if they receive any government assistance.[92] This idea that the poor shouldn't be allowed to vote—an issue most Americans probably thought had been settled generations ago—has been gaining traction on the right lately. Conservatives now openly raise the issue of property requirements for the franchise, suggesting, as has Rush Limbaugh, that if people can't "even feed and clothe themselves" perhaps they shouldn't be allowed to elect the nation's leaders.[93] Encouraging electoral participation among the "nonproductive" segments of society is not only inherently "un-American," as one prominent conservative put it recently, but amounts to "handing out burglary tools to criminals."[94] Ted Nugent has said that we should suspend the right to vote of "any American who is on welfare. Once they get off welfare and are self-sustaining, they get their right to vote restored.[95] And leading Tea Party activist Judson Phillips has exclaimed:

> The Founding Fathers originally . . . put certain restrictions on who gets the right to vote. It wasn't you were just a citizen and you got to vote. Some of the restrictions, you know, you obviously would not think about today. But one of those was you had to be a property owner. And that makes a lot of sense, because if you're a property owner you actually have a vested stake in the community.[96]

In other words, to Philips—who is perhaps the most prominent Tea Party activist in the country—not only the poor per se but also anyone who rents, most college students, the elderly in nursing homes, and anyone else who for whatever reason doesn't own property should be blocked from the most basic privilege of citizenship—voting. According to Bryan Fischer of the American Family Association, only property owners should be allowed to vote, because, "if somebody owns property in a community, they're invested in the community. If they're renters, they're going to be up and gone; they could leave the next day . . . they have no skin in the game. They don't care about the same things that somebody does who is rooted in the community."[97] In the eyes of prominent conservatives, people who rent don't care about their communities, the quality of their children's schools or the infrastructure of their neighborhoods; they are just transient slackers who care little for the broader well-being of the community. If you aren't a property owner, this is what the right thinks about you.

Though not advocating property requirements to vote, FOX morning co-host Elisabeth Hasselbeck recently suggested that perhaps one should have to pass a civics test before being allowed to cast a ballot. Putting aside the fact that such a requirement—a central feature of the Jim Crow South, regularly abused so as to prevent blacks from voting—has such a history of racist misuse, there is an irony in Hasselbeck's advocacy of it: namely, such tests have already been banned by Congress and are widely understood to be unconstitutional. To the extent Hasselbeck doesn't seem to know that and yet believes one should have to pass a civics test to vote, perhaps she should be the first to forfeit her voter registration card,[98] followed quickly by Ann Coulter[99] and Newt Gingrich,[100] both of whom have called for literacy or civics tests in order to vote, despite such instruments being outlawed by the Civil Rights Act of 1965.

For others, like venture capitalist Tom Perkins (about whom we'll have more to say later), it's not that people should necessarily be *prevented* from voting, but simply that the rich should get more votes than everyone else. The multibillionaire recently suggested that votes should be apportioned based on the dollar amount of taxes a person pays: in other words, "if you pay a million dollars in taxes, you get a million votes."[101] That such brazen calls for an official aristocracy of the rich and the eradication of democracy can be made with no sense of shame says a lot about how normalized the culture of cruelty and inequality has become.

Beyond merely restricting the freedom of poor people to vote, some on the right go quite a bit further, advocating that the poor should be forcibly sterilized by the state. For instance, former Arizona state senator Russell Pearce was recently forced to resign as vice-chair of the Arizona Republican Party after saying that women on Medicaid should have to get "Norplant birth-control implants, or tubal ligations."[102] It's an idea similar to one proposed by white supremacist David Duke in 1991, while he was serving in the Louisiana legislature.[103] Some conservative ideas never die, it seems, no matter how old, vicious, cruel or unconstitutional. Though such thinking may, as with Pierce, serve to embarrass the party of conservatives, it still seems worth mentioning how readily those on the right jump to such blatantly authoritarian and cruel policy proposals, only backtracking when their open hatred becomes a political liability for their more subtle peers.

Trivializing Hardship: Conservatives as Poverty Deniers

In 1981, Texas Senator Phil Gramm lamented: "We're the only

nation in the world where all our poor people are fat."[104] It was, to Gramm, clear evidence of how exaggerated the problem of economic hardship in America was, and how horrible the nation's welfare state had become. Apparently, poor people aren't really suffering or deserving of much sympathy until their rib cages are showing and their eye sockets have all but swallowed their eyes. If some poor people are fat, it's not because so many of the cheapest and most readily available foods in low-income communities are high in empty calories and non-nutritional ingredients—or because the American diet in general is less healthy than in other countries—rather, it must be because poor people have it too good and are able to do a lot of fancy eating at public expense.

Lack of compassion for people in need, which makes it so easy to engage in the viciousness examined in the last section, or to call for the repeal of poor folks' basic rights and freedoms, has long been fed by a belief among many that low-income families and underemployed people really aren't suffering that badly. Which brings us to the second device by which the right seeks to demonize the poor and struggling: denying that they're really struggling at all. Not only do they have a nifty disease like gout, as Charles Payne reminds us, which makes them similar to eighteenth-century royalty, but more importantly they are awash with other "stuff" that poor people shouldn't have, which proves that they aren't really doing that badly. This poverty denialism rests on three specific claims: first, that America's poor are fabulously wealthy by global standards, and thus should essentially stop complaining; second, that the poor buy expensive food with their SNAP benefits and have all manner of consumer goods in their homes, which means they aren't poor in any sense that should cause concern; and third, that large numbers of welfare recipients commit fraud in order to get benefits, and then misuse the benefits they receive. In short, these are not the deserving poor—their pain is not real.

As for the idea that the poor in America are not *really* poor, one can almost understand why this notion might seem persuasive even to those who are not particularly callous or cruel. Someone who has worked in the Peace Corps for instance, or the military, or has merely traveled widely and witnessed the kind of abject deprivation that is common in much of the world, where billions of people live on less than a dollar a day, might find this part of poverty denialism compelling. Most of us have seen at least one, if not several, late-night infomercials seeking charitable contributions to bring running water and vaccinations to the globe's poorest inhabitants. By comparison to the poverty highlighted by such efforts, one might not find the moral claims of America's poor to be particularly pressing.

That said, to diminish the real hardship faced by the poor in the United States solely because it is usually not as crushing as suffering elsewhere—and I say usually, because in some poor counties of America, conditions and life expectancy actually *do* rival those in some of the poorest nations on earth[105]—is neither a logical nor an ethical response to that hardship. Even though in absolute terms it is true that most persons in the United States do not suffer poverty in the same way and to the same extremes as say, *Sri Lanka's* poor, such a reassurance is likely not much comfort for America's struggling masses. After all, Americans are *not* Sri Lankans, and they are trying to stay afloat and compete in a society against other Americans. This is why the international standard for evaluating poverty is not simply a set dollar-equivalent amount, since poverty in a poor country is by definition different from poverty in a rich country, but is determined by looking at what percentage of a country's citizens live at half or less of the nation's median wage. To be at half or less of the median in any society, no matter what that median might be, is to be at a significant disadvantage relative to others in the job market and the housing market, in terms of the quality of education your children will likely receive, and in terms of the health care you can access. If the median income is well above your own, you will be effectively priced out of the market for any number of opportunities; as such, even if you are objectively richer than someone in

Bangladesh or Ghana, the life you will be able to carve out for yourself *in the place you actually live* will be far removed from the mainstream there.

This is why the reassurances of blogger Catherine Rampell at the *New York Times*, to the effect that "the bottom 5 percent of the American income distribution is still richer than 68 percent of the world's inhabitants," or that "America's poorest are, as a group, about as rich as India's richest," are vapid to a point that would be laughable were the subject matter not so serious.[106] Contrary to Rampell's breathless excitement at the chart demonstrating these fun facts—which she found in a book by World Bank economist Branko Milanovic and to which she refers as an "awesome chart" that "kinda blows your mind"—there is nothing awesome, mind-blowing, or even remotely relevant about the statistics in question. Nor are the protestations of Sean Hannity—who assures us that "poor in America is not poor like around the rest of the world"—helpful in understanding the real face of need in the United States.[107]

If anything, to be poor in a rich country, where one's worth is sadly too often presumed to be linked to one's possessions (unlike in a poor country, where people still know better) is to foster a particularly debilitating kind of relative deprivation. To be poor in a place where success is synonymous with being rich and famous increasingly means finding oneself voiceless, ignorable, criminalized and perceived as disposable. To live in a place where wealth is not only visible but flaunted, where the rich make no pretense to normalcy, and where one can regularly hear oneself being berated on the airwaves as losers and vermin and parasites *precisely because you are poor or working at a minimum-wage job*, is to be the victim of a cruelty that the citizenry of poor nations do not as likely experience. In a nation where poverty is distressingly normal for the vast majority, the poor are still likely to be viewed as belonging equally to a common humanity, unlike in a wealthy and powerful nation like the United States, where the humanity of poor people, and certainly their right to full citizenship, are increasingly under attack.

Ultimately, the politics of comparative suffering is always a losing and amoral proposition. It's precisely such politics that would justify telling a Japanese American who was herded into an American internment camp during World War II that they have nothing to complain about and should actually be grateful: after all, they could have been in Tokyo when we firebombed it, or in Hiroshima or Nagasaki when we dropped the atomic bombs. It's the kind of position that would rationalize saying to someone who survived the Holocaust of European Jewry that they had no legitimate complaint against the Nazis, since had they lived in the Soviet Union they may well have perished in Stalin's gulag (or, for that matter, the reverse of this argument). To forward this kind of position is like telling an African American during Jim Crow segregation to get over it, since King Leopold killed roughly ten million Africans in the Congo under Belgian colonialism. In other words, this kind of comparison between the suffering one is currently experiencing and the much greater suffering one could *theoretically* experience elsewhere lacks all moral and practical relevance.

Not to mention, there is something ironic about this kind of argument coming from the rich, who regularly push for greater tax breaks so they can have more money with which to "do great things," or just because they think they've earned it. After all, to whatever extent the poor in America are rich by global standards, surely the *wealthy* in America are far more so, and should perhaps rightly be seen as obsessive and gluttonous hoarders. *They* don't seem satisfied with the kind of wealth that would allow them to literally buy entire countries outright, and which certainly dwarfs the wealth of the so-called rich in less wealthy nations, but yet they have the temerity to lecture *poor people* about gratitude?

Consider a recent commercial paid for by the Charles Koch Foundation that seeks to remind Americans how good they have it by noting that even if one earns only $34,000 a year, that's enough to vault one into the top one percent of the world's population in terms of income.[108] Or consider the remarks of Bud Konheim, CEO and co-founder of fashion label Nicole Miller, who recently said those who are poor or working class in America should stop complaining, since their incomes would make them wealthy in India or China.[109] To whatever extent one finds this kind of thinking even remotely persuasive, shouldn't the logic of such an argument run both ways? Shouldn't the rich in the United States stop complaining about their taxes? The regulations they have to put up with? The minimum wage they have to pay employees? Talk about ingratitude! If they lived in any other industrialized nation, the taxes they paid would be higher, regulations would be just as strict or more so, and their workers would have far greater protections and safety nets than in the United States. So when it comes to shutting one's mouth and being grateful for what one has, perhaps the rich should lead by example.

In addition to comparing America's poor to those of the world and finding the former unworthy of concern by comparison, today's poverty deniers insist that those who claim to be struggling in the U.S. really aren't, and this we know because of all the extravagances they enjoy. To Rush Limbaugh, those who are out of work spend their unemployment benefits on lottery tickets, "Smirnoff Ice and chips," thereby demonstrating their personal irresponsibility.[110] FOX News commentator Andrea Tantaros says she wishes she could live on food stamps since it would make for a fantastic "dieting technique" that would make her "look great."[111] In short, there is no reason to be sympathetic to those who are out of work or have been forced to rely on SNAP benefits, since they only squander the assistance they receive anyway, and don't fully appreciate the weight-loss gift they've been given by virtue of their hardship.

One of the more prominent tropes of modern Scroogism is chastising the poor for possessing any material items remotely connected to middle-class normalcy, as if somehow the possession of modern conveniences like refrigerators, microwaves or televisions demonstrates that the poor in America aren't really suffering. In a segment from Bill O'Reilly's FOX program in July 2011, he and fellow talking head Lou Dobbs joked about the "stuff" one can find in the homes of the poor. Citing a report by the Heritage Foundation, which has long forwarded this kind of argument so as to undermine support for safety-net programs, O'Reilly noted incredulously:

> Eight-two percent have a microwave. This is 82 percent of American poor families. Seventy-eight percent have air conditioning. More than one television, 65 percent. Cable or satellite TV, 64 percent . . . Cell phones, 55 percent. Personal computer, 39 percent. So how can you be so poor and have all this stuff?[112]

Aside from the bizarre implication that air conditioning is a luxury the poor should not enjoy, there are a few obvious holes in O'Reilly's argument here. First, it should be apparent to even the most casual thinker that most of the poor live in apartments pre-rigged with A/C whether or not they can afford to actually run it. Second, cable is necessary in most parts of the country in order for a television to get reception at all, so the mere fact that one has cable says very little about the quality of one's television, let alone the extravagance of one's entertainment habits. And finally, cell phones are no more extravagant than landlines, having more or less replaced the older systems for millions of Americans, including those who are by no means poor. To not have a phone would render a person unable to remain connected to possible jobs, to family or to emergency services. Surely we do not expect poor families to be completely cut off from the world in order to deserve concern. Or perhaps for the Bill O'Reillys of the world, that is exactly what is required.

For Robert Rector of the Heritage Foundation, the poor aren't really suffering because per-person expenditures for the poorest fifth of Americans today are equal to the expenditures of the typical middle-class person in the early 1970s.[113] But, as with most everything said about the poor by the folks at Heritage, this too is fundamentally disingenuous. First, this seemingly impressive fact does not mean that poor folks are living in a style comparable to those middle-class persons from several decades ago. Rector's calculation is based on per-person spending, adjusted for the average consumer inflation rate. But certain items have inflated far faster than the general rate of inflation—namely, housing, education and health care—such that spending more for these things today is not tantamount to the receipt of greater luxuries. Today's poor are spending more for these things because they are so much more expensive than those same things were in 1973, and a generic inflation-rate adjustment like the one made by Heritage will not account for that. It is certainly not because they are doing that much better than the middle class of the early 1970s.

Second, even if Rector were right and poor and lower-income persons are now able to live like the middle class did thirty to forty years ago, what is the practical meaning of this information? It is also probably the case that the poor in the 1960s had "stuff" comparable to what middle-class Americans had in 1939, but so what? The poor today also doubtless have certain luxuries unknown even to the wealthiest Americans in the 1790s, what with indoor plumbing and all, but one wonders what the point of such a comparison is. Does anyone really believe that today's poor live better than Thomas Jefferson did, just because the latter had to crap in a chamber pot or an outhouse? Apparently, Rector and the folks at Heritage think so, as they have also made the argument that the poor in America today "live a better life than all but the richest persons a hundred years ago."[114] Though it should hardly need to be said, today's poor do not live in the early 1970s, let alone the nineteenth century; they live in the present, where the ability to feel part of the mainstream (and to *be* part of the mainstream) requires one to be able to do things and have things that previous generations didn't do or have. People didn't "need" the Internet in the 1970s, for instance, because the Internet didn't exist, but not having access to the web today can be seen as a pretty serious disadvantage. They didn't need cars in 1837 either, but try finding steady employment today without one.

What Rector and others ignore is that the ability of the poor to purchase electronics—the prices of which have actually come down in recent years—says little about their ability to afford more important amenities. Televisions, microwaves or any other consumer products in the homes of the poor will tend to be pretty cheap. What you won't as readily find is what really matters: namely, college degrees and high-quality preventive health care, the costs of which have far outpaced the rate of inflation. It is these things that an increasing number of Americans cannot afford, not because they have blown all their money on malt liquor and menthols but because they are not paid enough to purchase them, no matter the relatively cheap consumer goods with which they may entertain themselves, or which may cool the air in their apartments from time to time. The issue is not whether Americans are as poor today as the poor in Biafra, or as destitute as the poor were at the time of the Nixon administration or the Gettysburg Address or the landing of the Mayflower. The issue is whether the poor are situated in such a way as to compete with others in *this* country at *this* time, in such a way that they might move up the ladder and out of relative deprivation. A dishwasher will neither suffice for those purposes nor by virtue of its expense get in the way of them, but the lack of health care and education most certainly will.

To deny those who are struggling all manner of modern conveniences as the right appears prepared to do—even those that are increasingly necessary to stay connected to the mainstream and develop the cultural capital needed to make oneself employable—is to suggest that the poor should slug it out like the poor of old; it is to insist that they must suffer just as those in prior generations did before any sympathy can attach. Which is no doubt why conservative blogger Jim Hoft was so quick to criticize Lorain County, Ohio, for distributing air conditioners to needy elderly and disabled folks in the summer of 2012, during a record heat wave.[115] To Hoft and those of his mindset, the poor and aged (and those with respiratory disease who were particularly targeted by the effort) should suffer just as they would have in the days before air conditioning—because poor people should be miserable in the eyes of conservative America, perhaps even prostrate, covered by dirt and surrounded by flies in order to be seen as truly deserving society's assistance.

Notably, the common outrage over the possessions of the poor neglects to take heed of the obvious fact that for most, their consumer goods will likely represent items they were able to afford in better economic times before a layoff or medical emergency. If a family finds itself transitionally poor and having to turn temporarily to SNAP after the layoff of a parent, it's not as if the computer, the car or the Xbox they had before the layoff should be expected to disappear. Unless one wishes to suggest that upon a layoff one should pawn everything in one's possession before turning to the very government benefits that one's taxes previously paid for during periods of employment, expressing shock at the minor possessions of the poorest among us is absurd.[116]

Darlena Cunha, a former television producer turned stay-at-home mom, recently penned a column for the *Washington Post* in which she discussed her own experience as someone who ended up on SNAP after her husband lost his job and the economy imploded, leaving them owing more on their mortgage than their home was worth. As Cunha noted, when she went to pick up her Electronic Benefits Transfer card driving her Mercedes—a car she and her husband had owned long before hard times struck—she was acutely aware of how others were viewing her and how the contrast made her feel about herself. She also mentioned how friends would tell her that she and her husband couldn't be that bad off since they still had a luxury vehicle in their possession. And yet, as Cunha explained:

> [The Mercedes] wasn't a toy—it was paid off. My hus-

> band bought that car in full long before we met. Were we supposed to trade it in for a crappier car we'd have to make payments on? Only to have that less reliable car break down on us?[117]

Cunha's point is all the more pertinent given that supposed "luxury" items like vehicles help facilitate opportunities for unemployed and poor persons seeking better jobs.[118] To criticize the poor for having a car is to suggest that they should be without a vehicle so long as they receive government aid. But how can those in need better their situation if they have no reliable vehicle to get them from home to a job, especially if public transportation in their area is inconsistent or if the best job opportunities are far away?

Apparently it's a concern considered trivial by some, as suggested by a recent story in the *New York Times* concerning the increasing use of automobile GPS "de-activation" devices that debt collection agencies and car loan lenders can utilize so as to disable vehicles driven by people who fall behind on their car payments. According to the article, people with less than excellent credit are being lured into car loans with predatory interest rates and massive late-payment penalties. In other words, people with little money are being asked to pay *more* of what they don't have, and if they're late with a payment by just a few days, their cars can be immobilized remotely even while the car is on the interstate, in traffic, trying to get to one's job or to pick up one's children at school.[119] Aside from how dangerous such a practice can be, how can immobilizing a person's car help them pay for the vehicle? If they can't get to work, they can't earn money with which to make the payments. But none of that matters in a culture of cruelty—all that matters to such a culture and its enforcers is that an increasingly large percentage of the American citizenry can be financially squeezed, neglected and criminalized.

For many on the political right it isn't just luxuries like televisions and cars that they begrudge the poor. For some, like the editorial board of the *New York Post*, even providing a shelter for homeless families that is infested with rats, mold and roaches, and where "feces and vomit plug communal toilets"—as the city is apparently doing, according to a report in the *New York Times*—is "too generous" and relieves parents of the obligation to provide a decent home for their children.[120] For Rush Limbaugh, it's not merely a decrepit shelter or consumer products we should deny struggling Americans: even the idea that the poor should have teeth is pushing the envelope of acceptability for Rush. According to Limbaugh, if one is too poor to afford dentures, that is one's own fault, and surely it is not the responsibility of publicly funded health care to provide such a luxury. In his estimation, one who is too poor to afford fake teeth should be content to either recycle those belonging to one's dead uncle, or content oneself with the perpetual consumption of applesauce.[121]

Speaking of applesauce, conservatives have long been preoccupied with what poor people eat, as with the by now infamous stories that most of us have heard about persons buying expensive cuts of meat with food stamps or EBT cards. Tales of food stamp profligacy have been legion at least since Ronald Reagan's 1976 presidential campaign, when he told the tale about "strapping young bucks" buying T-bone steaks with food stamps. Of course, the allure of the rather pedestrian T-bone has dimmed considerably over time, such that stories of culinary overindulgence on the part of the poor now require a bit of an upgrade. Today, it's no longer mid-range quality steak for SNAP fraudsters, but rather king crab legs, according to Texas Congressman Louis Gohmert. In a recent speech on the House floor, Gohmert relayed a story supposedly told to him by a constituent who was angered that while he could only afford ground meat for himself and his family, he watched the person in front of him pay for crab legs with food stamps. That the constituent said the individual paid with stamps is itself an indication that the story was likely a lie (since there are no more actual food stamps in use), but that didn't stop Gohmert from repeating it and insisting that such a story proved why the nation should cut back on SNAP; this, despite the fact that the average monthly allotment for SNAP recipients as of 2013 was only $133 per person, and only $122 per month in Gohmert's own state.[122]

Clearly under the impression that the poor eat too well on the government dime, the aforementioned Arizona Republican activist Russell Pearce said recently that if it were up to him, families receiving assistance couldn't buy "Ding Dongs and Ho Hos," or "steak or frozen pizza," but would be limited to "15-pound bags of rice and beans, blocks of cheese and powdered milk."[123] So not only should the poor not have seafood or meat, let alone that extravagant luxury known as frozen pizza, they shouldn't be afforded the benefit of vegetables or even *liquid milk*, as these are properly understood to be the special purview of the rest of us.

But contrary to claims that the poor eat like royalty on the public dime, the evidence shows that most SNAP households are extremely thrifty with their food shopping. Far from blowing their benefits on crab legs or steak of any kind, they tend to shop inexpensively and responsibly to make the benefits last. According to a recent analysis of thousands of needy households, beneficiaries are bargain shoppers when they first receive SNAP and become even thriftier over time. Upon entering the program, nearly one in four households report purchasing food that is out of date or nearly expired, simply because those items are discounted, and this rate climbs to thirty percent for those same families after they have been on the program for six months. Likewise, eighty-five percent of new SNAP households buy food items on sale, and after six months of SNAP benefits about half of recipient households have learned to buy in bulk (so as to get discounts) and to clip coupons—practices that hardly afford one much lobster or very many premium cuts of steak.[124]

Importantly, pilot programs to encourage healthy eating among SNAP recipients show great promise—far more than punitive efforts to restrict what they can and cannot buy. For instance, the Department of Agriculture recently launched a project in Massachusetts to provide a credit of thirty cents for every dollar of SNAP spent on fresh fruits and vegetables. The result? A twenty-five percent jump in the consumption of these healthy items among SNAP recipients.[125] Likewise, there are dozens of programs across the country that provide SNAP recipients with $2 of produce for every dollar of SNAP benefits spent at farmers' markets, effectively matching such purchases and encouraging healthy eating.[126]

While the stories of SNAP extravagance say little about the reality of living and eating while poor, they speak volumes to the way in which more financially secure Americans think about those who are struggling. That anyone would believe SNAP recipients getting such paltry amounts in aid—again, $133 per person, per month, on average in 2013, or less than $1.50 per person per meal—would blow their benefits on crab legs or other expensive items, thereby reducing the amount of aid left for the rest of the month, says a lot about how families in need are perceived in this country. Those who repeat stories like this seem to believe that if and when the poor actually *do* splurge on pricey food items, they're somehow putting one over on the rest of us. But it's not as if their EBT cards are endless money pits that refill upon depletion like a cup of coffee at a Waffle House. If one blows all of one's money on beluga caviar and cedar-planked salmon, that's just less money for the rest of the month, which is why if a few among the poor spend in such a manner, they likely learn from their budget shortfalls and are unlikely to repeat the practice.

Although the facts suggest that impoverished families are far thriftier with their money, including government benefits, than commonly believed, it's still worth noting how fundamentally cruel it is to police the shopping habits of the poor in the first place. To deny to those who are struggling an occasional soda or candy bar or even cigarettes or beer is incredibly callous. While there are excellent health reasons to avoid all four, and certainly their overconsumption—and this is true for all of us, not only those who are poor—is it really necessary to resent the consumer habits of those who are economically hurting? Must they be not only poor but without any momentary relief? Without any of the escapes and diversions the rest of us take for granted? No snack food, no alcohol, no cable TV, and no movies with the kids? No anything to take their minds off the daily grind of trying to make ends meet? To insist that folks struggling with poverty be so indelibly miserable as to force them to spend every waking moment trying to find a better job seems sadistically cruel; it treats their situation as tantamount to a crime for which they are to be punished. It's the exact same thinking that animates resentment over prisoners receiving education while behind bars, or having any freedoms whatsoever—the idea that unless inmates are made to be utterly traumatized by their incarceration they won't fear coming back to prison. So too, under this logic, unless the poor are traumatized completely by their poverty, they won't work hard and get their lives together. Those who adhere to this thinking are making virtually no distinction between the blame they place on perpetrators of crime and the blame they place on victims of poverty.

This is far from mere hyperbole: those who struggle to survive readily articulate the way in which their reliance on public assistance has all but criminalized them, not only in the eyes of the public, but also in the eyes of those who oversee safety-net programs. In a recent column for the *Washington Post*, Kentucky-based writer Jeanine Grant Lister discussed her experiences as someone who once had to rely on food stamps and the national nutrition program for women, infants and children (WIC):

> In America today, being poor is tantamount to a criminal offense, one that costs you a number of rights and untold dignities, including, apparently, the ability to determine what foods you can put on the dinner table. . . . Utilizing American safety-net programs (which, by the way, I paid into for years before receiving any "entitlements") requires that I relinquish my privacy multiple

> times. I have to reveal how much I pay to live where I live, the amount of my utility and medical bills, what car I own, even whether I have a plot to be buried in when I die. I have to update the local office any time my income changes, or if a family member moves in or out, and even when my college-age children come home for the summer. When I used WIC to supplement the diets of myself and my two children, we were required to report to the Health Department quarterly for weight and wellness checks. My babies' blood was taken to look for lead exposure. When my daughter's test came back with sky-high lead levels, the Health Department came into my residence, crawled over the whole place, and took samples of windowsills, walls, soil, flooring and water, and found . . . nothing. Upon recheck, my daughter's lead levels were perfectly normal and deemed a false positive. What if they had had discovered metabolites consistent with drug exposure? Poppyseeds metabolize like opiates. Had I been living in Section 8 housing, that would have resulted in a search of my home for drugs, the loss of my home and quite probably the loss of my children.[127]

Sadly, stigmatizing the impoverished in this way—viewing them, speaking of them and treating them as presumed ne'er-do-wells—is just another day at the office for most right-wing activists and media mouthpieces. Criticisms of safety-net programs have long been rooted in grandiose notions of widespread abuse and waste by recipients. Kansas lawmakers recently passed legislation to prohibit TANF recipients from withdrawing cash on their debit cards and using the money on cruise ships or for psychics, tattoos or lingerie, despite presenting no evidence that any of the state's 17,000 recipients were splurging in such a fashion. Part of a larger welfare reform package, the Kansas law will also limit cash withdrawals using a TANF ATM card to a mere $25 per day.

While supporters claim this will prevent recipients from using benefits on nonessential items, such a limit will also make it difficult, if not impossible, for recipients without checking accounts to pay rent or utilities.[128]

Meanwhile, FOX has hyped a report from a group called Colorado Watchdog, purporting to show that welfare recipients in that state are withdrawing their subsidies at liquor stores, exotic vacation spots, casinos and at least one strip club.[129] According to the report, Coloradans withdrew $3.8 million in welfare benefits from ATM machines in states other than Colorado over a two-year period. Although nearly $1 million of this amount was in bordering states, which could simply reflect that residents live near the border and work in a neighboring state or shop there, the rest was withdrawn farther away, including $70,000 withdrawn in Las Vegas, about $6,500 in Hawaii, and $560 in the Virgin Islands.[130] Such anomalies make for plenty of right-wing outrage, but they clearly are not representative of a substantial fraud problem. The entire amount of TANF money withdrawn in states other than Colorado or its border states comes to only 1.7 percent of Colorado's TANF program dollars. The amount withdrawn in Vegas, Hawaii and St. Thomas combined amounts to less than five-hundredths of one percent (0.045) of all state benefits. To hype this handful of cases is less about truly rooting out a pattern of program abuse than about enraging a public already encouraged to think the worst of the poor and those on assistance.

As for withdrawals made in liquor stores, these too amount to less than one percent of TANF benefits withdrawn and involve less than one percent of households receiving benefits. Casino withdrawals, which amount to about $75,000 per year, could indicate that people are gambling with their benefits, but could also represent low-wage casino employees who make withdrawals at their place of employment because there isn't a closer or more convenient ATM around. When it comes to strip club withdrawals, there appears to have been a whopping $1,500 withdrawn at one Denver-area club over the course of two years: disturbing but hardly evidence of a common practice.[131] In all, making a public spectacle of these rare potential abuses of taxpayer monies ends up stigmatizing the ninety-nine percent or more of all recipients who play by the rules and don't misuse benefits. While it might be worthwhile to figure out ways to sanction this handful who take unfair advantage, is it really so important to catch and punish these few that the broad base of TANF families should be stigmatized? In a culture of cruelty, apparently the answer is yes: stopping a handful of abusers is so important on principle, that even if entire programs have to be stigmatized, chopped or ended altogether, the cost is worth it.

Likewise, commentators on the right have accused Colorado TANF recipients of using benefits to buy marijuana at the state's newly legalized weed stores, yet there have been only sixty-four cases of persons in the state using benefit cards to withdraw cash from ATMs located inside marijuana shops. This represents one and a half tenths of one percent (0.15) of all TANF-related withdrawals in Colorado during the month in which the usage was discovered; and the combined value of the withdrawals came to only $5,475, which is 4.4 thousandths of one percent (0.0044) of the state's annual TANF block grant. Not to mention, the stores in which these ATMs were located dispense marijuana for patients who use the drug for medicinal purposes, so to ban recipients from using TANF benefits this way would be to deny them a valid and legal form of medically authorized relief.[132]

For many on the right, however, evidence is a luxury hardly worth indulging. It is virtually axiomatic for some that Americans are often poor because of drug use. Bill O'Reilly, in one particularly disingenuous segment on his FOX program, suggested that because roughly thirteen percent of the population was poor and roughly thirteen percent of Americans currently use drugs, "maybe poverty is not exclusively an economic problem."[133] The implication was that the thirteen percent in poverty and the thirteen percent who use drugs were the same people. But of course they are not. Despite being nearly three times as likely as whites to be poor, African Americans use drugs at rates that are essentially identical to the rates at which whites use them. Latinos, despite being 2.5 times as likely as whites to be poor, are *less likely* to use drugs than whites.[134] And when it comes to drug abuse and dependence as opposed to mere recreational use, whites are *more likely* to abuse narcotics than people of color, despite being one-third as likely to be poor.[135] If there were a correlation between poverty and drug use, suffice it to say that these data would look very different.

But lack of evidentiary support for their presumptions hasn't stopped right-wing lawmakers from proposing drug testing for persons on public assistance. In the last several years, state legislatures have increasingly pushed through bills to require anyone receiving TANF or unemployment insurance to provide urine samples in order to prove they aren't drug users.[136] Although the bills have, in some cases, been found unconstitutional—and although the evidence suggests the cost of administering the drug testing exceeds the money saved from knocking drug users off the rolls—lawmakers persist, consumed with contempt for the poor and unemployed and committed to viewing them in the worst possible light.[137] And all this, despite clear evidence that persons receiving welfare benefits do not use drugs, let alone abuse them, at rates any higher than the general public—and certainly not at rates any higher than others who receive money from the taxpayers, including teachers, those working for private companies but on government contracts, or, for instance, those Wall Street executives whose entire industry was bailed out by the government.[138] Yet, none of these other recipients of public largesse are being drug tested, nor will they be.

Likewise, that so many Americans appear prepared to lecture the poor as to what they can eat (or even whether they should be able to purchase Valentine's candy for a loved one using SNAP benefits) is telling as to the selective way in which government program dollars are perceived. As Bryce Covert notes in *The Nation*, "When we give people assistance through the home-mortgage interest deduction, we don't feel entitled to tell them what house to buy or what neighborhood to live in; when we subsidize a college education through student loans, we don't tell students what school to go to or what to major in. When we tax capital gains income at a lower rate than income made from labor, we certainly don't tell those stock pickers what to do with the extra cash."[139] But of course, as Covert notes, while government programs like these benefit mostly middle-class and affluent taxpayers—and are "submerged" in the tax code or programs that are less visible to the public—food stamp EBTs are observed in the process of being used and help the poor and near-poor, who are presumed to be in that condition in the first place because of their irresponsibility. So even as those who are quite a bit better off receive the biggest benefits from government programs (funded by the government via direct payments or deferred taxes which result in the rest of us having to pick up the slack), it is the relatively small amount received by the poor that sets us on edge and makes us feel entitled to moralize.

Sadly, some simply cannot relinquish their commitment to the notion that the poor and those on public assistance are irresponsible and dishonest, scamming the system and taking advantage of hard-working taxpayers. When the Department of Agriculture recently released a report noting that 2012 had seen the lowest rate of SNAP payment errors in history, conservative commentators went ballistic. FOX Business anchor Stuart Varney excoriated the Department of Agriculture report, asking, "Since when has (a 3.42 percent error rate) been good?"[140] In fact, such a rate is extremely good and is the lowest in the history of the food stamp/SNAP program.[141] Even that error rate includes *underpayments* (i.e., payments that were lower than they should have been, or payments that were not made at all to persons who applied and should have received them but were unfairly rejected). When underpayments are subtracted from overpayments, the net amount of overpayment in SNAP falls to only around two percent of program dollars: one-eighth the amount of projected fraud in the area of tax collection.[142]

Importantly, the error rate in SNAP has declined rapidly despite the fact that program rolls increased during the recession. In the past decade, the SNAP error rate has fallen fifty-six percent even as participation grew by 134 percent due to the economic downturn. Likewise, although there is some degree of food stamp trafficking (in which recipients trade SNAP for cash, presumably so as to purchase items normally not covered by the program), it is estimated that for every dollar of SNAP benefits, only one penny is diverted through trafficking: half the amount that was being siphoned off a decade ago, and sixty percent below the amount being lost in the early 1990s to this kind of fraud.[143]

As for fraud by TANF recipients, there is no doubt that technical fraud occurs, meaning that recipients in some cases work for cash under the table by taking care of a neighbor's kids or cleaning their house—income that would result in a suspension or reduction of benefits were it reported. But considering that the average monthly benefit from TANF is only $162 per person,[144] and $387 *per family*—less than half the poverty line in every state and less than one-third the poverty line in most of them—is such under-the-table activity really surprising?[145] If benefits are set so low that even when SNAP is added to them the typical family on both kinds of assistance still remains below the poverty line, how is one supposed to survive without such side work? If anything, that kind of fraud speaks to the work ethic of the poor and their desire to earn income and take responsibility for themselves and their children. It suggests that the stereotype of lazy welfare recipients sitting around doing nothing is a complete contrivance.

In her 2011 book, *Cheating Welfare: Public Assistance and the Criminalization of Poverty*, University of Connecticut law professor Kaaryn Gustafson notes that although technical fraud is common, other types—like someone filling out multiple claim forms so as to procure excess benefits from the system—are exceedingly rare. In California, she notes, officials only identify about three such cases per month, only one of which has sufficient evidence of intentional fraud as to justify further investigation. According to Gustafson, efforts to detect criminal fraud through mechanisms like fingerprinting of recipients, intended to spot persons with criminal records who are legally barred from most program benefits, have proven superfluous. Not only do such efforts not result in much weeding out of criminals, they also are anything but cost-effective. In Texas, fingerprinting efforts ended up costing taxpayers $1.7 million in the first seven months of operation, and nearly $16 million by the end of 2000. But in four years, there were only nine criminal fraud charges filed by state prosecutors.[146] Indeed, serious fraud is so rare and expensive to detect and prosecute that anti-fraud initiatives typically exceed whatever amount of money is being lost from fraud in the first place. As Gustafson explains:

> When a welfare recipient is charged with fraud, she adds costs to the criminal justice system. In addition to the costs of investigation, the county has to pay for the time of both a prosecutor and a public defender. If the recipient goes through a welfare fraud diversion program, the county bears continuing administrative costs for collecting payments and monitoring her progress in the diversion program. If the welfare recipient is convicted and sent to jail or prison, then government costs soar. It is much more expensive to house a single inmate for a year than it is to provide for a typical family on welfare. If the head of a household does end up serving time in jail or prison, her children may be placed in the foster care system, where more money will be spent on the children than under the welfare system. All of these costs are ignored in calculations of the costs of investigating and prosecuting welfare fraud. In sum, the government cost savings that policymakers associate with punitive and criminalizing welfare policies may actually only be cost shifting—either between federal, state, and local coffers

or from the welfare system to the criminal justice and foster care systems.[147]

For some however, presuming the worst about the needy and unemployed is so reflexive an act, that they will quite purposely deceive the public. Recently, right-wing talking heads from Rush Limbaugh to FOX News personalities Bill Hemmer, Lou Dobbs, Shannon Bream and Charles Payne all publicized what they considered "stunning new evidence" about the irresponsibility of the unemployed.[148] Relying for their information on a popular right-wing website that naturally provided no links to its source, they trumpeted supposedly convincing data from the Labor Department to the effect that the unemployed spend more time shopping than looking for a job. In fact, the original article breathlessly exhorted its readers that the unemployed not only shop too much but also spend twice as much time during an average day in "socializing, relaxing or leisure" activities as they do searching for a job. They also seemed shocked and appalled at the amount of sleep that unemployed people report getting each day, as if this were indicative of how lazy the jobless are: "Nearly all of the unemployed—99.9 percent—reported sleeping on an average day. On average, they dedicated 9.24 hours to that activity."[149] Horrors.

But naturally, the article's author and the right-wing media figures who repeated that author's claims got it wrong. Despite Payne's suggestion that the data proves how welfare programs "do make people lazy. They make people comfortable. They make you want to take a chill pill,"[150] the actual statistics say nothing of the sort. The data source in question nowhere used the term "unemployed" to describe individuals being examined, nor was it specifying anything about those persons; rather it refers to persons "not employed," which is an entirely different thing, despite how similar it may sound. According to the report used to make this claim (the Labor Department's American Time Use Survey), those who are not employed include persons "not in the labor force,"[151] and *that* concept includes not only people who have simply quit looking for a job and might be on public assistance, but also those who are retired, disabled or full-time students, and those who are stay-at-home moms or dads with partners who earn enough to support them on their own. According to Census data, of all persons who are not working, two in five are retired, one in five are students, fifteen percent more are chronically ill or disabled, and another thirteen percent are caring for children or other family members (this would include many middle-class stay-at-home mothers). In other words, eighty-five out of a hundred people who are classified as not working or not employed fall into *these* categories.[152] So the fact that only nineteen percent of those classified as "not employed" engage in job searches or interviews on an average day, while 22.5 percent of those "not employed" shop for items other than groceries on an average day, means nothing. Those doing all that shopping and luxuriating are mostly *not* the people the right would have us envision: rather, they are people who are not in the labor force because they haven't the need to be due to a partner's earnings, or else they have already retired or are going to school.

The stay-at-home mom who spends her days shopping and getting her nails done and whose husband makes millions on Wall Street may be lazy and self-absorbed, and the seventy-five-year-old Florida snowbird who sits on the beach all day may have been a horrible human being during his work years, but they are surely not the individuals being chastised by the right with this data, even though they are the ones who are likely to be showing up in it. This is just one more prime example of how conservatives routinely distort data to further a narrative of cruelty toward America's most vulnerable.

Welfare Dependence and the Culture of Poverty: America's Zombie Lie

But no matter the evidence, there are many who simply fail to accept that their stereotypes of the poor are inaccurate. Not only do they continue to believe that the poor and those on public assistance are grifters, they insist that various safety-net programs are so generous as to have engendered intergenerational welfare dependence and a "culture of poverty," characterized by irresponsibility on the part of recipients. According to this line of thinking, programs from cash aid to SNAP to unemployment insurance (even Social Security and Medicare for the elderly) have rendered the United States a nation of "takers." It is this zombie lie—the kind that never seems to die no matter the counter-evidence—that one can hear articulated virtually any day on talk radio or on FOX. On his FOX Business show, former Judge Andrew Napolitano has claimed:

> Entitlements like Social Security, Medicare and Medicaid . . . make Americans dependent upon big government. And dependency is turning this country from a nation of makers who come up with new ideas, who employ new people, who risk their wealth and create wealth, into a nation of takers who primarily consume other people's wealth.[153]

While Napolitano is willing to throw all social programs including Social Security under the dependency bus—surely not endearing himself to the elderly who rely on it for their survival—the charge of dependency is more often thrown at programs aimed specifically at the poor, like TANF, SNAP benefits, or public housing. This is why when Congressman Paul Ryan recently introduced his new anti-poverty plan, he did so in terms that clearly suggested a belief that existing programs had contributed to cultural pathology and dependency. As Ryan put it:

> We have got this tailspin of culture, in our inner cities in particular, of men not working . . . generations of men not even thinking about working or learning the value and the culture of work, and so there is a real culture problem here that has to be dealt with.[154]

Aside from the implicitly racist framing of the issue—references to "inner cities" immediately conjure images of persons of color and are known to do so—Ryan's assumptions are based on falsehoods. His plan, which calls for welfare recipients to sign behavioral contracts with the government and then to be sanctioned for any failure to follow the terms of the contract, presumes that those on assistance are dysfunctional and little more than children in need of parental guidance and discipline.[155] Though said in a slightly less bombastic way, it's little different from the hateful ventilations of Ted Nugent, who has said antipoverty programs should be eliminated because poverty is the result of "poor decisions" that "we need to punish."[156] Because punishing poor people historically always managed to eliminate poverty—it's apparently an ancient wisdom we've forgotten.

The truth, of course, is quite the opposite: there is no logic or evidence to suggest that welfare programs have created a culture of poverty or permanent underclass. If there were a "culture of poverty," or if poverty were mostly the result of "bad decisions," we would expect most of the poor to remain poor for long periods. After all, few people trapped in a culture of pathology and dysfunction in January would likely have undergone a major cultural transformation by April, or even by Christmas; but most people who slip into poverty do not remain there long, suggesting that impoverishment is more about economic conditions and opportunity than about individual or cultural pathology. As Washington University professor Mark Rank explains:

> The average time most people spend in poverty is relatively short . . . the typical pattern is for an individual to experience poverty for a year or two, get above the poverty line for an extended period . . . and then perhaps encounter another spell at some later point. Events like losing a job, having work hours cut back, experiencing a family split or developing a serious medical problem all have the potential to throw households into poverty.[157]

Data clearly bear out Rank's point: Among persons entering poverty in the most recent period under review, forty-three percent remained poor for four months or less, 71.5 percent were poor for no more than a year, and only eighteen percent—or less than one in five—remained poor for more than twenty months in that period.[158] This is not to diminish the hardship faced by such families during their time in poverty (and of course, as mentioned earlier, even those who are not officially poor face substantial hardship and difficulty making ends meet), but merely to suggest that the notion that poverty becomes a "way of life" or is intergenerational in nature is almost entirely false.

Modern-day Scrooges might respond that although most of the poor might not be trapped in a long-term underclass culture, certain segments of the poverty population are, and especially those who rely on various forms of public welfare such as cash aid or nutrition assistance. But that position is also belied by the available data. For instance, the rates at which persons avail themselves of cash aid or SNAP have fluctuated from nearly seventeen percent of the population in 1993 to only 12.5 percent by 2000, then back to seventeen percent by 2008 at the onset of the recession, and then twenty-three percent by 2011. Rates of welfare *dependency*, which are calculated using a bipartisan formula developed by Congress in 1994, have also jumped around from six percent in 1993 down to three percent by 2000, back to four percent by the beginning of the economic collapse, and then 5.2 percent by 2011.[159] If rates of welfare receipt and dependence both fluctuate so dramatically, and especially in direct relation to the strength or weakness of the economy, it becomes difficult to believe in a widespread "culture of poverty" that plagues those at the bottom of the nation's economic barrel.

Finally, the fact that most so-called welfare recipients don't receive benefits for a long period of time also suggests that poverty and even welfare receipt itself are evidence not of cultural pathology so much as of economic conditions over which most Americans have little control. In the case of TANF, for instance, half of all persons who enter the program will be off of the rolls *entirely* within four months, and nearly eight in ten will leave the rolls within a year. As for SNAP recipients, fifty-two percent who come onto the program rolls will exit within a year, and two in three will be off the rolls within twenty months.[160]

Although conservatives claim that most welfare recipients receive benefits for long periods, they make this case by blatantly misinterpreting the available data. For instance, conservative advocacy groups will often point out that if you look at the TANF rolls at any given moment, the typical family receiving benefits will have been receiving TANF for roughly three years.[161] Likewise, for SNAP, they will note that many remain recipients for a long period—an average of seven years for about half of all persons receiving SNAP at a given moment.[162] But these statistics, while seemingly quite damning of those on assistance (or at least damning of the programs themselves for fostering long-term dependence, as per the conservative gospel) are thoroughly deceptive, and do not change the fact that most persons who come onto either the cash or nutrition assistance rolls will leave the programs in a short period. How can that be? How can most recipients get off the programs in a matter of months, and yet, most persons on the programs at any given moment still be long-term recipients? It sounds impossible for both of these things to be true, but it isn't. Both claims are accurate, but only one is relevant, and it isn't the one upon which conservatives focus.

The difference between the percentage of overall TANF or SNAP recipients who are short-term versus long-term beneficiaries, and the percentage of such recipients at *any given moment* who will be long-term beneficiaries is a large one. By definition, if a person is on the rolls at any given moment, that same person cannot also be *off* the rolls at that same moment. So if you look at the TANF or SNAP rolls in August, for instance, anyone who came onto one or both programs in January and then was off by June would not be captured in the data. But anyone who *was* a long-term recipient and was going to be on the rolls for several years most certainly would be. What one will see at any given moment will be a disproportionate number of long-term recipients, not because most who enter the programs actually remain on them for a long-time, but because anyone who *is* a long-term recipient is going to be captured in the data at whatever moment you take your statistical snapshot. But that says nothing about the effect of the programs themselves on recipients and their propensity to become dependent for long stretches of time.

As an analogy, consider the population of the nation's jails. On the one hand, most people jailed over the course of a given year will be locked up for relatively minor offenses, and will be released in a fairly short period of time, while a much smaller share will be tried and convicted of serious crimes and sentenced to do time in prison. But if you looked at the population of persons in jail who were awaiting trial *right now*, or at any given point in the course of a year, a disproportionate share of these individuals would likely be persons who had been accused of serious crimes and were facing long terms. Not because most lawbreakers are hard-core violent offenders who will receive long sentences, but because anyone who *is* a hard-core violent offender is likely to be captured in the data at whatever moment you sample it. Minor offenders, on the other hand, will have cycled in and out of jail, or they will have been released on bail awaiting trial; as such, they will not be evident to the same extent.

It would be the same for hospitals. If you were to look at those currently occupying beds in your local hospital, a disproportionate share of them would be suffering from serious conditions from which they might not recover, and certainly not quickly. And yet, if you were to look at the entry log of all persons who cycled through the hospital in a year, most would have come in for far less serious conditions, at which point they would have been fixed up by doctors and then sent on their way. If you assessed the efficacy of the doctors based solely on the share of chronically ill patients remaining in a hospital bed at any given moment, your assessment wouldn't be very good. But if you assessed their effectiveness by looking at the results obtained for all patients admitted, the hospital and its doctors would look far better. The same is true with welfare programs. The important point is that most people who enter the programs won't stay long, and this is why we can say that such initiatives do not foster dependence. If welfare benefits *did* foster dependence, let alone a *culture* of dependency, we would expect that large numbers and perhaps the majority of such persons coming onto the rolls would find themselves trapped on them, unable or unwilling to leave, and that is simply not the case. In other words, when someone like Wisconsin congressman Glenn Grothman insists that, "some people are arranging their life to be on [SNAP]," he is not only insulting the poor, he is also lying about them.[163]

The only way that someone could really believe that social welfare programs in the United States encourage dependence is by knowing almost nothing about the nation's welfare apparatus, because given the paltry nature of most program benefits and how few people actually receive them, becoming dependent on the benefits of those programs is virtually impossible. For example, by September 2013 there were only about 3.6 million people in the entire country receiving cash welfare under the TANF program, down from fourteen million who received such benefits in the early 1990s. Of these 3.6 million TANF beneficiaries, 2.8 million, or seventy-eight percent, are children,[164] and of those children who benefit from the program, three in four are under the age of twelve.[165] The percentage of the nation's adults currently receiving TANF sits at less than one-half of one percent (0.5) of the adult population, and less than 1.5 percent of the total population (including child recipients) is on the program. Far from encouraging a nation of dependent takers, the nation's primary cash aid effort reaches almost no one.[166]

In fact, not only do few Americans receive cash assistance, but most people living below the poverty line do not receive cash aid under TANF. Fewer than one in ten poor people in the United States receive cash assistance, down from over forty percent of the poor who did in the mid-1970s. Going back to the claim that welfare payments somehow create a permanent culture of poverty, how can such a claim be made when nine of ten poor people don't even receive them? Even among the somewhat smaller group of poor persons who are eligible for aid—because not all of the poor meet the various requirements of the law—most do not receive assistance. Whereas nearly eighty percent of those families who were eligible for cash assistance in 1981 actually received aid, today only about a third of eligible families do.[167] And how can such benefits engender dependence, when the value of those benefits remains so paltry? In 2012, families enrolled in TANF received an average *monthly* benefit of $387,[168] and even the *maximum* monthly benefit for a family of three with no other income averaged only $436.[169]

Not only does TANF reach very few, and not only are typical benefits quite low, but those it reaches look nothing like the common stereotype. One in four TANF recipients lives in a family with at least one *full-time* worker, four in ten live in a family with at least one person working either part time or full time, and six in ten live in a family where someone either currently works or is actively involved in searching for employment.[170] For those families where no adult recipient of TANF is in the labor force, a disproportionate share of such cases involve households where the adult member of the family is at home caring for small children or is disabled. When it comes to households on TANF where no one is working, looking for work or disabled—in other words, households with an able-bodied adult who is "doing nothing" in the eyes of the modern-day Scrooges—only nine out of every one hundred recipient households fit this description. With about 1.2 million recipient households in all, this means only about 108,000 of them could even theoretically represent the image held by conservatives.[171] At least ninety-one percent of such families fail to fit the image of those receiving welfare, yet the stereotype persists.

Among the most prevalent stereotypes of the poor, and especially those on public assistance, is that of the single mother who engages in irresponsible sexual activity, giving birth to children out of wedlock and thus increasing her monthly welfare stash. But it is simply not the case that welfare payments contribute to out-of-wedlock childbirth among single moms. Half of all families receiving cash welfare have only one child, and nearly eight in ten have only one or two.[172] What's more, and contrary to popular perception, there is no difference between the number of children in single-parent families that receive assistance and the number of kids in families that don't: in both instances, the statistical average number of children in the home is just under two.[173] Likewise, the typical household receiving SNAP benefits is composed of only two people—most often a parent and one child.[174]

As for commonly held racial stereotypes of welfare recipients, these too lie shattered before the facts. Although it is true that persons of color are disproportionately represented on the TANF rolls (because they are disproportionately poor, and poverty is what qualifies one for benefits), only about a third of recipients are black, while slightly less than a third are white and another 30 percent are Hispanic (all of them legally present in the country, by the way).[175] If there are 3.6 million TANF beneficiaries and only twenty-two percent of these are adults, as noted previously, and if one-third of these are African American, this means that there are only about 261,000 black adults *in the entire nation* receiving cash welfare benefits, out of a population of more than twenty-nine million black adults in all: about nine-tenths of one percent (0.9) of the overall adult black population. Considering that the "culture of poverty" is so often thought to be specifically a problem within the black community, the fact that not even one percent of the black adult population receives cash benefits renders such beliefs nothing short of preposterous. How a group of nearly forty million individuals (adults and kids combined) can be rendered culturally defective by programs that reach so few remains a mystery that those committed to the zombie lie feel no need to explain. Likewise, when it comes to SNAP, the common racial assumptions about who receives benefits (and how many black folks in particular do) are incredibly inaccurate. In 2013, forty-five percent of recipients were white, while thirty-one percent were black and nineteen percent were Latino/a.[176]

Much as with TANF, there is no evidence or logic to suggest that SNAP encourages dependence or cultural pathology. Although the rolls of SNAP beneficiaries did indeed grow dramatically after the onset of the recession in 2008, and have only recently begun to drop again—[177]down nearly two million persons in all from December 2012 to December 2014[178]—it is not the case that these benefits are sufficient to engender dependence on the part of those who receive them. First, benefit levels are hardly adequate to foster dependence. As of 2015, the average monthly SNAP allotment comes to only $128 per person, or approximately $4.27 per day, or $1.42 per meal.[179] In 2015, the *maximum* monthly benefit for a family of three is estimated to be $511, or roughly $1.90 per person per meal.[180] Second, to suggest that SNAP beneficiaries are rendered dependent by the program, or are part of some culture of poverty "unattached to work," as Paul Ryan argues, is to take no note of the facts regarding the population of SNAP recipients. To begin with, forty-four percent of all persons receiving SNAP are children who are obviously not expected to be in the workforce earning their keep. Another nine percent are elderly and another twelve percent are non-elderly adults who are disabled. These groups alone represent roughly two-thirds of SNAP beneficiaries: people who are not expected to be working.[181] Of those who are able-bodied adults, a little more than half already work or live in a household where another adult works, or they are actively looking for work but unable to find it.[182] According to the most recent evidence, eighty-six percent of SNAP recipients are either children, disabled persons, persons who are already working, or persons who are unemployed but actively and consistently seeking a job.[183] This means that the common image crafted by conservatives applies *at most* to one in seven persons benefiting from SNAP.

Despite the financial inadequacy of these two programs, conservatives continue to falsely insist that large numbers of families receive generous assistance from a huge basket of programs beyond these two. For instance, several FOX commentators recently twisted the findings of a Census Bureau report on various government benefits received by children so as to suggest that most American kids are now essentially wards of the state. According to the report, sixty-five percent of American children now live in a household that receives some form of public assistance during the course of a year. Roughly two-thirds of the nation's youth come from families that receive benefits from SNAP, TANF, Medicaid, WIC, and/or the school lunch program.[184] To FOX commentator and longtime actress Stacey Dash (whose most memorable role was, appropriately enough, in the film *Clueless*), such facts prove that government aid is "the new version of slavery."[185] Of course it is, because if you receive an EBT card or state-subsidized asthma medication it's exactly like being whipped, raped and stripped of all legal rights.

Putting aside Dash's absurd slavery analogy, the reaction from the right to the Census report could hardly be less honest. As for the raw facts, FOX more or less got them right. In 2011, approximately forty-eight million separate children lived in families receiving benefits from one or more of the above-mentioned programs, and this represented sixty-five percent of all children in the United States that year. Thirty-five million of these kids lived in homes where someone received benefits from the school lunch program; twenty-six million of them lived in homes where Medicaid benefits were utilized; seventeen million of them were in homes that received SNAP; six million were in homes that used WIC, and a little over two million were in homes that benefited from cash assistance under TANF. Although these numbers have come down a bit since then, for 2011 they are indeed accurate so far as they go. But this is roughly the point at which FOX proceeded to get everything else about the report horribly, horribly wrong.

To begin with, the period under review in the report stretches from 2008 to 2011. In other words, the report examines children's family conditions during the worst economic downturn since the Great Depression. Even the data for 2011 reflect family conditions at the tail end of the recession and while the after-shocks of job loss and wage stagnation in the previous three years were still reverberating for millions. That the number of kids in families having to turn to various government benefits would increase during an economic crisis unparalleled in the past seventy years should hardly surprise anyone.

Second, and as the report's author makes very clear, the primary challenges facing children—and particularly those in low- and moderate-income families—include disruptive life transitions such as parental unemployment or having to move to a new place often. These kinds of transitions, as the report indicates, are highly correlated with having to rely on one or another government program. As it turns out, forty-two percent of children in poor families (and about a third of all kids in the nation) moved at least once during the period under review, and forty-four percent of poor kids (and about a third of all children) had at least one parent who experienced a change in their job situation during the same period. This matters because, as the author notes:

> Parents who have steady employment may be better able to provide consistent economic support, while parents who go through many job changes may have unpredictable work schedules and irregular income.[186]

In other words, whatever the statistics might say, they suggest that use of these programs is less about culturally engendered dependence on benefits and more about serious and unexpected life drama that happens often to persons who are on the economic margins, and *especially* during an extraordinary economic recession.

Third, to argue that the sixty-five percent figure proves the so-called welfare state is creating a self-perpetuating culture of poverty (the standard right-wing interpretation) ignores the fact that most of the kids reaping the benefits from the listed programs are not officially poor, but they qualify for benefits because their family incomes are too low to bring them above eligibility levels. There were 16.6 million children living in "poor" families in America in 2011, for instance, but 47.9 million kids living in families receiving benefits from these programs that year. This means that two-thirds of the kids whose families benefit from these efforts are not living in poor homes, which in turn means that they will likely be in homes with parents who *earn income*, but not enough to make it without a little help. Many others live in homes that are poor but still have earned income from work. How the use of these programs can be blamed for fostering "dependence" or discouraging work when most of the beneficiaries live in homes with earned income is a mystery left unexamined by conservative hysterics.

So, for instance, let's look at the SNAP program. According to the most recent data from 2013, fifty-two percent of SNAP households with kids have earned income from work, and of those that don't, a large number of them have parents who are disabled. In fact, it is increasingly likely for SNAP households to have *earned* income, and less likely for them to rely on other forms of assistance, suggesting that receipt of this program's benefits has nothing to do with dependence, but rather, reflect the realities of low-wage work in a faltering economy. For instance, SNAP households are fifty percent more likely to have income from work today than they were in 1989, while the likelihood that they receive cash welfare has plummeted by *eighty-five percent*, from forty-two percent of such households to only 6.5 percent today.[187]

Or consider the school lunch program. According to the report that so concerns FOX, this is the program that appears to benefit the most children, with nearly half of all kids living in homes that benefit from this one government effort. But there are three huge problems with the way conservatives are reading the data. To begin with, eligibility for free or reduced-price lunch goes up to 185 percent of the poverty line, which means that many beneficiaries of this program are not poor, and thus reside in families that are hardly dependent on welfare benefits; rather, they work, albeit at jobs that don't pay enough to bring them above the eligibility limits. How a program can be rendering people dependent when they in fact work hard every day is again left unexplained by the right.

Second, according to the most recent data, nearly nine million kids who are counted as benefiting from the school lunch program—and who represent nearly *thirty percent* of current recipients—are called "full-pay" beneficiaries. These kids come from families whose income is high enough that they don't qualify for free meals, or even officially reduced-price lunches, but they are still receiving a slight price break relative to the actual cost of the food provided and are thus *counted in the data* as beneficiaries of the program. They may not even know that they're benefiting. They don't have to fill out paperwork or apply; rather, they just receive a slight subsidy for the cafeteria meals they purchase, and are therefore counted just like folks who get their meals for free. Clearly, even under the most absurd interpretation, these 8.7 million recipients cannot be considered "dependent."[188]

Third, many children who receive benefits from the school lunch program only do so because they live in high-poverty school districts where all students are automatically enrolled in the program (even if they aren't poor, and no matter how hard their parents work)—a policy implemented so as to reduce administrative costs, thereby allowing the program to operate more cheaply and efficiently. While we could perhaps end automatic enrollment and make all parents prove their low income in order to qualify for benefits, such a change would add to the costs of the program by increasing the kinds of bureaucratic paper-shuffling that the American right normally opposes.

In all, when you consider those kids who receive school lunch benefits but are a) not poor and who live in homes with a parent or parents who work; b) poor but whose parent or parents work; c) not poor at all but who benefit from the small subsidy provided even to "full-pay" recipients; or d) children who benefit automatically just because they attend a high poverty school but who may not be poor themselves, there is little doubt that the vast majority of the children and families claimed as beneficiaries are not caught in a cycle of dependence, and that none of them are being "enslaved" by the program. The need is real, but the dependence is not.

As for Medicaid, the assumption that families with kids who make use of this program are slackers who would rather let the government take care of them than work for a living couldn't be further from the truth. Fully *eighty-six percent* of children who receive benefits through Medicaid or the supplement to Medicaid known as the Children's Health Insurance Program (CHIP) come from families where at least one adult works.[189] Sadly, despite their earned income and even middle-class status in many cases, families in high-cost-of-living areas where health care inflation has been especially onerous are eligible for benefits and often have to make use of them. But doing so hardly suggests that the families are suffering from a debilitating mentality of dependence, nor that their children are being taught to rely on the state. The parents in these cases are doing their best; they're working and doing everything conservatives would have them do. Unfortunately their earnings have been insufficient to cover the spiraling costs of health care.

And when it comes to the WIC program for postpartum moms and their infants and toddlers, forty-three percent of beneficiaries live above the poverty line due to earned income, but still qualify for assistance. If nearly half of beneficiaries aren't even poor because they receive money from employment, how can the program be seen as encouraging dependence and laziness? And even for those beneficiaries who *are* poor, how can a program that provides assistance to children at special risk for nutritional deficiencies (like kids born prematurely or with particularly low birth weight), be ridiculed as an effort that fosters a culture of poverty?

Naturally, FOX is hardly alone in claiming that poor families are receiving massive government benefits. A recent study by the Cato Institute claims that the typical welfare family receives such huge handouts in most states that adults in these families have little incentive to work. According to Cato, welfare benefits make these families better off than they would be if one of its members were to get a full-time job.[190] But the report, much like an earlier one they issued in the mid-1990s, is entirely dishonest when it comes to how much a normal "welfare" family receives in benefits.

For instance, in order to claim that welfare benefits pay more than minimum wage in thirty-five states and are equivalent to a $15-an-hour job in thirteen of these, they divide the total amount spent on seven different welfare programs by the numbers of poor families with no currently employed member, and then assume that the resulting number is the average amount received by each such poor family. But this is dishonest on multiple levels. To begin with, few if any poor families receive benefits from *every single one* of the seven programs Cato references: TANF, SNAP, WIC, Medicaid, housing assistance, subsidies for utilities, and emergency food aid. As such, to presume that the typical "welfare" family takes home a basket of goodies anywhere near the amount Cato estimates is preposterous. For instance, as Cato admits in the report (though studiously finessing the implications of this fact), only about fourteen percent of TANF recipients also receive housing assistance;[191] and although most families receiving support from TANF receive SNAP benefits, very few persons who receive SNAP live in households where TANF benefits are received. According to the most recent data, only 6.5 percent of households that receive SNAP benefits also receive cash welfare under TANF.[192] To presume a common welfare basket involving both of these program's benefits (to say nothing of the others) is to grossly distort the picture for most persons who rely at one time or another on public assistance. Additionally, only eleven percent of SNAP recipients receive benefits from the WIC nutrition program for new moms and infants,[193] and only a little more than one in four SNAP beneficiaries receive any form of housing subsidy or public housing benefit,[194] indicating that Cato's assumptions about what a "typical" welfare family receives are completely off-the-mark. Even more fatal for Cato's principal claim—the idea that welfare programs discourage work among the poor because of their generosity—is the fact that since 1989 the percentage of SNAP recipient households also receiving cash has plummeted from forty-two percent of all households to only 6.5 percent, while the share receiving income from work has increased substantially, from only twenty percent of recipient households in 1989 to thirty-one percent with earnings now.[195] This being so, it is disingenuous to claim that SNAP discourages work, since SNAP families are working more than ever and relying on cash aid less than in the past.

Additionally, Cato ignores the fact that many of the benefits it references are received by persons who are not poor and who currently work, or those who work but in spite of their employment remain below the poverty line. SNAP expenditures, utility assistance expenditures, and Medicaid benefits are not all consumed by the unemployed poor; thus, simply dividing the amount spent on these efforts by the number of poor families with no member in the workforce will result in a gross overestimation of the amount being received by these kinds of families and overstate the supposed "disincentive" that these programs create for seeking employment. Given that large numbers of SNAP beneficiaries live in homes with at least one working family member, the entire idea of such a program creating a disincentive to employment is debunked.

Third, the methodology the Cato analysts use to calculate the value of non-cash benefits is so dubious as to suggest they concocted it with deliberate deception in mind. For instance, they presume that the value of the rent subsidy provided to those who receive housing benefits is equal to the average fair market rent in a recipient's state. But those who receive rent subsidies or live in public housing do not receive benefits equal to the *average* fair market rent. At most, the value of the benefit received should be considered relative to the typical rent at the *lowest end* of the rental market, since it is that kind of housing that poor people would be accessing in the absence of rental aid. By calculating the benefit relative to the average cost of housing in a state, Cato inflates the value of assistance by comparing it to middle-class rental housing. They are basically assuming that in the absence of public housing subsidies the poor and unemployed would find jobs that would allow them to afford an apartment in the mid-range of their local housing market, which is like saying that if poor people didn't receive housing subsidies they would suddenly become middle class—an idea so self-evidently preposterous as to be hardly worth serious consideration.

Cato also assumes that beneficiaries of housing assistance receive aid equal to the *full* cost of that housing, but this too is inaccurate. Persons in public housing or who receive Section 8 vouchers are expected to use roughly thirty percent of their income to pay rent. Although the unemployed may not contribute anything toward rent in those months when they are jobless, for many in public housing who work part time, roughly one-third of those earnings will be paid in rent. Since persons who work and receive housing subsidies are not counted in Cato's analysis—rather, all housing benefits are presumed to go to persons who do not work at all—Cato overstates the amount of the per-family subsidy, and especially how much is received by the supposedly "idle" poor. Cato also grossly distorts the percentage of persons who benefit from housing subsidies while also receiving benefits from other programs. Only half of those who receive rent assistance or other public housing benefits receive SNAP in a given month, while less than eight percent benefit from WIC, a far cry from Cato's accusation that housing aid comes along with a plethora of other programs.[196]

As for TANF, Cato's claims are even more preposterous: their analysis presumes that each poor family eligible for benefits actually receives those benefits, but most of the poor do not. Only one in ten poor people, and only a little more than one in four poor families, receive cash welfare benefits, meaning that such benefits cannot be a substantial cause of why such families presumably are poor or unemployed.[197] If you don't receive a benefit, it's pretty tough to conclude that said benefit is the reason you aren't currently working.

When it comes to Medicaid, the methodological dishonesty continues. Cato calculates the value of Medicaid benefits by comparing the per-family costs of the program to the premiums a person would have to pay under a typical private insurance policy providing the same coverage. In short, Cato assumes that in the absence of Medicaid the poor would use their own money to purchase comparable coverage, but such a claim is ridiculous. It's not as if people struggling with poverty are such shrewd and calculating mathematicians as to sit down and carefully calculate the cost of private care as opposed to public care and then simply opt for the latter so they can keep their own money for lottery tickets. In the absence of Medicaid, the poor would simply receive no health care at all, or rely on emergency room care when they became ill. Medicaid does not provide the poor with an income boost relative to what they would have in its absence; it does not allow them to keep more money in their own pockets that they would otherwise have spent on health care; rather, it provides them with needed medicine and other health services that they would otherwise likely *do without*. Not to mention, payments are made to health care providers and not the poor themselves: it is hardly fair to accuse those who benefit from heart surgery or blood pressure medicine of being enriched by welfare. One has to get sick in order to use the benefits, which is hardly something the poor—however crafty some may believe them to be—are likely to do on purpose.

And, of course, many of the Medicaid benefits that Cato presumes are going to the jobless poor are going to persons who, while poor enough to qualify for benefits, are actually in working families. As mentioned previously, nearly nine in ten low-income children who receive benefits through Medicaid or the Children's Health Insurance Program are in families where at least one adult works.[198] By ignoring these beneficiaries in employed homes, Cato overstates the value of benefits to each jobless family on assistance, thereby vastly exaggerating the supposed work disincentive provided by the program. Roughly half of families receiving benefits from Medicaid or CHIP are above 130 percent of the poverty line, but qualify for assistance because the cost of living in their communities is especially high and their wages make it impossible to afford health care on the private market. Medicaid cannot be blamed for discouraging work or locking people into poverty if half of recipients are earning income above the poverty line. Finally, even those who benefit from Medicaid often do not receive benefits from other programs, let alone all of the programs specified by Cato. For instance, less than forty percent of Medicaid beneficiaries also receive SNAP, and only ten percent receive benefits from WIC.[199]

Regarding WIC, Cato notes that since about sixty percent of eligible families participate in the program, it is therefore legitimate to include WIC benefits in the calculation of a typical welfare benefit package. But just because six in ten families eligible for this one program receive its benefits does not mean that the typical family in need receives the benefits of this program as well as all the rest Cato mentions, thereby providing a total benefit package sufficient to beat working for a living. Nor does it prove that all of those who are eligible for WIC are the jobless poor, and that therefore the program's benefits are all accruing to such persons and providing a possible work disincentive. Indeed, most of those who benefit from the other programs in Cato's presumptive "welfare basket" do not receive WIC, and most who receive WIC do not benefit from the other programs. Only eight of one hundred recipient families also benefit from TANF and only about one in four TANF beneficiaries also receive WIC (even then, only for a brief time, as they are only available to moms and their kids under the age of five).[200] Only forty percent of WIC beneficiaries also receive benefits under SNAP, meaning that the clear majority do not.[201] And since many low-income *working* moms qualify for WIC for themselves and their kids it is also unfair to calculate the average amount spent on this program as if it were all spent on persons in poor and unemployed families. More than forty percent of WIC families have incomes that are at least thirty percent *above* the poverty line, which means they have some kind of earned income. To blame such a program for discouraging work and locking people in poverty when some forty-three percent of its beneficiaries are above poverty and have income seems especially disingenuous.[202]

Overall, the evidence clearly negates any claim that government benefits for those in need discourage work. After all, according to the most recent evidence, three-quarters of all persons enrolled in major government benefit programs are in working families, and these families consume roughly two-thirds of all program benefit dollars.[203] As such, to suggest that government aid saps the work effort of its recipients, flies in the face of the facts, however much it might be commonly believed.

But however dishonest the Cato Institute might be, its deception is minor league compared to that of the far more professional liars who populate the Heritage Foundation. In their attempt to discredit government antipoverty efforts, Heritage publishes an "Index of Dependence on Government," which implies that the typical American has been rendered dependent on tens of thousands of dollars in annual cash and prizes from the state. They also have released several reports over the years professing to demonstrate how many trillions of dollars have been spent on antipoverty efforts, to no real effect. Yet Heritage's arguments are thoroughly dishonest, as anyone who actually reads the reports can readily see. For instance, when it comes to the antipoverty programs tallied by Heritage, their list includes things that very few people would consider welfare.[204] Among the programs that Heritage throws into the mix when bashing programs for the poor—and when claiming that trillions of dollars have been wasted on these efforts—one finds not only things like cash assistance, food stamps and housing programs, but also:

- Adoption assistance (typically paid to middle-class families who adopt neglected children);
- Foster care assistance (also typically paid to middle-class families who foster);
- Disability payments for disabled children;
- Emergency food and shelter assistance;
- Community health centers (where payments are made to the providers, not the poor);
- The nutritional program for the elderly;
- Rural housing insurance;
- The Title XX Block Grant (intended mostly to prevent child abuse);
- The Social Service Program for Refugees;
- Head Start (a popular and successful pre-school readiness program);
- Job training programs (intended to *reduce* welfare dependence);
- Pell Grants for college (also intended to boost future employability and wages, and reduce welfare dependence);
- AmeriCorps and other volunteer initiatives; and
- The Earned Income Tax Credit

Counting the Earned Income Tax Credit in the litany of "dependency-inducing" anti-poverty programs is especially egregious, since conservatives like Ronald Reagan specifically supported the EITC because it *reduces* dependence on other means-tested programs like cash and food assistance. The EITC rewards work by subsidizing earned income with tax refunds at low wage levels, and you can't receive the benefits if you don't work. By considering the EITC a form of welfare, Heritage inverts the meaning of the word and demonstrates its willingness to file every government program that benefits the poor under the rubric of the welfare state.

Of course, the bulk of the "massive" increase in welfare spending about which Heritage is so animated is in Medicaid, but two-thirds of Medicaid spending is for elderly people or the disabled, neither of whom even the most cold-hearted of modern Scrooges (one hopes) would expect to be in the workforce "earning their keep."[205] Twenty-one percent of Medicaid spending is for poor children, while only fifteen percent of program benefits are going to able-bodied adults.[206] So to calculate the size of the supposedly massive welfare state by throwing in the incredibly expensive health care expenditures on elderly, blind and disabled folks is to mislead the public about the amount being spent on the supposedly able-bodied poor.

Likewise, in its "Index of Dependence on Government," Heritage basically considers all government programs other than the military and K-12 education to be fair game for accusations of dependence-inducement.[207] So the Index authors include even Social Security and Medicare for the elderly as programs that foster dependence. The authors of the report romanticize the days when poor people (including the elderly) just relied on their families to care for them, or perhaps churches or "mutual aid societies." That such channels clearly weren't sufficient—large numbers of the elderly were poor in those days, which is precisely why Social Security was created—seems not to faze them. It's the same with housing: Heritage argues that the old days of private and religious groups providing housing (like orphanages, or Boy's Town, perhaps) were better than government-provided housing benefits. This is the vision the right offers to poor people: relying on some kindly old priest and his group home to take care of you, and if for whatever reason they can't manage it, that's too bad. They also argue that government-provided health care under Medicare and Medicaid has destroyed the wonderful private institutions that used to provide for people in need. But what evidence is there that such institutions ever covered the cost of high-dollar treatments like chemotherapy, radiation or organ transplants? Of course, they never did. Heritage seems to think people only get colds or the flu or chickenpox, and that armies of kindly old family doctors will gladly, out of the goodness of their hearts, provide care to them for free. But even if that were true for some, how would that address more long-term and costly care for serious conditions? It wouldn't, of course; rather, private, for-profit providers would end up refusing expensive care to those who couldn't afford it. It would be rationed care based solely on ability to pay—death panels, if you will, on which the panelists would be not doctors at all (and surely not the government), but insurance company representatives and hospital executives looking out for the bottom line.

Overall, the Index is calculated by throwing in pretty much every kind of government program imaginable and proclaiming them all guilty of making Americans dependent on the state. Among the programs deemed so destructive to personal independence, Heritage includes consumer and occupational safety spending, disease control funding, children and family services spending, all job training programs, disability insurance, agricultural research, and disaster relief. Even those who criticize programs like TANF, public housing or SNAP should be able to see that any measure of "Dependence on Government" that includes these things, as well as Social Security, Medicare and student loans, cannot be considered serious scholarship. It speaks to the ideological dishonesty of the right and those who seek to undo the various programs of the national safety net, and it should call into question their attacks on all programs, including the easier and more vulnerable targets like cash, food and housing aid.

The rhetoric of the culture of cruelty has been especially vicious of late with regard to the long-term unemployed and those who have been forced to rely on unemployment insurance. So those who have a solid work history and lost their jobs through no fault of their own (both conditions that have to be met in order to qualify for unemployment insurance) are increasingly incurring the wrath of the right. According to FOX commentators Stephen Moore and Eric Bolling, unemployment insurance is "like a paid vacation for people,"[208] which discourages the unemployed from looking for work. In a column for the *Wall Street Journal* in early 2013, Holman Jenkins claimed that unemployment insurance and Social Security disability payments encourage those who receive them to rely on "someone else to be productive."[209] Along those same lines, actor, commercial pitchman and onetime political speechwriter Ben Stein—apparently confusing the larger American public with Ferris Bueller, the main character in the only movie for which he is remembered—says that because of the availability of unemployment insurance, lots of unemployed people "would prefer not to go to work."[210] Rush Limbaugh concurs, noting that "extended unemployment benefits do nothing but incentivize people not to look for work,"[211] and that by advocating an extension of such benefits, President Obama is "in the process of creating and building a permanent underclass."[212]

Yet, contrary to right-wing belief, there is little evidence (or logic) to suggest that the availability of unemployment insurance contributes to long-term joblessness, or that the elimination of those benefits will suddenly lead the long-term unemployed to find jobs. In fact, a recent study by the Joint Economic Committee of Congress found that those persons who are out of work and receiving unemployment insurance spend more time looking for work than those who are unemployed but *not* receiving assistance.[213] Indeed, given that one can only qualify for unemployment benefits if one is actively searching for work, whatever relationship exists between unemployment insurance and increased joblessness is largely proof that the program is working, not failing. After all, if people receiving benefits remain in the job market (rather than dropping out altogether), and thereby are counted as unemployed, it's true that the unemployment rate could be marginally higher than it would have been had they simply stopped looking for work (at which point they would not be captured in the unemployment data). But surely it would be better to provide incentives to stay in the workforce and look for a job while receiving unemployment insurance, than for those out of work to simply give up hope, even if giving up hope managed to knock the unemployment rate down a few points.

It appears from the bulk of available evidence that extending unemployment benefits during an economic downturn results in *more jobs* being created rather than destroyed. Because these benefits are spent by their recipients, they serve to stimulate the economy, and according to the Congressional Budget Office, can produce as many as 300,000 jobs nationwide thanks to that stimulus.[214] That conservatives would attack the concept of unemployment insurance, even while more than three in four unemployed persons don't even receive any,[215] suggests the extent to which the right will blame the have-nots for economic problems they clearly did not cause.

The Real Reasons for Unemployment, Poverty and Welfare

Ultimately, it isn't a culture of poverty or individual irresponsibility that explains why a person is underemployed, unable to make ends meet, or in need of government assistance. It isn't a lack of values, or laziness. People are out of work because at any given moment there are rarely enough jobs available for all who are searching for one. People fall below the poverty line because they either can't find work, or do work but their wages are subsistence level. And people find themselves turning to government assistance because without work, or with only low-wage work, certain benefits from health care to housing subsidies to nutrition assistance become critical lifelines.

Far from not wanting to work, the unemployed desperately seek jobs; so much so in fact that the competition to get hired at Walmart can often prove more daunting than the competition to get into an Ivy League college. For instance, when Walmart opened a new store in Washington, D.C. in 2013, 23,000 people filled out applications in hopes of landing one of only six hundred jobs: an acceptance rate of 2.6 percent. By contrast, the overall Ivy League admissions rate is nearly nine percent, and even at Harvard about five percent of applicants manage to get in.[216] Likewise, only about six of every one hundred applicants for jobs at McDonalds get hired, suggesting that the problem is not a lack of willingness to work, but rather an insufficient number of positions for all who need and are seeking employment.[217]

Beyond the merely anecdotal, we know this is the problem in the larger economy. In June 2014 there were 4.7 million job openings, but there were 9.5 million people unemployed and actively searching for work.[218] In other words, for every job opening there were two people looking for employment, which is to say that no matter the work ethic of the unemployed and no matter their drive, determination, skills, values, sobriety, intelligence or anything else, half of all job seekers could not possibly find work. Although this is an improvement from 2013, when the ratio of job seekers to jobs was three to one, and far better than during the height of the recession when the ratio reached as high as seven to one,[219] it nonetheless suggests that the economy is not producing enough employment for all who want and need work. Considering that there are millions more who have grown so discouraged that they've given up looking for work altogether at this point, and who are no longer technically in the job market (nor counted in unemployment figures), the actual gap between persons needing work and available jobs is no doubt far worse than the official two-to-one ratio.

Among the challenges facing the unemployed, and especially the long-term unemployed, is discrimination. Presumimg them less competent or perhaps too desperate, employers are far less likely to provide interviews to long-term unemployed job seekers, no matter their qualifications. A recent study for the Boston Federal Reserve found that when qualifications and experience are otherwise similar, persons who have been out of work for longer periods of time are operating at a significant disadvantage. In the study, 4,800 résumés were sent out in response to six hundred job openings. Some résumés were of actual people, while others were fabricated to represent unemployed persons with various work histories and qualifications. For the unemployed, the study's author deliberately manipulated and altered certain factors such as how long the individual had been out of work, how often they had moved between jobs, and whether they had specific experience in the field for which they were applying.[220] Although the study confirmed that employers tend to favor those with industry-specific experience and stable work histories without too much job-hopping, these factors turned out to be far less important than the length of time a person had currently been unemployed. Applicants with industry-specific experience were *less* likely to get called back than those without such experience, if the more qualified applicant had been out of work for six months or longer, while the less qualified person had only been out of work for a short or medium period. People without relevant experience but whose spell of unemployment has been short are about three times as likely to be called back for an interview as those with relevant experience but who have been unemployed for six months or more.[221] In other words, when a person has been out of work for six months or longer, employers are simply screening them out regardless of experience and qualifications.[222] Unless there are specific measures established to bar discrimination against the long-term unemployed, or tax incentives for their hiring, or direct hiring of such persons by the government for new jobs programs, it is unlikely that the economic position of the long-term jobless is likely to improve. Unfortunately, any attempt to get employers to stop discriminating against the long-term unemployed is derided by the modern-day Scrooges as "punishing achievers," in the words of Rush Limbaugh.[223]

While reliance on benefits says little or nothing about the values of the poor, the need so many people have for these programs says quite a bit about the values of those for whom beneficiaries work, and from whom they receive such paltry wages as to leave them eligible for assistance. Companies like Walmart and

McDonalds pay their employees so little that workers at the companies often comprise the biggest group of Medicaid and SNAP beneficiaries in a given community,[224] and Walmart stores regularly set up food donation bins where they encourage their employees to buy and donate food for other employees who don't have enough to eat![225] By encouraging their employees to apply for public assistance, companies like McDonalds and Walmart get the taxpayers to subsidize them by shifting the burden of supporting workers from employers to the public. As many as eight in ten Walmart store associates rely on SNAP benefits so as to subsidize their paltry wages, and overall, taxpayers foot the bill for more than $6 billion in various welfare benefits for Walmart employees.[226] Although Walmart recently announced that it would boost wages for about 500,000 of its employees over the next two years—an issue to which we will return in a bit—many of these workers will remain eligible for public assistance even after the wage boost.

Cincinnati Walmart associate La'Randa Jackson's story, sadly, is all too typical. Although her family receives SNAP benefits, it's rarely enough to last the month. "I skip a lot of meals," she says. "The most important thing is food for the babies, then my younger brothers. Then, if there's enough, my mom and I eat." Sometimes she manages to get some extra food from the emergency food bank in town. As Jackson explains it, "The lady who works there knows we have babies at home."[227] Adding insult to injury, not only does Walmart pay such paltry wages that its associates are forced to turn to SNAP for food, but even worse, Walmart is the nation's largest food stamp redeemer as well. In other words, in many cases, their own employees are buying food at Walmart with the SNAP benefits they only have to rely on because their employer pays them so badly. This means that Walmart is making money on both ends: by paying poverty-level wages and then selling their own employees food, subsidized by the taxpayers. Annually, almost one in five dollars spent with SNAP benefits is spent at Walmart, bringing in approximately $13.5 billion in additional sales for the company.[228]

The picture is similar in the fast food industry. Current estimates suggest that fast-food workers and their families receive about $7 billion in public assistance of one form or another each year: a massive subsidy to low-wage employers, paid for by the taxpayers.[229] Indeed, the families of fast-food workers are about twice as likely as persons in the general population to rely on various forms of public assistance, with slightly more than half of such families receiving benefits from Medicaid, SNAP, TANF and/or the refundable portion of the Earned Income Tax Credit (EITC). Precisely because fast-food wages are so low (irrespective of the massive profits made by companies in that sector), the typical family of a fast-food employee receives nearly $8,000 annually in Medicaid benefits, and a few thousand more in food stamp and EITC benefits.[230]

Perhaps even more disturbing, given the mega-millions received by top bank executives (and the industry itself, due to recent government bailouts), a distressing number of bank tellers—perhaps the lowest rung in the industry's workforce, but nonetheless the one with which the public has the most interaction—are forced to rely on public assistance due to low wages. Nationally, nearly a third of all bank tellers' families benefit from at least one government aid program, from the Earned Income Tax Credit to Medicaid to SNAP, amounting to approximately $1 billion in total benefits. In New York, which is the fulcrum of the banking industry (and where top bankers receive six-figure bonuses as a matter of course), tellers make less than $13 per hour on average, forcing roughly forty percent of these workers' families to rely on one or another form of government aid.[231]

But rather than criticize companies for the inadequate pay offered to those who do the work that makes their profits possible, the wealthy economic minority and those on the right suggest that it is the value system of those low-wage workers that is to blame for their condition. Rather than advocating minimum wage hikes or livable wage legislation that would boost pay levels and purchasing power, thereby reducing the amount of public benefits received by these families, the rich oppose such wage boosts and advocate cutting the very programs that keep the families in the fast-food industry above complete destitution. Some go so far as to threaten workers with job loss if a minimum wage hike is successful, as did the Employment Policies Institute (a lobbying arm of the restaurant industry in California), which recently took out billboards in San Francisco, threatening to replace workers with iPads should the state's minimum wage be raised.[232]

Attempts by low-wage workers to organize for higher wages have been openly derided by FOX host Charles Payne, who seems especially upset that workers fighting for a livable wage would compare themselves to the foot soldiers of the civil rights movement. When FOX's Steve Doocy recently suggested that such a comparison was "insulting," Payne agreed, adding: "It's beyond the pale. Here is one of those things that insults almost everybody. Obviously, it would insult anyone who was involved in the civil rights movement, and also the workers."[233] Putting aside the bizarre notion that workers pushing for higher wages are somehow insulting themselves, it is worth noting that absolutely *no one* who was involved in the civil rights movement (which would exclude every prominent conservative in America, without a single exception) has objected to the analogy between the fight for decent wages and the fight for civil rights. Congressman John Lewis, who was repeatedly arrested and beaten in the struggle for racial equity, not only hasn't risen to the floor of the House of Representatives to denounce living wage activists; far from it, he actually supports them. Which makes sense, given the views of movement leader Martin Luther King Jr. on matters of economic justice for working people, which included strong support for labor unions, for higher minimum wages, and for guaranteed employment. In 1966, when addressing pending legislation to raise the minimum wage floor, King insisted, "A living wage should be the right of all working Americans." Indeed, he claimed that there was "no more crucial civil rights issue facing Congress" than the need to raise the minimum wage and extend its coverage to entire classes of workers, like farmworkers, to whom it did not yet (and still does not) apply, in most cases.[234]

For the modern-day Scrooges, the answer to any call for wage hikes at the bottom, or safety net protections, is essentially the equivalent of "Bah, Humbug!" To such persons as these, and their conservative mouthpieces in the media, attempts by workers to boost their pay, improve their work conditions, or mend the tattered safety net for the benefit of millions of families is little more than confiscation—the act of takers living off the work of the makers in society. Fundamentally, hostility to the poor and programs to support them comes down to an all-too-common belief that if those in poverty would simply try harder they wouldn't be in the shape they are. The attitude was expressed with no sense of misgiving in a recent *Daily Show* interview during which FOX Business commentator Todd Wilemon exhorted, "If you're poor, just *stop being poor*," thereby offering up the standard aristocratic advice to those who struggle to keep their heads above water.[235] In other words, it's your fault, so just stop it already. Get it together. Get a job. Be more like rich people.

Loving the One Percent: The Valorization of the Rich and Powerful

Which brings us to perhaps the most significant and telling example of modern Scroogism in recent years, and one of the pinnacle moments of the contemporary culture of cruelty: namely, the statement made by GOP presidential candidate Mitt Romney about the difference between the forty-seven percent of Americans who are essentially lazy, and the rest of us. In May 2012, at a private fundraiser, Romney issued his infamous "forty-seven percent" remark to those assembled, a statement that would go public a few months later when a video of the comments was leaked to the press. As Romney put it:

> There are forty-seven percent of the people who will

> vote for the president no matter what . . . forty-seven percent who are with him, who are dependent upon government, who believe they are victims, who believe the government has a responsibility to care for them, who believe that they are entitled to health care, to food, to housing, to you-name-it . . . the government should give it to them. And they will vote for this president no matter what. . . . These are people who pay no income tax. Forty-seven percent of Americans pay no income tax. So our message of low taxes doesn't connect. . . . My job is not to worry about those people. I'll never convince them they should take personal responsibility and care for their lives.[236]

In other words, to the standard bearer of the Republican Party roughly half of the American people are "dependent on government," suffer from an entitlement mentality, and refuse to take responsibility for their lives. For Romney's running mate, Congressman Paul Ryan, the numbers are even worse. According to statements made by Ryan in 2010, fully six in ten Americans are "takers" rather than "makers" because they receive some form of government benefit, from Medicare health coverage to unemployment insurance to nutrition assistance or the Earned Income Tax Credit, while not paying income taxes.[237]

Of Makers and Takers: Taxes, Public Subsidies and the Real Face of Entitlement

Ultimately, the thinking on display in the comments of both Romney and Ryan is clear: the poor are simply different from the rich in terms of values, work ethic and talent. While the latter create jobs and add value to the larger society, the former simply live off the more productive. Rather than criticize the wealthy, the poor and working class should be thanking them for all the good they do, or so the thinking goes. According to billionaire real estate investor Sam Zell, "the one percent work harder," and rather than criticize them, everyone else should emulate them.[238] Likewise, *Forbes* columnist Harry Binswanger has said in all seriousness that anyone "who earns a million dollars or more should be exempt from all income taxes," and because even *that* tax rate of zero is insufficient thanks for all the good they do for the world, "to augment the tax exemption, in an annual public ceremony, the year's top earner should be awarded the Congressional Medal of Honor."[239]

To question the prerogatives of the wealthy (let alone to actually advocate policies that might shrink the disparities between the wealthy economic minority and the rest of us) is to invite howls of protest that one is essentially the equivalent of a Nazi looking to march the rich into the ovens. To wit, the recent claim by venture capitalist Tom Perkins of San Francisco that those who fight for greater equality are essentially gearing up for their own "progressive Kristallnacht,"[240] reminiscent of what Hitler's legions launched against the Jews of Germany. Perkins, a billionaire who likes to brag about his $300,000 watch, is worried about poor people literally killing off the rich, which is ironic since it is *he*, a rich guy, who has actually been convicted of killing someone.[241] In 1996 while racing his yacht off the coast of France, Perkins collided with a smaller boat, killing a doctor in the process; Perkins was tried and convicted of manslaughter but only paid $10,000 as punishment.[242]

Although his remarks about the impending slaughter of the oligarchs, published in the letters section of the *Wall Street Journal*, provoked howls of outrage,[243] Perkins defended himself by noting that although the Nazi imagery was perhaps unfortunate, the underlying argument was true: demonizing the rich is no different from demonizing any other minority.[244] It's a position that the editorial page of the *Wall Street Journal* then ratified in the wake of the controversy,[245] as did FOX Business contributor Charles Payne, who defended Perkins's comments by claiming that the wealthy have a justified rage at those who would question their wealth, and that Perkins's predictions of a progressive

Kristallnacht were possibly overdrawn but not by much. As Payne explained it, in his typically grammar- and vocabulary-challenged style (neither of which serve as job disqualifiers at FOX):

> There is a war on success. It hasn't been violent, but that doesn't mean that it can't, or that it won't one day (sic). . . . We can snicker at Tom Perkins and his poor analogy, or we can look around and understand that his fears may one day spread to many others because the kind of anger based on envy can become uncontrollable. It can ravish (sic) an individual or a country once its spreads. Coupled with failed economic policy it can destroy. I don't think we should wait for people to be dragged out of their Park Avenue homes before we see how dangerous this war really is and can become.[246]

In other words, to Charles Payne, Tom Perkins was wrong but not really. The paranoid billionaire was just a few years ahead of the curve with his prediction.

In keeping with the progressives-as-Nazis theme, Home Depot founder Ken Langone has made it clear how he views the activism of people who express concerns about wealth inequality. "I hope it's not working," Langone has said. And then, descending into the pit of victimhood, he notes: "Because if you go back to 1933, with different words, this is what Hitler was saying in Germany. You don't survive as a society if you encourage and thrive on envy or jealousy."[247] For others, like AIG CEO Robert Benmosche, criticisms of the rich might not quite be equal to the Holocaust—after all, diminishing the horrors of Nazi genocide might be a bit dicey for a nice Jewish boy like Benmosche—but they certainly are comparable to the lynching of black people. After public outrage erupted over the massive bonuses paid to the company's executives (even as AIG had to be bailed out by the government), Benmosche claimed that the uproar "was intended to stir public anger, to get everybody out there with their pitchforks and their hangman nooses, and all that—sort of like what we did in the Deep South. . . . And I think it was just as bad and just as wrong."[248] Yes, because criticizing million-dollar bonuses for people who helped bring down the economy is exactly like the extra-judicial murder of black people.

The tendency to view the wealthy as virtual superheroes to whom the rest of us owe some debt of gratitude is becoming increasingly prevalent, and not only in the United States, but among the Anglo-elite in the U.K. as well. Boris Johnson, the Mayor of London, recently admonished the commoners in his own city that they should be "offering their humble and hearty thanks" to the super-rich, because, as he put it:

> These are the people who put bread on the tables of families who—if the rich didn't invest in supercars and employ eau de cologne–dabbers—might otherwise find themselves without a breadwinner.[249]

For clarification, an "eau de cologne–dabber" is someone who literally places perfumed water upon the temples of the rich, and is paid to do this because, naturally, the rich cannot put on their own perfume. The working class should be grateful, apparently, that the rich in London are so lazy; otherwise, how might the masses even manage to feed themselves? That such incredibly lazy souls as these have somehow managed to become millionaires and billionaires despite their pathetic indolence, apparently gives Johnson no pause. That people who can't even "pick up their own socks" (as Johnson himself puts it) can somehow control such an outsized portion of the world's wealth, causes no national reconsideration of the so-called merit of the wealthy, though among more sober-minded persons one might expect that it would.

Elsewhere, great inequalities of income and wealth are applauded as the only imaginable incentive for hard work on the part of the poor. Canadian millionaire Kevin O'Leary responded to a 2014 OXFAM report, which noted that the world's wealthiest eighty-five people were worth as much as the bottom half of the world's population (approximately 3.5 billion people), by exclaiming that the report was "fantastic news." Only such incredible inequality can spur the poor to better their condition, according to O'Leary. When asked if a poor African living on a dollar a day is truly inspired to harder work by the presence of the eighty-five wealthiest persons on the planet, and that they might actually think they are going to be the next Bill Gates, O'Leary felt no compunction in saying that such inequality and great wealth was exactly "the inspiration that everyone needs."[250] Inspiration or not, it appears that something in O'Leary's formula for success isn't quite working. Just a year after the announcement of the "fantastic news" of such enormous global inequality, things seemed to be getting worse rather than better. In 2015, it only took the world's wealthiest *eighty* people, rather than eighty-five, to equal the wealth of the poorest half of humanity.[251] At this rate, O'Leary's "inspiring" inequality will result in one person having the same net worth as 3.5 billion people by about 2030. Fantastic!

Central to aristocratic defensiveness about the extent of their wealth is the idea that the rich do more than enough for the rest of us, especially in terms of the nation's tax burden, which, in Romney's estimation, nearly half of Americans are skipping out on while the wealthy pick up the tab. It's not a particularly new position among conservatives. As early as 1975, when the Earned Income Tax Credit (EITC) was first passed so as to remove low-income Americans from the tax rolls by offering tax credits intended to subsidize work, some on the right were already screaming foul. Despite the fact that the program only benefited those who were working, and had the effect of reducing reliance on other forms of welfare that were not tied to employment, conservative firebrand Pat Buchanan was enraged. In his very first syndicated column, Buchanan, fresh off his stint working in the Nixon White House, blasted tax relief for the poor as "the redistribution of wealth, downward," and insisted that the 4.6 million low-income persons who were to be dropped from the tax rolls would be "reassigned to who expanding army of citizens who pay nothing in federal income taxes for the broad and widening array of social benefits they enjoy." They would, in Buchanan's estimation, come to represent "a new class in America, a vast constituency of millions with no interest whatsoever in reducing the power of government, and every incentive to support its continued growth."[252]

But actually, when it comes to who pays taxes and who doesn't, here too the position of the wealthy economic minority is without merit. When Cato Institute senior fellow Alan Reynolds says, "Poor people don't pay taxes in this country," or when FOX Business host Stuart Varney insists, "Yes, forty-seven percent of households pay not a single dime in taxes," they are lying.[253] And when FOX's Greg Gutfeld claims he envies those who are too poor to owe income taxes,[254] as if to suggest that minimum wage workers are living it up while highly paid media commentators like himself are oppressed, he makes no sense at all. I'm sure FOX would be happy to pay him $7.25 an hour if he'd like to experience life without income taxes (or much income), but somehow I'm guessing he won't request such a perk. Let's look at the facts.

On the one hand, yes, nearly half of the American population does not end up paying net federal income taxes, but this does not make the comments by Reynolds and Varney or the positions of Romney and Ryan accurate. To begin, it's important to understand why people who don't pay taxes enjoy that so-called luxury. One-fifth of those who don't pay income taxes are elderly and on fixed incomes, with nearly another fifth being students, the disabled or persons who are unemployed but actively seeking work.[255] The remaining three-fifths *do* work but simply don't earn enough to owe federal income tax. Why? Well surely it isn't because they have chosen to receive crappy pay just to get out of paying taxes. It's not as if the poor and struggling are turning down six-figure job offers just to avoid having to fork over a percentage to the government. They are not earning enough because they can't find a job that pays enough, and they are not paying taxes on what they earn because the poor and near-poor have been removed from the income tax rolls due to *bipartisan agreements* in place since the mid-1970s, intended to boost disposable income with programs like the Earned Income Tax Credit.

Additionally, although such persons may not pay income taxes, those individuals almost inevitably contribute to the overall tax pie via state and local sales taxes and payroll taxes, the latter of which only apply to the first $117,000 of income, thereby hitting middle- and working-class folks harder, proportionately, than the rich. In fact, when it comes to taxes other than those levied on income at the federal level, lower- and middle-income Americans actually pay quite a bit more, percentage-wise, than the affluent. State and local taxes, on average, take more than twice as much from the poorest residents (those in the bottom fifth of households) as from the top one percent: about 10.9 percent of income from those at the bottom, compared to only 5.4 percent from the wealthiest. The middle class too pays state and local taxes at a much higher rate than that paid by the nation's affluent economic minority. This is because state and local governments rely heavily on sales taxes, which take a higher share of income from those at the bottom than from those at the top. If a rich person and a poor person both buy a gallon of milk in Tennessee, for instance (which still levies sales taxes even on necessities like food), or clothes for their kids to start the school year, the taxes levied on these items will be the same as a share of the purchase price, but as a share of both shoppers' incomes, the tax bite will be more onerous to the lower-income shopper. Over the course of a year, taxes such as this add up to a substantial burden at the bottom of the economic pyramid, while amounting to only a very small burden for those at the top. In some states, the disproportionate burden for the working class and poor is especially crushing relative to that for the rich. In Washington State the poorest fifth of residents pay about seventeen percent of their annual income in state and local taxes: *seven times the percentage* paid by the wealthiest one percent, at only 2.4 percent of income. In Florida, the poorest residents pay 6.8 times as much as the richest, percentage-wise (12.9 percent as opposed to 1.9); in Texas, the ratio is more than four to one.[256]

Overall, there is not much difference between the tax burdens on the wealthy as opposed to the middle and working class, when all taxes (federal, state and local) are considered. Whereas the rich would have us believe they are carrying a disproportionate amount of the tax load, the data says something else altogether. The richest one percent of Americans pay twenty-four percent of all taxes, but they also earn twenty-two percent of all national income. The next richest four percent of Americans pay fifteen percent of all taxes, but they also earn fourteen percent of all income. In all, the top tenth of earners pay nearly half of all taxes, which may seem extreme, but they also bring in forty-six percent of all national income. Meanwhile, the middle fifth of income earners pays only ten percent of all taxes, which may seem as if they were not paying their fair share, but they only receive eleven percent of all income. So too, the poorest fifth of Americans contribute only two percent of all taxes paid in the country—a seemingly inadequate percentage—but this fifth only receives about three percent of all income.[257]

In terms of relative tax rates, the claims of an unfair burden on the rich also fall short. The top one percent, who had average incomes of $1.5 million in 2013, paid about thirty-three percent of that in overall taxes at all levels. But those with average incomes of only $75,000 (who found themselves in the upper-middle-class fifth of all earners) paid an almost equivalent rate of thirty percent; and the middle fifth of earners, with average incomes of only $45,500, paid about twenty-seven percent of their incomes in taxes. Even those in the lower middle class, with annual incomes averaging only around $28,000 per year, paid twenty-three percent of their incomes in taxes—less than the rate for the rich but not dramatically so. And surely twenty-three percent for someone making $28,000 is a much larger burden, in real terms, than a rate of thirty-three percent on someone who makes $1.3 million. Although the poorest fifth of Americans (whose annual incomes amount to only about $14,000 on average) have a much lower tax burden than others—since they have been removed from federal income taxes by the EITC and other income exemptions intended to reduce reliance on government programs—even they pay about nineteen percent of their paltry incomes in overall taxes. This is hardly evidence of freeloading, even by the poorest fifth of Americans, let alone by the forty-seven percent about whom Romney seemed so judgmental.[258]

Of course, it's not just with regard to taxation that the meme of the "makers versus the takers" is dishonest. The other implicit assumption of that narrative is that the rich, unlike the poor, don't rely on government for their success. According to elitist rhetoric, government is for the poor and life's losers, while the wealthy and successful prosper as a result of their own genius and the magic of the free market. But how anyone could believe that only the poor rely on government, especially in the wake of the government bailout of the banking industry and several American corporations, is beyond comprehension by the rational mind. The overall value of the various government-backed initiatives on behalf of industry since the economic meltdown includes not just the more than $800 billion disbursed to financial institutions by the Treasury Department under the Troubled Assets Relief Program (TARP), but also hundreds of billions in additional loans to banks to improve their ability to start lending again.[259] Without these bailouts, the banks in question would have gone under. Whether or not one believes that considering these institutions "too big to fail" might have been a necessary evil at the time of the bailouts, there can certainly be no doubt that it was *government*, not the magic of the marketplace or the genius of the leadership in these places, that allowed them to continue existing *at all*, let alone to prosper once again.

And yet, even as the U.S. government literally saved these institutions by bailing them out with taxpayer monies, the economic minority that benefited from that financial safety net remain ungrateful. Former AIG CEO Maurice "Hank" Greenberg, for instance, filed a lawsuit against the government for bailing out the company, because to Greenberg's way of thinking the terms of the bailout were insufficiently favorable to the company and its stockholders. According to Greenberg's attorney, by requiring AIG to give the government eighty percent equity ownership of the firm before agreeing to the $85 billion loan, the bailout resulted in injury to stockholders because limitations were placed on the amount of ownership (and thus income) they could enjoy privately.[260] That there would have been no AIG at all absent the loan matters not to economic aristocrats: they believe they deserve government assistance—corporate welfare—*and* that they should set the terms of such welfare at the same time. Because the rich believe that, unlike other beneficiaries of government benefits who are expected to meet certain conditions in order to qualify for assistance, the wealthy should receive public assistance with no strings attached at all. Rules are for the little people.[261]

Average hard-working Americans have certainly never received the kind of forbearance shown to the banks and their top leaders, and frankly, that's just how the rich like it. Far from relying on the marketplace, they quite openly insist that they *deserve* government assistance, even as those at the subsistence end of the economic spectrum do not. So consider the breathtakingly tone-deaf remarks of billionaire Charles Munger, vice-chair of Berkshire Hathaway: In 2010, while speaking at the University of Michigan, Munger told the audience that they should "thank God" for the bailouts of Wall Street, and rather than "bitching" about them, they should wish those bailouts had been "a little bigger." But when asked if it might also have been helpful to bail out homeowners who were underwater on their mortgages—in many cases because they were roped into terms that were unfavorable to them, though quite favorable to the bankers and rich investors—Munger was incredulous: "There's danger in just shoveling out money to people who say, 'My life is a little harder than it used to be'," Munger explained. "At a certain place you've got to say to the people, 'Suck it in and cope, buddy.'"[262] In other words, America's neediest families should suck it up and cope, while the rich sit back and enjoy corporate welfare to keep their highly profitable businesses humming along.

But it's not just the bank bailouts that demonstrate how dependent the rich are on taxpayer dollars, suckled from the very government they despise. From 2000 to 2012, not even including the bailouts, some of the world's wealthiest companies received $21.3 billion in *direct* government subsidies—about $200 million, on average, for each of the companies in the Fortune 100—in the form of subsidized loans, "technology development" grants and subsidized insurance, all of which use taxpayers' money to reduce operating costs and increase profits for corporate executives.[263] Overall, well over $100 billion in direct government subsidies have been handed out to businesses in recent years, the vast majority of it to huge corporations. Among the biggest recipients of government subsidies ranging from special financing deals to tax holidays to subsidized promotion of goods abroad, are Boeing, Dow Chemical, General Motors, Walmart, General Electric and FedEx. Most telling, even the current darlings of the right wing, the Koch brothers, have received substantial assistance from the government, to the tune of $88 million.[264]

In addition to direct subsidies, there are also indirect ways in which government benefits the corporate class. Because of what are known as "tax expenditures"—preferential tax treatment that reduces revenues available to the government, thereby operating like a spending program, but through the tax code rather than the normal budget process—corporations are able to artificially reduce what they have to contribute in taxes. In 2011, the government allowed corporations to defer paying $24 billion in taxes they otherwise would have owed by not taxing income earned abroad until those earnings are repatriated to the United States. So although the money has been earned and is available to benefit the company, as long as they reinvest those earnings in another country rather than in their homeland, taxes on those earnings go uncollected. Another $27 billion was lost due to "accelerated depreciation" rules, which allow companies to write off operating expenses for plant and equipment far more quickly than such costs actually occur.[265] And as discussed earlier, the preferential treatment of capital gains income—a *government* program that favors the income earned by the wealthy over the income earned by average Americans—provides a huge windfall to the rich, saving those who make over $1 million per year about $131,000 in taxes, as opposed to the EITC for poor and working-class families, which provides about $2,200 in relief to them.[266] So again, *who* is more dependent on government welfare? Who are the makers, and who are the takers?

Or consider the common practice of state and local tax abatements and special "economic development awards" granted to corporations so as to lure them to particular locations, ostensibly for the purpose of creating jobs. Surely such policies suggest that corporate success owes less to hard work or talent than public policy. Although supporters of the practice insist these special financing deals are a critical economic development tool, there is much reason to doubt their faith in the matter.[267] Whether hosting professional sports franchises or manufacturing plants, communities often end up giving away more in lost property tax revenue than they gain in payroll, sales taxes generated or other economic benefits.[268] And even if the incentives work as advertised—much as with the bailout of the large banks—the larger philosophical point remains: can we really claim these businesses are making it on their own, or are successful due to the talent of their executives, when they have to procure sweetheart deals from the taxpayers in order to produce such results? Wouldn't capitalist theory suggest that for an investment to be efficient and worthwhile, it should pay for itself in the market, without government giveaways? Indeed, don't such giveaways by definition suggest the inefficiency and thus market-illegitimacy of such investments? That some of the biggest recipients of these handouts are indeed among the nation's most profitable companies makes the practice all the more suspect. Perhaps if tax abatements were being given to small mom-and-pop businesses we could see their utility—after all, firms like that might have a hard time competing against larger companies (like big box retailers, for instance)—but those are not the companies reaping the rewards, by and large. Although large corporations have received only ten percent of all announced subsidy awards at the state and local level, these firms have pocketed at least seventy-five percent of the actual *dollars* given away by these efforts—an amount equal to about $110 billion in all. Among the largest recipients of such corporate welfare are Boeing (with over $13 billion in subsidies), Intel (with nearly $4 billion), GM and Ford (with $6 billion between them), Nike (with over $2 billion) and Dow Chemical (with $1.4 billion). Other brands often credited with success due to the genius and innovation of their corporate leadership have also been given significant handouts: Google has received over $600 million in state and local subsidies, FedEx and Apple have procured about $500 million each, and Amazon.com and Samsung have both benefitted from over $300 million in subsidies.[269]

Beyond corporate welfare itself, there are entire industries that rely on particular public policies in order to make profit. For instance, consider the way that private businesses profit from the rise of mass incarceration in America. As the number of persons in jail or prison has exploded, especially for nonviolent offenses and disproportionately for people of color,[270] companies such as Corrections Corporation of America (CCA) have developed entire business models that rely on the continuation of a public policy to lock people up. Their profits are not the result of innovation or business acumen. In a nation that didn't incarcerate so many people, no matter how bright their executives might be, and no matter how hard-working their employees, they simply could not be profitable. Their financial success—indeed their very existence—is due to government policy, which is why the industry hires lobbyists to push for longer prison sentences, even for relatively minor offenses.[271] Private prison operators require states to fulfill "occupancy guarantees" or else pay penalties to the company, if for some reason they can't find enough criminals to lock up.[272] Think about it: state officials are agreeing to lock up enough people to keep a private prison full, even before they know how much crime will be committed or how many dangerous offenders there will be in the coming year who might need to be detained. And if they fail to meet their incarceration targets, they agree to pay a penalty for underutilization. Which means that states will either have to find people to incarcerate (no matter how minor their offenses and no matter whether there might be more productive ways to deal with many offenders), or else pay the companies a penalty for having effectively reduced their local crime rates. What is that, if not a textbook example of private businesses subsisting on the public dole, where the government subsidy provided is not just money but the actual lives of people locked up to boost private profits?

But people who form companies to profit from the operation of private prisons are not the only ones making money from locking up Americans. So too are those companies that provide goods and services to prisons and prisoners, and those that make use of prison labor. As for the first of these categories, food providers like Aramark, despite being cited for multiple sanitation violations, rake in hundreds of millions of dollars annually from prison contracts. Global Tel*Link, which benefits from a virtual monopoly on phone service in prisons—and charges inflated collect call rates to those whom inmates call—makes half a billion in annual profits from prison calls. And even though health care is notoriously inadequate in prisons, Corizon, the nation's leading prison health provider, makes over $1.4 billion per year.[273]

As for companies that use prison labor, currently as many as a million prisoners in the United States are working as call center operators or taking hotel reservations or manufacturing textiles, shoes and clothing, while getting paid less than a dollar per day in some cases. This prison labor boosts profits for American businesses by giving them a cheap supply of virtual slave workers, while undermining employment opportunities for people on the outside. It's a practice for which we condemn China and other countries, but which we engage in without compunction.[274] Other inmates perform essentially free labor for the state—perhaps building furniture or cleaning up roadsides.[275] Not only are the jobs performed by inmates for pennies per hour taking jobs away, in many cases, from those in the so-called free world, but even worse, because inmate pay is far below what non-inmates would receive for the same work, the money that can be sent home to the inmate's family—thereby helping to support children left behind—is essentially nonexistent. This further undermines the economic base of the inmate's home community. Whether working for private companies or state agencies, the effect is the same: depressing the wages of working-class people, providing uncompensated (or barely compensated) benefits for economic aristocrats, and helping to perpetuate inequality.

Or consider the pharmaceutical industry. When drug companies develop new drugs, they often do so only after taking advantage of government-sponsored university research. The companies then market their branded products, for which they can charge exorbitant prices, in large part because of the government-granted patent monopolies that prevent generic drugs from competing with them for a number of years. As just one example, consider the recent case of the hepatitis-C drug Sovaldi, manufactured and sold by Gilead Sciences. Gilead's price schedule for a standard twelve-week treatment course of Sovaldi is $84,000, or $1000 per pill, even though the actual cost of production for the entire twelve-week treatment is between $68 and $136, or somewhere between eighty cents and $1.60 per pill. In other words, the price markup is on the order of one thousand to one. Since few individuals can afford the expense of such drugs, one might wonder how the company can get away with charging so much. But the answer to such a question is easy: private insurance and public insurance operated by the government will pick up the tab, thereby inflating the costs of health care for everyone. In just one year, Sovaldi and a companion drug raked in $12.4 billion for Gilead. And while pharmaceuticals are quick to defend these kinds of profits by claiming that the cost of developing drugs is massive, thereby requiring such prices to recoup corporate research and development costs, in the case of Sovaldi, as with so many other drugs, the argument falls flat. Turns out, the professor who developed the drug was working under government grants from the National Institutes of Health, and a disproportionate amount of the costs of research were borne by public dollars. Gilead's own contribution to the drug's R&D was likely no more than $300 million. Though hardly chump change, this amount was earned back by the company after just a few weeks of Sovaldi sales.[276]

Or what about the nation's various energy companies? Among the various forms of corporate welfare, which far and away dwarf most programs serving the needs of low-income and poor Americans, consider subsidies for the oil, gas and coal industries. Each year, a combination of special tax breaks, loan guarantees and direct subsidies for energy research and development cost taxpayers between $49 billion and $100 billion.[277] Even if one accepts the economic validity of such subsidies, the mere fact of their existence suggests that the companies and industries benefiting from such government largesse owe their success in large measure to the state and not merely to the genius of their executives, let alone the "magic of the marketplace."

Of course, to the ruling class, all of this makes perfect sense. To give taxpayers' money to the rich or to steer such money in that direction is different from giving money to average people. When you listen to a Charles Munger or Lloyd Blankfein, chief of Goldman Sachs—who has said that investment bankers are "doing God's work"[278] and who has defended the roughly $13 billion his firm got from the bailout of large insurer AIG[279]—it is hard to resist the conclusion that at some level, the wealthy economic minority simply believe that the rich and the poor are two distinct species. On the one hand, they insist that putting more money in the pockets of the wealthy via the bailouts or tax cuts can incentivize productive economic activity, and that when the rich have this extra money they can be guaranteed to do great things with it. They'll create jobs, start companies, and invest it wisely to the benefit of all. In other words, the rich respond *positively* to more money. On the other hand, the same voices assure us that putting more money in the pockets of the poor and struggling—via minimum wage hikes, overtime pay protections, the expansion of safety net programs or unemployment benefits—will do the opposite: it will strip the poor of the incentive to work, and if they have this extra money they will do horrible things with it; they'll buy narcotics, sit around all day doing nothing, or make babies they can't afford. In other words, the impoverished respond *dysfunctionally* to more money. The only thing that will properly incentivize *them* is the threat of destitution. Only the fear of homelessness, starvation and death in the gutter can possibly make struggling Americans do any work whatsoever. No overstatement, this is precisely the thinking of conservative economist and investor George Gilder—one of Ronald Reagan's favorite writers—who argued in his 1981 book, *Wealth and Poverty*, that "in order to succeed, the poor need most of all the spur of their poverty."[280] Only someone who believed that poor Americans were barely human, such that they don't respond to the same incentives the rest of us would, could make this kind of argument. And only someone who believed the rich were inherently superior could justify the benefits showered upon them by the state.

No, You **Didn't** *Build That: Confronting the Myth of Elite Talent*

Naturally, the economic aristocrats and the conservatives whom they bankroll firmly believe in their innate superiority. They sincerely preach the gospel of meritocracy and the idea that those who make it to the top of the power structure have done so by dint of their own hard work and talent. Research has found that dominant social groups—in the United States this means men, whites and those with higher incomes—are especially likely to think that they are smarter and more capable than others and have earned whatever they have by virtue of their own abilities.[281]

But what evidence actually supports this position? Looking at it historically, the idea that the wealthy have earned their great fortunes has never made much sense. White people who enslaved blacks formed the nation's original aristocracy, and relied not only on the stolen labor of Africans for their wealth but also on the willingness of government to defend their investment in human property by enshrining enslavement in the laws of the land and agreeing to the return of freedom-seeking blacks to their owners. Had it not been for the state's support in the maintenance of human trafficking and enslavement, the work and genius of the wealthy planter class would have meant nothing. They surely weren't prepared to pick the cotton or build the levees or construct the houses in which they lived, nor were they willing to pay market rates for that work. Their fortunes came from the barbaric exploitation of black families—men, women and children—and from no other source.

Interestingly, the wealthy planter class all but admitted their own dependence on enslaved black families and bragged about their own relative idleness, never noting the way such admissions contradicted whatever pretense they may have had to actually deserving their station. The thought of abolition frightened them because, if they could not force African peoples to work for them for free, their every luxury would be lost. Why? Because naturally it would be absurd to expect the rich to do the hard work needed to maintain the lifestyle to which they had become accustomed. That, after all, would make them little better than the slaves to whom they felt so naturally superior. As Herbert Gutman and the American Social History Project note in their epic volume, *Who Built America?*

> Chattel slavery discredited hard work, associating those who performed it with the slave's lowly status. Planters generally prided themselves on being men of leisure and culture, freed from labor and financial concerns.[282]

One especially honest (but not too self-aware) member of the South Carolina planter class summed up the thinking when he explained, "Slavery with us is no abstraction but a great and vital fact. Without it our every comfort would be taken from us. Our wives and children made unhappy . . . our people ruined forever."[283] One white Mississippi planter, lamenting the abolition of slavery after the South was vanquished in battle, put it this way: "I never did a day's work in my life, and don't know how to begin."[284] In short, the rich white Southerner, totally dependent on enslaving blacks for his fortune, was the ultimate lazy slacker, yet his laziness hardly prevented him from attaining monumental riches.

So too, the wealth of the early industrialists had less to do with their own hard work or intellect than with illegal activity and the intervention of the state. The Erie Canal, constructed with public money from 1817 to 1825, linked the Great Lakes and Ohio Valley to the Hudson River and New York City, vastly lowering shipping costs of goods to the nation's interior and boosting profits for private businesses, none of which spent their own cash to finance the project.[285] The further growth of the nation's economy in the late nineteenth century and the profits of the business class at that time were only made possible by the transcontinental railroad. But in order to make the railroad feasible at a profitable rate, officials with the Central Pacific and Union Pacific railroad companies bribed elected officials to give them free land on which to lay the track, engaged in illegal kick-back schemes, overcharged the government for the costs of construction and arranged for multiple public subsidies, allowing them to reap enormous profit at public expense. And, as with whites who trafficked and enslaved blacks, these economic aristocrats depended upon the use of exploited workers, mostly Irish and Chinese, to keep their profits high.[286] Between 1862 and 1872, Congress gave railroad companies more than one hundred million acres of previously public land, in addition to granting them tens of millions of dollars worth of tax concessions and loans.[287]

Additionally, beginning in the early 1860s, the government

began handing out large parcels of land to white families under the Homestead Act: hundreds of millions of acres upon which to farm and carve out a living. Although the work done on those homesteads was no doubt real, the ability of those farmers to access that land in the first place was due to government initiative.[288] For those denied access to the land, like African Americans, or those pushed off the land (like indigenous people or Mexicans who lost land claims after the war with Mexico), that government intervention also enshrined significant white racial privilege and advantage. And in many instances, even the small-scale white farmers were taken advantage of by big mining and lumber interests that would pay the individuals to stake claims for them under the Act, and then assume ownership after paying them a small pittance.[289]

By the early 1900s, the government was hard at work granting monopoly charters to corporations in a number of industries, from banking to transportation to insurance and others, thereby extending to the owners of these companies exclusive rights to engage in various types of enterprise. Their resulting fortunes, which were vast indeed, owed to government favoritism and graft, not to their own genius or having won a competition against less worthy competitors. Throughout this period, government forces were used to crush labor movement activity, including strikes by workers made to toil in often horrific conditions, suggesting that again, without the heavy arm of the state, their profits would have been much less certain.[290] And far from being self-made men, fully ninety-five percent of executives and financial tycoons at the beginning of the twentieth century were from upper-middle class or wealthy backgrounds. Throughout the nineteenth century only two percent of industrialists were born to working-class parents.[291]

But things are different today, some would insist. Surely the wealthy today earn their own keep, regardless of how the rich in earlier times might have procured theirs. Although it's possible—putting aside the fact that the wealthy of the 1700s, 1800s and early 1900s all would have said they had earned their fortunes too—in truth, the wealthy financial minority are no more justified in their positions now than in the past. First, recall the examples of direct government subsidy and preferential tax treatment mentioned earlier in this chapter, to say nothing of the government bailout of the financial industry, all of which demonstrate that the wealthy owe their position to the loving hand of a charitable state. But that isn't all. In 2008, for instance, less than one-fifth of the income earned by those making more than $10 million came from actual labor, while the rest came from interest, dividends and rents on properties these folks already owned.[292] In other words, even if they hadn't gotten out of bed for a single day of work, these individuals would have still made at least $8 million on average that year. What does that have to do with merit in any appreciable sense, let alone hard work?

Drilling down a bit more specifically, consider Wall Street traders. Far from making their fortunes due to their own skills, such folks are able to make hundreds of millions of dollars more than what they otherwise would, not because they're working harder, but simply by utilizing lightning-quick computers and software programs to which only they have access. These systems allow them to see trades that are in the process of being made—perhaps by individuals doing their own investing, or simply by investors who don't have such computers. Before the trade can go through, the high-speed traders can buy the same stock that's about to be purchased by the regular investor, and then sell it to that initial investor for a few pennies more than they were going to otherwise pay for it, all before the original trade is final. Although the practice has little discernible impact on the small investor, who likely won't notice the tiny markup, the practice, done millions of times a day, rakes in mega-profits for those engaged in it.[293] They are not producing anything of value. They are not making the companies whose stock is purchased worth more, allowing them to create jobs. They are simply skimming money off the top with a practice that is essentially the high-tech equivalent of mind reading or card counting in Vegas, only far more foolproof than either of those. It has nothing to do with merit or skill.

Likewise, to believe that America's corporate executives have "earned" their exorbitant pay and that income reflects effort or ability seems downright delusional. From 1978 to 2013, CEO compensation (base pay plus exercised stock options) increased by *937 percent.* Although it should be obvious that such an aristocratic bunch did not in fact manage to increase their work effort by this much, or become nearly a thousand percent smarter or more productive in that time, let there be no mistake: this boost in pay at the top was more than double the rise in the stock market over that same period. In other words, CEO pay grew twice as fast as the company value overseen by those CEOs. In the process, it far and away outstripped wage growth for the typical worker, whose pay barely budged, if at all, even as their productivity rose dramatically.[294]

In 1965, the ratio of CEO-to-worker compensation was only about twenty to one. By 1978 that ratio had grown, but still only stood at thirty to one. By 1995, however, the average CEO was bringing home 123 times what the average worker earned, and today, that ratio stands at 296 to 1.[295] The typical American CEO's annual bonus alone is sixty-two times greater than the average worker's annual pay.[296] To think that these numbers reflect merit not only requires one to assume that a typical CEO is worth three hundred times more than a typical worker, or works three hundred times harder, or is three hundred times more productive; more to the point, given the change over time, one would have to believe that CEOs were evolving at a scientifically unheard-of pace. After all, the top executive in 1965 was only twenty times more productive, according to this logic, and didn't really gain much in terms of ability or smarts over the next fourteen years. But then, suddenly, it's as if some biological breakthrough occurred, and although average workers stopped evolving, the species known as *homo executivis* enjoyed some amazing genetic leap to previously unimagined levels of talent and ability. And apparently, a few particular CEOs have evolved even more quickly and dramatically than their merely average peers, with former Walmart CEO Michael Duke receiving nearly a thousand times more than the average company employee, and Apple CEO Tim Cook taking home 6,258 times the wage of the typical Apple employee in 2011.[297] To believe that these kinds of financial chasms can be chalked up to merit and relative ability seems to stretch the bounds of credulity: after all, it would mean that Apple and Walmart either have especially superhuman executives or especially dull and unmeritorious hourly workers, or perhaps both, when compared to other corporations.

Surely it can't be merit that explains executive pay, considering that the highest-paid CEO in the United States—Charif Souki of Cheniere Energy—runs a company that has *never even claimed a profit.*[298] Or consider the $8.5 million raise given in 2013 to Jamie Dimon, the chair and CEO of JPMorgan Chase, which brought his total pay to $20 million that year, even after the company's profits fell sixteen percent, and after the company was forced to pay out roughly $20 billion to settle various legal claims.[299] Pay packages like this, despite mediocre or even negative performance, no doubt help explain why former AT&T Broadband CEO Leo Hindery insists that executive pay is "a fraud," which owes entirely to corporate "cronyism."[300] Meanwhile, the CEO of the Container Store, Kip Tindell, who has imposed limits on his own pay to no more than thirty-five times that of his average store employee—and who also pays those employees double the retail industry norm (around $50,000 per year on average)—is enjoying steady profits, suggesting that CEO pay is unrelated to excellence and that the tendency toward inflated executive compensation is more about greed than merit.[301]

Beyond the purely anecdotal, evidence seems to suggest that exorbitant CEO pay, and particularly "incentive pay" for performance, is *negatively* correlated with a company's stock returns in most cases. Not only is such compensation not a legitimate reward for a job well done; if anything, it may lead companies down the wrong road. According to a 2013 study by business school professors from Cambridge, Purdue and the University of Utah, firms whose CEOs rake in the very top levels of pay see their stock market returns fall by approximately eight percent over the three-year period immediately following the excess payouts. They suggest that excess pay leads to CEO overconfidence, which causes stock losses due to irresponsible over-investment and value-destroying mergers and acquisitions for which the company was not well suited.[302]

If we consider it logically, we must know that pay scales do not reflect hard work per se, let alone one's larger social value. Few among us, for instance, would actually accept the notion that a hedge fund manager like Steven Cohen really *earned* his $2.3 billion income in 2013, especially considering that the very same year he received this amount his firm pled guilty to insider trading, for which they were hit with a fine of $1.8 billion.[303] Doubtless, few of us have jobs that would allow us to commit a major financial crime and still remain on the free side of a jail cell, let alone able to walk away with a payday larger than the penalty we were asked to fork over. Likewise, it's hard to believe the earnings of Chris Levett, head of Clive Capital (a commodity hedge fund) are earned. After all, from 2011 to 2013, even as the firm lost money in both years for its investors, Levett was paid nearly $100 million.[304] In general, research finds that the average annual rate of return for hedge funds is actually no better, and is sometimes worse, than it is for low-risk or even no-risk investment instruments, and no better than the annual rate of return for the S&P 500.[305] In other words, most hedge fund managers aren't even outperforming the market or government bond rates, yet they rake in huge excess profits.

The absurdity of such hefty incomes for hedge fund managers is particularly obvious when the figures are contrasted with the incomes of many others in society, whom most would likely consider far more vital to the overall national well-being. As Robert Reich has noted:

> What's the worth to society of social workers who put in long and difficult hours dealing with patients suffering from mental illness or substance abuse? Probably higher than their average pay of $18.14 an hour, which translates into less than $38,000 a year. How much does society gain from personal-care aides who assist the elderly, convalescents, and persons with disabilities? Likely more than their average pay of $9.67 an hour, or just over $20,000 a year. What's the social worth of hospital orderlies who feed, bathe, dress, and move patients, and empty their bedpans? Surely higher than their median wage of $11.63 an hour, or $24,190 a year. Or of child care workers, who get $10.33 an hour, $21,490 a year? And preschool teachers, who earn $13.26 an hour, $27,570 a year?[306]

The list could go on for several pages: nurses, kindergarten teachers, firefighters, school counselors, food safety inspectors, farmers, hospice care workers and so on: all professions that most would consider pretty indispensable to the common good, and yet all of which pay far less than managing a hedge fund, moving money around for rich people, and apparently engaging in fraudulent behavior while doing it.

If you ask most people what jobs they consider the most important in the society, the list you'll get in response will always be pretty similar, and rarely if ever will they include jobs like "hedge fund manager" or "derivatives trader" or "real estate developer" or even "corporate executive." These are the jobs that pay the big money, but not because they have more objective value in the minds of Americans. Unless you asked this question of actual bond traders, it is unlikely that a single person would answer "bond trader" when pressed about the society's most important positions. In fact, I've conducted this little experiment before, and the list of the ten most important jobs is always top-heavy with professions that don't pay very much. With the exception of doctors, the jobs listed are some of the nation's lowest paying. Other than physicians, they typically include teachers, nurses, firefighters, police officers, soldiers, child care providers, elder care and nursing home providers, farmers, clergy and *mothers*. Occasionally, they will also include engineers—another high-paying profession—but rarely any other career that is particularly lucrative.

Now, compare the average person's list to the highest-paying careers, according to the Labor Department. In addition to investment bankers, the highest paid are physicians of various types, CEOs, petroleum engineers, lawyers, architectural and engineering managers (especially for the oil and gas industry), natural sciences managers, marketing managers, computer and IT managers and industrial psychologists.[307] No offense meant to anyone in one of those positions, but your pay hardly reflects the value placed on your jobs by the public. And let's be honest, no kid ever went to bed at night, clutched a teddy bear and said, "When I grow up, I want to sell highly leveraged mortgage-backed securities," even though doing so would no doubt make those kids a lot of money. Children don't think about things like money. They typically have more ethical concerns and far more admirable value systems.

According to the Bureau of Labor Statistics, almost none of the most socially useful jobs identified by the general public are among the best paid. Other than doctors—a broad category, in which various specialties almost always pay more than the general practice thought of by most when the term "physician" is used—the pay rates of the most socially useful jobs rank very low. Police and detective supervisors (not what most people are thinking of when they say police, in answer to the question), come in at number 180 on the list of best-paying professions, which is the highest ranking of any job other than physician that most folks mention. Criminal investigators rank 211; police detectives, 215; farmers, ranchers and agricultural managers rank 268; while no other socially useful jobs rank among the top three hundred.[308]

Ultimately, pay levels are not about merit or social value;

they're about power dynamics. They're about how much value is placed on various types of work, by people with lots of money to spend. So, for instance, if patients in nursing homes each managed to crap a flawless ten-carat diamond once they reached the age of ninety, rest assured, elder care workers would be paid like investment bankers, solely for their ability to keep old people alive until it was time for the diamond harvest. But as it is, they are paid horribly, since rich people see more value in office buildings and yachts and derivatives than they do in the people who care for their own grandparents.

Issues like the strength or weakness of labor unions, and how much influence the rich exercise over executive compensation packages set by company boards, further determine pay levels. We know power relations are more influential on pay than actual merit if for no other reason than this: the gaps between pay at the top and the bottom have grown drastically in recent decades, and far more quickly than could be explained by growing genius among the rich or falling IQ and output at the bottom of the scale. As Reich explains:

> Fifty years ago, when General Motors was the largest employer in America, the typical GM worker got paid $35 an hour in today's dollars. Today, America's largest employer is Walmart, and the typical Walmart worker earns $8.80 an hour. Does this mean the typical GM employee a half-century ago was worth four times what today's typical Walmart employee is worth? Not at all. That GM worker wasn't much better educated or productive. . . . The real difference is the GM worker a half-century ago had a strong union behind him that summoned the collective bargaining power of all autoworkers to get a substantial share of company revenues for its members. And the bargains those unions struck with employers raised the wages and benefits of non-unionized workers as well. Non-union firms knew

> they'd be unionized if they didn't come close to matching the union contracts. Today's Walmart workers don't have a union to negotiate a better deal. And because fewer than 7 percent of today's private-sector workers are unionized, non-union employers across America don't have to match union contracts. . . . The result has been a race to the bottom. By the same token, today's CEOs don't rake in 300 times the pay of average workers because they're "worth" it. They get these humongous pay packages because they appoint the compensation committees . . . that decide executive pay. Or their boards don't want to be seen by investors as having hired a "second-string" CEO who's paid less than the CEOs of their major competitors. Either way, the result has been a race to the top.[309]

Even though Walmart recently announced plans to offer a substantial wage boost to about half a million of their employees, this fact hardly changes the truth of Reich's statement. In fact, if anything, it only further demonstrates the wisdom of it. The announcement of pending raises at Walmart, though a positive sign for their employees (and many others whose wages may also be forced upward by such a jump at the nation's largest employer), actually proves the fundamental flaw at the heart of right-wing economic theory. First, and just to clarify what the raise does and doesn't mean, although Walmart recently announced plans to boost its lowest-level employees to $9 per hour ($10 per hour by 2016) and bring department managers to levels as high as $15 per hour, such news hardly suggests that the company values its employees at a level commensurate with their worth. As of now, Walmart extracts nearly $7,300 in net profit from each of its employees, on average, up from less than $6,000 per employee (which was still significant) just before the recession. In other words, as the economy tanked, the amount of surplus value the nation's largest company was able to skim from the work of their associates increased.[310] Although news of a pay hike is welcome, it will likely only bring their profit per worker back to pre-recession levels and merely reflects the tightening labor market, which has Walmart worried that if they didn't offer more pay, their employees might jump ship.

And it is this last point, more than anything, that proves the disconnect between the income workers receive and their actual work effort or productivity. That Walmart offered these raises proves that previously they had been paying so little not because that was all their workers were worth to them, but because they could get away with it in a weak economy where working people had fewer options. The lesson this reality affords us—both the previous wages being offered and the proposed pay hikes—is a significant one, and utterly debunks the dominant narrative about pay levels and people "getting what they're worth" in the market. After all, Walmart employees didn't become more productive in the last few months so as to justify the raises they appear poised to receive. Rather, economic conditions beyond the control of those workers changed, thereby necessitating a pay hike in the eyes of their employer. This is how the so-called free market works: it isn't about workers getting what they're worth; rather, it is about employers paying as little as they can get away with. The market as such does not exist; only power dynamics exist—who owns, who doesn't; who is in charge and who isn't.

Likewise, pay at the top hardly reflects merit or productivity either; it too is rooted in dynamics of power and influence. Reich has also explained, for instance, the particular disconnect between Wall Street bonuses paid to investment bankers and any notion of actual merit or talent on their part. In 2013, for instance, Wall Street bonuses skyrocketed to $26.7 billion overall, and averaged a fifteen percent boost from the previous year, bringing bonus levels to their highest point since the 2008 economic collapse. But as Reich explains, these bonuses had nothing to do with a fifteen percent gain in productivity, or indeed any measurable notion of merit. Instead of merit, these bonuses (and indeed the entire profitability of these banks) were made possible by government policy, and the indirect subsidy received by these entities ever since the government bailout rendered the investment banks, and especially the largest of them, "too big to fail." By bailing out the investment banks and sending a clear signal that these institutions—as opposed to smaller depository institutions, like your local bank branch—will not be allowed to go under, the government indirectly subsidized the larger banks by making it more attractive for persons to park their money with Goldman Sachs, for instance, than with a smaller bank. Even though the investment banks pay out a smaller interest rate on the money deposited with their institutions, the security purchased by "too big to fail" steers money to the large firms that would otherwise have gone elsewhere; as such, it results in more money for investment banks, and higher bonuses for investment bankers on Wall Street. If the government had not made Wall Street investments so artificially attractive with the bailout, roughly $83 billion less would have been deposited on Wall Street last year, according to recent estimates.[311]

Needless to say, without that $83 billion, which only exists because of government policy and has nothing to do with the genius of bankers, there is no way investment banks could have paid out nearly $30 billion in bonuses last year. In fact, the amount of the predicted subsidy received by just the "big five" investment banks was roughly equal to those companies' profits last year. In other words, without government helping to steer money to those institutions, they would have barely broken even, let alone have been able to pay out such massive bonuses. It is more accurate then to think of investment banks and bankers as charity cases and welfare recipients, rather than as hard-working and highly skilled business folks.

Even beyond the bailout and its salutary effects for current banking profits, the everyday operations of Wall Street are made easier by government actions (or perhaps we should say, inactions). Investment banks have reaped significant profits above and beyond what otherwise could have been possible, thanks to the deregulation of the financial industry in the 1990s—a government decision that made possible several investment instruments and practices that previously would have been disallowed. In short, had it not been for the power of the banking lobby to incentivize lawmakers to loosen the rules for Wall Street, no matter the genius and hard work of the investment class, hundreds of billions, even trillions of dollars simply wouldn't have been made. That's not about a magical marketplace, but about naked political clout. Likewise, the lack of a sales tax on financial transactions, despite sales taxes on virtually all other consumer purchases, amounts to a form of preferential government treatment of one type of market activity, and in this case, one most likely to further profit the already wealthy. When Americans have to pay sales tax on baby formula and fresh produce worth a few dollars but not on stock purchases worth trillions, it seems obvious that certain types of market activity are being favored over others, to the benefit of the wealthy.

Even those upper-income individuals unrelated to the banking industry reap substantial benefits from government. Every year, just one preferential tax policy—the home mortgage interest deduction—costs the government over $100 billion in revenue that would otherwise have been collected. This kind of policy, known as a tax expenditure, is every bit as much a government program as direct housing subsidies for Americans in need. It is no different from writing checks to homeowners to help pay their mortgages, because not collecting taxes that would otherwise be owed deprives the government of money in the same way as collecting it through taxes and then turning around and giving it back out again. And this benefit, which costs more than twice the amount spent annually on low-income housing programs, disproportionately benefits wealthier Americans, because the value of the deduction increases percentage-wise, depending on one's tax bracket. Also, of course, since there is no similar deduction or tax credit for renters, such a policy by definition subsidizes more affluent homeowners but not less-well-off families that rent.

Although the deduction has long been defended as a way to encourage homeownership, it is questionable whether it truly serves this purpose. Since wealthy homeowners are likely to buy a house with or without the deductibility of mortgage interest, the only possible effect for them would be to encourage them to buy a bigger house than they might otherwise purchase: hardly as noble a goal as encouraging homeownership in general. And for persons whose incomes put them on the cusp of buying as opposed to renting, for whom an interest deduction might make the difference, it is doubtful that the deduction as currently constituted does much good. Why? Because the deduction is only available to people who itemize their taxes (which most moderate-income families do not), and because the value of the deduction is tied to a person's tax bracket. So the average benefit for homeowners with income between $40,000 and $75,000 a year, for instance, only comes to $523, or about $44 each month. Is that benefit sizable enough to encourage them to purchase a home rather than rent? Not likely. In other words, the mortgage-interest deduction is mostly a tax giveaway to upper-middle-income and affluent homeowners—and for all those who reap the benefits (my family included, thank you very much), it amounts to a government program that puts more money in our pockets.[312]

The facts are all too clear: rather than talent determining income or wealth, it is a combination of luck, connections, government assistance and public policy like financial deregulation which ultimately make the difference. And let's not forget making money the old-fashioned way: inheriting it. No matter how much we may like to believe that dynastic wealth is a feature of life only in other nations, inherited wealth continues to skew the class structure in the United States as well. Before the economic meltdown, estimates suggested that from 1998 until 2017, about $7 trillion in assets were in the process of being handed down via inheritance. By 2061, that number is expected to reach $36 trillion in intergenerational wealth transfers, nearly ninety percent of which will flow from the wealthiest fifth of Americans to their heirs.[313] Although there is no doubt that the economic collapse may have put a temporary damper on the assets of some among the affluent, as we've seen previously, most of their wealth has been recouped and then some; thus there is little reason to suspect that these numbers will have declined, and much reason to expect them to climb in coming decades. Not to mention, these numbers only refer to assets transferred at death, but what are called *inter vivos* transfers—gifts essentially—from parents to children while those parents are still alive (such as help with a down payment on a house, or college tuition) actually account for a larger share of intergenerational wealth transfers than direct inheritance.[314] That numbers like these drive a stake through the heart of the idea that the well-off simply "earn" their position should be obvious.

Most important, perhaps, is the simple reality that the rich almost always depend on squeezing the working class for whatever fortunes they manage to build. The idea that the poor and working class *need* the wealthy, rather than the other way around—though a common perception, it appears—couldn't be more backwards. Without workers, whom they pay less than the value of the work performed, no capitalist could ever become successful. It is only by paying workers less than the value of what they do for you that you are able to make a profit. It seems axiomatic that if you do a job for me that I could not and would not do for myself, and which enriches me to the tune of $100, but I only pay you $70 for your effort, I have taken advantage of you. To that argument the defender of capitalism would reply that without the capitalist to offer the job, the worker would have made nothing. But this equation continues to miss the obvious: without prior workers, there would have been no capitalist. The wealth held by the capitalist came from somewhere, and in almost no instance did it come from their own direct labor; rather, it came from someone else's labor—either people the capitalist hired, or those his predecessor hired; or it came from state-sanctioned violence and the forcible expropriation of land. The railroad tycoons did not lay their own track and dig their own tunnels, not even for one day, let alone long enough to save up the money with which they were able to hire all those other folks to continue the effort. They inherited their companies or knew the right people and had the power of the state at their disposal to make their profits possible. To give thanks to the capitalist for the job offer he is able to make, without acknowledging the complete reliance upon labor that made the capitalist possible, and without which he or she could not exist, is to invert the cause-and-effect relationship between work and wealth. It was something that Abraham Lincoln understood quite clearly, however much his words might appear radical by comparison to today's political boilerplate:

> Labor is prior to and independent of capital. Capital is only the fruit of labor, and could never have existed if labor had not first existed. Labor is the superior of capital and deserves much the higher consideration.[315]

In short, the rich didn't build their fortunes: the labor of others who were underpaid for their trouble did. Capitalists, it turns out, may be the most dependent people on the planet.

A Culture of Predatory Affluence: Examining the Inverted Values of the Rich

Not only are talent and hard work inadequate to explain the inflated incomes of the super-rich; so too, their value systems and personal integrity fail to justify their positions. Indeed, while the wealthy and their conservative media megaphones spend time and energy bashing the so-called "culture of poverty" and suggesting that it is the poor and unemployed whose values are dysfunctional, pathological and destructive, the reality is almost entirely the opposite of that charge. If anything, it is the culture and values of the affluent that are the most dysfunctional and destructive to the social good.

Consider, for instance, the value system of executives at one of America's largest corporations—General Motors. Recently it was revealed that GM had made the conscious decision not to replace faulty ignition switches on certain of their cars, even though they knew that the switches could turn off unintentionally, thereby disabling power steering, airbags and power brakes and leading to dangerous and potentially deadly accidents. According to internal GM documents, the flaw was known to exist and the decision as to whether or not the company would recall the vehicles and make the necessary fix was debated internally. Ultimately, it was decided there would be no recall and no fix for the existing vehicles, because the costs were prohibitive. And what were these? Less than $1 per car, and about $400,000 in various other costs. Ultimately, much as Ford had done in the 1970s with its release of the known-to-be-dangerous Pinto, GM decided it would cost less to pay off the families of those killed in accidents related to the faulty switch, or to pay the bills of those injured, than to make the fix on all the flawed vehicles they had put on the road. In short, a multibillion-dollar company decided that their money was more important than other people's lives—a calculation that ultimately resulted in the deaths of at least thirteen people.[316] If a drug dealer were to make this calculation preceding a deadly drive-by shooting intended to take out his gang rival (and thus protect his financial interests), we would call that criminal, we would seek to jail him, and we would probably consider his actions evidence of an inherently pathological culture. If corporate executives and engineers make this calculation, as was the case at GM (and several decades ago at Ford), the dominant analysis in the media and among the nation's business class is that the result has been a terrible tragedy, but that it does not reflect anything meaningful about the value systems of the wealthy people upon whom blame ultimately resides.

It's certainly not the poor who took advantage of investors by selling them risky and even useless mortgages in large bundles, knowing full well the dangers posed by those investment instruments; it was JP Morgan that did that, and Citigroup and Bank of America, among others, all of which are now ponying up tens of billions of dollars in settlements with the Justice Department for their questionable, unethical and in many cases blatantly fraudulent activities—although, as we'll explore shortly, these fines amount to very little in the larger scheme of things, and essentially amount to a slap on the wrist.[317]

The tendency to recklessness and risk-taking that was central to the banking crisis stems directly from the value systems and psychology of those who make their livings as investment bankers. And according to recent studies, such persons are actually more likely to engage in reckless and risky behavior than even certified psychopaths. In one study, Swiss researchers tested stock traders on measures of cooperation and egotism, using computer simulations and standard intelligence tests, ultimately finding that the traders "behaved *more* egotistically and were more willing to take risks than a group of psychopaths who took the same test." Particularly disturbing was the observed tendency of the investment bankers to deliberately seek to damage their opponents in the experiment. Rather than simply trying to outperform others on their own merits, the traders seemed especially interested in harming others in order to get ahead. As one of the research team put it, it was as if the stockbrokers discovered that their neighbor had the same car as they did, "and they took after it with a baseball bat so they could look better themselves."[318]

When it comes to the defective value systems of the nation's wealthy economic minority, there are few better examples than that provided by the investment bank Goldman Sachs. The firm, which received more in bailout funds and government subsidies than any other investment bank, used millions in taxpayer money to pay top executives, even as the bank's actions had helped bring the economy to the brink of utter collapse. From 2009 to 2011, after receiving bailout funds from the government, Goldman Sachs paid its senior officials nearly $50 billion in bonuses. And this they did despite a history of unethical, destructive activity responsible for the suffering and even death of millions, through the deliberate manipulation of food prices. As Chris Hedges has noted:

> Goldman Sachs' commodities index is the most heavily traded in the world. Goldman Sachs hoards rice, wheat, corn, sugar and livestock and jacks up commodity prices around the globe so that poor families can no longer afford basic staples and literally starve. Goldman Sachs is able to carry out its malfeasance at home and in global markets because it has former officials filtered throughout the government and lavishly funds compliant politicians—including Barack Obama, who received $1 million from employees at Goldman Sachs in 2008 when he ran for president. These politicians, in return, permit Goldman Sachs to ignore security laws that under a functioning judiciary system would see the firm indicted for felony fraud. Or, as in the case of Bill Clinton, these politicians pass laws such as the 2000 Commodity Futures Modernization Act that effectively removed all oversight and outside control over the speculation in commodities, one of the major reasons food prices have soared. In 2008 and again in 2010 prices for crops such as rice, wheat and corn doubled and even tripled, making life precarious for hundreds of millions of people. And it was all done so a few corporate oligarchs, the 1 percent, could make personal fortunes in the tens and hundreds of millions of dollars. Despite a damning 650-page Senate subcommittee investigation report, no individual at Goldman Sachs has been indicted, although the report accuses Goldman of defrauding its clients.[319]

But the manipulation of food prices is only part of Goldman Sachs's pathological culture. All throughout the economic run-up to the Great Recession, and in moves that helped contribute directly to it, Goldman was misleading investors about the value of the investments they peddled, making the investments sound like guaranteed money makers even as they were actively betting against their own recommendations with still other investments—all to ensure they could make money either way. No matter what happened to the persons whom they tricked into buying securities they knew were junk, Goldman covered their assets (or more to their point, their asses), with little concern for the effect of their actions. When the dust settled, it was the taxpayers who got stuck with the bill.

That all of this reckless and irresponsible investment behavior was neither the creation of poor people nor the outgrowth of so-called underclass cultural pathology should be apparent. These tools of economic manipulation were the product of wealthy and highly educated individuals and the institutions for which they worked. If anything, they are the effluent of affluence, or more importantly, indicative of a culture of "predatory affluence," within which people seek to make money without actually working, without having to create anything of lasting value, and without having to worry about the impact of their actions on others. They are the result of a kind of rapacious and ravenous greed of which the poor cannot even conceive. A poor person's greed might lead them to steal $200 worth of goods from a store, or your purse, or your iPhone. Though unfortunate, and wrongheaded, and unethical, it isn't likely to have a dramatic impact on the larger society. And of course, if apprehended, the perpetrator of such robbery whose greed (or even desperation in some cases) led them to steal your stuff will likely go to jail. But the greed of the rich, which causes them to be unsatisfied with six-figure salaries and to seek out hundreds of millions, or even billions in loot, will cause them to figure out ways to game the entire economy, to play fast and loose with other people's livelihoods, to inflate the demand for risky mortgages so that they can make money off the misfortune of others, and if the economy collapses, oh well. They still made a killing on the deal, and in all likelihood, none of them will go to jail—even the people who created investment instruments they knew would likely bring immense loss to others. Fraud and deceit on that level is considered "too big to jail," and the institutions that perpetrated all that risk and fraud "too big to fail." And so, despite their inverted value systems, their "short-term orientation," and their sociopathic disregard for the well-being of others (all of which we are told characterize the underclass, but really fit the wealthy Wall Street speculators far better), they remain unpunished and available for the veneration of fellow aristocrats who game the system while acting as if they are making vital contributions to our society and the world.

Even rich people who are repeatedly caught committing crimes often get off with only minor punishments. A 2011 *New York Times* analysis uncovered more than fifty cases over the past fifteen years in which Wall Street bankers violated anti-fraud laws. Once caught, the violators promised never to break the laws again, and then proceeded to do so over and over with virtually no consequence. In many of the most prominent cases, top executives at the fraudulent firms got huge raises even after the misdeeds had been uncovered, and the fines imposed in most instances only amounted to between one and five percent of revenues—hardly sufficient to deter future financial crimes.[320]

Frankly, even when the rich make their money from perfectly legal means, there are still valid questions to be asked as to the ethics of their operations. Just as conservatives condemn the ethics of the poor for supposedly relying on government aid (which is entirely legal), so too should it be acceptable to challenge the ethics of companies and individuals at the top of the nation's economic pyramid—especially considering how many of these make their money from less than entirely laudable means. So consider, for instance, the operations of the Blackstone Group: an investment group based in New York, which over the past few years has bought up tens of thousands of foreclosed properties and is now the largest single landlord in the nation, even renting out those properties in some cases to the very individuals who owned them previously.[321] To hear the experts tell it, Blackstone is one of the "hottest investments" on Wall Street, and as such, it is making plenty of money. But are its operations ethical?

To make that determination it helps to think about what

foreclosure meant to the more than seven million families that lost their homes during the Great Recession. For those who found themselves unable to make their mortgage payments, the American Dream came crashing down around them. Many were families that had never been able to own a home until relatively recently, but thanks to the proliferation of subprime loan instruments, which allowed people in the banking business to make mega-profits off inflated interest rates, they suddenly could. Lenders were offering loans to people who they knew would likely have difficulty making payments, but it didn't matter. If the borrowers defaulted, they could always reclaim the property and sell it again, and ultimately the risk was low: most subprime mortgages were being repackaged in large bundles and sold to wealthy investors in the form of mortgage-backed securities. If some of the loans went bad, it would be the investors who lost their money, not the banks themselves. So there was very little incentive for lenders to worry about whether the loans were too risky for the borrowers. And the borrowers, not understanding the finer points of things like "adjustable rate mortgages" (which start out small and affordable but then balloon after a few years), got caught in a system intended to make short-term profits without much regard for the effect on the borrowers over time.

So into the breach of foreclosure came a number of investors seeking to snap up foreclosed properties. At first, the process likely helped stabilize the housing market and allowed mostly small investors to buy up a handful of properties. Initially, this process of buying up blighted and vacant housing was likely a net plus for the communities in which so many foreclosures had occurred, but now, several years later, buying up foreclosed homes has become less a way to stabilize communities and more a strategy for making bucketloads of money. By snapping up so many properties, big investors like Blackstone reduce the pool of moderately priced housing options for families to purchase and begin building equity. Because investment groups like Blackstone have so much cash on hand to allow them to buy up single-family homes for rental, individuals who might be able to buy foreclosed houses at auction for a good price are inevitably outbid, and end up renting at a higher cost than what a fair mortgage would run them. The net result is fewer homeowners, less equity built up among the working class, and less affordable housing for moderate-income individuals, while wealthy investors make ten percent profits annually on each rental unit. And, of course, as Blackstone and others bundle all these rental properties into packages for wealthy investors, the risk to the economy grows. Just as mortgage-backed securities brought down the economy when too many people couldn't pay their notes due to inflated interest rates, so too could rental-backed securities create problems if tenants can't keep up with their rents. In an economy that isn't producing rising wages for most workers—and certainly not the kind of workers who normally rent—that risk is quite real.

So how do we assess the ethics of such a practice? Is it ethical to make money off of the pain of others, who lost their homes? And to engage in a practice that ultimately increases the cost of living to moderate-income persons and reduces the ability of such persons to buy their own homes? Is the value of moneymaking at all costs, and as quickly as possible, a value we wish to promote? Or should such a value and those who adhere to it be questioned? Ironically, one of the principal critiques of the so-called "culture of poverty" has long been that those trapped in this supposed culture have a "short-term orientation" and don't plan for the future sufficiently; yet with groups like Blackstone, the very same short-term thinking—make money now, and lots of it, without regard for the risk that such actions might be introducing into the economy—is seen as normal, legitimate, even laudable in the eyes of the wealthy minority. By ratifying such practices and allowing them to proceed with very little regulation or oversight, we begin down a road similar to the one that has already caused so much pain for so many people.

Beyond individual examples like Blackstone, or the phenomenon of widespread unethical financial activity in the United

States, there is reason to believe that the larger culture of affluence and great wealth itself poses a significant risk to the society we share. A recent analysis of seven separate studies found that the wealthy actually behave less ethically than the poor: they are more likely to break driving laws, more likely to exhibit unethical decision-making tendencies, to take valued goods from others, to lie in negotiations, to cheat so as to increase their chances of winning a prize, and to openly endorse unethical behavior to get ahead at work. According to the studies, the unethical tendencies of the upper class stem mostly from their more favorable attitudes toward greed when compared to those in lower-income groups.[322]

Likewise, four additional studies have recently found that lower-income persons are more generous than the wealthy, more trusting and more likely to help someone in need. The research finds that people who are categorized as poor and working class are more likely to act in pro-social ways because of their greater commitment to egalitarian values and greater levels of compassion.[323] As explained by those who have studied the link between wealth and unethical behavior:

> The answer may have something to do with how wealth and abundance give us a sense of freedom and independence from others. The less we have to rely on others, the less we may care about their feelings. This leads us towards being more self-focused. Another reason has to do with our attitudes towards greed. Like Gordon Gekko [in the fiction film *Wall Street*], upper-class people may be more likely to endorse the idea that "greed is good." [Researcher Paul K.] Piff and his colleagues found that wealthier people are more likely to agree with statements that greed is justified, beneficial, and morally defensible. These attitudes ended up predicting participants' likelihood of engaging in unethical behavior.[324]

Researchers who have explored the connection between

wealth, power and cold-hearted, even cruel behaviors, have uniformly found the connection to be strong. In experimental settings, they have been able to induce feelings of power among subjects that lead to a substantially increased tendency to engage in self-aggrandizing, callous and cruel behaviors toward others. According to the research, wealth and power produce a kind of implicit, if not explicit, narcissism:

> Even thoughts of being wealthy can create a feeling of increased entitlement—you start to feel superior to everyone else and thus more deserving. . . . Wealthier people were more likely to agree with statements like, "I honestly feel I'm just more deserving than other people. . . . " This had straightforward and clearly measurable effects on behavior. . . . For example, when told that they would have their photograph taken, well-off people were more likely to rush to the mirror to check themselves out and adjust their appearance. Asked to draw symbols, like circles, to represent how they saw themselves and others, more affluent people drew much larger circles for themselves and smaller ones for the rest of humankind. If you think of yourself as larger than life, larger and more important than other people, it is hardly surprising that your behavior would become oriented towards getting what you think you deserve.[325]

Perhaps this is why polling data indicate the wealthy are so much less sympathetic to the lives and struggles of hard-working but still poor Americans. So whereas the general public says by an overwhelming margin (about four to one) that the minimum wage should be high enough to ensure that no family with a full-time worker at that wage should remain poor, only forty percent of the wealthy agree.[326] In this regard, it appears that the values of the rich clearly are at odds with the larger society's values. Interestingly, even though this fact renders the values of the wealthy pathological by definition—since pathology refers to something in an abnormal state—one rarely if ever hears discussion of the rich as a pathological "overclass" that manifests dysfunctional and abnormal values.

According to still more research, when people experience power their brains become less sensitive to others. As Canadian psychologists Michael Inzlicht and Sukhvinder Obhi note:

> The human brain can be exquisitely attuned to other people, thanks in part to its so-called mirror system. The mirror system is composed of a network of brain regions that become active both when you perform an action . . . and when you observe someone else who performs the same action. . . . Our brains appear to be able to intimately resonate with others' actions, and this process may allow us not only to understand what they are doing, but also, in some sense, to experience it ourselves—i.e., to empathize.
>
> In our study, we induced a set of participants to temporarily feel varying levels of power by asking them to write a brief essay about a moment in their lives. Some wrote about a time when they felt powerful . . . others wrote about a time when they felt powerless . . . Next, the participants watched a video of a human hand repeatedly squeezing a rubber ball. While they watched, we assessed the degree of motor excitation occurring in the brain—a measure that is widely used to infer activation of the mirror system . . . by the application of transcranial magnetic stimulation and the measurement of electrical muscle activation in the subject's hand. We sought to determine the degree to which the participants' brains became active during the observation of rubber ball squeezing, relative to a period in which they observed no action.
>
> We found that for those participants who were in-

> duced to experience feelings of power, their brains showed virtually no resonance with the actions of others; conversely, for those participants who were induced to experience feelings of powerlessness, their brains resonated quite a bit. In short, the brains of powerful people did not mirror the actions of other people. And when we analyzed the text of the participants' essays, using established techniques for coding and measuring themes, we found that the more power that people expressed, the less their brains resonated. Power, it appears, changes how the brain itself responds to others.[327]

Additional research in two different countries has found that when individuals are placed in experimental settings and are led to believe they have just beaten someone else in a particular task (although in truth there was no competitor), they behave more aggressively toward the imaginary "other" than when they are led to believe they had lost the competition. Researchers suggest the studies demonstrate that winning makes one more aggressive, reducing empathy to those one has defeated.[328] This too could have implications for how those in a hyper-competitive economy act upon "winning" the various competitions of everyday life: by beating someone out for a job, or by making more money than one's fellow citizens, for instance.

A lack of empathy flows from a culture of cruelty and predatory affluence rather than anything over which the poor and unemployed have control. Unethical behavior makes perfect sense in a culture where getting ahead at all costs is the only supreme value. As David Callahan explains in his book *The Cheating Culture:*

> In today's competitive economy, where success and job security can't be taken for granted, it's increasingly tempting to leave your ethics at home every morning. Students are cheating more now that getting a good education is a matter of economic life and death. Lawyers

> are overbilling as they've been pushed to bring in more money for the firm and as it's gotten harder to make partner. Doctors are accepting bribes from drug makers as HMOs have squeezed their incomes. . . . A CEO will inflate earnings reports to please Wall Street—and increase the value of his stock options by $50 million.[329]

And it's not just corporate executives; even mere wealthy parents game the system on behalf of their kids. Affluent parents often pay tutors not only to help their children in certain subjects, but even to write papers *for* them; and it's entirely the norm, it seems, for rich parents to pay psychologists thousands of dollars for a "learning disability" diagnosis for their kids, so those children can get extra time on standardized tests like the SAT. Of the 30,000 test takers who are granted disability status each year, the overwhelming majority are wealthy; meanwhile, low-income kids who might actually *have* learning disabilities, but not the money to pay for the diagnosis, are expected to play by the normal rules, and as a result, they are put at a disadvantage on a test that already favored the rich in the first place, if only because of the quality of their K–12 schooling.[330]

Though it doesn't happen often, occasionally, members of the economic minority will themselves acknowledge the way in which great wealth can distort one's value system. Former hedge fund manager Sam Polk took to the pages of the *New York Times* in early 2014 to note the way his earnings—which he now could readily acknowledge had been unrelated to anything socially productive—had changed him, turning him into a wealth junkie, much as drugs can become addicting.

> I wanted a billion dollars. It's staggering to think that in the course of five years, I'd gone from being thrilled at my first bonus—$40,000—to being disappointed when, my second year at the hedge fund, I was paid "only" $1.5 million.

As Polk put it, his greed overtook any moral qualms he had about misleading investors and ruining people's financial lives.

> Not only was I not helping to fix any problems in the world, but I was profiting from them. During the market crash in 2008, I'd made a ton of money by shorting the derivatives of risky companies. As the world crumbled, I profited. I'd seen the crash coming, but instead of trying to help the people it would hurt the most—people who didn't have a million dollars in the bank—I'd made money off it.[331]

Although Polk ultimately "got clean" by walking away from the hedge-fund world and the riches that came from it, and now is engaged in a number of truly inspiring projects intended to empower persons in marginalized communities, for every reformed money-junkie there are several others who are still ensnared in a culture of predatory affluence, manipulating financial instruments for their personal gain. It is a mindset that is at once entirely psychopathic and yet normalized within the system of capitalism to which Americans are wedded. Ultimately, folks like Polk were only able to become addicted to outrageous fortune in the first place because the society in which they live allows such grotesque profits to flow to those whose economic activity is so corrosive of the greater good. In short, it is the pathological values of policymakers and the economic aristocrats who call the tunes to which they so eagerly dance, which are to blame for the Sam Polks of the world. We create them, systemically, and by the antisocial, money-obsessed ideologies we teach to the people of the nation every day. Waste, disposability, selfish materialism, celebrity superficiality and the never-ending quest for *more, more, more* seem to have won out over the advance of citizenship, public interest, community building and the common good.

It is a mindset that does virtually nothing valuable for communities or the world, unlike other, far less well-paying professions, as Polk himself notes in the *Times* piece:

> Yes, I was sharp, good with numbers. I had marketable talents. But in the end I didn't really do anything. I was a derivatives trader, and it occurred to me the world would hardly change at all if credit derivatives ceased to exist. Not so nurse practitioners.[332]

In some ways, that the wealthy turn out to be moral and ethical reprobates should hardly surprise us. To a large extent dishonesty and predation are the values inculcated by the nation's most elite finishing schools for bankers and others who are trained to siphon all they can out of the system. At Harvard Business School, for instance, students are told, "Speak with conviction. Even if you believe something only 55 percent, say it as if you believe it 100 percent."[333] Lying is not only something that rogues do to make an extra buck; rather, it is virtually built-in to the process of enormous money-making. According to the evidence, top executives are fully aware of and endorse that reality. One recent survey of five hundred top executives in the U.S. and the UK found that one in four said they knew of ethical and legal wrongdoing in the workplace, and the same number agreed that success in the financial services sector may actually *require* conduct that is unethical or illegal. One in seven of the executives said they would commit insider trading if they believed they could get away with it, and nearly one in three said that their compensation plans created incentives to violate the law or one's own ethical standards.[334]

Jim Cramer, formerly a hedge fund manager and now a major television personality who gives investment advice to millions of people who hang on his every word (even though his investment advice is notoriously mediocre),[335] has made the thinking very clear: "What's important when you are in that hedge-fund mode is to not do anything remotely truthful because the truth is so against your view, that it's important to create a new truth, to develop a fiction."[336]

You can probably imagine the reaction if a poor person were to describe the importance of creative dishonesty so as to procure food stamp benefits or disability payments. Conservatives would point to them as proof positive of the dysfunctional and destructive values bred within the so-called underclass. But when rich white men like Jim Cramer encourage deceit as a way of life, so as to make billions of dollars, they are praised as genius investors worthy of significant tax concessions. While the nation is treated to a never-ending stream of warnings about the culture of poverty and the dysfunctional underclass pathologies of the struggling, the much more significant and destructive pathologies and inverted value systems of the rich go uninterrogated.

With Justice for None: The Real World Implications of a Culture of Cruelty

It's important to note, however, that the culture of cruelty and the assorted rhetorical devices used to maintain and further it are far from mere academic matters: there are real-world implications to the kind of callousness displayed toward the poor and those in need; so too, there are policy implications to the veneration of predatory financial minorities and the myths that are propagated to defend their excess wealth. As mentioned previously, such thinking stokes support for cuts in social safety-net programs and provides rhetorical ammunition for those who seek to limit the availability of unemployment insurance. But it does more than this.

The culture of affluence and cruelty contributes to the kind of obeisance to corporations that leads directly to death and suffering around the globe. So consider pharmaceutical companies that manufacture drugs meant to treat HIV/AIDS. On the one hand, we know that several drugs developed for those with HIV have extended life in the United States for hundreds of thousands of people. That's the good news. But because of intellectual property laws, which protect these pharmaceuticals from competition by generic drug makers, when South Africa passed a law that would have allowed South African drug companies to make generic versions of the same drugs, U.S. lawmakers and trade representatives cried foul. Even though international law allows and even calls for such actions to be permitted in cases of national emergency (which the AIDS crisis in South Africa surely was), lawmakers objected, deferring to corporations and their supposed property rights over and above the needs of desperately ill people to receive medicine at an affordable price. Although GlaxoSmith-Kline (the company that makes the main anti-AIDS drug, AZT) reached an agreement to allow a South African manufacturer to make the drug, they required the generic version to be sold only in that nation, and insisted on a thirty percent royalty on all sales. Interestingly, Glaxo thinks it deserves credit and money for AZT, even though researchers at the Michigan Cancer Institute and Duke University, who were working under government grant monies from the National Cancer Institute, actually discovered it. Because of trade policies that prioritize the intellectual property rights of American companies, millions of people around the world suffer, priced out of the market for needed medicine.[337]

The culture of cruelty facilitates a callous disregard for the suffering of Americans as well. After the passage of the Affordable Care Act (ACA, commonly referred to as "Obamacare"), conservatives repeatedly pledged to torpedo the law, either by repealing it in Congress or by seeking to have it deemed unconstitutional by the courts. Although the Supreme Court upheld the law's constitutionality, it also stipulated that states could not be compelled, as the law had called for, to expand their Medicaid rolls to persons who normally would not have qualified for benefits under the program. Relieved of the obligation to cover more patients under Medicaid, twenty-five states, mostly led by conservative Republicans, have refused to expand their Medicaid rolls, leaving five million low-income workers without access to affordable care.[338]

Because several of these states set absurdly stringent Medicaid eligibility levels—Texas and Louisiana won't cover a family of three making more than $5,000 in annual income—even people living at only a bit more than a fourth of the poverty line will be "too rich" to qualify for Medicaid.[339]

The fact that opposition to the ACA is largely about cruelty and a callous disregard for the poor and working class should be obvious. Rush Limbaugh, for instance, has openly derided the centerpiece of the law—the idea that insurance companies should not be allowed to deny coverage to those with pre-existing conditions—by calling such a requirement nothing more than "welfare" and "nonsense."[340] In other words, to leading conservatives, if you have chronic asthma, or a history of cancer, or high blood pressure, or a thyroid condition, insurers should be allowed to reject you entirely for coverage, and to give coverage to anyone in such a condition is to make them welfare recipients. This is modern fiscal conservatism in a nutshell: the right of corporations to make money and make decisions that kill people is more sacrosanct than the right of American families to survive or receive health care that might help them live healthy and productive lives.

And in what seems like a direct mirror of the Dickensian thinking that led off this chapter, there has actually been a resurrection not only of hateful rhetoric toward the poor and struggling, but also the mechanisms of punishment for poverty that were so prevalent in Dickens's time, and which were supported by the likes of Ebenezer Scrooge. Debtors' prisons, although technically illegal, seem to be making a comeback. In several states, poor people are being incarcerated for failure to pay various fines and fees (for traffic tickets or other low-level offenses), under laws governing contempt of court, thereby allowing officials to avoid the impression that they are locking people up for poverty, but ultimately amounting to just that.

Consider the case of Kristy and Timothy Fugatt. In 2010, police in Childersberg, Alabama, ticketed them for driving with expired tags. The fine came to $296 in all, with an additional $198 for Kristy, because her license had also expired. Because they were unable to pay, they were put on probation. Their probation was overseen by a private company called Judicial Correction Services, which charges $45 per month to each probationer they handle. Once the Fugatts fell behind on their payments for the initial violations—in large part because their infant child was hospitalized with a rare brain disease, and caring for him made it difficult to hold down steady employment[341] —they were charged additional fees and threatened with incarceration. In 2012, a police officer arrested them, threatened them with a Taser, and told them that their kids would be taken away and placed in state custody. They only gained release after relatives came to the jail and paid off their outstanding debt.[342]

Although locking up indigent defendants for failure to pay fees and fines makes no sense economically—it costs more to jail people for noncompliance than the value of the debt those people have failed to pay[343]—the practice seems to be growing in popularity.[344] Even worse, in Arkansas, persons who are late on their rent can actually be incarcerated. In such cases, if a landlord issues an eviction notice, rather than going through the civil courts if a resident falls behind or refuses to pay, tenants can be arrested for a criminal violation and locked up. Even if a tenant is only one day late with rent, he or she can be evicted on ten days' notice. If they haven't vacated within those ten days, the landlord can have them arrested.[345]

Meanwhile, as the poor are incarcerated for minor offenses or for failure to pay fines and fees to the courts after receiving traffic tickets, the rich manage to avoid jail or prison time, even if their crimes are far more serious. Despite the persistent fraud that was at the heart of Wall Street's activities for much of the first decade of the 2000s, and which ultimately cratered the economy for the rest of us, no investment bankers have gone to jail for their misdeeds. At most, their companies pay fines that can then be written off on the company's next tax return.

In the case of JPMorgan Chase, the deal cut with the government is a perfect example of how the state soft-pedals white-collar crime on a gargantuan scale, even as it furiously prosecutes low-level street criminals. Of the $9 billion ultimately paid to the government by Chase, only about $2 billion was defined in the settlement as a fine or penalty for wrongdoing; this means that the remaining $7 billion could be written off on the company's taxes the following year. Then, because the settlement terms gave Chase immunity from further civil liability, the firm's stock shot up by six percent upon news of the deal, pumping roughly $12 billion of added value into the company's stock, essentially making the settlement a *money-maker* for a firm that had defrauded investors by selling mortgage-backed securities they knew full well were junk. Chase then further insulated itself from the cost of its actions by laying off 7,500 low-level employees, which then allowed them to offer nice raises to upper management, including a seventy-four percent raise for CEO Jamie Dimon, bringing his overall compensation package to nearly $20 million.[346]

Author and journalist Matt Taibbi explains the magnitude of the problem, and makes clear how economic privilege insulates the nation's financial aristocracy from the kinds of punishment that would surely await average Americans guilty of even a fraction of the illegality engaged in by the banking class:

> Not a single executive who ran the companies that cooked up and cashed in on the phony financial boom—an industrywide scam that involved the mass sale of mismarked, fraudulent mortgage-backed securities—has ever been convicted. Their names by now are familiar to even the most casual Middle American news consumer: companies like AIG, Goldman Sachs, Lehman Brothers, JP Morgan Chase, Bank of America and Morgan Stanley. Most of these firms were directly involved in elaborate fraud and theft. Lehman Brothers hid billions in loans from its investors. Bank of America lied about billions in bonuses. Goldman Sachs failed to tell

> clients how it put together the born-to-lose toxic mortgage deals it was selling. What's more, many of these companies had corporate chieftains whose actions cost investors billions—from AIG derivatives chief Joe Cassano, who assured investors they would not lose even "one dollar" just months before his unit imploded, to the $263 million in compensation that former Lehman chief Dick "The Gorilla" Fuld conveniently failed to disclose. Yet not one of them has faced time behind bars.[347]

Even when a bank such as HSBC engages in money laundering for drug cartels and the Iranian government, and agrees to pay a nearly $2 billion fine for these actions, it remains untouched by criminal prosecution, for fear that an indictment would collapse the bank and set off a chain reaction that could destroy the economy.[348] Taibbi contrasted the kid-glove approach taken with HSBC to the routine prosecution of low-level drug users in an April 2014 interview with Amy Goodman of *Democracy Now*:

> This idea that some companies are too big to jail, it makes some sense in the abstract. . . . If you have a company . . . that employs tens (of thousands) or maybe even 100,000 people, you may not want to criminally charge that company willy-nilly and wreck the company and cause lots of people to lose their jobs. But . . . there's no reason you can't proceed against individuals in those companies. . . . In the case of a company like HSBC, which admitted to laundering $850 million for a pair of Central and South American drug cartels, somebody has to go to jail in that case. If you're going to put people in jail for having a joint in their pocket or for slinging dime bags on the corner in a city street, you cannot let people who laundered $800 million for the worst drug offenders in the world walk. . . . In that case, they paid a fine;

> they paid a $1.9 billion fine. And some of the executives had to defer their bonuses for a period of five years—not give them up, defer them . . . and nobody did a single day in jail in that case [but] somebody at the bottom, he's a consumer of the illegal narcotics business, and he's going to jail, and then you have these people who are at the very top of the illegal narcotics business, and they're getting a complete walk.[349]

Despite the economic calamities wrought by bankers and financial workers who clearly have no problem destroying the economic security of millions of American families, virtually no one among the nation's political leadership has been willing to advocate serious punishment, let alone jail time, for their actions. President Obama and his Justice Department have been utterly unwilling to punish financial crimes with any degree of seriousness or even to speak forcefully about the criminality of Wall Street. Unlike the forceful language of FDR, who openly challenged the economic aristocracy he hailed from, it is rare to hear anything remotely as brave from the mouths of modern politicians. Consider these words from Franklin Roosevelt, spoken in October 1936, and ask how often such straightforward sentiments are to be heard from elected officials in the twenty-first century:

> We know now that Government by organized money is just as dangerous as Government by organized mob. Never before in all our history have these forces been so united against one candidate as they stand today. They are unanimous in their hate for me—and I welcome their hatred. I should like to have it said of my first Administration that in it the forces of selfishness and of lust for power met their match. I should like to have it said of my second Administration that in it these forces met their master.[350]

In the modern era, few people appear brave enough to fully challenge the hatred emanating from the financial class, or to invite the anger of the wealthy. Today, politicians are far too dependent on the campaign contributions of such persons to speak truth in the way Roosevelt did.

Meanwhile, as America seems incapable of arresting and prosecuting bankers whose actions very nearly destroyed the world economy, some among us have no problem with the thought of further criminalizing poor people whose only crime is asking for money. Since 2001, the nation has lost about thirteen percent of its low-income housing, thereby contributing to increased homelessness, yet restrictions on loitering, begging or resting in public have proliferated. Eighteen percent of all American cities ban sleeping in public, and a little more than four in ten have even made it illegal to sleep in one's vehicle.[351] Recently, the police chief in San Antonio (where panhandling has been essentially banned since 2011) suggested that *giving* money to someone who begs for it should also be illegal, and something for which the charitable are ticketed.[352] Because giving money to homeless people is apparently a far more serious offense than ripping off investors and homeowners to the tune of hundreds of billions, even trillions of dollars.

Further demonstrating the way that valorization of the rich and the business class skews the dispensation of justice in America, consider the epidemic problem of wage theft and the nation's pathetic response to it. Wage theft refers to a number of practices that result in business owners keeping money for themselves that has been earned by their employees. Examples include not paying for overtime work, paying less than minimum wage, cheating workers out of tips, or paying workers less than the prevailing wage required on union-negotiated contracts. According to a recent study by the Economic Policy Institute, wage theft of this sort costs workers billions of dollars each year—potentially as much as $50 billion annually—and amounts to transferring money from the hands of employees to the hands of business owners, thereby furthering income inequality. Considering that most wage theft affects low-wage employees who already struggle financially, siphoning off even small amounts from individual workers not only adds up to a huge windfall for bosses, but also can seriously impair the ability of these workers to support themselves and their families.[353]

Far from a minor concern, according to the FBI, the amount being lost to wage theft dwarfs the amount stolen in all robberies, burglaries, larcenies and motor vehicle thefts *combined.* Even if we only consider the money *recovered* by employees whose bosses stole wages from them and who discovered the violation, filed a complaint or hired a private attorney—obviously only a small portion of those from whom wages were stolen—the amount would be almost three times the total amount of money and property taken in all bank, residential, convenience store, gas station and street robberies *combined.* Yet, whereas those who rob a convenience store or break into your house and steal jewelry, cash or electronics face serious criminal penalties, felony records and possible jail time, people who steal from their employees need not worry about being subjected to such an indignity. There are only eleven hundred investigators in the Department of Labor capable of looking into the problem of wage theft, and the penalties, even for deliberate and repeated violations of the law, are hardly onerous: a maximum of $1,100 for failing to pay minimum wage or required overtime, for instance.

But it's not only for workplace-related wrongdoing that the wealthy are let off easy: even rather standard crimes manage to go unpunished if one has enough money. In the last few years there have been a number of cases indicating that inequality is not just an economic matter, but a matter of unequal justice as well. In 2013, a sixteen-year-old boy from one of the nation's wealthiest communities received probation after driving drunk and killing four people.[354] Ethan Couch, who according to a psychologist called by his defense team suffers from "affluenza" (in other words, too much privilege and not enough accountability), received yet more privilege and was relieved of accountability by the judge who sentenced him.

Joseph Goodman, a wealthy business owner in Washington State, led police on a high-speed chase while drunk, and despite having a blood alcohol level twice the legal limit (and despite the fact that it was his *seventh* DUI), he was given a year of work-release from jail, requiring him to spend nights and weekends in jail but allowing him to go to work in the day. In February 2014, he was even allowed to travel to New York for the Super Bowl. Why such lenience? Because according to the judge, to jail him outright would harm his business and employees.[355] It's the same logic that led a Colorado prosecutor not to seek felony charges against Martin Joel Erzinger after he ran over a bicyclist and fled the scene in 2010. Erzinger, a hedge fund manager for Smith Barney, was considered too important to jail. In the words of District Attorney Mark Hurlbert, "Felony convictions have some pretty serious job implications for someone in Mr. Erzinger's profession." Because Erzinger oversees more than $1 billion in assets for his rich clients, the D.A. feared that serious punishment would harm the interests of those "ultra-high net worth" individuals, and so he sought only misdemeanor charges that would not carry jail time. Even though Erzinger left the critically injured cyclist for dead and failed to report the incident, prosecutors thought it best to go easy on him.[356]

The courts are especially lenient on those who are heirs to large fortunes. In the past year, heirs to S.C. Johnson and Sons and DuPont managed to get off lightly for serious offenses in a way that no poor defendant in their position could have. Billionaire Samuel Curtis Johnson III confessed to sexually assaulting his stepdaughter on numerous occasions but was only given four months in prison. His attorney argued, and the judge apparently agreed, that hard time should be reserved for "maximum defendants" rather than wealthy scions like Johnson.[357] As for the DuPont heir, although convicted of raping his daughter, Robert Richards IV avoided jail time and was only sentenced to sex offender treatment, because, as the judge put it, he would "not fare well" in prison.[358] Apparently if you're wealthy and white, prison is too harsh for you no matter your crimes, while for Americans who are poor (and especially Americans of color), incarceration is still the preferred option. Such is a justice system in a culture of cruelty, operating under the affluence of a small self-valorizing minority that is given permission to prey upon the citizenry. Clearly, when modern-day Scrooges ask, "Are there no workhouses? No prisons?" they are only inquiring as to their availability for the poor and struggling.

CHAPTER III

REDEEMING SCROOGE: FOSTERING A CULTURE OF COMPASSION

Revisiting the imagery of Ebenezer Scrooge and the normalization of Scroogism in America, it is worth remembering that in the end of Dickens's tale, the villain was redeemed. Shown visions of his past, his present and the grim future that would await him were he not to change, Scrooge undergoes a transformation. The hopefulness of such a message—the idea that even the coldest of hearts can be warmed—may be at turns sappy or sentimental, but it nonetheless speaks to a deeply held human belief that most of us appear to share: the notion that most people are good and caring and compassionate. We are turned cold and callous by various forces—perhaps our upbringing, by things that happen to us throughout life, or even by a culture that fosters selfish insensitivity—but we are redeemable, capable of co-creating an egalitarian, just and democratic nation.

To whatever extent that hope of metamorphosis is justified in the case of one person, so too must it be possible for many people collectively, for entire societies in fact. As a nation and culture we too can be redeemed; we can become more just and loving and complete, we can live out the words of our national creed however much they have been regularly violated thus far. But it won't happen if we don't face the reality before us. It can't happen unless we remove the blinders from our eyes and make note of how we got here.

If you've made it this far, you know the bad news: the American ideal of the U.S. as a land of opportunity is daily mocked by rising inequality, stagnating wages and the dynastic concentration of wealth among the richest fraction of the national population. Much as that ideal has always been vitiated by the nation's history of white supremacy and racism, so too does the class structure render America unrecognizable to its most vaunted principles. Upward mobility is becoming a fleeting memory of an earlier time, while downward mobility has become a distressing reality for millions. Not only is the economic picture dim for the vast majority of the American people, but sadly the way that we are being encouraged to view those who are struggling is also increasingly negative. Relentlessly hostile rhetoric from talk show hosts and reactionary pundits poisons the minds of millions, encouraging contempt for those Americans who have become poor, underemployed or underpaid. That rhetoric serves to rationalize inequality, to justify harsh public policies that weaken the safety net for millions who need it, and to legitimize policies that further aggrandize the wealthy minority.

And all of this inequality is, simply put, *bad for us*; not just for those at the bottom of the economic ladder, for whom it obviously isn't working, but for American society as a whole. The evidence is rather overwhelming: on virtually any measure of social well-being that one might choose to examine, countries that are more unequal in their distribution of income rank lower than countries that are more egalitarian. On measures of health (life expectancy, infant mortality, drug use); on measures of social cohesion ("trust in others," the status of women, homicide rates); and on measures of educational accomplishment, more equitable societies are far more successful. On virtually all of these measures the United States looks awful by comparison to most every other industrialized nation on the planet.[1]

Among the reasons why inequality seems to have such deleterious effects on health and well-being, scholars suggest that the chief factor is the psychological (and thus, in many cases, physiological) stress "of relative deprivation . . . the stress of being at the bottom end of an unequal pecking order, especially when the dominant ideology attributes being at the bottom to individual deficiencies."[2] And then, for those who are not at the bottom, a concomitant stress may exist, specifically around the desire to maintain one's edge and advantage so as not to slip up or be surpassed by others. If we think of the phenomenon of "keeping up with the Joneses," whereby we feel the need to have a house or car as nice as or nicer than our neighbor's, or secretly wonder if a colleague or friend is making more than we make at our respective jobs, we can easily imagine the way that even people doing well in a society of great inequality could be stressed, with deleterious health effects for all involved. In other words, when it comes to building a healthy and functional society, for any of our children or ourselves, *we're doing it wrong.*

But knowing how bad things have gotten isn't enough, and wringing our hands about the damage done within a culture of cruelty won't help move us to a culture of compassion. To do that, we'll have to develop a new way of speaking about these issues. We'll have to craft counter-narratives that can sustain movements for justice in the face of the new Scroogism.

I should warn readers now: I am not going to be making concrete policy proposals to address growing inequality and the culture of cruelty, per se. Not because I don't support certain ideas floated by others, but merely because no policy proposals I could make would stand a chance of going anywhere until we have sufficient support to effectively push for them; and to develop that base of support and build a movement that could effectively win any of the changes we seek, we will have to develop the narrative, the strategy and the vision first. During the nearly twenty years that conservatives wandered in the political wilderness after the defeat of Barry Goldwater in 1964, they didn't spend time focused on particular policy details; they focused on crafting a story with which to reclaim the country for the policies they would push through once they took power.

While the right has long understood the importance of the

narrative and controlling the storyline, the liberal left has too often focused on calling for specific policies, as if the mere logic of their appeal, or the facts we can muster in support of them, would suffice. But even though I've spent much of this book providing facts, I know that those facts alone won't matter if there isn't a storyline to go with them. Likewise, the more radical left, of which I have long been a part (and remain), has typically operated on the assumption that mass mobilization and protest movements will suffice to turn things around: if we can just get enough people in the streets, we can force the power structure to bend to our will. But while I support tactics of mass mobilization, the left is misreading history if we believe past protest movements succeeded because of protest alone. In each case of successful protest, or for that matter liberal reform, it was the existence and propagation of a clear counter-narrative—a storyline—that paved the way for victory. The civil rights pioneers did not win because of sheer numbers. They won what they won because they were able to deploy a message of dreams deferred, to articulate a vision of an America that had betrayed its promise and was in need of fulfillment. It is not clear to me that the left today, in either its liberal or radical stripes has nearly so clear a narrative. This seems to be the piece given short shrift by liberals and radicals alike, content to either put forward facts and policy proposals on the one hand or raise hell on the other, in hopes that somehow one or both of these will turn the tide. In both cases, their hopes are incredibly naïve, for reasons we will explore below.

The culture of cruelty has triumphed thus far, not because the American people are inherently committed to injustice—far from it. The culture of cruelty has triumphed because we haven't understood its roots, and therefore haven't known where to start digging in order to uproot it. It has triumphed because we haven't understood the psychology behind it, and because we have underestimated its allure for millions. Too often, progressives and leftists look at those who follow the siren song of the right as fools, or naïve, or suffering from "false consciousness" or some such thing; we ask, "Why do these people vote against their own self-interest," supporting cuts in the very programs they themselves might need one day? Why do middle-class and working-class voters support candidates who promise only tax cuts for the wealthy? But even the way in which that question is framed—specifically in terms of what it doesn't mention about those "middle-class and working-class voters"—suggests the answer, as we'll see below. Only by understanding why the culture of cruelty has been given such a long shelf life in America can we hope to transform it.

How Did We Get Here? The Importance of Seeing the Roadblocks Clearly

Americans are quick to compare our nation to the rest of the world, usually in ways that seek to reassure us, if not others, of our national greatness. We proclaim: "We're number one!" And we do this even when we're not, at least not when it comes to most any category in which one would hope to be the world leader. Our pride and hubris have long tended to get the better of us, much to the amusement of persons around the globe, and quite often to their horror. After all, people who believe themselves smarter, wiser, more imbued with insight, and inspired by providence can be both incredibly domineering and dangerous.

When progressives and those on the left compare the United States with other nations, we take a far more sober assessment of our national position, and we often stand aghast at how far behind America seems to be when it comes to things like reducing child poverty, guaranteeing health care for our people, or providing one or another safety net program for persons in need. Noticing how much stronger are those safety-nets in most every industrialized nation with which the United States likes to compare itself, we routinely pose the question: What is it about America that makes us such an outlier among modern so-called democracies when it comes to these matters? Why is our sense of solidarity with one another so neglected and incomplete by comparison? Why do American families have fewer protections than those in other "rich" countries?

Normally, when that question is asked, at least in my experience, there are two answers that typically come back in reply. The first is that the influence of the conservative Protestant colonists early on in the American experiment set the tone for the kind of society that the United States was to become. A zealous commitment to the so-called Protestant work ethic and the inherently individualistic nature of the colonial enterprise is to blame. Having seen themselves as carving out a society from nothing—an inherently racist notion, of course, as there was surely something here before white people arrived from Europe—the ideology of early Americanism was directed toward self-reliance and to eschew government intervention in matters of economics and social welfare. The second explanation commonly offered is that, unlike most nations of Europe, in the United States we don't have the same history of a strong labor movement—no labor party, for instance, and never the kind of union strength typical in the rest of the industrialized world. As such, there has been less pressure on people with capital to share the wealth, so to speak, and less pressure on politicians to create policies that would empower workers and low-income individuals and families.

In both of these explanations for a weaker safety net here, one can no doubt find some truth. And yet, something about these two arguments fails to satisfy, mostly because they raise more questions than they answer. Among them: Why was the hyper-individualistic Protestant work ethic such an influence here but less so elsewhere, in nations where there are also plenty of Protestants, many of them no doubt just as individualistic, hard-working and even ascetic in their lifestyle? And why is it that in spite of that history, most of those same hard-working Protestants embraced a substantial role for government intervention in the economy and safety-net programs in the wake of the Depression, but seem to have slid backwards and to increasingly oppose such efforts now? And *why* have labor unions and the labor movement generally been weaker in America than elsewhere? Is there something specific to the American experiment that can explain these things? I contend there are two such forces, both of which we'll need to address in order to move from a culture of cruelty to one of compassion: first, the national faith in rugged individualism and meritocracy; and second, the use of racism as a force to divide working-class people and discredit social safety nets for the poor and struggling.

Rugged Individualism & the Myth of Meritocracy: Cornerstones of the Culture of Cruelty

For those of us born and reared in the United States—and even for those born elsewhere who have come to the United States and spent any significant time here—there is one idea that has been taught to all of us, by parents, teachers, preachers, politicians, the media, from all corners of the society. It has been taught to us regardless of race, ethnicity, gender, sexuality, religion, disability status or economic class, so much so that it can rightly be considered our national creation myth. It is the idea of meritocracy: the notion that, in America, anyone can make it if they try hard enough, and that all obstacles will vanish in the presence of the determined will. Rugged individualism triumphs over all else, and if one fails to succeed, that is the fault of the individual who either didn't try hard enough or wasn't good enough to make it. Conversely, those who attain great fortune have done so because they put forth maximum effort, or were simply better than the rest of us.

On the one hand, it might appear at first glance that this notion has served our society reasonably well. Unlike past feudal systems where opportunity was limited to those of royal lineage or persons directly connected to the ruling class, in the United States, the notion that merit should determine who gets ahead and falls behind has generated more openness and mobility—at least historically speaking—than has been enjoyed in most of the world. It's an idea that is intoxicating and initially even empowering: I am the master of my own fate; I can do anything if I put my mind to it. It is hard to imagine a more invigorating mantra for a child to hear. It is, for that reason, something that most parents tell their children. We want them to believe in themselves, to take risks, to always do their best, and to never let anything stand in the way of their dreams. To introduce sticky concepts—like the idea that systemic injustices and obstacles exist, and that these are capable of derailing even the most determined of persons—is to inject uncertainty into an otherwise simple and more reassuring worldview. It is to surrender a degree of control, and is for this reason terrifying to people raised on a steady diet of optimism and the power of positive thinking—both hallmarks of the American cultural narrative. Just as fundamentalist practitioners of religious faiths have a need to believe in the one true path to God—one that they feel confident they can control by believing the right thing, saying the right thing and praying the right words—so too are Americans raised to believe that our economic fates are in our hands, that we can enter the kingdom of financial heaven if we just work hard enough.

But underneath the encouraging words of our national ideology rests a much more problematic truth: namely, the reality is always more complex than the mantra. At some level we all know this, and not just those of us steeped in liberal-left ideology or sociological theory. Most of us know people who have worked incredibly hard their entire lives but have little to show for it. So too, we probably have met at least a few individuals who were essentially born on third base but are firmly convinced they hit a triple and earned their place there. We can look around and see many examples of persons at the top and bottom who hardly deserve their station based on their own morality, work effort and talents. Yet the ideology remains. We assume that these individuals are outliers, exceptions to an otherwise meritocratic rule. We want to believe the mantra, and who can blame us? To believe that we are in control of where we end up in life seems far more empowering than to accept that perhaps there are systems and institutional arrangements in place that can block opportunities for people, regardless of their talent. If we reject the idea of America as a meritocracy, we have to confront the possibility that our fates may be determined at least in part by others, and that is simply too frightening for many to consider, especially if they are white, and/or male, and/or middle class—or really any combination of relatively advantaged groups—which makes it so much easier to miss the ways in which our personal success or failure is socially structured.

For me, I know that it can be difficult to add the asterisk to the promise of America when discussing these issues with our daughters, by which I mean the asterisk that points out the reality of sexism and misogyny in a society that claims to be about equity and justice for all. It's difficult, because I want our girls to believe they can do anything, be anything, and go as far and as high as their determination and talent can take them. But however difficult, the asterisk is still necessary, because it speaks to a truth that is just as real, and sometimes more so, than the promise itself. To not let them know that there are some who will view them as lesser because they are girls, soon to be women, would be tantamount to sending them down a dark alley at night, aware that there is an electric fence at the end that may or may not be turned on, but not telling them for fear of making them neurotic. Better to tell the truth and prepare them for the obstacles that are out there, so they may figure out strategies for overcoming them, both individually and collectively. The same is true for the society at large, but as a country, we are not good at the asterisk; we forget to add it, or avoid adding it deliberately, so desperate are we to believe that the aspirational nation is an actualized reality.

Think about how entrenched this ideology of meritocracy really is for a second. The notion of individual merit as the sole arbiter of where one ends up—or at least the primary one—is an idea so ingrained in the nation's psyche that it managed to survive even during times when this nation was *overtly* and *consciously* committed to the maintenance of formal white supremacy. Even during a time when millions of Africans were enslaved on these shores, the idea that anyone could make it if they tried was widely trumpeted, as was the notion that those who did make it (almost exclusively whites) had actually *earned* what they had, rather than being unjustly favored in every arena of life. Even during a time when indigenous land was being stolen and indigenous cultures uprooted, most believed that anyone could make it if they tried, and that those who had managed to do so, had done so by dint of their own talents and efforts, owing nothing to the stolen land and resources upon which their newfound wealth was based. When immigrants were being blocked from entering the U.S. for reasons of blatant racial and ethnic bias, or mistreated once here, it was still believed by most that anyone could make it in America, and that those who had managed to succeed had only themselves to credit for such prosperity, rather than the restrictions against others that had elevated them in the job market or in higher education by protecting them from competition. When hundreds of thousands of Mexican American citizens of the United States were deported to Mexico to free up jobs for white men in the 1930s—a shameful story that few Americans have learned in our history books—the national faith in meritocracy held firm.[3] When segregation ruled the South (and was the de facto reality everywhere else), and when lynchings were a common occurrence, and when millions were denied the ability to vote for reasons of color, the confidence that the United States was a society of opportunity for all, where initiative and determination were what mattered, still managed to remain intact. While people of color obviously questioned the national commitment to these principles, for most whites the contradictions were invisible. We believed the lie even as the truth was staring us in the face. That's how intoxicating and alluring the myth can be.

This is an ideology that, more than anything else, distinguishes the United States from most other Western nations not only in the present day but also throughout history. Over the centuries, most such nations had class structures that were firmly fixed: one was either nobility or commoner, and if one was the latter, one was not going to become the former. In systems such as that, class consciousness is relatively easy to come by. If you are a landless peasant you know it, and you know that no matter your work ethic or determination, you will likely live and die a landless peasant, barring some revolution that alters the power structure in your society. But in America, the ideological glue of meritocracy—what really amounts to the nation's creation myth—provides us with an almost perfect philosophical mechanism for justifying and rationalizing inequality. The irony of Ebenezer Scrooge is that his attitude toward the poor should not have been all that common or persuasive in a place like England, which could hardly have denied its embedded class structure during the days in which Dickens was writing; but in the United States Scrooge makes perfect sense. Scroogism, in that regard, can be seen as a completely American concept. If one can truly be anything one wants in America, then if there are vast disparities between those who achieve and those who don't, such outcomes can be written off to differential talent or effort. There is no need on this account for the state to intervene or to provide opportunity. With an ideology such as this in hand, not only can those inequalities be rationalized, but the development of a callous and even cruel disposition towards those at the bottom of the structure can come to seem quite normal and acceptable.

Even more perniciously, the notion of meritocracy not only serves as a source of narcissism for the rich—encouraged to view themselves as virtual super-humans who have earned all they have—but also as a source of self-doubt among the poor and struggling, because they too have been taught the lie. They too have internalized in many cases its stifling logic. So having not succeeded, it becomes easier for the poor person, or the person who's out of work or can't afford health care for their family, to blame themselves. It becomes easier to wonder what's wrong, not with the society that doesn't provide sufficient opportunity, but with oneself. Then, if you blame yourself for being less successful than you had hoped to be, you will be far less likely to organize for social transformation or a more just economic order—instead, you will simply double down on the personal effort that the system tells you is sufficient to make it. You'll work harder, sacrifice more and never question the larger structures within which you're laboring.

The destructive genius of the nation's secular gospel is precisely this: whether you succeed or fail, the myth of meritocracy is calculated to encourage you to look inward for the source of either outcome. If you attain great professional and financial reward, then that was all about *you*. The society is due no credit, nor the government, nor those who helped you along the way. As such, you owe nothing to anyone, and are surely not obligated to assist those who for whatever reason have failed to attain the same heights. And if you fall short professionally or financially, then that too was all about *you*. The society and its institutions are due no blame. As such, you are owed nothing more—not better schools, not better housing access, nor a neighborhood free from toxic waste facilities, nor affordable health care, nor a sufficient safety net when you stumble. You are own your own, win or lose. In the supreme irony then, one of the most foundational elements of the dominant American ideology—the thing that so often binds us together collectively, at least at the level of narrative—is an idea that at its core is the antithesis of a collective at all. Our collective and community identity is actually *anti-community*. It is hyper-individualism as the essence of one's group identity, and ultimately keeps us pitted against one another. There are winners and losers, and one's goal in life under such a system is to make sure you are the former and not the latter.

In his critique of modern society, *The Culture of Make Believe*, author, activist and philosopher Derrick Jensen explains the way in which such a mentality is destructive of the very notion of compassion:

> If you believe that the fundamental organizing principle of the world is competition (or if the fundamental organizing principle of your society *is* competition) you will perceive the world as full of ruthless competitors, all of whom will victimize you if they get the chance. The world as you perceive it will begin to devolve into consisting entirely or almost entirely of victims and perpetrators; those who do, and those who get done to; the fuckers, and the fucked. Your society will devolve—not in perception but in all truth—into these roles you have projected onto the world at large. You will begin to believe that everyone is out to get you. And why not? After all, you are certainly out to get them.[4]

In the wake of the economic meltdown of recent years, one might expect that faith in meritocracy would have diminished. With so many people thrown out of work, it would seem logical for Americans to begin questioning their faith in the idea that effort is sufficient for success and that one is solely responsible for one's own economic outcome. With the economy failing so many, one might expect that, if for no other reason than to maintain a sense of self-worth, Americans would begin to question the idea that their station owed to their own effort or lack thereof. After all, the psychological cost of believing the myth, even as you find yourself out of work and unable to pay your bills, is no minor matter. But even in 2009, at the height of the Great Recession, fully seventy-one percent of Americans said that hard work and personal skill were the main ingredients for success.[5] A look at a recent Pew Research Center poll makes clear that the lure of meritocracy remains strong. Despite an awareness that the economic system "unfairly favors the powerful" (something about which respondents agreed by a two-to-one margin), and that too much power is "concentrated in the hands of a few large companies" (affirmed by a three-to-one margin), the same poll found that two-thirds of Americans still answer "yes" when asked if hard work is sufficient to get ahead in America.[6] This percentage is roughly the same as the share of Americans who have believed this for the past several decades, whenever the question has been asked. Naturally, eight in ten conservatives agree with this key notion of meritocratic thinking, but so do majorities of most liberal subgroups, according to Pew.

How can faith in the meritocratic notion remain so high, even as so many were obviously harmed by the recent economic crisis? On the one hand, there is the national *need* to keep believing, if for no other reason than to offer some hope that with just a little more effort and initiative one can pull out of the hole into which one may have fallen. In other words, even though the evidence may tell us that something is seriously wrong, there is still the psychological boost one gets (at least in the short term) from continuing to believe that despite the chaos, one is still in charge of one's own destiny. But in addition, there may be something else at work, unique to the modern era, which was not an issue in the same way after the economic collapse of the 1930s: namely, the influence of popular culture on the way we perceive issues like social mobility. Unlike the 1930s, during which time there were no mass media regularly broadcasting images of wealth and affluence and success to American families via 24-hour television cycles, today, images of the good life, success and opulence immerse us wherever we go. Any evening of the week we can turn on the television and see not just one program providing us with images of success—as in the 1980s with *Lifestyles of the Rich and Famous*—but dozens of programs, from news shows to programs claiming to be "reality TV," which provide narratives of people who have made it despite in many cases being pretty mediocre in terms of talent. As Imara Jones has explained:

> Despite the fact that half of Americans are struggling to get by, the truth is that we still revere aspirational wealth culture as if it were before the crash . . . whole networks are built off of the concept of living gilded lives, like

> the cable network Bravo, and transformation from poverty to the world of multimillionaires is at the core of the number one reality show in the history of television, A&E's controversial "Duck Dynasty." . . . Additionally the super rich have their own dedicated channel, CNBC—like Fox News for conservatives—to reinforce it all. Ostensibly a financial news channel focused on the world's stock markets, CNBC is a daily parade of the 1 percent and the values they hold dear. In what might be a surprise to non-viewers, the network dedicates all three hours of primetime on Wednesdays to a show called the "Secret Lives of the Super Rich" where the 1 percent can learn everything from which firms specialize in super-rich security, to which luxury watch brands require an application to purchase them, to how to hide luxury cars in secret uber-secure facilities away from everyone else.[7]

Programs that push material acquisition and flaunt so-called success in purely economic terms prime the public to aspire to those things and to revere those who have managed to acquire them. Combined with programming that seems to demonstrate how even folks starting from nothing can go on to make it, the mass media message reinforces the notion of meritocracy at every turn. In a society where Honey Boo-Boo could get her own show, or where the Hillbilly Hand Fishing guys or the Real Housewives of (fill in the blank) can become celebrities—even though few of them are more educated or accomplished than millions of others (and in some cases they're quite a bit less so)—it becomes increasingly difficult to imagine there are persistent obstacles to success. Already imbued with the ideology of meritocracy as a condition of simply living in America, we can look around, see all these "proofs" of that ideology—folks who came from nothing and now have their own show, lots of money and fame—and then fail to question if what we're seeing is really representative of a larger truth. When people can go on one or another talent show, from *American Idol* to *So You Think You Can Dance?* and become overnight sensations, or develop a YouTube station or Snapchat or Instagram following with just a bit of creativity and a gimmick, it becomes ever easier for people to believe that anyone can make it, and if you don't, you have only yourself to blame.

Also, to the extent so many of the reality shows revolve around competition, in which individuals are seeking to outdo others (to become the last person on the island, to be the best chef according to a handful of pompous judges, to become the best fashion designer or drag queen, or to snag the bachelor or bachelorette), the mentality that competition is the key to success is reinforced. Don't misunderstand: these shows can be entertaining, and occasionally, in spite of themselves, they might even manage to teach valuable lessons. But competition is no more natural to human existence and success than cooperation and collaboration. Yet the motif of most reality TV is about the former and not the latter: it plays to one part of the national and even human experience while largely neglecting the other. If the competition were merely of the kind one can see in an athletic event, it wouldn't be so ideological in nature; after all, most of us realize that professional athletes have rare skills, and that not everyone can make it in such a field. But reality shows, by virtue of featuring incredibly average people in most cases, are different. We can see ourselves as the Storage Wars people, or that guy who owns the pawnshop in Detroit or the Orange County Chopper folks; not literally, of course, but in the sense that they are average, hard-working people who have made a name for themselves, and so why can't we, why can't you, why can't *anybody?*

Beyond mere speculation, recent research on television viewing, and especially genre-specific viewing of reality shows, confirms a correlation between watching such programming and a greater likelihood of believing in meritocracy, even after other factors that can influence such belief systems are held constant.[8] Granted, there are shows in the reality genre that offer a very different message. *Undercover Boss*, for instance, sends company CEOs into the workplace as average low-wage employees, their identity unknown to their co-workers, and in each episode the boss learns something valuable about how hard their employees work, and how much their own success depends upon the effort of those below them. It is a powerful episodic rebuttal to the myth of meritocracy. But sadly, it is one show in a sea of others that daily reinforce the dominant narrative.

Whatever the source of meritocratic faith, there is little argument that it has demonstrated a remarkable staying power over the generations and that it complicates attempts by progressives to successfully push for policies that would reduce inequalities of income and wealth. Yet it appears as though most liberals are deathly afraid of challenging the notion of meritocracy or questioning the rugged-individualist narrative that undergirds it. It is the rare politician of either party, or the rare political commentator who doesn't appear compelled to mouth the words of this secular gospel. We are just as likely to hear Barack Obama or Hillary Clinton express confidence that the United States is "the greatest nation on earth," or that "anyone can make it in America," or that one can "be and do anything if you're willing to work for it," as we are to hear those sentiments from Mitt Romney or Rush Limbaugh. Oh sure, the former may say these things a bit less bombastically, but they say them nonetheless.

At the Democratic National Convention in 2012, one after another speaker proclaimed their faith in America as a uniquely good and great nation. San Antonio mayor Julian Castro delivered the keynote address, in which he exclaimed: "Ours is a nation like no other. . . . No matter who you are or where you come from, the path is always forward." Then, First Lady Michelle Obama, speaking of the people she had met during the campaign, added: "Every day they make me proud. Every day they remind me how blessed we are to live in the greatest nation on earth." Finally, it was the president's turn to offer up homilies to the nation's greatness, and he did not disappoint, exhorting the audience that, "We keep our eyes fixed on that distant horizon knowing that Providence is with us and that we are surely blessed to be citizens of the greatest nation on earth."[9] In other words, not only are we the best, and a land where anyone can make it, but God Almighty is on our side as well. And if you can't manage to make it with *God* riding shotgun, then seriously, what in the world is wrong with you? On other occasions, President Obama has specifically nodded to American greatness with reference to the supposed economic opportunity the nation provides, as in 2011, when he noted: "What's great about this country is our belief that anyone can make it and everybody should be able to try—the idea that any one of us can open a business or have an idea and make us millionaires or billionaires. This is the land of opportunity."[10] Indeed, and contrary to conservative criticisms that the president doesn't accept the sacrosanct notion of American exceptionalism—accusations recently made yet again by former New York City mayor Rudy Giuliani—*Slate* magazine recently compiled video, taken from thirteen different speeches between 2004 and 2014 in which the president has explicitly bowed to the idea that the United States is the greatest nation on earth.[11]

Though we have come to expect such rhetoric and to consider it almost obligatory within our political system, the articulation of such uncritical praise and confidence carries a cost. When our leaders on both sides of the dominant political aisle reinforce the notion of the United States as an land of unfettered opportunity, it makes seeing the existence of systemic barriers to opportunity more difficult. And for progressives, it makes pushing for real change incredibly complicated. The president is a good example of someone who often mixes a stated faith in meritocracy with calls for substantive change (to health care or the tax structure for instance), and in so doing often fails to convince large segments of the public. And he fails not because of the inadequacy of his rhetoric, but because it is rhetoric with a mixed message, and one that cannot compete in many ways with the much less complicated message of the right.

For instance, when the president says America is essentially awesome, but then says that despite our awesomeness, we really need to change some things because there are very serious problems—inadequate health care coverage, inadequate schools for millions, not enough job opportunities, and a tax structure that doesn't ask enough from the wealthy—the second part of the comment is thoroughly undermined by the first, especially when the other side makes things much easier. To conservatives, we don't need change. America is the best: always was, always will be; we don't need to fundamentally alter anything about our policies or our system of governance. This is a much easier message to hear, and for those with the luxury of believing in meritocracy (especially white men, who have increasingly become the base of Republican voting), the less complicated message hits home, while the mixed message of "we're the best, but we could be better" gets lost in translation. People of color might still support progressive policies because their experience tells them that meritocracy is an unfulfilled and often hollow promise, but for white Americans who have experienced just enough opportunity and privilege to believe the myth, progressive policies (even the watered-down versions offered by the president) are a bridge too far. Given the choice between the cheerleader party and debate team party, it's not surprising which one the dominant group is more likely to choose.

Only by directly confronting the myth of meritocracy—indeed the very idea that the United States is, at present, a land of unfettered opportunity—might progressives build the kinds of coalitions needed to truly replace a culture of cruelty with a culture of compassion. But how might we go about doing it? The thought of pushing back against the central organizing principle of a society can be daunting, somewhat like questioning the existence of God while sitting in the front pew of a church. To question the secular gospel of one's society is to be seen as hostile to the nation itself. This is doubtless why the more radical left has often failed to gain much steam, what with our tendencies to rail against the institutional evils of the American empire as if those evils were immutable, indelible and unalterable flaws that rendered the nation worthy of utter collapse. But surely it doesn't have to be that way. The problem, or so it seems, is not with the *concept* of meritocracy, let alone equal opportunity in the abstract; the problem is that the *ideology* of meritocracy and equal opportunity is at war with the ideal. America is living a fundamental contradiction, forcing its people to accept a horrific moral compromise in the process.

Ideologies and ideals are not the same. An ideal is something to which we aspire, and something we are hoping to become, either as individuals or societies. To aspire to be a place where opportunity is open and equal for all is a noble goal. The notion that America should be a place where anyone and everyone can carve out a life for themselves and their families—a place where everyone has the chance to truly offer their unique gifts and talents to the larger society—is a valuable one. It is a concept that transcends ideological lines and speaks to an ideal of a society in which there are no systemic impediments to the exercise of individual initiative, autonomy and creativity. The ideal of achieving such a place where persons are free to pursue their own dreams and interests is an admirable quest to be sure.

But an ideology is a philosophical prism through which one tries to make sense of the world as it is; looked at that way, meritocracy becomes a straitjacket—an almost scriptural explanation for everything, nearly as concrete and powerful as Biblical injunctions themselves. Armed with the *ideology* of freedom and meritocracy, a nation becomes less self-reflective. Such a nation is not aspiring to anything, because it already *is* an exceptional place with exceptional people; it needn't change, evolve or grow in any real sense; it is not an infant but a fully realized and actualized adult—the greatest nation in the history of the world.

To the extent that the ideology of individualism and meritocracy is at war with the *ideal* of equal opportunity and mobility, Americans will have to choose which is more important to them.

Are we more committed to the ideology than the ideal? Or do we value the ideal more than the mantra? To the extent we remain wedded to the ideology of an equal-opportunity meritocracy, the ideal of an *actual* equal-opportunity society becomes almost impossible to obtain. They cannot coexist, because if one already believes America is that place, then faced with the unemployed, underemployed or poor, one isn't likely to give them much of a chance: to hire them, to invest in their business idea, or to view them in the classroom as truly capable. The ability of such persons to actually get a shot to prove their talents becomes more remote, precisely because we are given to viewing them as damaged goods. There must be something *wrong* with them if they've been out of work for twenty-six weeks, or if they live in *that* part of town, or if they receive a housing voucher to help pay their rent. Only by relinquishing faith in the ideology of meritocracy might we actually ever develop into one, because only by divorcing the ideology can we expect people to get the chance to fully and equitably demonstrate their abilities, talents and gifts.

More complicated still, if we choose the ideal over the ideology, how do we challenge those who are still committed to the last of these? How do we get people to hear us when we say that America is living a lie? How do we persuade people, most of whom have internalized the meritocratic notion for their entire lives, that we are not a place of equal opportunity, but rather, a place where the game is rigged, and increasingly so, to the benefit of a few and against the interests of the rest? It's no easy sale, but it seems to me that there is a way. As I've demonstrated earlier, there is ample evidence that the affluent minority is undermining the ideal of America, and that *they* are subverting Americanism in its best sense. It is *their* tax breaks, *their* preferential treatment in the courts, *their* dynastic wealth, and the subsidies *they* receive from the government—from banker bailouts to annual tax subsidies—that undermine the ideal of meritocracy, equal opportunity and justice for all. Far from junking the ideal of meritocracy and equal opportunity, the left must reclaim it by demonstrating that it is the financial elitists who are at war with those notions. Importantly, it isn't sufficient to make that case in purely data-driven terms. We must make it in cultural terms, flipping the script on the common and derogatory critiques of the poor by casting our judgmental eyes directly to the wealthy. It isn't the culture of poverty we should be concerned about, but the culture of predatory affluence. The right, in other words, is correct: The problem in America is a values problem. But the values that are the problem are not the values of the poor and working class. The values that should disturb us are those that reside at the top. As the old saying goes: the fish rots from the head down.

One thing is for sure: by failing to directly confront the notions of meritocracy and rugged individualism as the key to success, progressives will struggle to build large-scale movements for change. So long as meritocracy is accepted as a reality rather than an aspiration, and so long as equal opportunity is understood not as an ideal but as an existential fact, any call for significant changes in the society and its policies will fail to resonate. Only by moving forward with a narrative of aspiration—and only by demonstrating how the aspiration is blocked by the economic aristocracy to the detriment of the rest of us and the society we share—can we undermine the cornerstone of the culture of cruelty. The myth of meritocracy is the bedrock upon which that culture was constructed. It won't be taken apart unless we dig it up. We'll return to how this might be done, but first, let's look at the second force that helps perpetuate a culture of cruelty, and has fed hostility against the poor and underemployed in recent years. Unless we understand this one too, movements for economic justice will likely fall short.

Racism, White Resentment and the Culture of Cruelty

As mentioned earlier, many are quick to point to the historical weakness of the labor movement and the lack of a labor-based party in the U.S. as a central reason for weaker safety nets in America, when contrasted to other Western industrialized nations. It's an argument with significant historical resonance, but it still begs the question *why*? Why has it been so much harder for labor unions to gain strength in the United States? Why has there been no effective labor party to develop in America, even as such parties have been quite common elsewhere? Why have working-class consciousness and the political movements that typically flow from that consciousness been generally weaker here than in other nations?

Although there are likely several answers to these questions, among the most accurate would be the role of racism in dividing working-class folks along lines of racial and ethnic identities. The development of the class structure in the United States has been, from the beginning, interwoven with the development of white supremacy. Indeed, a fair reading of those dual histories suggests that white supremacy and the elevation of whites *as whites* above persons of color, even when both shared similar class positions, has been critical in the shoring up of class division. Race, in other words, has been a weapon with which the rich have divided working people from one another and prevented white working folks from developing a strong identification with their counterparts of color. Unless we address racial inequity and racism—and especially as linchpins to the maintenance of economic inequity and class division—it will be impossible to solve these issues. Sadly, most Americans appear not to comprehend this truism. So, for instance, in a recent survey, while eighty percent claimed the government should focus "a lot" or "a great deal" of effort on addressing economic inequality, only twenty-six percent said the same about the issue of racism and racial inequity, suggesting that the connections between the two are not well understood.[12]

The history of whiteness as a wedge between working-class people—and as a key element in the perpetuation of economic inequity—goes back to the early colonies in the Americas. As theologian and scholar Thandeka explains, discussing the late seventeenth and early eighteenth centuries:

> The legislators (in the Virginia colony) also raised the status of white servants, workers, and the white poor. . . . Until then the European indentured servants had lived and worked under the same conditions as the African slaves, the chief difference in their status being that the Europeans' servitude was contracted for a specified period whereas the slaves, and their progeny, served for life. In 1705, the assembly required masters to provide white servants at the end of their indentureship with corn, money, a gun, clothing, and 50 acres of land. The poll tax was also reduced. As a result of these legally sanctioned changes in poor whites' economic position, they gained legal, political, emotional, social, and financial status that depended directly on the concomitant degradation of Indians and Negroes.[13]

The decision to elevate poor and landless Europeans above blacks and indigenous peoples was a conscious one, made so as to safeguard the position of the economic minority relative to the general citizenry from whom they feared cross-racial, class-based rebellion. Collaborations between poor Europeans and Africans, and militant resistance to economic oppression, had frightened the Virginia planter class during Bacon's Rebellion in 1676, leading to the passage of the above-mentioned laws granting so-called whites privileges previously denied to the poor. Fear of further cross-racial alliances led to the abolition of European indentured servitude altogether in the first decade of the eighteenth century, much as it had led colonial leaders in the British West Indies to halt the importation of Irish servants to the island of Nevis, due to previous rebellions against the rich fomented by a combination of poor Europeans and African slaves there.

To limit the prospects for working-class and peasant-class consciousness across racial lines, the colonial ruling class passed further laws requiring plantation owners to employ a certain number of whites for every African they held in bondage, thereby yoking white employment opportunities to the institution of slavery. Other laws barred blacks from certain trades altogether, in effect reserving those for whites, further linking the enslavement of blacks to the relative elevation of whites, even those without land.[14] Still other laws required whites to serve on slave patrols and help control blacks, thereby creating the perception among even poor European peoples that they were members of one big team, along with the rich.

It was a powerful trick. After all, logic would suggest that poor and landless Europeans should have recognized the economic harm done to their own interests from human trafficking and enslavement. Obviously, if a plantation owner has to pay white people to work on their farm but can force black people to do it for free because he actively enslaves them, the employment and wage base for white workers is effectively undermined. But by way of these laws meant to create racialized status for poor Europeans (now and for the first time called white), the wealthy managed to elevate such peasants just sufficiently to make their objective class interests literally pale in comparison to their racial ones.

It was this elevation of whiteness at the expense of class interests that helped convince most white Southerners to support secession and the maintenance of a free market in buying, selling and trafficking black families. Even though the wealthy were able to escape military service during the civil war if they owned a sufficient number of Africans—a kind of class privilege one might expect to rankle poor whites who would have to take up the slack and risk their own lives to protect the power of the planter elite—working-class whites typically fell in line, fighting and dying to protect a way of life the benefits of which were mostly enjoyed by persons unlike themselves. Indeed, the Southern aristocracy knew that only by seceding from the union and rebelling openly against the anti-slavery Republican party of Lincoln might poor whites be kept in line. Three-quarters of Southern whites didn't enslave blacks; as such they might not be as committed to maintaining the market in human beings, or white supremacy—the institution that Confederate vice-president Alexander Stephens called the "cornerstone" of the breakaway government. In 1859, giving voice to concerns that poor and landless whites may prove insufficient support for wealthy interests in the face of class-conscious anti-slavery forces, one South Carolina politician exclaimed: "I mistrust our own people more than I fear all the efforts of the Abolitionists."[15] It was for this reason that Southern lawmakers often tried to pass laws encouraging all whites to own at least one slave and even offering tax breaks and financial incentives to make such ownership possible. Why? Because, as one Tennessee planter explained it: "The minute you put it out of the power of common farmers to purchase a Negro man or woman . . . you make him an abolitionist at once."[16]

In 1860, Stephen Hale of Alabama wrote to the governor of Kentucky in his official capacity as Commissioner to that state, in an attempt to convince him of the propriety of joining the Confederate government. Therein, he appealed directly to the importance of maintaining white supremacy even for the non-slaveholding class:

> If the policy of the Republicans is carried out . . . and the South submits, degradation and ruin must overwhelm alike all classes of citizens in the Southern States. The slaveholder and non-slave-holder must ultimately share the same fate—all be degraded to a position of equality with free Negroes, stand side by side with them at the polls, and fraternize in all the social relations of life. . . . Who can look upon such a picture without a shudder? What Southern man, be he slave-holder or non-slave-holder, can without indignation and horror contemplate the triumph of negro equality, and see his own sons and daughters, in the not distant future, associating with free negroes upon terms of political and social equality, and the white man stripped, by the Heaven-daring hand

> of fanaticism of that title to superiority over the black race which God himself has bestowed?[17]

Even in the North, these kinds of appeals were common. During the Civil War, Democratic politicians in places like New York appealed to Irish working-class racism, warning that if blacks were emancipated, it would cause a human flood northward to "steal the work and the bread of the honest Irish."[18] In short, the rich sought to sow fear of racial equality, appealing to whiteness as a virtually corporate identity, even as most poor whites—South and North—would have been better off financially had white enslavement of blacks been abolished. Linking the degradation of people of color to the elevation of whites was a narrative and material strategy deployed so as to create a very particular kind of class consciousness in the majority population: a class consciousness that would prioritize one's racial class (or perhaps more properly, *caste*) over economic station.

After the Civil War, industrial capitalism and the organizing of working-class Americans in both North and South followed the developing racial script as well. Convinced that integrated labor federations would somehow "degrade" the quality of work or the social status of white workers, most labor leaders expressed openly racist and hostile views about blacks and Asian labor, about Mexicans and all workers of color. Furthermore, people of color were kept from most of the largest trade unions for generations, as white workers sought to elevate their racial status above their class interests.[19] As one Texas railroader put it, faced with the prospect of admitting blacks to his union: "We would rather be absolute slaves of capital than to take the negro into our lodges as an equal and brother."[20]

The great sociologist W.E.B. Du Bois wrote extensively about the importance of working-class white racism in the early labor movement, and how white workers saw their short-term interests as being served by racial bonding against persons of color, given the white supremacist society in which they were living.

Even as racism diminished the strength of the labor movement in the long term—by providing bosses with a desperate pool of black and brown workers whom they could use to break strikes and to limit the militance of union demands—the "psychological wage" of whiteness remained real and was difficult to dilute. Du Bois noted that as regards white workers:

> While they received a low wage they were compensated in part by a sort of public and psychological wage. They were given public deference . . . because they were white. They were admitted freely, with all classes of white people, to public functions. . . . The police were drawn from their ranks, and the courts dependent upon their votes treated them with leniency.[21]

Not only in regard to black labor, but also to the labor of Chinese railroad workers, whites found their class status elevated ever so slightly by way of racial domination. When tens of thousands of Chinese were brought to America to help lay the transcontinental railroad, white workers were pacified by promises that far from taking white men's jobs, Chinese "mudsills" would create a need for new foremen who would exercise authority over the Asian newcomers. During a Congressional investigation into the use of Chinese labor in the 1870s, Charles Crocker—who was a board member of the Central Pacific Railroad Company—explained the way in which the exploitation of Chinese workers had elevated white labor:

> I believe that the effect of Chinese labor upon white labor has an elevating instead of degrading tendency. I think that every white man who is intelligent and able to work, who is more than a digger in a ditch . . . who has the capacity of being something else, can get to be something else by the presence of Chinese labor. [A]fter we got Chinamen to work, we took the more intelligent

> of the white laborers and made foremen of them. I know of several of them now who never expected, never had a dream that they were going to be anything but shovelers of dirt, hewers of wood and drawers of water, and they are now respectable farmers, owning farms. They got their start by controlling Chinese labor on our railroad.[22]

Discussing Du Bois's analysis, historian David Roediger notes, "The pleasures of whiteness could function as a 'wage' for white workers." That is, "status and privileges conferred by race could be used to make up for alienating and exploitative class relationships."[23] The problem, of course, was that by opting for the "property" of whiteness (as UCLA law professor Cheryl Harris has termed it), white workers and their labor unions managed to trade class interests for racial ones, and in so doing limited the ability of unions *as unions* to raise labor's negotiating power here to levels that were seen elsewhere. The whites turned into foremen on the railroads may have benefited from their newfound middle-management positions, but for most whites (who indeed were not so elevated), the promise of advancement was little more than a trick; it was ultimately a way to dampen class-based discontent and keep white workers in line as the new go-between, running interference for the white aristocracy against workers of color. Racism ultimately created real material advancement for a few, but at the cost of splitting the economic coalitions that would likely have otherwise developed. It is in much the same way that the late nineteenth-century Populist Party (an early iteration of a labor-farmer party in America) was ultimately weakened by racism, when white workers in the movement were turned against workers of color by blatant appeals to white supremacy.[24]

This history matters: it is one thing, after all, to note the relative weakness of labor in the United States when compared to labor organizing in other nations—something most all on the left are quick to do—but it is quite another to confront the role that the racism of white people has played in that comparative weakness and then seek to address it directly. Consider, for instance, how much more vital the American labor movement could have been, had it not fallen prey to the kind of racism voiced in the main publication of the American Federation of Labor (AFL) in 1910, regarding Mexican labor from over the border:

> Cheap labor, yes, at the sacrifice of manhood and homes and all that go to build up and sustain a community. Cheap labor—at the cost of every ideal cherished in the heart of every member of the white race, utterly destroyed and buried beneath the greedy ambitions of a few grasping money gluttons. . . . True Americans do not want or advocate the importation of any people who cannot be absorbed into full citizenship, who cannot eventually be raised to our highest social standard.[25]

In short, rather than embrace Mexican working people and bring them into the unions—where they would then have helped to form a broader force of workers—here, the leaders of the nation's largest union federation were suggesting that the enemy was other working people. They were willing to make permanent outsiders of brown-skinned "foreign" labor—ostensibly to better fight the money-grubbing of the wealthy, whom they recognized as using Mexican workers for less pay—never noticing that in so doing they would force an alliance between those workers of color and the employers, while doing little to help themselves. Again, racism ultimately weakened the position of workers—all workers—relative to capital.

The sorry process was repeated with regard to blacks. In 1917, the horrific anti-black pogrom that touched off in East St. Louis, Illinois—in which 150 were killed, including thirty-nine children—was sparked by the hiring of blacks by companies there, seeking to break white unions. By promising job opportunities to blacks willing to move from the South, these companies took advantage of union racism and sought to pit struggling blacks against struggling whites. And it worked; when large numbers of African Americans made the journey to East St. Louis, settling there in hopes of steady employment, white anger grew, not against the bosses who were using both groups of workers, but against the burgeoning black community, finally erupting in an orgy of violence.[26]

By the 1920s, playing upon the unwillingness of white unions to integrate, managers in the stockyards and packing houses actually helped create an all-black union—but one that was beholden to the company and its leadership. Led by an African American promoter named Richard Parker, the "American Unity Labor Union" worked to sow suspicion of the dominant white labor movement and white workers, all so as to benefit the interests of company elites. Announcing that the black union did not believe in strikes, and that all differences "between laborers and capitalists can be arbitrated" (and mixing in a dose of pseudo-black nationalism so as to promote race pride and unity) Parker's group did the bidding of capital—the point being, such a thing was only possible because the white unions had sought to remain segregated in the first place.[27]

Elsewhere, in places like New Orleans, employers began hiring Irish, and then Italians, to replace blacks in canal building and hospitality jobs such as in restaurants and hotels, as well as barbering, janitorial work and catering.[28] Though none of these positions paid exorbitant wages, they provided new economic niches for recent white immigrants, once again creating a link—both material and psychological—between the subordination of African Americans and the relative elevation of whites; it was a link that held despite the fact that those white workers remained dominated in the larger class structure by economic minorities who, in the end, cared little more for them than for those persons of color whose mistreatment had been longstanding.

In addition to weakening the labor movement—and thereby helping to enhance the class position of the nation's ruling aristocracy and the culture of cruelty over which it presides—there is another important way in which racism has furthered the economic inequality and injustice that are the hallmarks of that culture. Specifically, racism has been critical to driving down support for any form of safety nets or social programs to benefit low-income, unemployed and impoverished Americans. It is impossible to understand the last forty-plus years of backlash to safety-net programs and taxation, or the growing opposition to government intervention in the economy, without understanding the politics of race. Although not all persons opposed to such efforts are racists, the anti-tax, anti–government spending, anti–welfare state narrative since the mid-1960s has been intimately intertwined with issues of white resentment toward people of color, especially blacks; and that narrative linkage has impacted the way in which the white public has come to understand efforts that are portrayed as examples of "big government."

That the culture of cruelty is beholden to the racialization of social policy is hardly arguable among those who have closely observed American politics over the past half-century. By deliberately linking poverty and economic need with an image of African Americans, and by encouraging resentments against social programs for the poor by linking them to people of color—all while crafting a narrative that those persons of color are undeserving, lazy, culturally pathological and defective—conservatives have managed to indelibly smear programs of social uplift, and key elements of a safety net that a few generations before had been popular.

In the 1930s and 1940s, New Deal programs and other government interventions to shore up job and housing opportunity enjoyed widespread support. Although the rich no doubt viewed the unemployed and poor as moral slackers who deserved their plight—and surely saw themselves as superior in intellect, work ethic and character—few among the masses would have believed either of those things to be true. The idea that the rich had more because they were better, and the poor and unemployed lacked because of their own defects would have struck most average folks as absurd, at least when applied to white Americans. These kinds of hostile views about blacks and other people of color were quite common, but when it came to white farmers in the Dust Bowl Midwest, or white factory workers, or whites on bread lines or riding the rails looking for jobs, the general consensus would have been that these were hard-working, salt-of-the-earth types whose misfortune owed little to their own character, but rather, were the result of structural forces beyond their control. The wealthy minority despised him, but the hobo was a hero to many, about whom some of the nation's most beloved folks songs were written.

Thanks to the widespread pain experienced by millions during the Depression, and the resulting recognition that state intervention was critical in making real the American dream, government job programs were overwhelmingly popular. Likewise, housing programs initiated by the government, like those of the Federal Housing Administration and the Home Owners Loan Corporation (HOLC)—which provided low-interest loans to millions of families who otherwise could never have qualified for a mortgage—were well received. Few voices among the masses could have been heard critiquing such efforts as "big government" intrusions into the magic of the free market. The masses had gotten a dose of what the free market had to offer, and most of them were none too impressed.

So long as these efforts—which pumped billions of dollars of income and capital into almost exclusively white hands, and created the white middle class[29]—were racially restrictive, they remained popular.[30] In fact, it was precisely the exclusion of blacks and other racial minorities from these programs that allowed them to be passed by Congress in the first place. Southern congressmen, seeking to maintain authoritarian control of blacks and prevent them from having alternatives to low-wage, segregated employment, pushed President Roosevelt to accept provisions in his social programs that would elevate whites and marginalize persons of color, as a condition of gaining their support. Only by excluding agricultural and domestic workers from Social Security for instance—an exclusion that would remain in place for two decades—could FDR secure the votes of Southerners in his own party for the creation of the government retirement program. Because eighty percent or more of blacks in the South worked in those two areas, excluding them from Social Security meant that racist control of black labor could continue unabated, and white employers would be freed from the burden of contributing to retirement funds for their black employees.

So too, the Federal Housing Administration guaranteed low-interest loans for families, but relied on neighborhood "desirability" criteria that all but guaranteed the beneficiaries would be exclusively white. As Rudolph Alexander explains:

> Because the federal government was guaranteeing mortgages [it] did not want to make these highly desirable terms available to all people in the United States. Thus the federal government sought to evaluate all properties so that banks would know what type of property merited a federally backed loan. This enormous task of classifying properties fell to a newly created agency in 1936—the Home Owners Loan Corporation (HOLC). HOLC established strict standards. A surveyor looked for any sign . . . that a neighborhood was in decline. The surveyor would look for any sign of minorities. . . . Even one African American in a neighborhood would disqualify the entire neighborhood from getting any federally backed loans.[31]

Maintaining economic apartheid and ratifying white privilege in the housing market became central to the offering of government-backed loans under the FHA program. Indeed, the FHA stipulated as a condition of underwriting properties, "If a neighborhood is to retain stability, it is necessary that properties shall continue to be occupied by the same social and racial classes."[32] In effect, this meant that people of color couldn't get loans in rapidly growing white suburbs throughout the 1940s and 1950s, locking them within crowded urban spaces, while freeing up opportunity for whites whose only chance at accessing such loans would be in all-white communities outside the cities.

In this sense, the U.S. government subsidized racial isolation and separation—apartheid—in the process helping to pump billions of dollars worth of housing equity into white hands, while denying the same to people of color. Needless to say, throughout this period, few if any white families complained about the "heavy hand of government" when it came to housing policy; after all, that hand was literally lining their pockets to the exclusion of African Americans and other persons of color. Complaints about taxes being too high so as to finance these big government initiatives were few and far between, even though tax rates were far higher throughout this period than they are today, with the top rate holding at ninety-one percent for most of the 1950s.[33] Apparently, white people didn't mind government spending so long as the presumptive beneficiaries looked like them. If anything, receiving an FHA loan, or taking advantage of the G.I. Bill—job and educational benefits that were theoretically open to all veterans, but were administered in blatantly racist ways—was a badge of honor for millions.

It was only when people of color began to gain significant access to government programs (and once they became the public face of government programs more broadly) that suddenly the so-called evil of an overly intrusive "nanny state" came to be seen as a problem. Even cash welfare for mothers with children—originally created as "mothers' pensions" as a way to allow white moms to stay home with their kids if their husbands had died or if they had left the family to look for work—had been relatively popular. The thinking, though clearly sexist for how it characterized the "proper" domain of women, was widely accepted:

> By providing mothers a pension—essentially small cash payments from the government—the program would

> enable single mothers to forgo paid work and attend to children in their own home. Advocates suggested that mothers would no longer suffer the fear of leaving children with strangers, the strain of working all day in a factory, or the pain of having their families separated. A mothers' pension would restore the proper—even sacred—domestic role to those women who struggled alone without a male breadwinner to make ends meet.[34]

Although there were expressed concerns about these efforts even for white women—some believed, for instance, that too generous a pension for mothers would relieve women of the "need" for a husband—and although there were harsh regulations put in place that sought to police the sexual morality of recipients, administrators were especially frugal about distributing monies to African American women. By 1933, only three percent of mother's pensions went to black women, despite their far greater level of economic need.[35]

Once mothers' pensions were formally replaced by ADC, restrictions on black access to the program continued, in large measure at the behest of Southern administrators who policed the boundaries of the program in explicitly racist ways, deeming the homes of African American women "unfit" for benefits.[36] The extent to which race drove growing hostility to cash welfare was most apparent in states like Louisiana, where lawmakers passed a "suitable home" law in 1960 that bumped nearly 30,000 mothers and children—ninety-five percent of them black—from the ADC rolls. The bill, supported by Governor Jimmy Davis, who had previously called mothers receiving assistance "a bunch of prostitutes," was part of a larger package of legislative initiatives in response to desegregation efforts in Louisiana schools—a kind of payback for even the smallest victories over institutional white supremacy.[37]

Throughout the 1960s, as women of color increasingly gained access to cash assistance (now renamed AFDC), opposition to the efforts proliferated, as did attacks on recipients. Thanks to the efforts of the welfare rights movement, AFDC enrollment rolls nearly tripled over a ten-year period from the mid-1960s to the mid-1970s, in large measure by allowing backlogged cases of black applicants to move through the process.[38] On the one hand, this opening of the rolls was of real benefit to black families, allowing them to better support themselves; but on the other, the increasing 'blackness' of such programs in the white imagination helped plant the seeds of backlash with which we are still grappling. Thanks to the "blackening" of welfare in the public mind, ideas like a guaranteed minimum income for all families—prominently endorsed for a brief while by several on both the right and left of the political spectrum (though differing on the specifics)—ultimately were scuttled. In 1972, during Senate Finance Committee hearings on the Family Assistance Plan (President Nixon's guaranteed income proposal), Senator Russell Long of Louisiana explained his opposition by noting that if poor women were guaranteed a minimal income he wouldn't be able to find anyone "to iron my shirts." In other words, and especially in the South, state support for the poor through AFDC or with a guaranteed income would cause a shortage of domestic help performed mostly by black women in white homes.[39]

By the mid to late 1970s, with the image of welfare thoroughly racialized thanks to persistent media imagery that reinforced these notions,[40] it became easy for manipulative politicians to play to those tropes, knowing that appeals to "less government," advocating "lower taxes" and attacking "welfare fraud" would pay dividends at the polls. Occasionally, conservatives would even admit this had been their strategy. Lee Atwater, for instance—among the most successful and powerful Republican campaign operatives in the past half-century—acknowledged the racial subtext of his party's rhetoric on matters of government, taxes and the like. In a now-infamous 1981 interview, Atwater explained how people like him and the candidates he worked for (including Ronald Reagan), deftly used abstract racial imagery to make the same appeals that a generation before would have been far more explicit.

> You start out in 1954 by saying, "Nigger, nigger, nigger. . . . " By 1968 you can't say "nigger"—that hurts you. Backfires. So you say stuff like forced busing, states' rights and all that stuff. You're getting so abstract now [that] you're talking about cutting taxes, and all these things you're talking about are totally economic things and a byproduct of them is [that] blacks get hurt worse than whites. . . . Obviously sitting around saying, "We want to cut this," is much more abstract than even the busing thing, and a hell of a lot more abstract than "Nigger, nigger."[41]

In a similar vein, and in keeping with the importance of covering up the racist underbelly of conservative politics with language that wasn't explicitly bigoted, consider the words of Richard Nixon's White House chief of staff, H.R. Haldeman: In his diary, Haldeman made note of Nixon's insistence that "you have to face the fact that the whole problem is really the blacks. The key is to devise a system that recognized this while not appearing to."[42]

As conservatives and the Republican Party increasingly pushed buttons of racial resentment, while studiously avoiding the kinds of explicitly racist rhetoric common to previous reactionary politicians, the linkage between liberal social policy and handouts to African Americans became firmly concretized in the public mind. This was especially true for the working class whites who had long been a key part of the Democratic Party's base. As David Dante Troutt notes in his recent book, *The Price of Paradise:*

> By 1984, when Ronald Reagan and George Bush beat Walter Mondale and Geraldine Ferraro in the presidential election, many white Democratic voters had come to read their own party's messages through what Edsall calls a "racial filter." In their minds, higher taxes were directly attributable to policies of a growing federal government;

> they were footing the bill for minority preference programs. If the public argument was cast as wasteful spending on people of weak values, the private discussions were explicitly racial. For instance, Edsall quotes polling studies of "Reagan Democrats" in Macomb County—the union friendly Detroit suburbs that won the battle to prevent cross-district school desegregation plans in 1973—that presents poignant evidence of voter anger: "These white Democratic defectors express a profound distaste for blacks, a sentiment that pervades almost everything they think about government and politics. . . . Blacks constitute the explanation for [white defectors'] vulnerability and for almost everything that has gone wrong in their lives; not being black is what constitutes being middle class; not living with blacks is what makes a neighborhood a decent place to live. These sentiments have important implications for Democrats, as virtually all progressive symbols and themes have been redefined in racial and pejorative terms."[43]

It was this racialization of liberal and Democratic social policy, more than any other factor, which convinced white working-class and middle-class voters to support supply-side economics. After all, the fundamental premise of conservative economic policy by the 1980s was that taxes should be slashed for the wealthy so that the benefits might "trickle down" to the rest of us. It was a notion that would have met with widespread derision from most voters in the past, and which had never held much sway for them in previous decades, where direct government intervention to boost wages and job opportunities had long been the favored policies. But once taxes came to be seen largely as a redistribution scheme in which "productive" (read: white) people were burdened so as to benefit "lazy" (read: black) people, calls for tax cuts no longer required that one agree with or even understand the economic rationale for them; all that mattered now was that such cuts would stick it to blacks on behalf of a beleaguered and fiscally burdened white electorate. As Troutt explains, "Only racism could achieve the ideological union of the Republican rich with the working man (and woman). Nothing else could fuse their naturally opposed interests."

And when one considers that Reagan-era policies actually resulted in a *higher* tax burden for most working-class and middle-class Americans—and a cut only for wealthier types—it becomes even harder to square white working-class support for such policies with any notion of actual material self-interest. It was the rhetoric of smaller government and cutting taxes on the rich (envisioned as hard-working, as contrasted with folks of color) that made the difference, no matter the practical impact of trickle-down policies. Troutt continues:

> Edsall provides data on the combined federal tax rate that includes all taxes—income, Social Security, and so forth. Between 1980 and 1990, families in the bottom fifth of all earners saw their rates increase by 16.1 percent; [they] increased by 6 percent for those in the second-lowest fifth [and] by 1.2 percent for those in the middle fifth. . . . But those in the second-highest fifth of all income earners saw a cut in their tax rate by 2.2 percent . . . those in the top fifth got a 5.5 percent decrease [and] the richest 10 percent of American earners received a 7.3 percent decrease in their combined federal tax rate. The top 1 percent? A 14.4 percent cut . . . this hurt the middle class, as the vaunted trickle down never arrived. But it was working-class whites who bought the message that this model of fiscal conservatism, married to social conservatism in the form of a rollback of redistributive programs they perceived to favor blacks, would benefit them. It did not. Yet it established a popular political rhetoric by which lower-income whites can be counted on to take up against "liberal" policies that may

> actually serve their interests as long as opposition can be wrapped in the trappings of "traditional values," "law and order," "special interests," "reverse racism," and "smaller government." This was . . . based on an erroneous notion . . . that whatever "the blacks" get hurts me.[44]

Ultimately it was the moral posturing of middle- and working-class whites—the sense that they were arbiters of decency, values and "proper" behavior, contrasted with blacks, who were violators of all three—which allowed so many of them to vote against their direct and immediate material interests, or at least to define those interests in highly racialized ways. It is this moral wage—a slight deviation from what Du Bois called the "psychological wage" of whiteness—that traditional liberals, progressives and leftists have always managed to underestimate. So when asking "What's the Matter with Kansas?" as political theorist Thomas Frank has done in an attempt to understand why working-class and middle-class whites support policies that cater to the rich, the role of racial resentment is inevitably downplayed in favor of an analysis that focuses on religious manipulation over issues like abortion—anything but race.[45] Even progressive writers and theorists like Robert Reich, whom I've referenced several times, rarely talk much about racism and its centrality to white opposition to equity initiatives. And the Occupy movement, even as it raised issues of income and wealth inequality in America, largely ignored the centrality of race and racism to that inequality and the nation's larger ambivalence to it. It's as if white liberals and the white left are afraid to call out the obvious: Anger about big government is largely about the racialization of government efforts on behalf of the have-nots and have-lessers. Unless this reality is confronted, support for progressive social policy will be undermined, because a significant reason for opposition to such policies will go unaddressed.

Recent examples of how race frames our discussions about social policy abound, especially in the way that notions of moral deservingness influence that racial analysis. So, for instance, consider the way that the right talks about unemployment and poverty in the black community. As mentioned previously, it is common for conservatives to raise the issue of out-of-wedlock childbirth (or what they call "illegitimacy") as the supposed "real problem" confronting the poor, and particularly the African American poor. If black women, according to this argument, would just stop having babies outside of marriage, the problems would essentially disappear. To this end, they regularly claim that the "rate of out-of-wedlock births" in the black community has skyrocketed, presumably because welfare programs have encouraged this tendency, or at least not done enough to discourage it. The argument conjures images of sexually libidinous and irresponsible black women—literally breeding new generations of dangerous, un-fathered *others*—as literal incubators of social decay. Such an image engenders contempt for poor women and their families and allows the notion of "personal responsibility" for that condition to remain intact. And it is persuasive despite the fact that the narrative is *entirely false*.

Make no mistake: it is undeniably true that seventy-two percent of all African American babies born today are born to unwed mothers, and it is also the case that this percentage is nearly double the rate of black kids who were born to unwed moms in 1970, at which point only 37.5 percent of black children were born out of wedlock.[46] However, this figure does not mean what conservatives claim it means. While the political right uses these data to insist that black women and their male partners—and the larger culture from which they come—are increasingly irresponsible, the reality is, even though the share of out-of-wedlock births as a percentage of all black births has nearly doubled, the actual rate of births to unmarried black women has fallen dramatically. If these seemingly contradictory realities appear confusing to you, it's not your fault. Almost no one explains it, in some cases because they don't understand what's going on, and in others because they have a political motivation to lie.

Here's the thing: according to the Centers for Disease Control, the birth rate for unmarried black women *fell* by nearly a third between 1970 and 2010, from 95.5 births per 1,000 unmarried black women at the beginning of that period to only 65.3 births per 1,000 such women by the end of the period. Among black teenagers between fifteen and nineteen years of age (almost all of whom are unmarried), birth rates have plummeted since 1991, from 118.2 births for every 1,000 such girls to only 51.5 births per 1,000 such girls in 2010.[47] So just twenty years ago, black teens were having 2.3 times more children per capita than they are today. From 1970 to 2009, black teens between the ages of fifteen and nineteen cut their birth rates by sixty percent, while those between eighteen and nineteen reduced theirs by a third.[48] As a result of this apparently positive trend—but one that conservatives ignore—the black teen birth rate is at an all-time low. In other words, and whether we look at teens or adults, unmarried black women are *already doing* exactly what conservatives would have them do: namely, having fewer children. This means that if we are to view out-of-wedlock childbearing as evidence of cultural pathology, black culture must be getting healthier and *less* pathological, rather than more so.

So what about that seventy-two percent figure? The reason that the *share* of births that are out of wedlock has increased to seventy-two percent as opposed to the prior figure of 37.5 in 1970, is because although births to black unmarried women have fallen considerably, married black couples have cut back even *further* on childbearing.[49] So if married black couples are having far fewer children than before, and are cutting back even faster than single women, the overall percentage of births that are out of wedlock will rise, owing nothing to the supposedly irresponsible behaviors of single black folks. One could bring down the seventy-two percent figure just as easily by having married black couples each have ten kids, as by lecturing single black women to do what they're already doing—only *faster!* Strangely, no one on the right ever suggests *this* solution to the "problem," because—and

I'm just guessing here—they probably don't want lots more black people in America, whether or not those black people are growing up in two-parent homes. The hysteria over out-of-wedlock childbirth in the black community is little more than conjured fear-mongering—a conscious attempt to push buttons of racial anxiety and resentment rather to honestly examine cultural trends within our country.

Or consider the deft racialization of the health care debate in 2009. Although the Obama health care plan was criticized as far too moderate by most all persons on the left, conservatives managed to characterize it as a big government boondoggle, making it one of the most despised national efforts to help Americans in recent memory. Additionally, to help mobilize antipathy the right characterized it in blatantly racial terms. Conservative commentator Glenn Beck, for instance, said that the president's desire for broader health care availability was driven by his belief in "reparations for slavery," simply because people of color are disproportionately the ones lacking insurance, and thus would reap disproportionate benefits. On an intellectual level, the argument was quite obviously absurd (after all, what kind of reparations require beneficiaries to get sick first in order to get paid?), but it was genius politically, in that it was perfectly calculated to get a reaction.[50] By suggesting that any policy disproportionately benefiting those with lower income can be viewed as "payback for slavery"—since African Americans are disproportionately to be found among the poor—Beck could essentially prime the racial resentment that had animated white opposition to the notion of safety nets for forty-plus years. *Any* policy to assist the poor or unemployed, from unemployment insurance to college loan assistance to emergency food aid to early childhood education funding, can be seen as an anti-white confiscation scheme under this logic, thereby pushing buttons of racial resentment on cue when conjured by those like Beck.

And it wasn't only Beck who tried to link health care reform and racial payback in the public's mind. Rush Limbaugh said the same thing several months later,[51] referring to the president's health care reform proposal as a "civil rights bill" and "reparations," as did the folks at the FOX Nation website and *Investor's Business Daily*, the latter of which went so far as to refer to health care reform as "affirmative action on steroids," to make sure the message wasn't lost on anyone.[52]

Though one could perhaps argue that these claims are so ridiculous as to be entirely unpersuasive, there is evidence that such appeals can be quite effective in fostering race-based opposition to real policy proposals, even when those proposals are intended to bring universal and broad-based benefit. So consider public support for health care reform in the wake of Barack Obama's election as president. When studies were conducted in which white respondents were given a description of a health care reform plan and told it was Bill Clinton's 1993 proposal, they overwhelmingly supported it. Given the same proposal but told it was Barack Obama's health care reform plan, they overwhelmingly opposed it. And when it came to explaining the difference, the research found that whites who scored high on measures of racial resentment—believing, for instance, that blacks get "more than they deserve" from government—were the most likely to alter their perception of the proposal when they thought it was Obama's as opposed to Clinton's. Those who expressed the greatest level of racial resentment and were most likely to accept negative stereotypes of African Americans were nearly twice as likely as those with low levels of racial resentment to oppose health care reform when they thought Obama was its proponent as opposed to Clinton, suggesting that something other than mere partisanship can explain white opposition to health care reform.[53]

In other words, white opposition to national safety-net programs, from health care to cash assistance to nutrition aid and housing assistance, is shaped by the perception that the beneficiaries will be mostly people of color, and thus, undeserving. And this perception retains influence in spite of the reality that it is not mostly people of color who receive the benefits from government programs. While black folks comprise about twelve percent of the population, they receive only fourteen percent of government benefits, roughly in line with their population share and well below their percentage of the nation's poor, which stands at twenty-two percent. Although African Americans receive certain benefits disproportionately (because they are more likely to be from a low-income bracket and benefits are only available to persons earning less than a certain level of income), those disproportions are small. So, for instance, blacks receive about twenty-eight percent of SNAP benefits, which is roughly in keeping with their percentage of the population that is either poor or near poor and thus eligible. They receive only thirteen percent of unemployment benefits, which is below their share of the unemployed at any given moment. They receive twenty-one percent of school lunch benefits (in line with their share of those who qualify for them based on income), only thirteen percent of Medicare benefits, and twenty-two percent of Medicaid benefits, equal to their share of the poverty population.

Likewise, Latinos, who comprise sixteen percent of the population, and twenty-nine percent of the nation's poor, receive only twelve percent of government benefits. This includes only thirteen percent of unemployment compensation, twenty-three percent of SNAP benefits, five percent of Medicare benefits and twenty-one percent of Medicaid dollars spent. Meanwhile, whites, at forty-two percent of the nation's poverty population (and sixty-four percent of the overall population), receive sixty-nine percent of all government benefits. Although many of these dollars represent Social Security payments (which, it can be argued, were "earned" by defined contributions into the system during one's working years), it is still the case that whites receive sixty-eight percent of unemployment benefits, fifty-two percent of SSI benefits (mostly for those with disabilities), and forty-two percent of SNAP, as well as consuming eighty percent of Medicare expenditures and nearly six in ten Medicaid dollars.[54]

Right-wing commentators have consistently race-baited in

the Obama era, even attributing the president's re-election in 2012 to government handouts to voters of color. In case his listeners didn't fully appreciate the centrality of race to the welfare state, Limbaugh sought to make it clear in the immediate aftermath of the election, insisting that the only reason Obama defeated Mitt Romney was because, "We're talking about Santa Claus for the past couple, three days. Let's reach out to the Hispanic community and make sure they get the message here." Limbaugh then played Feliz Navidad on his show, while referring to the president as Baracka Claus, and comparing him to Papa Noel: the Spanish version of Santa, handing out gifts to people. That Rush is not much for subtlety should be obvious.[55]

The notion that Obama has "given things" to constituents of color, and that these handouts made the difference in his victories, has been central to the Republican spin on their 2012 electoral defeat. Mitt Romney said that the president won because he had effectively courted "especially the African-American community, the Hispanic community and young people. . . . In each case they were very generous in what they gave to those groups," as if to suggest that it was merely government handouts of one form or another that allowed President Obama to win re-election.[56] This position was further endorsed by former New Hampshire governor and Romney adviser John Sununu, who claimed that the reason for Obama's victory is that "they aggressively got out the base of their base, the base of their base that's dependent, to a great extent economically, on government policy and government programs."[57] FOX host Stuart Varney insisted that President Obama and the Democratic Party are using SNAP benefits as a way to buy voter loyalty in interim elections—yet another attempt to play upon racialized and classist anger to stigmatize the nation's safety net and its recipients.[58] Suggesting that government handouts helped secure the re-election of Barack Obama, or that he uses welfare benefits to maintain political power, is a none-too-subtle way of telling voters that not only are black and brown folks sucking up taxpayer dollars, but more important, they are literally stealing elections from the more deserving white folks who used to run the show. The strategy and narrative is entirely one of implicit, if not explicit, white nationalism.

So long as progressives fail to openly confront the way that racial resentment against folks of color has been used to weaken support for safety-net efforts, attempts to strengthen those safety nets will likely fail. According to a study from the Harvard Institute of Economic Research, it is white racial resentment and bias—and specifically, fear that blacks will take advantage of social programs—more than *any other factor*, that explains opposition to safety-net efforts in America.[59] This means that appeals to self-interest, or even the larger economic benefit of such programs, will likely be ignored unless the racialized root of white opposition is confronted. If whites are being encouraged to defend their interests in *racial* terms rather than class terms, only by challenging that tendency and exposing it for the deliberately manipulative and cynical strategy it is, might we hope to pare off enough whites from the conservative ranks to join with people of color in defending a more equitable society.

Such a strategy won't be easy, of course, but ignoring the way safety nets have been racialized will allow the subtle and implicit biases upon which the Becks and Limbaughs of the world capitalize to go unexamined. What the research on subconscious and implicit bias has shown us is that those kinds of biases are more effective and do more harm when they are uninterrogated and allowed to remain in the background. By forcing them into the light of day, we force those who may be operating on the basis of those biases to confront their prejudices; and since most Americans wish not to be seen as operating on the basis of racial bias, that confrontation with the gap between aspiration and achievement can potentially prompt significant numbers of white Americans to rise to the level of their aspirations rather than sink to the level of their fears. I discussed this issue of implicit bias and how conscious reflection on prejudice can help inhibit it in my book *Colorblind*, but it is worth quoting Emory University psychology professor Drew Westen here as well on this point, and how directly confronting racial triggers might help inhibit their operationalization. As Westen explains:

> The scientific data suggest two strategies that are . . . effective in addressing unconscious prejudice. . . . The first is to remind people of their conscious values, which tend to be our better angels on race [and] the second is to speak directly to the conflict between those values and the attitudes we hold at some level that we wish we didn't. . . . It's about talking to people like grown ups. . . . The best antidote to unconscious bias is self-reflection. And the best way to foster that self-reflection is through telling the truth.[60]

Making it plain that the right has been manipulating white racial resentment and playing upon deeply ingrained prejudices in their tirades against social safety-net programs can force whites whose racism is not blatant or deliberate, but implicit and subconscious (who are the only ones likely reachable to begin with), to see that they are being used. And not just used, but used by people who ultimately think so little of them that they assume their biases can forever and always trump their sense of justice, and are willing to bank on that cynical view.

Beyond Facts: The Importance of Storytelling

As the previous section demonstrates, the power of stories is incredibly important. Because the right has been successful in telling a story about the poor, the unemployed and those in need of public assistance, they have been able to successfully pare back the contours of the so-called welfare state over the course of two generations. When the dominant narratives about such persons in the 1930s and 1940s concerned down-and-out white folks, buffeted by circumstances beyond their control, the operative response from most was one of sympathy and solidarity. Once those dominant narratives turned to stories about black families (and Latino families too), that sympathy dimmed considerably. Suddenly, the programs that had been popular became unpopular, and the very idea of government intervention on behalf of those in need became suspect. It wasn't data or facts that changed; it was the narrative and who controlled it.

To pull out of the culture of cruelty and to live out the creedal notions that are so central to the ideal of America, we will need to tell very different stories. Facts and data, though helpful, cannot convince enough Americans that we desperately need to go in a different direction. After all, the facts have always been on the side of justice, but the other side has had the better story. Likewise, the left has long been good at mass mobilization and protest activity, and yet it seems as though every victory obtained by such movements, from the labor struggle to civil rights to the fight for women's liberation, has been undermined, at least in part, because there hasn't been a strong enough narrative to sustain them. The right has had the story of a land of opportunity, the story of rugged individualism, the story of welfare queens (like those Ronald Reagan was fond of telling), and the stories of Horatio Alger: the author (and as it turns out, apparent child-molester) who spun tales of young men who came from nothing and achieved greatness.[61] Their stories are intoxicating and persuasive, irrespective of how divorced from the facts they may be. Until and unless progressives get better at telling stories—only in our case, stories that actually comport with sociological reality—we will continue to watch reactionaries dominate the discourse and set the policy agenda. After all, legislative victories for greater equity that occur today against the backdrop of a still embedded narrative of meritocracy can only go so far. Eventually, such victories will be undone by a storyline that suggests such policies are no longer needed, or have even gone "too far," as with various social programs or equity efforts like affirmative action or desegregation. Likewise, if protest movements succeed in forcing current lawmakers to make certain concessions, so be it—and we should certainly try to bring about such results. But without a storyline to sustain those victories, the next crop of lawmakers may well come in and undo all that was done, having themselves never faced the wrath of the public in the same way. Having to reinvent the protest wheel in every new generation so as to force lawmakers to bend to our will is merely a long-term strategy for unending protest for protest's sake; it is hardly a strategy for social change. For that, we need better stories; in academic terms we need counter-hegemonic narratives that can speak to a different reality—both the reality that exists today and the one we wish to create tomorrow. But what kind of stories should we tell? How can we craft a narrative that challenges meritocracy and effectively questions the notion that we all end up where we do because of our own individual effort? How might storytelling help us defeat the notion that government aid is for "losers," in Rick Santelli's terms, and that the poor, the unemployed and the struggling have only themselves to blame?

These are questions quite similar to those I have often engaged regarding how to discuss matters of racism in America. As someone who has lectured around the country for twenty-plus years and written six previous books on race, I am constantly grappling with how best to make the case to mostly white audiences that not only do people of color continue to face discrimination, but whites enjoy unearned advantages over people of color, and that we need to be accountable for those privileges in order to help foster a society of true fairness. What I have come to conclude from that experience is that white Americans must be honest enough to tell our stories. These include stories about the assistance we've received from old-boys' networks for jobs; stories about parental wealth or connections; stories about the schools we were able to attend; and stories about the benefit of the doubt we've been given by teachers, employers and police. And it's especially important to tell these stories when we didn't come from wealthy families—many of these advantages flowed to us despite not being particularly well off, and even if we struggled economically. Until we tell those stories and challenge other white people to reflect on the many ways we too have benefited from unequal opportunity, it will be much easier for most whites to tune out the discussion. We can view race and racism as black or brown issues only, as things that only others need worry about, and not as subjects that shape our lives too.

By the same token, all of us, regardless of color, who have benefited from government programs or interventions in the economy need to tell *our* stories, to make it clear just how much help *we've* received, and how government, more so than the free market, has been heavily implicated in our success. So too with parental help or help from various connections, without which we could not have begun to accomplish the things we have. The culture of cruelty operates on the assumption that government aid is for the poor or those who can't make it on their own. But if we tell stories of our own success that are laden with examples of how that success owes much to government aid, or help from others, and is not simply a reflection of our own talent and determination, the narrative of meritocracy can be undermined, the reliance on rugged individualism diminished, and a collective sense of responsibility for one another rebuilt. By showing others how our own successes owe to fortuitous circumstance and the collective efforts of the larger society, we can de-stigmatize the notion of government aid and commit to extending to others those public blessings bestowed upon us.

How many of us, after all, would be where we are today were it not for loans for college, underwritten by the government? If not for low-interest housing loans created by the government under the FHA program, which may have financed our parents' or grandparent's homes if not our own? Where would so many be if not for the G.I. Bill, or for rural electrification programs? If not for the mortgage interest deduction: a government tax subsidy that disproportionately benefits upper-middle-class families? If not for Medicare, which might be paying our health care bills, or those of an elderly relative, or Social Security or disability benefits? If not for the government-sponsored research that was critical to the creation of the Internet? If not for Small Business Administration loans, or the interstate highway program, which reduced the cost of getting goods to market for millions of American businesses? Although we sometimes overlook the ways we have benefited from government programs, we all have, in some way. Anyone who runs a business and has employees who keep that business successful owes a debt to the public school teachers who helped educate most all of those workers, and helped to make them some of the most productive workers in the world. Any of us who attended one of those public schools wouldn't be where we are today but for the teachers who inspired us, all of them paid from the public purse.

So we have to come out of the closet, as it were—the closet marked "government beneficiary"—and insist that there is no shame in any of that. To reduce the stigma associated with relying on the government, or on others generally, we need to show one another how much we ourselves have benefited. I use the closet metaphor here deliberately. It is hard to deny, for instance, that much of the recent progress in the struggle for LGBT equality has come less from political efforts and protest activity (though both have been important) and more from the fact that as more of our LGBT brothers and sisters came out, millions of straight and cisgendered folks have come to the realization that people whom they love and respect are indeed lesbian, gay, bisexual or transgendered. Personal relationships and connections have allowed for a counter-hegemonic narrative to develop, and that has made a huge difference: it de-stigmatizes the LGBT community by humanizing the issues faced by its members. Likewise, if we admit the help we've received from government, family, friends and identities that have nothing to do with talent, we can begin to de-stigmatize things such as publicly provided health care, nutrition assistance, housing aid and unemployment insurance. We can begin to chip away at the individualist narrative that makes us so quick to deify the rich and demonize impoverished and struggling Americans.

Currently, the problem is that most Americans who have benefited from government programs (often several of them) don't see it, and unless those who do are willing to openly claim their status as beneficiaries, it may remain hard for this consciousness to spread. According to a poll in 2008, fifty-seven percent of Americans say they have never used a government social program. But when asked specifically if they had received benefits from Social Security, or ever received unemployment benefits, had student loans or taken a mortgage-interest deduction, nearly nine in ten of those who said they had not received government assistance actually had; indeed, the typical respondent in the survey had benefited from four different government programs.[62] Because government programs for those who aren't poor are more sublimated—or as Cornell government professor Suzanne Mettler calls them, "submerged"—and do not require recipients to regularly interact with government officials or bureaucrats (the way the poor do, when they interact with case workers, for instance), it is easy for those who reap the largesse of such efforts to remain in denial about the aid they receive. As Mettler explains:

> The submerged state obscures the role of government and exaggerates that of the market. It leaves citizens unaware of the source of programs and unable to form meaningful opinions about them. Until political leaders reveal government benefits for what they are by talking openly about them, we cannot have an honest discussion about spending, taxes or deficits. The stipulation in the new health care reform law that W-2 forms must indicate the value of untaxed employer-provided health care benefits is a step in the right direction. The government should also provide "receipts" that inform people of the size of each benefit they get through the tax code. The threat to democracy today is not the size of gov-

> ernment but rather the hidden form that so much of its growth has taken. If those who assume government has never helped them could see how it has, it might help defuse our polarized political climate and reinvigorate informed citizenship.[63]

For myself, acknowledging the help I've received irrespective of merit is easy. I've done well as a writer and educator, lecturing in all fifty states, and in three countries. I've written six previous books. Although none of them have exactly been bestsellers, they've been well reviewed and endorsed by some of the nation's leading civil rights and human rights voices, including leading scholars on race and racial equality, and are used in scores of college classrooms. I've appeared on dozens of television programs and been featured in several documentary films. Although far from wealthy, I make more than a decent living and am able to provide things for my children that my own parents were not able to provide for me. But it isn't because I've worked harder, nor because I am smarter in any real sense than they or millions of others who haven't achieved the same status. My mother, for her part, worked as hard as anyone I know to put food on the table and keep a roof over our head, though she has little to show for it. I am where I am, and doing what I'm doing, solely because of circumstances beyond my control. Some of those circumstances, obviously, have to do with blatant racial privilege: simply put, and sadly, as a white person—and especially as a white man—I am listened to when I speak out against racism in ways that too often, people of color are not. But many of those circumstances have also been shaped by government policies.

As I mentioned in the introduction, my first job out of college was working in the campaigns against neo-Nazi David Duke, when he ran for office in Louisiana. That was a critical springboard for me, without which it is doubtful I'd be doing what I'm doing today. Had I not been in New Orleans at the time, I wouldn't have had a chance to get that job and thus be thrust into antiracism work at a high and nationally prominent level. But the only reason I was in New Orleans, where I would meet the two men who offered me the position (one a college professor of mine and the other a friend and graduate student), was because I had gone to Tulane University; and the only reason I was at Tulane was because despite not having the money to afford the school, I was able to cobble together just enough to attend. Where did these resources come from? Two places: government grants and loans, including those specifically for low- and moderate-income students, and then a private loan from a bank, which my mother was able to secure so as to make up the difference between what school was going to cost that first year, and how much we were able to get in financial aid.

But even that private loan had public origins, which are important to acknowledge. My mother, despite having no collateral of her own was able to get that loan, for $12,000, by using *her* mother's house as collateral and having my grandmother co-sign. It was a nice house in a "nice neighborhood," which my grandfather (who had been dead six years by then) had been able to purchase with cash, and which my grandmother now owned, free and clear. How had he been able to do that? Easy enough: he bought it with proceeds from the sale of his previous house, which he had also bought with cash—cash generated by the sale of his house before that, which was also bought with cash; and in that case, cash generated from the sale of his first house, purchased in 1950 with a mortgage, which he paid off in fifteen years. And the story of how he managed to get *that* house, and then pay it off so quickly, is one that despite his hard work, has little to do with merit.

First off, he was white. Had he not been, there is simply no way he could have procured a loan for a house in the neighborhood where he bought—not at that time, and not in that place. Although the Supreme Court had, two years earlier, outlawed the enforcement of restrictive covenants barring the sale of homes to people of color, those covenants still existed, and unless a family of color was prepared to file a lawsuit after being denied a particular home, the court decision meant very little. Not to mention, just because a home couldn't have a legally enforceable restrictive covenant didn't mean that discrimination in housing itself had been outlawed. It simply prohibited the enforcement of blatant racial restrictions in the deeds themselves. Banks could still deny loans to blacks, and did so. Real estate agents could still refuse to show certain homes in certain neighborhoods to blacks, and did so. And, of course, threats of violence against blacks who moved into white areas ensured that few if any persons of color would have been capable, especially in Nashville during segregation, to get the home my grandfather did, the house where my mother grew up. Of course, he still had to work to make the payments on that first house. He did that, thanks to a secure, good-paying career with the *government*: first as a military officer and then in the Corps of Engineers as a civil servant. Though his positions hardly left him a rich man, they were more than sufficient for a solid middle-class lifestyle. And having obtained those jobs during a time of segregation, when those positions would have been all but off-limits to persons of color, he benefited directly from government and then government-enforced *policies* that elevated him above others.

In a very real sense, if not for his government-sponsored jobs—and his whiteness—my grandmother doesn't have that house, which is to say that we don't get that loan, I don't go to Tulane, and I don't meet the two men who would give me that first job; all of which ultimately means I'm not likely doing what I'm doing today, you're not reading this book, and my children aren't in the position they're in either. This is how non-merit factors such as race or government-provided opportunities can keep on giving, even generations later, and even if that assistance hasn't made possible a huge inheritance. Just a small head start can snowball, so that children who never even knew their great-grandfather are today reaping the benefits of his race, employment and class status some thirty-five years after his passing.

It's a point I tried to make a few years back to a young man in an audience of mine who was none too pleased with the suggestion that he might have benefited from white racial privilege. I was speaking at St. John's, an all-boy's school in Danvers, Massachusetts, and after my speech a young man, probably sixteen, indicated his discomfort with the suggestion that his position at St. John's had been anything but deserved. His father, he explained, had worked in the textile mills, long and hard hours, just to provide his children with a better life than the one he had lived. He had worked and worked and saved and saved, and as a result of his sacrifice he could now afford to send his son to a prep school as fine (and pricey) as St. John's. After he was done with his praise for his father's work ethic—a work ethic which, I noted, he was justifiably proud of and which he should be very grateful for—I made the suggestion that in my estimation there was no doubt that his dad was an incredible person and a hard worker, who had by all means earned the right to attend St. John's. The young man looked confused by my remark, clarifying that his dad was in his late fifties and hardly a candidate for admission there. I assured him that I knew this. I was under no illusion that his father was likely to be looking to re-enroll in high school. My point was simply that he had spent the last five minutes explaining to me how great his father was, and he had convinced me, beyond any doubt, that this rendering was accurate; and yet, I explained, I was having a hard time understanding what in the world this fact had to do with *him*, the son. He, after all, was sixteen and had done exactly *nothing*, beyond perhaps acing his Algebra II final. The accomplishments, the hard work, the determination and the sacrifice had been his father's doing. Unless the son believed that somehow he had *earned* his father, perhaps in a past life (which I felt confident, seeing as how this was a Catholic school, he was not likely to suggest), it struck me that his story had just made *my* point: that we often benefit from unearned head starts afforded by others. Even if the young man didn't want to accept that his father had benefited from whiteness at all (and frankly, he had, because those mill jobs paid well, and whites had been afforded a leg up for the best positions), there was no question that the son himself was benefiting from something over which he had no control, and for which he was due no credit.

This is a vitally important point to understand: even if someone really did "make it on their own," without help from anyone else—an absurdity, but one we can indulge for the sake of the point I wish to make—by the time they pass any of the benefits of those accomplishments down to children, we are no longer talking about something that is earned or deserved. At that point, we are talking about being able to start a race ahead of someone else for reasons owing neither to one's own merit nor to another's deficit. Even if meritocracy were real, it could only last for one generation before we'd have to provide boosts in opportunity for those whose prior family members had lost the previous race. After all, it would hardly be fair to attain a real equal opportunity society, and then after a generation of that, take the children of those who ended up poor in the first generation—people who had the misfortune of being born to those who were less successful—and say, "O.K., now because your parents were such losers, you'll just to have to run faster than the kids whose parents were winners. Suck it up and good luck." How would that be just? How would that be any different from a society based on royal lineage and pure aristocracy? It wouldn't be different at all. By the second generation of that, and certainly the fourth or fifth or twentieth, we would have subverted meritocracy all over again, by ensuring such an unfair starting point in each new race that those who started out behind would rarely have a real chance to prove their worth, while those who started out ahead would have less and less need to even bother proving theirs.

For those on the right who insist they believe in "equal opportunity" but not "equal results" take note: If results are profoundly unequal, they subvert the prospects for equal opportunity in the next competition. At least the NFL draft gives the first-round draft pick to the team with the worst record the previous year, in the hopes that perhaps the opportunity to win can be made more equal. But in the larger culture we ignore the logic of such a practice, opting instead for a process that favors the favored and provides advantages to the advantaged, while thinking nothing of the injustice of such a thing. The way we operate the society is exactly the opposite of the way in which the NFL draft functions. In the larger society we essentially give the economic equivalent of the Super Bowl champions the first-round pick, allowing them to build on their pre-existing advantage and continue to beat the economic losers senseless year after year, running up the financial scoreboard into a perpetual blowout.

By telling our stories and acknowledging the extent to which we have all been dependent on others (family, friends, mentors, the kindness of strangers, policies of the state) and even plain luck and good timing, we can move in a more honest and humble direction. And of course, to also speak forthrightly about the various advantages that come from other identities we possess is crucial. If we're white, male, straight or cisgender, and/or able-bodied, discussing how those dominant-group identities have helped us along the way can allow us to put aside the self-absorbed and dishonest narratives about rugged individualism and merit being the keys to success. We can begin to acknowledge that whatever success any of us have, if we have it, is due to a combination of effort and circumstance as anything intrinsic to us as individuals. Digging even deeper into my own story illustrates this point quite clearly. So it wasn't only because of my whiteness and government loans that I ended up at Tulane and was therefore in a position to meet the two men who gave me my first job fighting racism; there's actually another aspect of that story that's even more telling—and even less related to my own merit. It's a story of luck, pure and simple (and interestingly, a combination of good *and* bad luck all at the same time).

Fact is, at the conclusion of my junior year of high school, as I began to consider which college I might attend, Tulane wasn't even on my radar screen. I had never thought of it even once. As a high school debater, I was planning on debating in college and was only looking at schools with debate programs, which Tulane didn't have at the time. My heart was actually set on Emory University in Atlanta. I knew the debate coach well, had met with a recruiter from there and had taken an official campus tour. But that summer I attended a three-week debate camp at American University in Washington, D.C., where I met a girl from Louisiana and almost instantly, in the manner of a sixteen-year-old, fell in love. Suddenly, and also in the manner of a sixteen-year-old, all my life plans immediately changed. Since she was going to be attending Louisiana State, the only way we'd be able to see each other once college started (and of course, we just *knew* we'd still be together in a year, because what high school relationship *doesn't* last?) would be for me to go to Tulane. So off to New Orleans it was. In other words, if I hadn't gone to that particular debate camp—and there were many others from which I could have chosen—I would never have met Monica, never have gone to Tulane and never have been in a position to get the job fighting David Duke upon graduation.

But actually, it's even deeper than that. The only reason I was a high school debater in the first place, and thus in a position to go to debate camp at all, was because when I had been a freshman in high school, I had been inexplicably cut from the baseball team. I say inexplicably because I had always been a good baseball player, so much so that I'd actually had college recruiters at my games going back to when I was eleven. I had long figured, in fact, that baseball was going to be my ticket to college. But for some reason, when I tried out for my high school it was as if I'd never played the game before. I couldn't hit, couldn't field and could no longer pitch. My baseball dreams dashed, I had to find another activity, and debate it would be. Had I made the baseball team, there would have been no time for debate, and certainly no time for debate camp at American or anywhere else—summers would have been spent playing more baseball.

So even my *bad luck* at getting cut from the baseball team ultimately helped to secure my future: it led me to debate, which led me to American, which led me to Monica, which led me to Tulane, which led me to the guys who hired me to organize against David Duke, which led to everything that has come after. Among those things was my decision to stay in New Orleans for six more years to do community work, and then return to my hometown of Nashville after getting out on the road for lectures. If I had gone to a different college and embarked on a different career, I likely wouldn't have returned home when I did, for the simple reason that I likely wouldn't have had the flexibility to live wherever I wanted—a flexibility that came from being an activist and speaker on the national lecture circuit and not having a normal job. And had I not returned home at exactly the time I did, I would have been either too early or too late to move in with the two women who would become my roommates; and if I hadn't met them, I would never have met my wife, because it was one of those roommates who introduced me to her—all of which means that our children would not exist. In other words, I owe every good thing that has happened in my life to that asshole who cut me from the baseball team. So to coach Cantrell, let me now offer a sincere *thank you!* I seriously couldn't have done it without you.

Though I know there are some who insist that there is no such thing as luck, or that we "make our own luck," I cannot fathom how I made any of the above happen. Yes, once I made the jump to debate I worked hard at it and did well, but it was only luck that allowed me to have the time to pursue the activity, and it was just coincidence that Monica and I had chosen the same summer camp to attend. Nothing about that was remotely associated with talent or hard work. It was timing and serendipity, and it has made all the difference.

Importantly, timing and serendipity explain more than just my own success. In his book *Outliers*, Malcolm Gladwell discusses the ways that non-merit factors—even things like the month or year in which one is born—can significantly correlate with achievement. For instance, according to research by economists studying grade-level performance on common math and science tests, there is a significant relationship between higher scores and the month of a child's birth. Why? Because birth month is, in turn, highly correlated with the point at which a child will begin school (at least in the United States). Fourth graders who are at the upper end of the age range in their class tend to score significantly higher than those in their class who are at the younger end of the range. The older kids, who were generally born in summer and held out of school an extra year by their parents so as not to spend all of kindergarten as a five-year old, have an extra year to mature. Once they are several grades in, these students are more likely to be placed in accelerated classes and offered challenging material, either because, being several months older, they really *are* more advanced than their younger peers in the class, or because teachers are confusing maturity with talent and placing them in accelerated classes as a result. Either way, because of the month of their birth, and the parental decision to hold their kids back from school for an extra year (and school policies that allow this), certain kids end up with an edge in key academic disciplines, relative to their classmates, independent of any inherent abilities or particular effort.[64] So the difference between something as trivial as a November birthday versus one in July can produce significant differences in achievement going forward through one's academic career. And to the extent that our academic performance can influence everything from professional career decisions to future earnings, even something as trivial as birth month can end up influencing our longer-term life outcomes.

The *year* of one's birth can also make a difference. If the economy undergoes a major transformation, like the industrial revolution or the computer revolution, and you're a few years too young to get in on the ground floor of the emerging industries, or a little too old and already doing something else, you're out of luck. Of the seventy-five wealthiest people in the history of the world—using today's dollar equivalent amount to gauge their wealth relative to the present—fourteen were Americans born between 1831 and 1840. What are the odds of such a thing? For one-fifth of the wealthiest people in the history of the world to have come from one country and essentially one decade, must mean something. What it means, of course, is rather apparent if we think about it for a few seconds: simply put, they came of age right at the time when the industrial revolution was hitting its stride, and these men made their fortunes with companies and industries that were instrumental to that revolution. If they had been born ten years earlier, they would likely have been involved in other careers and unable to get in on the boom; likewise, had they been born ten years later, they would have missed out by being too late to the game. Luckily for them, they were born right in the sweet spot for entering new industries in their critical early stages, and that made all the difference. Likewise, as Gladwell notes, a disproportionate number of the leading individuals in the computer revolution and the development of Silicon Valley were born between 1953 and 1956, because these dates would put them at just the right age to get in on the initial computer explosion of the 1970s.[65] In other words, if Steve Jobs and Steve Wozniak had been born in the 1940s or 1960s instead of the 1950s, iPhones may never have been invented. Although they would surely have made something of themselves, it likely would have been something very different than what we know them for now.

Bill Gates is a particularly good example of how timing (and even location) plays such an important role in success. While it is often claimed that Gates—in most years, the world's wealthiest individual—was self-made, simply because he didn't come from a family of millionaires, the story is considerably more complicated than that. Gates's father was a successful, well-off attorney, and his mother was the daughter of a successful banker (and ultimately served on a bank Board of Directors herself). In short, he wasn't born into poverty and hardship. Indeed, the family had sufficient resources to send him to the Lakeside School, one of Seattle's most prestigious prep schools. In 1968, Gates's second year at Lakeside, the school started a computer club and bought its first computer terminal from funds raised by a rummage sale. And far from being the punch-card type of computer so common in those days, the one Lakeside bought was a much more advanced time-sharing terminal that was connected to a huge mainframe in downtown Seattle. As Gladwell explains:

> Bill Gates got to do real-time programming *as an eighth grader in 1968*. . . . He and a number of others began to teach themselves how to use this strange new device [and] then a group of programmers at the University of Washington formed an outfit called Computer Center Corporation (or C-Cubed), which leased computer time to local companies. . . . One of the founders of the firm—Monique Rona—had a son at Lakeside, a year ahead of Gates. Would the Lakeside computer club, Rona wondered, like to test out the company's software programs on the weekends in exchange for free programming time? Absolutely! After school, Gates took the bus to the C-Cubed offices and programmed long into the evening. C-Cubed eventually went bankrupt, so Gates and his friends started hanging around the computer center at the University of Washington. Before long, they latched onto an outfit called ISI (Information Services Inc.), which agreed to let them have free computer time in exchange for working on a piece of software that could be used to automate company payrolls. In one seven-month period in 1971, Gates and his cohorts ran up 1,575 hours of computer time on the ISI mainframe, which averages out to eight hours a day, seven days a week.[66]

In other words, Bill Gates was in the right place at the right time to take advantage of computing opportunities that others, every bit as capable and hard-working as he, simply did not have. Not only would he have missed out on these opportunities had he remained in the public schools where he spent the first six years, but even had he gone to a *different prep school* he would have missed out. As the story continues, it turns out that Gates and Paul Allen (his colleague and now another one of the wealthiest people in the world) got kicked out of ISI for stealing passwords and crashing their system. But Allen had discovered a computer he could use for free at the University between three and six in the morning. Gates would sneak out and walk or take the bus to the college and program for three hours most days. Then ISI got a call from another company that was setting up a computer system at a power plant in the southern part of the state, and needed programmers who were familiar with the software programs the company was using. One of the ISI founders immediately thought of Gates and his schoolmates and steered the power company to them. Gates then convinced officials at Lakeside, where he was still a senior, to let him move several hours away and write code for the power station as an "independent study" project.[67] So by the time Gates founded his own software company a little more than two years later, he'd been programming continually for nearly seven years—something that virtually no other person his age in the world would be able to say. As Gates himself puts it: "I had better exposure to software development at a young age than I think anyone did in that period of time, and all because of an incredibly lucky series of events."[68]

Indeed, the success of entire groups can often owe significantly to timing and circumstance every bit as much as to hard work and effort. Though many are quick to credit cultural attributes for the disproportionate economic success of American Jews—and even many in the Jewish community are quick to embrace this notion—the facts are quite a bit more complex. As Stephen Steinberg documents in his book *The Ethnic Myth: Race, Ethnicity and Class in America*, Jewish immigrants from Eastern Europe in the late 1800s and early 1900s, unlike many of their non-Jewish European counterparts, were likely to have been skilled labor in their home countries. Between 1899 and 1910, two-thirds of Jewish immigrants were skilled workers in manufacturing or commerce, or artisans of some sort, compared to only forty-nine percent of English immigrants who had such skills, only thirty percent of Germans, fifteen percent of Southern Italians, thirteen percent of Irish immigrants and six percent of Poles. But not only did they possess that pre-existing class advantage relative to other immigrants, their professional experience was especially pronounced in the garment-making industry—an industry that was growing two to three times faster than the larger industrial average. Because fine clothing was a luxury for which the affluent were willing to pay a premium, Jewish tailors, haberdashers, furriers and dressmakers were able to make an excellent living and move up the ladder in their newly adopted country. Yes, they had skills and talent, and yes, they worked hard. But they also happened to be in the right country at the right time, with precisely the right skills and experience needed to benefit from an economic boom in a given industry.[69]

None of this is to detract from the efforts or talents of those who have been successful—whether myself, or someone like Bill Gates, or a disproportionate number of American Jews, including, for that matter, one of my own great-grandfathers. It is simply to say that effort and talent, unless mixed with opportunity, access and good timing, combined with a little dumb luck, often amounts to very little.

For one final example, consider the recent admission of self-professed plutocrat Nick Hanauer (whom I referenced in an earlier chapter) as to the real sources of his outsize success. Hanauer, who has founded, co-founded or provided start-up funding for thirty companies, co-owns his own bank and is worth billions, recently dished as to how he made all that money, and suffice it to say, it wasn't simply a matter of skill and hard work. According to Hanauer—whose essay was meant as an open letter of sorts to his fellow oligarchs—his success owes mostly to timing and luck. Although Hanauer professes a certain degree of savvy and insight, not to mention a healthy willingness to embrace risk, he also notes that these things would have meant nothing had he not known the right people. As it turns out, one of his close friends is Jeff Bezos (founder of Amazon), and when Bezos told him of his idea for the book-selling company he was thinking of launching, Hanauer was able to get in on the ground floor. Thanks to that serendipitous circumstance, as Hanauer puts it, "Now I own a very nice yacht."

Though still firmly committed to the idea of capitalism, and certainly unapologetic about his own success, at least Hanauer is self-aware enough to go against the grain of the dominant cultural narrative. As he puts it, calling out his fellow one-percenters:

> My family . . . started in Germany selling feathers and pillows. They got chased out of Germany by Hitler and ended up in Seattle owning another pillow company. Three generations later, I benefited from that. Then I got as lucky as a person could possibly get in the Internet age by having a buddy in Seattle named Bezos. I look at the average Joe on the street, and I say, "There but for the grace of Jeff go I." Even the best of us, in the worst of circumstances, are barefoot, standing by a dirt road, selling fruit. We should never forget that, or forget that the United States of America and its middle class made us, rather than the other way around.

His essay not only critiques the myth of meritocracy, but even more, warns of the dangers inherent in the current and growing economic cleavages in America. As Hanauer explains it, while proudly supporting Seattle's recent hike in the minimum wage to $15 an hour, and calling for a newly invigorated New Deal for American workers and average families:

> No society can sustain this kind of rising inequality. In fact, there is no example in human history where wealth accumulated like this and the pitchforks didn't eventually come out. You show me a highly unequal society,

> and I will show you a police state. Or an uprising. There are no counterexamples. None. It's not if, it's when.[70]

While those of us on the left might welcome the thought of such an uprising—indeed might well be hopeful that such an event would transpire—it's probably worth contemplating the likely outcome of such a thing in the face of increasing repression and inequality. To believe that the forces of justice and equality would prevail in such an encounter is to ignore most of human history, and betrays an utter ignorance as to the strength of the American oligarchy. Before the first battle of any revolution could be won, let alone before the power of the ruling class could be brought down by force, the stewards of global capitalism could push a button and transfer billions of dollars to overseas investment banks, push another button and book themselves on the next plane to some island paradise, and then skip town. With that, they could leave the rest of us to pick up the pieces of a completely shattered society that they had rigged to implode without the continued infusion of the capital they had accumulated off the work of others. While we could certainly do fine without them in the long run, the short-term horror of such a scenario is not to be toyed with. Their money and property is easily transferable and transportable. Even were they to stay, they have the guns, they have the military, they have the apparatus of law enforcement, and they have the material resources to crush such an uprising long before it delivered anything of value to the people. Dreams of revolution from below forcing a capitulation of capital to the masses are the stuff of left fantasy, engaged in by people who know so little of global economics as to believe it possible to expropriate excess wealth the way revolutionary movements were once able to do in past eras. But the world is different. An attempted revolution of that sort would be met with a true police state almost certainly, and absent a well-established counter-narrative that has effectively challenged the fundamental assumptions of American ideology *first*, it would be a police state likely welcomed and cheered by the majority. In short, if there is ever to be truly transformative change in America, it will require the clear development of a new politics and vision first: one that can be popularized across the society and embedded in the national dialogue.

Some Things Are Not Negotiable: Developing a Vision of a Culture of Compassion

To move toward a culture of compassion, and beyond the importance of crafting effective personal narratives to chip away at the key props to the culture of cruelty, it is important that social justice activists—and the American people more broadly—forward a vision of the society we want. Although that vision will need to be worked out in collaboration with many different voices weighing in on what true justice would involve, it might be helpful here to articulate at least a core set of basic principles upon which to organize a just society. These would be the essential notions that are necessary for a culture of compassion, without which no true turn from the culture of cruelty could proceed, let alone ultimately arise victorious.

And this is more important, at least at this stage, than crafting a set of policy proposals for how we get there. One of the common mistakes of the left, it seems to me, is our tendency to want very specific ideas—some reformist, some revolutionary—about how we get from point A to point Z, without first attending to this all-important step of changing the narrative and the vision currently running through the heads of most Americans. If the narrative people are hearing is one about meritocracy and how "you can be anything you want if you just work hard enough," then nothing we propose has much chance of going very far, because the need for any significant cultural and social change would be rejected. You don't need major changes when the society is basically fair already, the thinking goes. At best, that narrative will limit our possible vision to a handful of piecemeal policy options: a slight minimum-wage boost here, a slight change in tax rates there, or a little more funding for a handful of policy initiatives.

Not to mention, putting forward a set of specific policy options will immediately cause the discussion to default to those specific ideas—Can *this* proposal raise enough revenue for the programs we have in mind? Will *this* proposal sufficiently limit the power of corporations and the wealthy? Will this other idea cause capital flight by the rich?—rather than keeping focused on the philosophical premises of the movement we need to build and sustain. Instead of keeping our eyes on the principles and the support for them that we need, we'll end up debating marginal tax rates and the minutiae of trade policy, election finance specifics and the particular responsibilities of the Federal Reserve. We'll get to all that, and we must. The problem is, though there have been plenty of good policy proposals out there for a while now, none of them have gained much headway because there has been no clear vision of the future that would recommend those initiatives, outside the confines of the public policy community or a handful of activist groups.

The vision of the future needed to help us emerge from "under the affluence" can be one that begins with some of the fundamental elements of the longstanding national creed—however, drastically it has typically been betrayed—while also adding to it and developing it further for our modern realities. As I noted in the introduction, the national ideal, so often encapsulated by the phrase "American dream," has long been one that yoked individual liberties to broader collective and communal uplift. The fact that the ideal has regularly and consistently been violated can, of course, suggest that the national character is not up to the task, that perhaps we are incapable of fulfilling the promises we have made on paper. Or, alternatively, perhaps it simply means that we have never clearly articulated a vision of what would be necessary in order to fulfill those promises. Perhaps it indicates that such a lofty vision requires more than parchment and platitudes, more than faith and abstract freedom. Perhaps it requires that we make commitments to some broad-stroke concepts that would more fully concretize that vision. It is to that end that I now turn my attention.

People often ask me after my speeches: What is your vision of a just society? On the one hand, I don't think it is my role to offer a complete picture of that because visions for progressive and transformative change have to come from the people, working in concert with one another to craft the world they hope to see. To rely on any one person to tell you how to proceed would be horribly ill advised, especially if that advice comes from someone like myself who is white and male and straight and upper middle class. Given those identities, despite my best intentionality and lifelong commitment to justice, I am still going to be operating from behind some very strong lenses that could distort my range of vision. When it comes to the larger concept of the society we want and the specifics about how we get there, that is not for experts and writers and policy wonks to dictate. That is for all of us to decide, and for those ready to do the difficult work of organizing to help determine.

Yet, there are some broad contours of a vision that I feel I can put forward as an initiating conversation about the society we'd like to bring to fruition, while leaving the finer brush strokes to others in a more collective capacity. This is the answer I give when asked, and though it might strike some as rather basic, it is far from anything remotely being discussed in the mainstream political culture—which is to say that it is aspirational, not practical as of yet. But practicality isn't getting us anywhere. Bill Clinton was being "practical" when he signed the horrific 1996 welfare reform bill and deregulated the financial industry. Barack Obama was being practical when he agreed to the government sequester resolution and decided to take any real public option for health care off the table so as to keep the insurance industry on board with his health care reform, regardless of its impact on the public. Practical has often made things worse, or at least only moderately better, as with health care. Perhaps now it's time to dream a bit. It strikes me that America hasn't been able to dream for a long time, so beholden have we become to a small group of economic aristocrats, commercial mass media that increasingly narrow debate, and a political culture rooted in acrimony and name-calling.

For me, one way of thinking about all this is as a parent. More so than my role as a writer, activist or educator, being a father has caused me to reflect on the issue of social justice in a new way. This is not because parenting naturally confers superior insight, so please don't misunderstand; it is simply to say that parenthood is one more identity that provides a set of lenses through which one views reality. Just as race and gender and class and sexuality shape our understanding of the world—because they shape our experience of it—so too does one's status as a parent.

As a dad, I often think about how our political outlook desperately needs to align more closely with what most parents know about maintaining a healthy home environment for our partners, for our children, and also for ourselves. Especially because the culture of cruelty—*our* culture—violates virtually every lesson that responsible parents the world over teach our kids: about caring, compassion, respect, the importance of sharing and taking care of one another. No responsible parent would instruct their child to look down on a weaker classmate, let alone to bully them because of their relative weakness. No decent parent would encourage their son or daughter to view the classmate whose family just lost their home to foreclosure as a "loser." Even more to the point, no responsible parent would dole out portions at the dinner table based on which of their children had done the most chores, or gotten the better grade on a test. While we might reward or sanction certain behaviors when in comes to luxuries (like how much screen time a child gets with their electronics, or whether they can go hang out with friends) based on their school performance, or whether they had done various chores, no decent parent would do the same when it came to basic necessities like food, shelter or medicine.

Yet the culture of cruelty does *exactly* that: it says, in effect, that one's ability to access the basic things that one needs for survival (and certainly for the ability to exercise true human autonomy) should be based on whether or not one wins certain races in life. They should be commodities, up for grabs just like smartphones or big-screen TVs, luxury cars or vacation cruises. Such an idea flies in the face of the way we run our families, if we have them, and likely the families in which we were raised. A parent who doled out food, medicine or shelter to his or her children in this way would be brought up on charges of cruelty, endangerment and abuse. But when we do the same thing as a country, we call that the workings of a "free society" and the "magic of the marketplace." Clearly, something is amiss when we can deem just and proper in the larger society things that we would just as quickly condemn in the familial setting.

Likewise, something is askew when we can speak of justice and liberty for all as a nation, while discussing large swaths of our nation's people as barely worthy of human consideration. Something is dangerously upside down from a moral perspective, when policymakers can cut what meager lifelines have been provided for one sector of American citizens while seriously aiding and abetting financial excess for some of the most grotesquely rich Americans the country has ever produced.

It is time for us to set things right, and perhaps by building a movement for the needed cultural change around this principle—that necessities are not up for negotiation, but rather, are things to which we are entitled as human beings—we might begin to shift not only the consciousness of Americans regarding life in our own nation, but our nation's relationship to the rest of the world. Indeed, this notion is far from unimaginable; it is already given voice in the United Nation's Universal Declaration of Human Rights. It is one thing for a person to have a nicer stereo than someone else, or a fancier phone or car, or to take more vacations than the next person down the block, but quite another to differ markedly in our access to the necessities of life. If you have an iPhone 6 and I can only afford the old-school flip phone, life goes on; so too, if

I'm driving an eleven-year-old vehicle (I was, by the way, until a recent accident), while you just bought the latest model, it's really no big deal. But if you can get preventive health care and medicine when you're ill and my kids can't, because I can't afford it, or because my state didn't expand the programs that could make it available, then we have a problem. If my family and I are assured a roof over our heads and adequate nutrition, while you and your children are wondering where you'll sleep tonight and whether or not there will be enough food to eat, then we have more than a problem: we have a moral crisis. In that situation, we are living in a national culture that has failed in its basic ethical obligations to treat people as equals, and we are surely betraying our national aspirations and ideals.

There can be no equal opportunity in the absence of some sense of security, and not just physical security, but the kind of security that comes from knowing that your children will eat and have health care and a place to live. Without those things assured as a matter of human right and yes, *entitlement*, people are really never free to be who they are capable of becoming. If you have to sweat basic matters of survival, you aren't as likely to follow your passions, take a risk and start your own business or nonprofit group, pursue the education you've always wanted, or even take the time to breathe and contemplate who you are and who you want to become. If you have to worry about those basic necessities, you'll toil away at a job you hate for years, just to put food on the table and keep the metaphorical wolf from the door, but you'll never become the person you were meant to be.

I saw my mother do this. I watched her sacrifice much of who she was (an artist and a dancer) because she had to, and had to get a barely adequate-paying job just to keep it together—*for me*. On the one hand, I am grateful that she sacrificed as she did, for had she not, I have no doubt things would have turned out quite differently and quite a bit worse. But I can't help but resent a culture that requires a person to put aside what she loves in order to do something she doesn't, all in the name of supposed practicality. She has been a wonderful mom, and so perhaps that was her calling after all. But I know she had other gifts, too; I wish she had been able to at least truly *decide* whether to share them and follow the dreams she once had, rather than having that decision made for her by economic circumstance. Maybe she would have still made the choices she did, and if so, that would be fine. But that's the point: so long as families are worried about basic matters of survival, they aren't really free to make choices in any true sense. The person who is poor can obviously choose not to accept a crappy job offer, but in most cases won't, because such a choice will leave them destitute. Real choice, *meaningful* choice, requires a modicum of stability and security. Without those things, the ability to truly weigh options, to consider all the possibilities, and to pursue our passions is sacrificed.

This is the irony of the dominant meritocratic and competitive free-market narrative that holds such power at present. To those who worship at the altar of capitalism, government intervention in the economy stifles innovation and discourages risk-taking, entrepreneurship and determination. But imagine how much *more* willing to take risks a person might be, if he or she knew their failure wouldn't mean the inability to feed or house their family? It's easy to take risks when you're already rich, because you have your own safety net. For poor and working-class families however, taking the same risks—quitting a low-wage job to start up that bakery they always wanted to own, or to make their own furniture, or market their own jewelry line—would be putting too much at risk. It would be too big a gamble. Not so were we to make certain things non-negotiable.

Conservatives and the wealthy get just about everything wrong when it comes to human nature. They think innovation and risk-taking derives from free-market insecurity and uncertainty, and they appear to believe that only the promise of great fortune or the prospects of utter destitution can motivate people to do anything. They act as though unless people know they can become filthy rich without having their mega-earnings taxed away, they won't work hard. But is this what we really believe about our fellow human beings? That the only thing that gets them out of bed in the morning is the prospect of more *stuff*? How can that be true, especially for the bulk of the world's population for whom dreams of riches are self-evidently absurd? What gets *them* moving each day? Surely it can't be thoughts of Silicon Valley riches and hedge funds, collateralized debt obligations and Cayman Island tax shelters. What motivates most of the world's population must be something else, something more meaningful, having to do with survival and love and caring for their children and protecting them from the dangers that exist around every turn. Or for artists, musicians, poets and even parents, for that matter: is it the promise of money and material riches that motivates such persons? You'd best hope not. Art motivated by the goal of money will pander to the whims of others, not the truth of the artist, burning to be expressed; and any parent whose primary concern was the size of their bank account should probably, in a perfect world, be relieved of their children. There is surely little good they will be able to do for them with such a value system in place.

So too, the rich seem to believe that for the poor and struggling, only the prospects of *continued poverty and struggle* could possibly motivate them to hard work and success. If people are poor, then they must not be poor *enough*, on this rendering, for if they were, surely they would have gotten sufficiently motivated so as to not be poor any more. Make no mistake; this is the thinking of the sadist, akin to those who say we should make prisons as awful as possible so as to deter people from committing crime. It's tantamount to insisting that we need to beat our children when they misbehave, as if cruelty ever motivated any of us to be better or to do better, as if cruelty did not inevitably wear off on its targets and instill in them the very same penchant for inhumanity that had previously been beaten into them or taught indirectly by the hostility of others. Just as the mistreatment of incarcerated people feeds their capacity for brutality upon release—and indeed most will one day exit the prisons within which some would prefer them brutalized—so too, the idea that we can scare needy communities into not being poor has never worked anywhere. All it has done is heap pain upon pain, exponentially adding to the net sum of brutality in the society within which the poor and the rest of us are trying to make our way. It is beneath the dignity of humanity to treat our brothers and sisters in such a fashion. It is a violation of every ethical principle, religious or secular, to which we claim some allegiance.

Moving to Self-Determination: Empowering Communities to Control Their Destiny

In addition to a guarantee of food, shelter and medicine as core components of a just and compassionate society—and one in which a modicum of security will better allow individuals to pursue their interests and passions—there is one more principle to which a larger movement for equity must be committed: namely, the idea that those who have been marginalized by poverty and economic hardship, by racial subordination and oppression of all kinds, have the capacity for exercising autonomy and self-governance and must be trusted to do so. A key element of the culture of cruelty, and something taught to us as a nation "under the affluence," is that the poor need the guidance of the rest of us; that their condition indicates something fundamentally flawed about *them*—above all their incapacity for competently managing their own lives. And so this is why lawmakers seek to police the boundaries of their diets and recreational activities (if they receive SNAP or TANF), or to require them to prove that they aren't using drugs with their paltry unemployment benefits. To truly turn the tide toward justice, we'll need to begin moving away from this paternalistic contempt for the poor and the communities in which they live; we'll need to foster a society in which such persons have more say about their lives, not less—more self-determination, as opposed to more micro-managing and domination from above. One can imagine the importance of such a concept in two of the most problematic arenas of daily life for poor communities and those who live there: the criminal justice system, especially as regards the interactions of poor communities with police, and the educational system within which low-income children are educated.

As for the justice system, we have seen in recent months the extent of the disconnect between impoverished communities (particularly of color) and police, in ways more telling and graphic than most white Americans had probably imagined possible. Beginning with the killing of Michael Brown in Ferguson, Missouri in August 2014, followed by other high-profile incidents in which police took the lives of unarmed people of color—Eric Garner in New York,[71] Tamir Rice in Cleveland,[72] John Crawford outside of Dayton,[73] Rekia Boyd in Chicago,[74] Yvette Smith in Texas,[75] Walter Scott in South Carolina,[76] and Freddie Gray in Baltimore[77]—the extent to which law enforcement sees persons of color as dangerous and deserving of violent, even lethal, confrontation has never been clearer. The outrage and indignation felt by communities of color at the way their neighborhoods are policed—subjected to racial profiling and harassment,[78] or given tickets for minor infractions as a way to fundraise for local government, as happened in Ferguson[79]—though often not understood by whites in more affluent communities, speaks to the long-standing sense of the nation's people of color that they are seen as domestic enemies by police and the courts, as people in need of occupation and domination rather than protection and compassionate service.

Although an extended discourse about racialized and economically oppressive policing is beyond the scope of this volume, at the very least what the growing conflict between police and the poor of color tells us is that there is a profound mistrust between the two. The police view too many of the persons in those communities negatively, and the community fears and mistrusts the cops as well. Though much has been said about the need for body cameras on officers, so as to better safeguard against brutality and misconduct on their part, much less has been said about the deeper structural and cultural disconnect between the police and the people they are supposed to "protect and serve." When officers are drawn from outside the community—and especially when white, middle-class officers are working in mostly black and brown communities far different from their own—the opportunities for mistrust and conflict are vast. While it might not be possible to require all officers to live in the communities they police—after all, locals might not want the job and there may not be sufficient housing availability to allow outsiders to move in—surely there are other ways to provide greater local control over police in such spaces.

For instance, imagine how different policing in low-income communities (of color and mostly white) might look if new officers were required to spend the first sixty to ninety days in a probationary period during which they would not carry weapons or have the power to arrest criminal suspects, but would be expected to meet with community stakeholders and get to know them: religious leaders, teachers and school administrators, business owners, and everyday average folks, in cafes, barber shops and the corner market, or on their front porch stoops. What if officers were expected to go door to door, introducing themselves to the community, offering their vision of law enforcement to the people there, and making sure that the residents saw them, knew them, and felt a connection to them from the beginning? And then, what if, at the end of the probationary period, the community got to vote on who does and doesn't get to be a cop in their neighborhood? Having sized up the new recruits, the people would make the call. If a recruit came off as too domineering, unwilling to listen and work with the people, or hostile to them, they wouldn't be hired; on the other hand, those who showed themselves capable and willing to work with the people there would get the green light.

It seems reasonable to assume that such a process in low-income communities (regardless of race) would foster greater trust between law enforcement and the folks who live there—which would actually be good for both the citizenry and the police. Likewise, it would reverse the common assumption in a culture of cruelty that those in poverty are incapable of determining their own fate, unable to control their own affairs, and untrustworthy when it comes to exercising autonomous decision making. By creating opportunities like this for the marginalized to demonstrate concrete forms of self-governance, the common perception of the poor as irretrievably damaged and incompetent can be challenged and diminished.

One can also imagine a comparable process and how it might work in the educational system. As for schools, there is little doubt that at present, low-income persons and communities have very little input on the way their children are educated or for what purpose. Impoverished kids of color—and even similar white children—are routinely herded into overcrowded schools, given very different materials than kids receive in affluent public or private schools, forced to drill for standardized tests in order to graduate, and turned into little more than raw material on an educational conveyor belt that seems almost tailor made for filling low-wage job slots. The charter school movement, predicated on the notion that what schools need is less regulation, more competition and more rigid discipline, has been foisted upon low-income communities as the solution to their problems, even as very little evidence suggests that charters, on balance, do any better than regular schools. Even the much touted pro-charter propaganda film *Waiting for Superman* acknowledged that only one in five charters produce the incredible educational outcomes touted by the movie—and even this may be overly generous. According to a large national study of charters by Stanford economist Margaret Raymond, only seventeen percent of charters produce results that are in any way superior to comparable public schools—let alone truly amazing gains in learning and performance—while thirty-seven percent perform worse and forty-six percent produce no change at all in student performance.[80] Indeed, when charters do show marked improvements in student outcomes, it is often the result of their ability to remove low-performing students, or exclude low-performing kids from the start, leaving them with a more select bunch than the typical school, which has a legal obligation to educate all children who walk through the door and exclude no one.

Although charter schools are sometimes locally controlled by people from the communities they serve, more often than not charter schools are run by large companies located far from the places where they operate. Locals have very little input as to their policies, their governance, their curricula, the quality and preparation of their teachers, or any other aspect of daily school life, which is likely why many such institutions end up treating the children in their care horribly, subjecting them to cruelties and harsh discipline that would land their operators in jail were they to try such things in the tony halls of elite academies.[81] Among these: throwing kids in padded rooms, making them sit on bare cement floors for days until they can "earn" their own desk, making them sit on a bench with signs demeaning their intelligence and character hanging from their necks, sitting them in front of computers for hours at a time rather than engaging them in active learning with professional educators, and various forms of public shaming for any disciplinary infractions, however minor (such as not looking a teacher in the eye or not sitting up perfectly straight).[82]

If parents and communities had more direct say as to who will be allowed to teach in their kids' schools, who will be allowed to serve as principals, and who will serve as guidance counselors, surely we can imagine a very different process. Community leaders and parents would be able to size up teachers and evaluate their level of compassion and understanding for their children, as well as the extent to which they were culturally competent to work in a community that is so often very different, racially and economically, from the ones where the teachers, administrators and counselors live. Rather than being satisfied with a teacher having basic content knowledge or professional credentials, communities could play a role in choosing the educators for their kids based on the extent to which those educators are willing to work *with* the community and draw upon the strengths of that community—not merely view it as a compendium of deficits to be "fixed"—so as to make the schools work better. Teachers with experience in racially and economically marginalized communities, and who have a proven track record in successfully educating students from such spaces, would be prioritized for employment in such a system. Those who see low-income communities as spaces of perseverance, determination and untapped strengths would be the first hired, while those who view the members of those communities as damaged goods, or persons suffering from a tangle of pathology in need of discipline and regimentation, would be shown the door. In other words, prospective teachers would have to demonstrate *to the satisfaction of the community and the parents in that community* that they were to be trusted with the community's children, and that their perception of those families and the community itself was not laden with the kinds of race and class stereotypes that so often torpedo effective learning.

Again, by investing low-income persons with a sense of self-determination, such a process would help reconnect parents to a school system from which they have often felt alienated. Such a process would capture the largest ostensible benefit of "school choice" or charters—touted as greater parental involvement—while avoiding the pitfalls of those systems as they exist at present: namely, top-down management, culturally incompetent pedagogy and course content, unprepared teachers, and presumptions that poor children need more harsh discipline in order to learn. It would help create an educational model in low-income communities rooted in a sense of the capacity of even desperately marginalized people to govern their own affairs, rather than relying—as does the current deficit model of schooling in such spaces—on presumptions of pathology and dysfunction that need to be broken by outsiders with no intrinsic connection to the people being served.

Taken together, these concepts—of certain basic needs being non-negotiable matters of human rights and entitlement, and the idea that the poor as much as anyone else deserve the right to exercise control over their own communities—can begin to push back substantially on the culture of cruelty. Such thinking can help us as we seek to crawl from under the affluence to a place more equitable and just than the culture that faces us today.

Conclusion: Maintaining Hope Amid Struggle

As Americans, we are not deserving of more than anyone else, but make no mistake, we have been given quite a bit more by dint of circumstance, including the heritage of monumental injustices perpetrated over many generations: conquest, genocide, enslavement, segregation and the economic exploitation of much of the planet for the benefit of global capital (so much of it centered in the U.S.). Not only have we inherited a nation that is arguably the richest and most powerful in the history of humankind, so too have we been left a society whose founding principles are among the most progressive and advanced in that history, however much we have always violated them and made ourselves hypocrites by mouthing them even as we oppressed large segments of the national family on the basis of race, religion, class, gender, sex, sexuality and disability. Having been given so much, we are especially obligated to prove ourselves worthy of such advantages.

As of now, it remains to be seen whether we are capable of establishing true liberty and justice for all, not only on paper but in practice, not only on sheets of parchment but on the streets of our cities, not only in our lofty rhetoric but in our humble reality. From their words and actions it appears that the country's wealthy minority do not believe this is possible, and, more to the point, do not wish it so. They are profoundly un-American in the only way that really matters—in terms of whether one believes in the principles of equal opportunity and fairness upon which we have staked so much as a people. They have made their desire clear. They want the world for themselves and others like them; they see it as their personal playground, within which their prerogatives, desires and whims take precedence over antiquated concepts like freedom and liberty. Or perhaps they simply view the world as a place where those quaint words can and should be redefined to mean freedom and liberty for them and their money. As for that other value, democracy? They never much bought into that one to begin with. Why should they? After all, they can manage to get what they want without it.

But no matter the designs of the moneyed class, I refuse to believe that most Americans are so cynical as to think we can't do better. Surely we are capable of something more. I believe in justice, even though I've never seen it. I believe in equity, even though I've never experienced a society in which it was operative. Now, if I'm being fully honest I have to admit that I don't know for sure if genuine justice is possible. Having never seen it, I have to remain agnostic, if only for intellectual reasons. But that said, I *choose* to believe in the possibility of humankind. Why? Because what other choice is there? Cynical pessimism and a jaundiced view of humanity have brought us very near the brink of collapse. We cannot afford to nurture such a mentality even if, in the end, humanity—and especially that American portion of it—turns out to be a monumental failure. We have to proceed as if we were capable of getting it right. If we are wrong, in other words, let us be wrong in the interest of justice, not in the service of self-doubt.

In 1963, the eminent psychologist Kenneth Clark interviewed James Baldwin, inarguably one of the finest writers and thinkers to ever set pen to paper in this or any other nation. In that interview, Clark asked Baldwin—whose primary literary wheelhouse was the subject of American racism, but who also had profound things to say about class and gender and sexuality—whether he was an optimist or a pessimist when it came to the future of America. It's a question I've spent many hours thinking about. It has haunted me for years, in fact, as I've often found myself vacillating between the two depending upon my mood on any given day. But Baldwin's answer to that question cut to the real heart of the matter, and captures now my own thinking on the subject. Asked the question by Clark, Baldwin took a long drag on his cigarette, as was his way, and offered the following:

> Well, I'm both glad and sorry that you asked me that question, and I'll do my best to answer it. I can't be a pessimist, because I'm alive. To be a pessimist means you agree that human life is an academic matter. So I'm forced to be an optimist. I'm forced to believe that we can survive whatever we need to survive.[83]

Although Baldwin was speaking about the racial crisis in the country in the early 1960s, his remarks then are just as applicable today, and not only about the crucible of race but about the larger issue of inequality. One has to retain a measure of hope in our capacity to get things right and to do what has to be done, or else dreams die. At the same time, I am mindful of the words of Derrick Jensen—next to Baldwin, perhaps my favorite thinker—who has reminded us of the inadequacy of hope, and even its destructive potential when manifested in a vacuum. As Jensen explains it, hope means that one has given away one's own power to effect change. In his book *Endgame*, Jensen explains:

> I'm not, for example, going to say I hope I eat something tomorrow. I'll just do it. I don't hope I take another breath right now, nor that I finish writing this sentence. I just do them. On the other hand, I hope that the next time I get on a plane it doesn't crash. To hope for some result means you have no agency concerning it. . . . When we realize the degree of agency we actually do have, we no longer have to "hope" at all. We simply do the work. . . . We do whatever it takes.[84]

In short, to the extent, hope is so often devoid of a commitment to concrete *action*, it becomes sterile and meaningless. We cannot hope our way out of the crisis we're in. But neither can we lose all confidence in our ability to save ourselves from the future as currently scripted.

It is time to take pen in hand and write our own next act. Up to this point, we have let too much of the script be written by others, and the one they are crafting is a tragedy to be sure— a national horror story with no happy ending and very little chance at a quality sequel. But there's still time: time to think and organize and collaborate. All over the country it's already happening. And not just in the usual hotbeds for organizing and activism, but in places like Ferguson, Missouri, where young people, mostly of color, are leading the charge against racially biased law enforcement in the wake of the killing of Mike Brown—and tying that to the economic conditions in the St. Louis area, which have been a persistent tale of two cities (or perhaps a dozen cities) for decades. It's happening in North Carolina, where religious and civic leaders like Reverend William Barber are leading thousands of people in the "Moral Mondays" movement: standing up to budget cuts in programs for the poor, and demanding better health care, job opportunities and fully funded and equitable schooling. In other words, we are not without inspiring examples of collective action; we are not without direction; and we are not without—or at least should not be without—a belief in our ability to change our future and, as Baldwin once said, "achieve our country."

It is in this sense that we must push back against the common and thoroughly despicable rhetoric of the right, to the effect that we of the left—whether the watered-down and liberal version of it presented by President Obama or the more radical version of it manifested in the Moral Mondays, Occupy and #BlackLivesMatter movements—somehow "don't love" and perhaps even hate America, that *we* are the ones who are cynical about our nation and its people. Though we who are leftists are sometimes reluctant to embrace the notion of patriotism—and I, for one, believe patriotism to be a dangerous ideology, too wedded to destructive and divisive nationalism to ever make for a just world—that doesn't mean we don't love our country and those who call it home. While patriotism typically devolves into a blind and militant devotion to one's nation and renders one unable or unwilling to engage in the kind of critique needed to make the nation worthy of praise, true love of country suggests quite the opposite. Loving one's country, as with loving one's children, means struggling with that nation in hopes of making it better. A parent who didn't correct his or her children's flaws or misbehaviors—who refused to so much as acknowledge a child's imperfections for fear of besmirching that child's self-image—would be no parent at all. They would be cheerleaders, absentee mentors, ultimately guilty of a self-absorbed and dangerous form of parenting-by-chaos. Children nurtured in such an uncritical fashion as this would be dangerous, too narcissistic to contribute to the society they share with others. If loving one's children means correcting them, guiding them and seeing them for *all they are*—which is, as with all of us, a mix of better and worse traits and tendencies—then so too must loving one's nation require such complexity.

Let us proclaim it loudly and clearly: it is not we of the left—we who struggle for a more just and equitable nation—who hate that nation. If anything, those who hate the nation and are cynical about its people are those who throw up their hands in the face of massive inequalities and say, in effect, "Oh well, I guess that's the best we can do." Those who hate the country and are cynical about its people are those who insist that we are not capable of ending child poverty, not capable of ensuring health care for all our people, not capable of providing employment for all who are able to work, and not smart enough to create equitable schools and an economic system that works for everyone. What is more cynical, more hateful? To believe that we can do better or to be content at the prospects of a society in which persons of color will remain roughly twice as likely to be unemployed and three times as likely to be poor, and will enjoy one-twentieth the net worth and nine years less life expectancy than those who are white? The answers seem self-evident. It is not the left that hates the country, let alone its people; it is the right, it is the financially affluent minority who would mortgage the future of that country, its people and all of its principles for the sake of their own continued privileges and power.

So let us be bold in our efforts and even bolder in our vision. Let us tell the story of an America becoming—of a nation breaking free from the limits of its own arrested development and transforming into the place we were told about in school but which never really existed as such. Just because that place has been a cruel and taunting mirage for so long does not mean we cannot mold it into a reality. As the Student Non-Violent Coordinating Committee (SNCC)—one of the premier civil rights groups of our nation's history—used to say: Come, let us build a new world together.

NOTES

INTRODUCTION

1. Please know, I am fully aware of the problematic nature of using the term "America" when referring to the United States. I am cognizant of the argument, made especially by many of my Latino and Latina brothers and sisters, to the effect that doing so amounts to appropriating to one nation the principal name of an entire continent, encompassing many nations. The Americas are more than us, in other words, and it is understandable that using the term for the U.S. alone could strike some as an act of linguistic colonialism. That said, I use the term America often throughout this book when discussing the United States, for the following reasons. First, however much I agree with the critique of its use, the term "America" as a signifier is recognizable to most readers, and as a writer, connecting to readers is the most important task—and specifically, to readers who may not be versed in post-colonial, critical race theory. Second, to substitute "United States" for "America" each time the latter is used—as opposed to alternating between them as I do here—would become incredibly unwieldy. It might mean using "United States" twice in the same sentence clause, for instance. However ideologically preferable such a move might be for some, junking up a narrative with repetitive formal nouns of any kind so as to make a larger philosophical point (which will likely be lost on most readers anyway) is a conceit I won't indulge simply to remain ideologically pure and sufficiently leftist in the eyes of some. So too, using "USAmericans" when referring to people in the United States (though I've used it in previous essays) can be ridiculously confusing, and "United States-ians," which I've heard in some circles is even more absurd. Fact is, persons in other nations within the Americas have never called themselves "Americans," so it's not as if we in the U.S. have stolen the term from others who were actually using it. As such, referring to persons in the United States as Americans is accurate (however non-exclusively accurate it quite obviously is) and entirely appropriate, or so it seems to me. In the end, reaching the uninitiated in a language they actually speak, rather than the one we might prefer they knew, is more important than displaying radical linguistic credibility to the already existing left.
2. Michelle Higgins, "Buy Condo, Then Add Parking Spot for $1 Million," http://www.nytimes.com/2014/09/10/realestate/million-dollar-parking-spot.html?hp&action=click&pgtype=Homepage&version=HpSum&module=second-column-region®ion=top-news&WT.nav=top-news&_r=0 *New York Times* (September 9, 2014).
3. Chloe Albanesius, "New 'Facebook for Rich People' Costs Just $9,000 to Join," http://www.pcmag.com/article2/0,2817,2468652,00.asp *PC Magazine* (September 16, 2014).
4. Ben Yakas, "Brunch Hate Reads: NYC Kids Choose Multi-Million Dollar Apartments For Their Parents," http://gothamist.com/2015/03/20/ny_times_definitely_wants_to_spark_class_warfare.php, *Gothamist* (March 20, 2015).
5. Ben Yakas, "The Struggle Is Real: 22-Yr-Old Settles For $3700/Month Apartment," http://gothamist.com/2014/10/19/the_struggle_is_real_22-yr-old_sett.php, *Gothamist* (October 19, 2014).
6. Melissa Korn, "Forget the Old College Try, Ring the Concierge," http://

online.wsj.com/news/articles/SB10001424127887323452204578290183202447320?mod=WSJ_article_comments&mg=reno64-wsj&url=http%3A%2F%2Fonline.wsj.com%2Farticle%2FSB10001424127887323452204578290183202447320.html%3Fmod%3DWSJ_article_comments *The Wall Street Journal* (March 5, 2013).

7. Bryce Covert, "New York City Pantries Ran Out Of Food After Food Stamps Were Cut,"
http://thinkprogress.org/economy/2014/01/23/3195501/york-city-food-pantries-food-stamps/ *Think Progress* (January 23, 2014).

8. Kate Briquelet, "City OKs UWS development with 'poor door' for residents," http://nypost.com/2014/07/20/city-oks-uws-development-with-poor-door-for-residents/ *New York Post* (July 20, 2014).

9. Ronda Kaysen, "What's Next, a Bouncer?" http://www.nytimes.com/2014/05/18/realestate/rent-regulated-tenants-excluded-from-amenities.html?_r=0 *New York Times* (May 16, 2014).

10. Kate Briquelet, "Luxury building fences off low-rent tenants' terraces," http://nypost.com/2014/12/07/luxury-bulding-fences-off-rent-stabilized-tenants-terraces/ *New York Post* (December 10, 2014).

11. Heather Knight, "Income inequality on par with developing nations," http://www.sfgate.com/bayarea/article/Income-inequality-on-par-with-developing-nations-5486434.php *San Francisco Chronicle* (June 25, 2014).

12. "Most Income Inequality: U.S. Cities," Bloomberg.com, http://www.bloomberg.com/visual-data/best-and-worst/most-income-inequality-us-cities.

13. http://media.nola.com/politics/photo/11315388-large.jpg

14. Jarvis DeBerry, "Photo of boy in public housing with an iPad prompts debate over what the poor should have," *New Orleans Times-Picayune* (July 22, 2012), http://www.nola.com/opinions/index.ssf/2012/07/photo_of_boy_in_the_projects_w.html

15. Robert Tracinski, "An Unnatural Disaster: A Hurricane Exposes the Man-Made Disaster of the Welfare State," *The Intellectual Activist* (An Objectivist Review) (September 2, 2005).

16. U.S. Census Bureau, *American FactFinder, 2004*, (New Orleans city, Louisiana — Selected Economic Characteristics: 2004, Data Set: 2004) American Community Survey.

17. U.S. Census Bureau, *American FactFinder, 2004*, (New Orleans city, Louisiana — Selected Economic Characteristics: 2004, Data Set: 2004), American Community Survey

18. U.S. Census Bureau, *American FactFinder, 2004*, (New Orleans city, Louisiana — Selected Economic Characteristics: 2004, Data Set: 2004), American Community Survey.

19. U.S. Bureau of the Census, Census 2000 Sample Characteristics (SF3), compiled by the Greater New Orleans Community Data Center, www.gnocdc.org.

20. http://gnocdc.org/NeighborhoodData/4/IbervilleDevelopment/index.html

21. http://media.nola.com/politics/photo/graphic-iberville-070411jpg-038076f8c-426ba49.jpg

22. "Budget of the United States Government," *Historical Tables, Fiscal Year 2015*, http://www.whitehouse.gov/sites/default/files/omb/budget/fy2015/assets/hist01z1.xls.

23. Thomas Frank, "Right-wing obstruction could have been fought: An ineffective and gutless presidency's legacy is failure," http://www.salon.com/2014/07/20/

right_wing_obstruction_could_have_been_fought_an_ineffective_and_gutless_presidencys_legacy_is_failure/ *Salon* (July 20, 2014).
24. Bill Curry, "GOP's new moral monstrosity: Trickle-down lies enrich the 1 percent, as wing-nuts assert control," http://www.salon.com/2015/03/22/gops_new_moral_monstrosity_trickle_down_lies_enrich_the_1_percent_as_wing_nuts_assert_control/ *Salon* (March 22, 2015).
25. I have deliberately chosen to refer to the economic "elite" as an "economic minority" throughout the book, rather than using the term elite, principally because of what each concept connotes. Too often, we use the term "elite" not merely to denote financial status, but also quality, moral value and talent (think "elite" cheerleading squads, youth soccer teams, military units, limousine services, etc). As such, to refer to the wealthiest and most powerful one percent or 0.1 percent as "elite," while certainly accurate financially, runs the risk of reinscribing however subtly and subconsciously this notion of deserved status, moral superiority and quality. To the extent my argument here is that their status is undeserved, and often the result of moral and ethical misconduct, it would be ironic to continue to label them in such a salutary way. On the other hand, the term "minority" has come to be seen as a word that signifies something lesser than, not merely in terms of numbers but also in terms of status and deservingness. As such, peoples of color have increasingly moved away from using it. First, because indeed peoples of color are the majority of the world's population (and will soon be roughly half of the United States' population as well)—and thus, the term minority either doesn't fit at all, or will no longer fit very shortly—and because to use it is to continue to "minoritize" such folks (hat tip to my friend Michael Benitez for this term) in terms of influence and moral deservingness. In this case, however, to use "minority" to describe the wealthy and powerful is not only numerically accurate—*they* are the minority, not the rest of us—but also flips the script on their ability to claim greater virtue or worthiness. Since a large part of my argument in chapter three is that creating counter-hegemonic narratives is a key element of defeating the culture of cruelty and emerging from "under the affluence," best to begin here, by deliberately altering my own language and encouraging others to do likewise.
26. Sarah Churchwell, "The Great Gatsby and the American dream," http://www.theguardian.com/books/2012/may/25/american-dream-great-gatsby *The Guardian* (May 25, 2012).

CHAPTER I

1. Plato, *The Republic, Book IV* (translated by Benjamin Jowett), http://classics.mit.edu/Plato/republic.5.iv.html
2. Theodore Dreiser, *Sister Carrie* (New York: Doubleday, Page, 1900).
3. John Steinbeck, *The Grapes of Wrath* (New York: Viking Press, 1939).
4. James Baldwin, "A Talk to Teachers," *The Price of the Ticket, Collected Non-Fiction 1948-1985* (New York: Saint Martins, Marek: 1985).
5. "Stock Market Closes at Record High," http://abcnews.go.com/Business/wireStory/stock-market-closes-record-high-25183927 *ABC News* (August 29, 2014).
6. "Corporate Profits Grow and Wages Slide," http://www.nytimes.com/2014/04/05/business/economy/corporate-profits-grow-ever-larger-as-slice-of-economy-as-wages-slide.html?_r=0 *New York Times* (April 14, 2014).
7. Bryce Covert, "Corporate Profits Hit A New Record High Last Year," http://

thinkprogress.org/economy/2014/03/27/3420092/corporate-profits-record-2013/ *Think Progress* (March 27, 2014).

8. Emmanuel Saez, *Striking it Richer: The Evolution of Top Incomes in the United States*, http://elsa.berkeley.edu/~saez/saez-UStopincomes-2012.pdf (University of California Berkeley, September 3, 2013), 3.

9. Lex Haris, "The Super-Rich are Mad as Hell — and Doing Great," *CNN Money*, http://money.cnn.com/2014/01/28/news/economy/super-rich-attack/?iid=EL (January 28, 2014).

10. Emmanuel Saez, *Striking it Richer: The Evolution of Top Incomes in the United States*, http://elsa.berkeley.edu/~saez/saez-UStopincomes-2012.pdf (University of California Berkeley, September 3, 2013).

11. Pavlina R. Tcherneva, "Growth for Whom?" http://www.levyinstitute.org/pubs/op_47.pdf (Bard College, Levy Economics Institute, October 6, 2014).

12. Matthew Phillips, "Goldman: Corporate Profits Grew Five Times Faster Than Wages in 2013," http://www.businessweek.com/articles/2014-01-24/goldman-2013-corporate-profits-grew-five-times-faster-than-wages (January 14, 2014).

13. United States Department of Labor, Bureau of Labor Statistics, "News Release: The Employment Situation, January, 2015," http://www.bls.gov/news.release/pdf/empsit.pdf (February 6, 2015).

14. Dionne Searcey, "After a Bounce, Wage Growth Slumps to 0.1%," http://www.nytimes.com/2015/03/07/business/economy/jobs-report-unemployment-february.html?_r=1 *New York Times* (March 6, 2015).

15. United States Department of Labor, Bureau of Labor Statistics, "The Employment Situation – March 2015," http://www.bls.gov/news.release/pdf/empsit.pdf (April 3, 2015).

16. United States Department of Labor, Bureau of Labor Statistics, "The Employment Situation – April 2015," http://www.bls.gov/news.release/pdf/empsit.pdf (May 8, 2015).

17. Elise Gould, "Nominal Wage Growth Still Far Below Target," http://www.epi.org/blog/nominal-wage-growth-still-far-below-target/ *Working Economics* (February 6, 2015).

18. Robert Kuttner, "Will the Recovery Finally Translate into Better Wages?" http://www.huffingtonpost.com/robert-kuttner/will-the-recovery-finally_b_6642236.html *Huffington Post* (February 8, 2015).

19. Dean Baker, "The Federal Reserve Board's Plan to Kill Jobs," http://www.huffingtonpost.com/dean-baker/the-federal-reserve-board_b_6788040.html *Huffington Post* (March 2, 2015).

20. United States Department of Labor, Bureau of Labor Statistics, "The Employment Situation – April 2015," http://www.bls.gov/news.release/pdf/empsit.pdf (May 8, 2015).

21. Michael Grunwald, "Everything is Awesome," http://www.politico.com/magazine/story/2014/12/everything-is-awesome-113801.html#.VNelCYcf7dt *Politico* (December 24, 2014).

22. National Employment Law Project, "The Low-Wage Recovery: Industry Employment and Wages Four Years into the Recovery," (Data Brief), http://www.nelp.org/page/-/reports/low-wage-recovery-industry-employment-wages-2014-report.pdf?nocdn=1 (April 2014).

23. United States Department of Labor, Bureau of Labor Statistics, "The Employ-

ment Situation – April 2015," http://www.bls.gov/news.release/pdf/empsit.pdf (May 8, 2015).

24. Chris Kirkham, "Economic recovery marked by lower-paying jobs, analysis finds," http://www.latimes.com/business/la-fi-income-inequality-20140812-story.html *Los Angeles Times* (August 11, 2014).

25. United States Department of Labor, Bureau of Labor Statistics, "The Employment Situation – April 2015," http://www.bls.gov/news.release/pdf/empsit.pdf (May 8, 2015). Please note, the relative racial unemployment rates in the official data will look slightly different than what I am claiming here. This is because the Labor Department does not break Hispanics out of the other racial categories when tabulating monthly unemployment figures. Although there is a separate table for Latino/a labor force data, the Hispanic folks captured in that data are also represented in the data for whites, blacks and Asians to varying degrees, since Hispanic is not a separate racial category, but rather an ethnic category whose members can be of any so-called race. The problem is that by leaving Hispanics in the other racial categories—especially the white category, in which eighty-nine percent of Hispanics are to be found according to the Labor Department document referenced in the next footnote—the white unemployment totals and rate are skewed upward, since Latinos have higher rates of unemployment than whites. Because Hispanics (including "white Hispanics") are likely to be perceived as persons of color within the nation's racialized institutions, including nearly nine out of ten of them in the white category will artificially inflate the unemployment picture for whites, making it hard to discern the true racial opportunity gaps between whites and various persons of color. So for these calculations I have performed the necessary extractions of Hispanics from the white data. It's an easy calculation: I simply took the number provided in table A-3 for Hispanics in the civilian labor force (26.2 million) and multiplied it by .89 (the share of Hispanics who are also counted as white in the racial data), leaving a total of about 23.3 million Hispanics who are also to be found in the "white" labor force numbers, which are provided in table A-2. I then extracted that 23.3 million from the 123.5 million whites in the civilian labor force to leave a total of 100.2 million non-Hispanic whites in the overall civilian labor force. Then, I took the number for Hispanics who are unemployed (1.8 million) and multiplied that by .89 (the share of unemployed Hispanics who are also to be found in the white totals), leaving a total of about 1.6 million "Hispanic whites" who are unemployed. Then I subtracted the 1.6 million from the provided white unemployment numbers (5.8 million), to leave a total of 4.2 million non-Hispanic whites who are unemployed. Finally, I divided the unemployment numbers by the labor force numbers for non-Hispanic whites (4.2 million/100.2 million), leaving a real unemployment rate for non-Hispanic whites of 4.2 percent, which is a full half point lower than what one sees in the official data.

26. U.S. Bureau of Labor Statistics, *Labor Force Characteristics by Race and Ethnicity, 2013*, http://www.bls.gov/cps/cpsrace2013.pdf, Report 1050 (August, 2014). As with the previous note, these calculations are slightly different than the raw data in Table 6 of this particular report, because the table, as presented, does not extract Hispanics classified racially as white from the overall white totals for unemployment, by level of education. As with the above note, I have performed the extractions here, using the same assumption as above; namely, that 89 percent of Hispanics are classified as racially white, which we know from the text on page two of this report.

27. Patricia Cohen, "For Recent Black College Graduates, a Tougher Road to Em-

ployment," http://www.nytimes.com/2014/12/25/business/for-recent-black-college-graduates-a-tougher-road-to-employment.html?_r=1 *New York Times* (December 24, 2014).
28. Janelle Jones and John Schmitt, *A College Degree is No Guarantee*, http://www.cepr.net/documents/black-coll-grads-2014-05.pdf (Washington, DC: Center for Economic and Policy Research, May 2014).
29. Rory O'Sullivan, Konrad Mugglestone and Tom Allison, *Closing the Race Gap: Alleviating Young African American Unemployment Through Education*, https://d3n8a8pro7vhmx.cloudfront.net/yicare/pages/141/attachments/original/1403804069/Closing_the_Race_Gap_Ntnl_6.25.14.pdf?1403804069 (Washington DC: Young Invincibles, June 2014), 8.
30. United States Department of Labor, Bureau of Labor Statistics, "The Employment Situation – April 2015," http://www.bls.gov/news.release/pdf/empsit.pdf (May 8, 2015).
31. Rich Morin and Rakesh Kochhar, "Lost Income, Lost Friends – and Loss of Self-Respect" (Pew Research Center), *Social and Demographic Trends*, http://www.pewsocialtrends.org/2010/07/22/hard-times-have-hit-nearly-everyone-and-hammered-the-long-term-unemployed/ (July 22, 2010).
32. Brad Plumer, "7 reasons why Congress's failure to extend unemployment insurance matters," *Washington Post*, http://www.washingtonpost.com/blogs/wonkblog/wp/2014/01/14/an-extension-of-unemployment-insurance-just-failed-in-the-senate/ (January 14, 2014).
33. Mark Trumbull, "Child poverty rate declines in America for first time since 2000," http://www.csmonitor.com/USA/2014/0917/Child-poverty-rate-declines-in-America-for-first-time-since-2000-video *Christian Science Monitor* (September 17, 2014).
34. Carmen DeNavas-Walt and Bernadette D. Proctor, U.S. Census Bureau, Current Population Reports, P60-249, http://www.census.gov/content/dam/Census/library/publications/2014/demo/p60-249.pdf *Income and Poverty in the United States: 2013* (U.S. Government Printing Office, Washington, DC, 2014), 43.
35. Carmen DeNavas-Walt and Bernadette D. Proctor, U.S. Census Bureau, Current Population Reports, P60-249, http://www.census.gov/content/dam/Census/library/publications/2014/demo/p60-249.pdf *Income and Poverty in the United States: 2013* (U.S. Government Printing Office, Washington, DC, 2014), 17.
36. Peter Edelman, *So Rich, So Poor: Why It's So Hard to End Poverty in America* (New York: The New Press, 2012), xvii.
37. Carmen DeNavas-Walt and Bernadette D. Proctor, U.S. Census Bureau, Current Population Reports, P60-249, http://www.census.gov/content/dam/Census/library/publications/2014/demo/p60-249.pdf *Income and Poverty in the United States: 2013* (U.S. Government Printing Office, Washington, DC, 2014), 13.
38. Carmen DeNavas-Walt and Bernadette D. Proctor, U.S. Census Bureau, Current Population Reports, P60-249, http://www.census.gov/content/dam/Census/library/publications/2014/demo/p60-249.pdf *Income and Poverty in the United States: 2013* (U.S. Government Printing Office, Washington, DC, 2014), 13.
39. "Reservation Poverty," *Wikipedia*, http://en.wikipedia.org/wiki/Reservation_poverty
40. U.S. Census Bureau, Current Population Survey, 2009 Annual Social and Economic Supplement, http://www.census.gov/hhes/www/cpstables/032009/perinc/

new04_013.htm, and also, http://www.census.gov/hhes/www/cpstables/032009/perinc/new04_017.htm "Educational Attainment--People 18 Years Old and Over, by Total Money Earnings in 2008, Work Experience in 2008 Age, Race, Hispanic Origin, and Sex."

41. There are a number of problems with claims about Asian American success and the data used to prove those claims. Although Asian American household income is higher than the median for white households, this hardly suggests that racism is a thing of the past. First, Asian American households, on average, have one to two more members per household and one to two more earners in the household as well. In other words, it takes more people working to make just a little bit more than whites can make with fewer persons in the labor force; and with more mouths to feed, that additional income has to stretch farther as well. In other words, actual per capita income is generally lower for Asian Americans than for whites. Second, Asian Americans are far more likely than whites to have college degrees or advanced degrees, in large part because a significant number of Asian immigrants came with those degrees already or were pursuing them upon arrival. This means that we would expect Asian Americans to make more money: a group with far greater educational attainment would naturally earn more. But considering the greater level of educational accomplishment, the income premium for Asians (i.e., their return on education in terms of earnings) is quite low. Finally, there are large differences between various Asian sub-groups: those who came to America with substantial economic advantage to begin with generally are doing better than whites (which makes sense, since one is a self-selected minority and the other a broadly distributed majority), while those who came as refugees or escaping political turmoil, and who lacked advanced degrees or middle class backgrounds, have persistently high poverty rates and high rates of welfare receipt. For data on these matters, see my previous book, *Colorblind: The Rise of Post-Racial Politics and the Retreat from Racial Equity*, in which I discuss the "model minority myth" and provide several citations on the matter, in addition to those provided in the text here.

42. Elizabeth M. Hoeffel, Sonya Rastogi, Myoung Ouk Kim, and Hasan Shahid, *The Asian Population: 2010*, http://www.census.gov/prod/cen2010/briefs/c2010br-11.pdf (U.S. Census Bureau, 2010 Census Briefs, March 2012).

43. Nancy Rivera Brooks, "Study Attacks Belief in Asian American Affluence, Privilege," *San Jose Mercury News* (May 19, 1994).

44. Carmen DeNavas-Walt and Bernadette D. Proctor, U.S. Census Bureau, Current Population Reports, P60-249, http://www.census.gov/content/dam/Census/library/publications/2014/demo/p60-249.pdf *Income and Poverty in the United States: 2013* (U.S. Government Printing Office, Washington, DC, 2014), 17.

45. Brian Miller, *State of the Dream, 2014: Health Care for Whom? Enduring Racial Disparities* (Boston: United for a Fair Economy, January, 2014), 16.

46. Brian Smedley, et.al, "Race, Racial Inequality and Health Inequities: Separating Myth from Fact," http://www.unnaturalcauses.org/assets/uploads/file/Race_Racial_Inequality_Health.pdf *Unnatural Causes* (California Newsreel, December, 2013), 7-8.

47. Carmen DeNavas-Walt and Bernadette D. Proctor, U.S. Census Bureau, Current Population Reports, P60-249, http://www.census.gov/content/dam/Census/library/publications/2014/demo/p60-249.pdf *Income and Poverty in the United States: 2013* (U.S. Government Printing Office, Washington, DC, 2014), 13.

48. Southern Education Foundation, "A New Majority Research Bulletin: Low

Income Students Now a Majority in the Nation's Public Schools," http://www.southerneducation.org/Our-Strategies/Research-and-Publications/New-Majority-Diverse-Majority-Report-Series/A-New-Majority-2015-Update-Low-Income-Students-Now (2015).
49. Robert Sanders, "EEGs show brain differences between poor and rich kids," http://berkeley.edu/news/media/releases/2008/12/02_cortex.shtml *UC Berkeley News* (Press Release, December 2, 2008).
50. Clive Cookson, "Poverty Mars Formation of Infant Brains," *Financial Times* (February 16, 2008).
51. Jamilah King, "The PTSD Crisis That's Plaguing America's Poorest Neighborhoods," http://colorlines.com/archives/2014/02/the_ptsd_crisis_thats_plaguing_americas_poorest_neighborhoods.html *Colorlines* (February 4, 2014).
52. Angela Johnson, "76% of Americans are living paycheck-to-paycheck," *CNN Money*, http://money.cnn.com/2013/06/24/pf/emergency-savings/ (June 24, 2013).
53. Carmen DeNavas-Walt and Bernadette D. Proctor, U.S. Census Bureau, Current Population Reports, P60-249, http://www.census.gov/content/dam/Census/library/publications/2014/demo/p60-249.pdf *Income and Poverty in the United States: 2013* (U.S. Government Printing Office, Washington, DC, 2014), 17.
54. Ilyce Glink, "Housing crisis: Fewer homeowners underwater," http://www.cbsnews.com/news/housing-crisis-fewer-homeowners-underwater/ *CBS MoneyWatch* (Novemeber 19, 2012).
55. Joint Center for Housing Studies of Harvard University, *America's Rental Housing: Evolving Markets and Needs* http://www.jchs.harvard.edu/sites/jchs.harvard.edu/files/jchs_americas_rental_housing_2013_1_0.pdf (Harvard College: 2013).
56. Erik Eckholm, "Victims' Dilemma: 911 Calls Can Bring Eviction," http://www.nytimes.com/2013/08/17/us/victims-dilemma-911-calls-can-bring-eviction.html?hp&_r=3& *New York Times* (August 16, 2013).
57. Lauren Feeney and Cameron Hickey, "Tent Cities Are Cropping Up in the Same Place Where Tech Millionaires Are Being Minted," http://www.alternet.org/hard-times-usa/tent-cities-are-cropping-same-place-where-tech-millionaires-are-being-minted, *Alternet* (April 8, 2013).
58. "HUD Reports Slight Decline in Homelessness in 2012," http://portal.hud.gov/hudportal/HUD?src=/press/press_releases_media_advisories/2012/HUDNo.12-191 (December 10, 2012).
59. Scott Keyes, "At Least Five Homeless People Froze to Death Last Week," *Think Progress*, http://thinkprogress.org/economy/2014/01/24/3200211/homeless-deaths/ (January 24, 2014).
60. *America's Youngest Outcasts: A Report Card on Child Homelessness.* http://www.homelesschildrenamerica.org/mediadocs/280.pdf (Waltham, MA: The National Center on Family Homelessness at American Institutes for Research, November, 2014).
61. Steven Perlberg, "Peter Schiff And Barry Ritholtz Battled Over The Minimum Wage On Last Night's Daily Show," http://www.businessinsider.com/peter-schiff-barr-ritholtz-daily-show-2014-1, *Business Insider*, (January 29, 2014).
62. U.S. Department of Agriculture, *Fiscal Year 2013 Budget Summary and Annual Performance Plan*, http://www.obpa.usda.gov/budsum/FY13budsum.pdf (Washington, D.C.: U.S. Department of Agriculture, 2013).
63. Jordan Weissmann, "The Number of Hungry Americans Has Barely Fallen

Since the Recession," http://www.slate.com/blogs/moneybox/2014/09/03/hunger_in_america_food_insecurity_has_barely_fallen_since_the_recession.html?wpsrc=slatest_newsletter *Slate* (September 3, 2014).
64. Mike Glenn, "Homeless man ticketed for looking for a meal in trash," http://www.chron.com/news/houston-texas/houston/article/Homeless-vet-ticketed-for-looking-for-a-meal-in-4346621.php *Houston Chronicle* (March 11, 2013).
65. Alex Kane, "McDonald's Advice To Underpaid Employees: Break Food Into Pieces To Keep You Full," http://www.alternet.org/mcdonalds-advice-employees-break-food-pieces-keep-you-full *Alternet* (November 19, 2013).
66. Michael Grunwald, "Everything is Awesome," http://www.politico.com/magazine/story/2014/12/everything-is-awesome-113801.html#.VNelCYcf7dt *Politico* (December 24, 2014).
67. Brian Miller, *State of the Dream, 2014: Health Care for Whom? Enduring Racial Disparities* (Boston: United for a Fair Economy, January, 2014), 5.
68. D.U. Himmelstein, D. Thorne, E. Warren, and S. Woolhandler, "Medical bankruptcy in the United States, 2007: results of a national study," *American Journal of Medicine* 122:8 (August, 2009): 741-6.
69. "What are we doing with our lives?" *TIME* (September 8-15, 2014), 60.]
70. Brian Miller, *State of the Dream, 2014: Health Care for Whom? Enduring Racial Disparities* (Boston: United for a Fair Economy, January, 2014): 27.
71. David Callahan, *The Cheating Culture: Why More Americans are Doing Wrong to Get Ahead* (New York: Harcourt, 2004), 214.
72. Peter Edelman, *So Rich, So Poor: Why It's So Hard to End Poverty in America* (New York: The New Press, 2012), 32--33.
73. U.S. Department of Labor, Bureau of Labor Statistics, "Real GDP Per Hour Worked in the United States" http://research.stlouisfed.org/fred2/data/USARGDPH.txt (December, 2012).
74. Elise Gould, "Why America's Workers Need Faster Wage Growth—And What We Can Do About It," http://www.epi.org/publication/why-americas-workers-need-faster-wage-growth/ (Economic Policy Institute: August 27, 2014).
75. Stephen J. McNamee and Robert K. Miller, Jr., *The Meritocracy Myth* (Lanham, MD: Rowman and Littlefield, 2009), 247.
76. Heidi Shierholz and Lawrence Mishel, "A Decade of Flat Wages," http://www.epi.org/publication/a-decade-of-flat-wages-the-key-barrier-to-shared-prosperity-and-a-rising-middle-class/ (Washington, DC: Economic Policy Institute, August 21, 2013).
77. David Leonhardt, "The Great Wage Slowdown, Looming Over Politics," http://www.nytimes.com/2014/11/11/upshot/the-great-wage-slowdown-looming-over-politics.html?_r=2&abt=0002&abg=1 *New York Times* (November 11, 2014).
78. Mark Gimein, "For U.S. Men, 40 Years of Falling Income," http://go.bloomberg.com/market-now/2013/12/31/for-us-men-40-years-of-falling-income/ *Bloomberg* (December 31, 2013).
79. Alan Dunn, "Average America vs the One Percent," http://www.forbes.com/sites/moneywisewomen/2012/03/21/average-america-vs-the-one-percent/ *Forbes* (March 21, 2012).
80. John Marsh, *Class Dismissed: Why We Cannot Teach or Learn Our Way out of Inequality* (NY: Monthly Review Press, 2011), 40.

81. Brian Miller, *State of the Dream, 2014: Health Care for Whom? Enduring Racial Disparities* (Boston: United for a Fair Economy, January, 2014): 13.
82. John Marsh, *Class Dismissed: Why We Cannot Teach or Learn Our Way out of Inequality* (NY: Monthly Review Press, 2011), 35.
83. Congressional Budget Office, *Trends in the Distribution of Household Income Between 1979 and 2007*, Pub. 4031, http://www.cbo.gov/sites/default/files/cbofiles/attachments/10-25-HouseholdIncome.pdf (Washington D.C.October 2011).
84. Emmanuel Saez, *Striking it Richer: The Evolution of Top Incomes in the United States*, http://elsa.berkeley.edu/~saez/saez-UStopincomes-2012.pdf (University of California Berkeley, September 3, 2013), 3.
85. Sarah Anderson, "Wall Street Bonuses vs the Minimum Wage," *Other Words*, http://otherwords.org/wall-street-bonuses-vs-minimum-wage/ (March 12, 2014).
86. Les Leopold, *How to Make a Million Dollars an Hour: Why Hedge Funds Get Away With Siphoning Off America's Wealth* (NY: Wiley, 2013).
87. Sylvia Allegretto, "The State of Working America's Wealth, 2011" http://epi.3cdn.net/2a7ccb3e9e618f0bbc_3nm6idnax.pdf (Washington, DC: Economic Policy Institute, March 23, 2011), 1.
88. Anthony Shorrocks, Jim Davies and Rodrigo Lluberas, *Global Wealth Databook*, http://www.international-adviser.com/ia/media/Media/Credit-Suisse-Global-Wealth-Databook-2013.pdf (Switzerland: Credit Suisse Research Institute, October, 2013), 15-16; 146.
89. G. William Domhoff, "Wealth, Income and Power," http://www2.ucsc.edu/whorulesamerica/power/wealth.html?print *WhoRulesAmerica.net* (retrieved, September 3, 2014).
90. W. Scheidel, and S. Friesen, "The Size of the Economy and the Distribution of Income in the Roman Empire," *Journal of Roman Studies*, 99 (2010).
91. "Forget the 1%," http://www.economist.com/news/finance-and-economics/21631129-it-001-who-are-really-getting-ahead-america-forget-1 *The Economist* (November 8, 2014).
92. "Forbes Announces Its 33rd Annual Forbes 400 Ranking Of The Richest Americans," http://www.forbes.com/sites/forbespr/2014/09/29/forbes-announces-its-33rd-annual-forbes-400-ranking-of-the-richest-americans/ *Forbes* (September 29, 2014).
93. Luisa Kroll, "Inside The 2013 Forbes 400: Facts And Figures On America's Richest," *Forbes*, http://www.forbes.com/sites/luisakroll/2013/09/16/inside-the-2013-forbes-400-facts-and-figures-on-americas-richest/ (September 16, 2013).
94. Sam Pizzigati, "America's Ridiculously Rich: The 2014 Edition," http://ourfuture.org/20141005/americas-ridiculously-rich-the-2014-edition?utm_source=pmupdate&utm_medium=email&utm_campaign=20141006 *Campaign for America's Future* (October 5, 2014).
95. Paul Buchheit, "4 Shocking Examples of American Inequality," *Alternet*, http://www.alternet.org/economy/4-shocking-examples-american-inequality (February 2, 2014).
96. Paul Buchheit, "4 Reasons You Should Be Taking America's Inequality Very Personally," http://www.alternet.org/economy/4-reasons-you-should-be-taking-americas-inequality-very-personally *Alternet* (October 12, 2014).
97. http://geography.about.com/library/faq/blqzcircumference.htm.
98. "Top Ten Things You Didn't Know About the Moon," http://content.time.com/

time/specials/packages/article/0,28804,1929328_1929325_1929310,00.html *Time.*
99. Hedrick Smith, *Who Stole the American Dream?* (New York: Random House, 2013).
100. Tommy Unger, "Which billionaire could buy your city?" http://www.redfin.com/research/reports/special-reports/2014/us-cities-that-billionaires-could-buy.html?utm_content=buffer8bb40&utm_medium=social&utm_source=twitter.com&utm_campaign=buffer#.VC7if5HSJfP (Redfin Research Center, June 5, 2014).
101. "The World's Billionaires," http://www.forbes.com/billionaires/ *Forbes* (March 2, 2015).
102. Melvin Oliver and Thomas Shapiro, *Black Wealth, White Wealth: A New Perspective on Racial Inequality* (New York: Routledge, 1996).
103. According to a recent analysis by the Pew Research Center, from 2005 to 2009, inflation-adjusted median wealth fell by two-thirds among Latino households and by over half among black households, compared with only a 16 percent decline among white households. Mike Brunker, "Wealth in America: Whites-Minorities Gap is Now a Chasm," http://www.nbcnews.com/id/43887485/ns/business-eye_on_the_economy/t/wealth-america-whites-leave-minorities-behind/#.VAFpRpHSLnY *NBC News* (July 26, 2011).
104. Laura Sullivan, Tatjana Meschede, Lars Dietrich, Thomas Shapiro, Amy Traub, Catherine Ruetschlin and Tamara Draut, *The Racial Wealth Gap: Why Policy Matters* http://www.demos.org/sites/default/files/publications/RacialWealthGap_1.pdf (Institute for Assets and Social Policy/Demos, March 2015).
105. Paul Buchheit, "5 Ways Most Americans Are Blind to How Their Country Is Stacked for the Wealthy," http://www.alternet.org/economy/5-ways-most-americans-are-blind-how-their-country-stacked-wealthy *Alternet* (November 15, 2012); Sylvia Allegretto, "The State of Working America's Wealth, 2011" http://epi.3cdn.net/2a7ccb3e9e618f0bbc_3nm6idnax.pdf (Washington, DC: Economic Policy Institute, March 23, 2011), 10.
106. Matt Bruenig, "In Reality, Middle-Class Blacks And Middle-Class Whites Have Vastly Different Fortunes," http://www.demos.org/blog/8/29/13/reality-middle-class-blacks-and-middle-class-whites-have-vastly-different-fortunes *Demos* (August 29, 2013).
107. Matt Bruenig, "White High School Dropouts Have More Wealth Than Black And Hispanic College Graduates," http://www.demos.org/blog/9/23/14/white-high-school-dropouts-have-more-wealth-black-and-hispanic-college-graduates *Demos* (September 23, 2014).
108. Algernon Austin, "A good credit score did not protect Latino and black borrowers," http://www.epi.org/publication/latino-black-borrowers-high-rate-subprime-mortgages/ *Economic Snapshot* (Economic Policy Institute), January 19, 2012.
109. Pro Publica, "One of the nation's largest banks discriminates against blacks, Latinos and Asians, lawsuit claims," http://www.rawstory.com/rs/2015/02/one-of-the-nations-largest-banks-discriminates-against-blacks-latinos-and-asians-lawsuit-claims/ *Raw Story* (February 9, 2015).
110. Michael Powell, "Bank Accused of Pushing Mortgage Deals on Blacks," http://www.nytimes.com/2009/06/07/us/07baltimore.html?pagewanted=all&_r=0 *New York Times* (June 6, 2009).
111. Stephen J. McNamee and Robert K. Miller, Jr., *The Meritocracy Myth* (Lanham, MD: Rowman and Littlefield, 2009), 69.

112. Bob Lord, "Dr. King's Nightmare," http://otherwords.org/dr-kings-nightmare-racial-wealth-gap-forbes400/, *Other Words* (January 15, 2014).
113. John Marsh, *Class Dismissed: Why We Cannot Teach or Learn Our Way out of Inequality* (NY: Monthly Review Press, 2011), 30.
114. Center on Budget and Policy Priorities, "Today's Safety Net Cuts Poverty Nearly in Half, Provides Health Care to Millions, and Has Long-Term Benefits for Children," *Chart Book: The War on Poverty at 50*, (Washington DC: Center on Budget and Policy Priorities, January 7, 2014), 11.
115. John Marsh, *Class Dismissed: Why We Cannot Teach or Learn Our Way out of Inequality* (NY: Monthly Review Press, 2011), 36-7.
116. Paul Buchheit, "4 Shocking Examples of American Inequality," *Alternet*, http://www.alternet.org/economy/4-shocking-examples-american-inequality (February 2, 2014).
117. Paul Buchheit, "4 Shocking Examples of American Inequality," *Alternet*, http://www.alternet.org/economy/4-shocking-examples-american-inequality (February 2, 2014); Anthony Shorrocks, Jim Davies and Rodrigo Lluberas, *Global Wealth Databook*, http://www.international-adviser.com/ia/media/Media/Credit-Suisse-Global-Wealth-Databook-2013.pdf (Switzerland: Credit Suisse Research Institute, October, 2013).
118. Tami Luhby, "Wealth gap between middle class and rich widest ever," http://money.cnn.com/2014/12/17/news/economy/wealth-gap-middle-class-rich/index.html?iid=EL *CNN Money* (December 17, 2014).
119. "Rubio: 'We Are A Nation Of Haves And Soon-To-Haves,' (press release), http://www.rubio.senate.gov/public/index.cfm/press-releases?ID=66bd09d9-2acc-41c0-b853-b43ee6f27ad2 (December 26, 2011).
120. Anthony Shorrocks, Jim Davies and Rodrigo Lluberas, *Global Wealth Databook*, http://www.internationaladviser.com/ia/media/Media/Credit-Suisse-Global-Wealth-Databook-2013.pdf (Switzerland: Credit Suisse Research Institute, October, 2013).
121. Nick Bunker, "Middle Class Series: 5 Charts that Show How Increasing Income Inequality Leads to Less Opportunity," http://www.americanprogress.org/issues/economy/news/2012/12/05/46817/5-charts-that-show-how-increasing-income-inequality-leads-to-less-opportunity/ (Center for American Progress, December 5, 2012).
122. Richard V. Reeves and Isabel V. Sawhill, "Equality of Opportunity: Definitions, Trends, and Interventions," Conference Paper, http://www.bostonfed.org/inequality2014/papers/reeves-sawhill.pdf (Federal Reserve Bank of Boston, October 2014), 12.
123. Sean McElwee, "The Myth Destroying America: Why Social Mobility Is Beyond Ordinary People's Control," http://www.alternet.org/myth-destroying-america-why-social-mobility-beyond-ordinary-peoples-control *Alternet* (March 7, 2015).
124. Katharine Bradbury and Jane Katz, "Trends in U.S. Family Income Mobility, 1967–2004," http://www.bostonfed.org/economic/wp/wp2009/wp0907.pdf, Working Papers No. 09-7 (Federal Reserve Bank of Boston: August 20, 2009).
125. Dalton Conley and Rebecca Glauber, *Wealth Mobility and Volatility in Black and White* http://cdn.americanprogress.org/wp-content/uploads/issues/2008/07/pdf/wealth_mobility.pdf (Washington, DC: Center for American Progress, July, 2008).
126. Richard V. Reeves and Isabel V. Sawhill, "Equality of Opportunity: Definitions, Trends, and Interventions," Conference Paper, http://www.bostonfed.org/inequal-

ity2014/papers/reeves-sawhill.pdf (Federal Reserve Bank of Boston, October 2014), 13 and figures 8 and 9.
127. Richard V. Reeves and Isabel V. Sawhill, "Equality of Opportunity: Definitions, Trends, and Interventions," Conference Paper, http://www.bostonfed.org/inequality2014/papers/reeves-sawhill.pdf (Federal Reserve Bank of Boston, October 2014), 14 and figures 8 and 9.
128. Dalton Conley and Rebecca Glauber, *Wealth Mobility and Volatility in Black and White* http://cdn.americanprogress.org/wp-content/uploads/issues/2008/07/pdf/wealth_mobility.pdf (Washington, DC: Center for American Progress, July, 2008).
129. Richard V. Reeves and Isabel V. Sawhill, "Equality of Opportunity: Definitions, Trends, and Interventions," Conference Paper, http://www.bostonfed.org/inequality2014/papers/reeves-sawhill.pdf (Federal Reserve Bank of Boston, October 2014), 17-18.
130. Josh Bivens, *Globalization, American Wages, and Inequality: Past, Present, and Future.* (EPI Working Paper) http://s1.epi.org/files/page/-/old/workingpapers/wp279.pdf. (Washington D.C.: Economic Policy Institute, September 6, 2007).
131. Peter Edelman, *So Rich, So Poor: Why It's So Hard to End Poverty in America* (New York: The New Press, 2012), 56.
132. John Schmitt, "Minimum Wage: Catching up to Productivity," *Democracy: A Journal of Ideas*, http://www.democracyjournal.org/29/minimum-wage-catching-up-to-productivity.php, Issue 29 (Summer, 2013).
133. Peter Edelman, *So Rich, So Poor: Why It's So Hard to End Poverty in America* (New York: The New Press, 2012), 53.
134. Alexandrea Boguhn, "Bill O'Reilly Downplays Impact Of Minimum Wage Increase For Low-Income Workers," http://mediamatters.org/blog/2015/01/21/bill-oreilly-downplays-impact-of-minimum-wage-i/202230 *Media Matters* (January 21, 2015).
135. Congressional Budget Office, "The Effects of a Minimum-Wage Increase on Employment and Family Income," http://www.cbo.gov/sites/default/files/44995-MinimumWage_OneColumn.pdf (February, 2014).
136. David Cooper, "Raising the Federal Minimum Wage to $10.10 Would Lift Wages for Millions and Provide a Modest Economic Boost," http://www.epi.org/publication/raising-federal-minimum-wage-to-1010/ (Washington, DC: Economic Policy Institute, December 19, 2013).
137. John Schmitt, "Why Does the Minimum Wage Have No Discernible Effect on Employment?" http://www.cepr.net/documents/publications/min-wage-2013-02.pdf (Center for Economic and Policy Research: Washington, D.C., February, 2013).
138. Nick Hanauer, "The Pitchforks Are Coming . . . For Us Plutocrats," http://www.politico.com/magazine/story/2014/06/the-pitchforks-are-coming-for-us-plutocrats-108014.html#.VE_KwJHSJfM *Politico* (July/August 2014).
139. Bethany Jean Clement, "Truth Needle: Is $15 wage dooming Seattle restaurants? Owners say no," http://www.seattletimes.com/seattle-news/politics/truth-needle-is-15-wage-dooming-seattle-restaurants-owners-say-no/ *Seattle Times* (March 19, 2015).
140. Ben Wolcott, "2014 Job Creation Faster in States that Raised the Minimum Wage," http://www.cepr.net/index.php/blogs/cepr-blog/2014-job-creation-in-states-that-raised-the-minimum-wage *Center for Economic and Policy Research* (June 30, 2014). There is a particularly pernicious version of the argument that higher mini-

mum wages destroy jobs, which has been increasingly common among some conservatives, and which is worth mentioning briefly here. Posing as defenders of job opportunities for young African Americans, some on the right insist that by raising the minimum wage (or even having a minimum wage at all), policymakers inadvertently price young blacks out of the labor market by making it too costly for employers to hire them in particular. The claim rests on two principal sub-arguments: 1) that the history of the initial creation of the minimum wage was tied to racism among labor unions and the white working class, which wanted to protect their wages from competition with persons of color, whom they feared would drive down pay scales if they were hired for the same jobs as whites; and, 2) that employers might be willing to hire young blacks if the minimum wage were lower, or if it were repealed altogether, but if it is raised they will not, because the work performed would not likely be worth more than the current minimum, if even that much. Because of these "facts," conservatives have taken to insisting that the minimum wage itself is racist.

The problems with this line of reasoning are myriad, of course, even beyond the general fallacy already discussed, about the minimum wage being a job-killer. First, although it is true that the history of the minimum wage's creation was indeed connected to white working class racism, that fact has little relevance to the debate today. After all, most every policy ever created in the history of the country was tied to white racism: the founding of most all colleges, which discriminated against persons of color; the creation of public schooling from which persons of color were regularly excluded; and research into various methods of birth control, as just a few examples. If a policy or practice's historical connection to racism renders it illegitimate in the present day, we would have to close most colleges, ban all forms of birth control, and actually abolish the United States altogether, since the entire nation's history was embedded in white supremacy.

Second, the argument is itself somewhat racist, in that it presumes young blacks are so devoid of skills and abilities that they aren't even worth $7.25 per hour. Presumably, in the eyes of those who make this argument, blacks are uniquely unskilled at inherently unskilled labor, so that even flipping fries or busing tables is something for which they are unprepared at such a beneficent wage; as such, employers won't hire them, but they would if they could only pay them three or four bucks an hour instead. But does anyone really believe this? Can anyone really believe that the marginal productivity differences at the bottom of the wage scale are so vast as to justify this line of thinking? Third, how could employers add jobs just because the minimum wage had been repealed? Is there really a backlog of persons currently unable to get served at McDonalds, or a shortage of persons to stock shelves at Walmart, such that getting labor even cheaper than they currently do would incentivize new hiring? Of course not. McDonalds doesn't need new stores to meet demand, nor more persons to work their registers. So lowering worker wages wouldn't spur job creation for anyone. It would simply save the company money and make their executives richer, especially since they wouldn't likely lower the prices of their products just because now the workers were paid less.

Finally, even if they did suddenly need new workers in such positions, why should we expect they would hire African Americans for those openings? After all, if conservatives are correct, and blacks are that much less productive than their white counterparts (such that employers will only hire them at below the current minimum wage), then if the minimum wage were abolished why wouldn't those employers just go hire more whites? If the argument were true, the whites would still be better workers, so the bosses could still stick with the better employees and save money at the same time. If the minimum wage were abolished, the whites would be desperate too, after all, and have no choice but to work at whatever wages the company offers. If they really make better fry cooks or grocery clerks or busboys, then the employers will just hire more of them. And if whites are *not* that much more productive, then the entire conservative argument on this score is undermined, and there is no other reason, other than racism, for why employers refuse to hire blacks for minimum wage jobs in sufficient numbers presently

141. Tim Koechlin, "Which Side Are You On? Inequality and the Case for Unions," http://www.huffingtonpost.com/tim-koechlin/which-side-are-you-on-unions_b_5517913.html *Huffington Post* (June 24, 2014).

142. Ross Eisenbrey, "Management—bad management—crippled the auto industry's Big Three, not the UAW," http://www.epi.org/blog/bad-management-crippled-auto-industry-big-three/ *Working Economics* (Economic Policy Institute, May 24, 2012).

143. Robert Borosage, *Inequality: Rebuilding the Middle Class Requires Reviving Strong Unions* (Washington, DC: Campaign for America's Future, 2012), 2.

144. Peter Edelman, *So Rich, So Poor: Why It's So Hard to End Poverty in America* (New York: The New Press, 2012), 52.

145. Tax Foundation, "Federal Individual Income Tax Rates History, Nominal Dollars Income Years 1913-2013," http://taxfoundation.org/sites/taxfoundation.org/files/docs/fed_individual_rate_history_nominal.pdf

146. Thomas, L. Hungerford, "Changes in Income Inequality Among U.S. Tax Filers between 1991 and 2006: The Role of Wages, Capital Income, and Taxes," http://papers.ssrn.com/sol3/papers.cfm?abstract_id=2207372 (January 23, 2013).

147. Troy Kravitz and Leonard Burman, "Capital Gains Tax Rates, Stock Markets, and Growth," http://www.taxpolicycenter.org/UploadedPDF/1000851_Tax_Fact_11-7-05.pdf *Tax Notes* (Tax Policy Center, November 7, 2005).

148. Tax Policy Center, "Tax Facts: Financial Assets, Median Value of Holdings—Family Holdings of Financial Assets: Median Value of Holding for Families Holding Asset, by Selected Characteristics of Families and Type of Asset, 2010," http://www.taxpolicycenter.org/taxfacts/displayafact.cfm?Docid=549&Topic2id=49 (Urban Institute/Brookings Institution, February 5, 2014).

149. Tax Policy Center, "Tax Facts: Financial Assets, Percentage Holding Asset—Family Holdings of Financial Assets: Percentage of Families Holding Asset, by Selected Characteristics and Type of Asset, 2010," http://www.taxpolicycenter.org/taxfacts/displayafact.cfm?Docid=548&Topic2id=49 (Urban Institute/Brookings Institution, Feb 5, 2014).

150. Seth Hanlon, "Tax Expenditure of the Week: Capital Gains," http://www.americanprogress.org/issues/open-government/news/2011/02/23/9163/tax-expenditure-of-the-week-capital-gains/ (Center for American Progress, February 23, 2011).

151. Tax Policy Center, "Tax Benefit of the Preferential Rates on Long-Term Capital Gains and Qualified Dividends; Baseline: Current Law; Distribution of Federal Tax Change by Expanded Cash Income Level, 2015," http://www.taxpolicycenter.org/numbers/displayatab.cfm?DocID=4035 (Urban Institute/Brookings Institution, December 18, 2013).

152. Paul Buchheit, "3 Facts That Poverty-Deniers Don't Want to Hear," http://

www.alternet.org/print/economy/3-facts-poverty-deniers-dont-want-hear *Alternet* (August 3, 2014).
153. Paul Buchheit, "Four Contemptible Examples of Corporate Tax Avoidance," http://www.nationofchange.org/four-contemptible-examples-corporate-tax-avoidance-1373297031 *Nation of Change* (July 8, 2013).
154. Robert Scheer, "If Corporations Dodge Taxes, Why Shouldn't You?" http://www.alternet.org/if-corporations-dodge-taxes-why-shouldnt-you *Alternet* (March 13, 2013).
155. Robert S. McIntyre, Matthew Gardner and Richard Phillips, *The Sorry State of Corporate Taxes: What Fortune 500 Firms Pay (or Don't Pay) in the USA and What They Pay Abroad — 2008 to 2012* (Washington, DC: Citizens for Tax Justice and the Institute on Taxation and Economic Policy, February 2014), 1
156. Tax Policy Center, "Tax Facts: Corporate Income Tax as a Share of GDP, 1946-2012," http://www.taxpolicycenter.org/taxfacts/displayafact.cfm?Docid=263 (Urban Institute/Brookings Institution, May 17, 2013)
157. Tax Policy Center, "Tax Facts: Historical Amount of Revenue by Source, Receipts by Source: 1934-2018," http://www.taxpolicycenter.org/taxfacts/displayafact.cfm?Docid=203 (Urban Institute/Brookings Institute, May 9, 2013).
158. Tax Policy Center, "Tax Facts: Type of Tax as a Share of Federal Revenues, 1934 - 2011," http://www.taxpolicycenter.org/taxfacts/displayafact.cfm?Docid=264 (Urban Institute/Brookings Institution).
159. Pat Garofalo, "U.S. Corporate Tax Rate Plunges To 40 Year Low Of 12.1 Percent," http://thinkprogress.org/economy/2012/02/03/418171/corporate-taxes-40-year-low/ *ThinkProgress* (February 3, 2012).
160. Scott Klinger and Sarah Anderson, *Fleecing Uncle Sam* http://www.ips-dc.org/wp-content/uploads/2014/11/IPS_Fleecing_Uncle_Sam_Report_Nov2014.pdf (Washington DC: Institute for Policy Studies and Center for Effective Government, 2014).
161. Lydia DePillis, "Why companies are rewarding shareholders instead of investing in the real economy," http://www.washingtonpost.com/blogs/wonkblog/wp/2015/02/25/why-companies-are-rewarding-shareholders-instead-of-investing-in-the-real-economy/ *Washington Post* (February 15, 2015).
162. William Lazonic, "Profits Without Prosperity," *Harvard Business Review* (September 2014), https://archive.harvardbusiness.org/cla/web/pl/product.seam?c=34792&i=34794&cs=ea368ca3777a1ed5a98b709c7a 8bb969
163. Lu Wang and Callie Bost, "S&P 500 Companies Spend Almost All Profits on Buybacks," http://www.bloomberg.com/news/articles/2014-10-06/s-p-500-companies-spend-almost-all-profits-on-buybacks-payouts *Bloomberg Business* (October 5, 2014).
164. William Lazonic, "Profits Without Prosperity," https://archive.harvardbusiness.org/cla/web/pl/product.seam?c=34792&i=34794&cs=ea368ca3777a1ed5a98b709c7a 8bb969 *Harvard Business Review* (September 2014).
165. "Republican Party Platform of 1956," http://www.presidency.ucsb.edu/ws/?pid=25838 (August 20, 1956).
166. "Coulter: Hoffa Represents 'Useless' Workers Like 'Kindergarten Teachers' Instead of 'Men Who Have Actual Jobs'," http://mediamatters.org/video/2011/09/07/coulter-hoffa-represents-useless-workers-like-k/181907 *Media Matters* (September 7, 2011).

167."Limbaugh Calls Union Workers 'Freeloaders' as Opposed to 'Real Working Non-Unionized People'," http://mediamatters.org/video/2011/02/17/limbaugh-calls-union-workers-freeloaders-as-opp/176572 *Media Matters* (February 17, 2011).
168.Leo Gerard, "GOP's Blind Hate of Labor Union Members," http://www.huffingtonpost.com/leo-w-gerard/gops-blind-hate-of-labor_b_6778702.html *Huffington Post* (March 2, 2015).
169.Andy Sher, "Sen. Bo Watson slams VW over labor policies, UAW recognition," http://www.timesfreepress.com/news/business/aroundregion/story/2015/mar/18/watsquestions-volkswagen-over-labor-policies/293841/ *Chattanooga Times Free Press* (March 18, 2015).
170.Bryce Covert, "Republican Senator Calls For Abolishing The Minimum Wage," *ThinkProgress*, http://thinkprogress.org/economy/2013/06/26/2216671/republican-senator-calls-for-abolishing-the-minimum-wage/ (June 26, 2013).
171.Christopher Cousins, "LePage's efforts to remove child labor barriers to continue in January," *Bangor Daily News*, http://bangordailynews.com/2013/12/02/politics/lepages-efforts-to-remove-child-labor-barriers-to-continue-in-january/ (December 2, 2013).
172."Fox's Bolling: We Should Emulate China With No Labor Laws Or Minimum Wage," http://mediamatters.org/video/2014/04/15/foxs-bolling-we-should-emulate-china-with-no-la/198904 *Media Matters* (April 15, 2014).
173.Helen Pow, "White America's fears for the future: Survey reveals massive gulf between pessimistic Caucasians and optimistic minorities," http://www.dailymail.co.uk/news/article-2677127/New-polls-reveal-pessimism-white-America-Less-quarter-believe-hard-work-pays-majority-think-country-going-wrong-direction.html *London Daily Mail* (July 1, 2014).
174.Rick Marin, "Can Manhood Survive the Recession?" *Newsweek*, http://www.newsweek.com/can-manhood-survive-recession-66607 (April 17, 2011).
175."Black And Latino Wealth Falls Further Behind," http://www.npr.org/2013/05/06/181601018/black-and-latino-wealth-falls-further-behind *NPR* (May 6, 2013).

CHAPTER II

1. Dale C. Andrews, "Dickens' A Christmas Carol," *SleuthSayers*, http://www.sleuthsayers.org/2011/12/dickens-christmas-carol.html, (December 20, 2011).
2. "A Christmas Carol," http://en.wikipedia.org/wiki/A_Christmas_Carol
3. Charles Dickens, *A Christmas Carol* (London: Chapman and Hall, 1843); full text available at, http://www.stormfax.com/1dickens.htm
4. Peter Edelman, *So Rich, So Poor: Why It's So Hard to End Poverty in America* (New York: The New Press, 2012), xv.
5. Max Weber, *The Protestant Ethic and the Spirit of Capitalism* (Translated by Talcott Parsons) (London: George Allen & Unwin, 1930), p. 163.
6. Joseph Townsend, *A Dissertation on the Poor Laws by a Well-Wisher to Mankind* (Berkeley, CA: University of California Press, 1971), 23.
7. Paul Bernstein, *American Work Values: Their Origin and Development* (Albany, NY: State University of New York Press, 1997), p. 137.
8. Lydia Morris, *Dangerous Classes: The Underclass and Social Citizenship* (New York: Routledge, 1994), p. 59
9. John Marsh, *Class Dismissed: Why We Cannot Teach or Learn Our Way out of*

Inequality (NY: Monthly Review Press, 2011), 110.
10. Howard Zinn, *A People's History of the United States* (New York: Harper Perrenial, 1980), 256.
11. Herbert G. Gutman and the American Social History Project, *Who Built America: Working People and the Nation's Economy, Politics, Culture and Society - Volume I* (New York, Pantheon, 1989), 547-8.
12. Frances Fox Piven and Richard A. Cloward, *The New Class War: Reagan's Attack on the Welfare State and Its Consequences* (New York: Pantheon, 1985), 64.
13. Marta Cook and John Halpin, *The Role of Faith in the Progressive Movement: Part Six of the Progressive Tradition Series* (Center for American Progress, October, 2010.)
14. Henry George, "The Chinese in California," *New York Daily-Tribune* (May 1, 1869): 1-2, excerpted in S.T. Joshi, ed., *Documents of American Prejudice* (New York: Basic Books, 1999), 425-436.
15. Marta Cook and John Halpin, *The Role of Faith in the Progressive Movement: Part Six of the Progressive Tradition Series* (Center for American Progress, October, 2010.)
16. Marta Cook and John Halpin, "Progressive Traditions: The Role of Faith in the Progressive Movement," http://www.americanprogress.org/issues/progressive-movement/report/2010/10/08/8490/the-role-of-faith-in-the-progressive-movement/ (Center for American Progress, October 8, 2010).
17. Moshe Adler, *Economics for the Rest of Us: Debunking the Science That Makes Life Dismal* (New York: New Press, 2010), 9.
18. "Hull House," http://en.wikipedia.org/wiki/Hull_House
19. Premilla Nadasen, Jennifer Middelstadt and Marissa Chappel, *Welfare in the United States: A History with Documents, 1935-1996* (New York: Routledge, 2009), Kindle Location 456.
20. Clifford M. Johnson, Amy Rynell and Melissa Young, *Publicly Funded Jobs: An Essential Strategy for Reducing Poverty and Economic Distress Throughout the Business Cycle.* http://www.urban.org/uploadedpdf/412070_publicly_funded_jobs.pdf. (The Urban Institute, March, 2010).
21. Francis Fox Piven and Richard Cloward, *Regulating the Poor: The Functions of Public Welfare* (New York: Vintage, 1993).
22. Douglas S. Massey and Nancy A. Denton, *American Apartheid: Segregation and the Making of the Underclass* (Cambridge, Massachusetts: Harvard University, 1998).
23. Philip F. Rubio, *A History of Affirmative Action, 1619-2000* (Oxford, MS: University Press of Mississippi, 2012).
24. Tax Foundation, "Federal Individual Income Tax Rates History, Nominal Dollars Income Years 1913-2013," http://taxfoundation.org/sites/taxfoundation.org/files/docs/fed_individual_rate_history_nominal.pdf.
25. Joan Walsh, "The radical MLK we need today," Salon, January 20, 2014, http://www.salon.com/2014/01/20/the_radical_mlk_we_need_today/. Martin Luther King, Jr., *Where Do We Go From Here? Chaos or Community?* (Boston: Beacon Press, 1967).
26. Josh Levin, "The Welfare Queen," http://www.slate.com/articles/news_and_politics/history/2013/12/linda_taylor_welfare_queen_ronald_reagan_made_her_a_notorious_american_villain.html, *Slate* (December 19, 2013).
27. Rick Perlstein, *The Invisible Bridge: The Fall of Nixon and the Rise of Reagan* (New York: Simon & Schuster, 2014, Kindle Edition), Kindle Locations 9159-9160.
28. Ernest Dumas, "The 'Welfare Queen' lives on in food-stamp myth," http://www.arktimes.com/arkansas/the-welfare-queen-lives-on-in-food-stamp-myth/

Content?oid=2977935, *Arkansas Times* (July 18, 2013).
29. Frances Fox Piven and Richard A. Cloward, *The New Class War: Reagan's Attack on the Welfare State and Its Consequences* (New York: Pantheon, 1985).
30. Frances Fox Piven and Richard A. Cloward, *The New Class War: Reagan's Attack on the Welfare State and Its Consequences* (New York: Pantheon, 1985), 158. This is an especially important point given the continued claims of some conservative economists that lower tax rates for the wealthy actually *boost* overall tax revenue. The argument, put forward by economists like Arthur Laffer (considered fringe by most mainstream economists, but regularly interviewed on FOX) is that lower tax rates spark so much additional economic activity that incomes will rise and thus taxes collected will also climb. It was Laffer's analysis (known as the "Laffer Curve"), literally drawn on the back of a cocktail napkin, which formed the basis for much of Reagan's early economic policy. And yet, there have always been multiple and obvious problems with the position. These problems are in addition to the fact that virtually all academic economists consider it laughable (no pun intended), and the fact that it has never been demonstrated true at any point in economic history for tax cuts as deep as Laffer proposed and Reagan managed to push through. Among those problems, perhaps this is the most utterly devastating: Does it really seem likely that officials who insisted one of the biggest problems in Washington was government waste, would then support economic policies that they honestly believed would give that same wasteful government even more money to spend? Why would people whose entire worldview involved shrinking the size of government push for tax policies that would have the exact opposite effect? Obviously, by internally discussing the hope that the budget cuts and massive spending increases for the military would balloon the deficit, thereby forcing domestic spending cuts, the Reaganites essentially admitted the intellectual absurdity of Laffer's claims. They knew revenues would fall, and indeed, that was their goal.
31. "Oscar Lewis," http://en.wikipedia.org/wiki/Oscar_Lewis
32. William Ryan, *Blaming the Victim* (New York, Vintage Books, 1976).
33. Premilla Nadasen, Jennifer Mittelstadt, and Marissa Chappell, *Welfare in the United States: A History with Documents, 1935-1996* (New York: Routledge, 2009).
34. U.S. Department of Health and Human Services, *Temporary Assistance for Needy Families Program (TANF), Eighth Annual Report to Congress* (Washington, DC, 2009).
35. Michelle Chen, "How Reforming Welfare and Gutting Programs for the Poor Became a Bipartisan Platform," *Alternet* (September 8, 2012)
36. Steven Perlberg, "Rick Santelli Started The Tea Party With A Rant Exactly 5 Years Ago Today — Here's How He Feels About It Now," http://www.businessinsider.com/rick-santelli-tea-party-rant-2014-2 *Business Insider* (February 19, 2014).
37. Jocelyn Fong, "Cunningham: '[P]eople are poor in America . . . because they lack values, morals, and ethics'," http://mediamatters.org/video/2008/10/29/cunningham-people-are-poor-in-america-because-t/145918 *Media Matters* (October 29, 2008).
38. "Obama chastises black fathers," http://www.capitolhillblue.com/node/8828 *Capitol Hill Blue* (June 15, 2008).
39. Ta-Nehisi Coates, "How the Obama Administration Talks to Black America," http://www.theatlantic.com/politics/archive/2013/05/how-the-obama-administration-talks-to-black-america/276015/ *The Atlantic* (May 20, 2013).
40. United States Department of Labor, Office of Policy Planning and Research,

The Negro Family: The Case for National Action (Washington, DC: U.S. Department of Labor, March, 1965).
41. Peter Edelman, *So Rich, So Poor: Why It's So Hard to End Poverty in America* (New York: The New Press, 2012), 14.
42. Peter Edelman, *So Rich, So Poor: Why It's So Hard to End Poverty in America* (New York: The New Press, 2012), 19.
43. Elspeth Reeve, "E.W. Jackson Says the Government Is Worse for Black People Than Slavery," http://www.thewire.com/politics/2013/06/ew-jackson-government-slavery/66451/ *The Wire* (June 20, 2013).
44. Jamelle Bouie, "What Cliven Bundy Knows About 'The Negro'," http://www.slate.com/blogs/weigel/2014/04/24/cliven_bundy_and_some_conservative_pundits_are_not_so_different.html *Slate* (April 24, 2014).
45. U.S. Department of Agriculture, Food and Nutrition Service, Office of Policy Support, *Characteristics of Supplemental Nutrition Assistance Program Households: Fiscal Year 2013*, http://www.fns.usda.gov/sites/default/files/ops/Characteristics2013.pdf (December 2014).
46. Carmen DeNavas-Walt, Bernadette D. Proctor, and Jessica C. Smith, *Income, Poverty, and Health Insurance Coverage in the United States: 2012* http://www.census.gov/prod/2013pubs/p60-245.pdf (U.S. Census Bureau, Current Population Reports, P60-245, 2013), 21.
47. Hilary W. Hoynes, Diane Whitmore Schanzenbach, Douglas Almond, "Long Run Impacts of Childhood Access to the Safety Net," NBER Working Paper, No. 18535, http://www.nber.org/papers/w18535 (National Bureau of Economic Research, November, 2012)
48. Jeffrey Grogger, "The Effects of Time Limits, the EITC, and Other Policy Changes on Welfare Use, Work, and Income among Female-Headed Families," *The Review of Economics and Statistics* 85: 2 (May 2003), 394-408.
49. "Policy Basics: Introduction to Medicaid," http://www.cbpp.org/sites/default/files/atoms/files/policybasics-medicaid.pdf (Washington DC: Center on Budget and Policy Priorities, May 8, 2013).
50. Lisa Gray-Garcia, "The Hater Party: How Right-Wing Candidates Have Turned Hate Into Political Currency," http://www.alternet.org/story/148657/the_hater_party%3A_how_right-wing_candidates_have_turned_hate_into_political_currency *Alternet* (October 28, 2010).
51. Beth Fouhy, "Carl Paladino Backs Welfare Prison Dorms, Hygiene Classes," http://www.huffingtonpost.com/2010/08/22/carl-paladino-backs-welfa_n_690284.html *Huffington Post* (August 22, 2010).
52. "Limbaugh: 'Do You Know Any Low-Income People Who Want To Get A Better Job? . . . Do They Even Want To Work?'" http://mediamatters.org/video/2011/04/21/limbaugh-do-you-know-any-low-income-people-who/178940 *Media Matters* (April 21, 2011).
53. Molly K. Hooper and Bob Cusack, "Boehner: Suicide over minimum wage hike," http://thehill.com/homenews/house/198856-boehner-id-rather-kill-myself-than-raise-the-minimum-wage#ixzz30Tsx379t *The Hill* (February 21, 2014).
54. Arthur Delaney, "John Boehner Is Done Being Nice About The Unemployed," http://www.huffingtonpost.com/2014/09/19/john-boehner-unemployment_n_5849742.html *Huffington Post* (September 19, 2014).
55. Lis Power, "Congressional Progressive Caucus Denounces Erick Erickson's

"Degrading Remarks" About Minimum Wage Workers," http://mediamatters.org/blog/2014/09/04/congressional-progressive-caucus-denounces-eric/200653 *Media Matters* (September 4, 2014).

56. "Limbaugh says non-profit organization employees are "lazy idiots" and "rapists in terms of finance and economy," http://mediamatters.org/video/2010/08/12/limbaugh-says-non-profit-organization-employees/169145 *Media Matters* (August 12, 2010).

57. Craig Harrington, "Fox's Varney On Furloughed Federal Employees: 'I Want To Punish These People'," http://mediamatters.org/blog/2013/10/03/foxs-varney-on-furloughed-federal-employees-i-w/196261 *Media Matters* (October 3, 2013).

58. "Limbaugh Compares Welfare Recipients To Wild Animals That Become Dependent On People For Food," http://mediamatters.org/video/2012/04/04/limbaugh-compares-welfare-recipients-to-wild-an/186252 *Media Matters* (April 4, 2012).

59. "Limbaugh Compares Students Who Receive Free School Meals To Family Pets," http://mediamatters.org/video/2013/09/06/limbaugh-compares-students-who-receive-free-sch/195761 *Media Matters* (September 6, 2013).

60. "Limbaugh Calls Poor Children Receiving Free School Meals 'Wanton Little Waifs And Serfs Dependent On The State'," http://mediamatters.org/video/2011/12/12/limbaugh-calls-poor-children-receiving-free-sch/185173 *Media Matters* (December 12, 2011).

61. Oliver Willis, "The 10 Worst Advertiser-Sponsored Moments Limbaugh Laughed At Human Suffering," http://mediamatters.org/blog/2012/03/11/the-10-worst-advertiser-sponsored-moments-limba/185470 *Media Matters* (March 11, 2012).

62. "Hannity Compares Individuals On Government Programs To Animals That Become Dependent On People For Food," http://mediamatters.org/video/2013/01/03/hannity-compares-individuals-on-government-prog/192013 *Media Matters* (January 3, 2013).

63. "Ann Coulter: 'Welfare' Creates 'Generations of Utterly Irresponsible Animals'," http://mediamatters.org/video/2011/08/15/ann-coulter-welfare-creates-generations-of-utte/182020 *Media Matters* (August 15, 2011).

64. Ted Nugent, "Four More Years of Debt and Class Warfare," http://www.washingtontimes.com/news/2012/nov/8/four-more-years-of-debt-and-class-warfare/ *Washington Times* (November 8, 2012).

65. Kaaryn S. Gustafson, *Cheating Welfare: Public Assistance and the Criminalization of Poverty* (New York: NYU Press, 2011), 61.

66. Zachary Pleat, "Fox Regular Neal Boortz Calls 'The Poor' The 'Toenail Fungus' Of America." http://mediamatters.org/blog/2012/02/01/fox-regular-neal-boortz-calls-the-poor-the-toen/184463 *Media Matters* (February 1, 2012).

67. Julie Millican, Andrew Seifter, and Trevor Zimmer, "Boortz: '[P]rimary blame' for Katrina goes to 'worthless parasites who lived in New Orleans'," http://mediamatters.org/video/2008/02/01/boortz-primary-blame-for-katrina-goes-to-worthl/142414 *Media Matters* (February 1, 2008).

68. Alfred Lubrano, "Reacting to the poor - negatively," http://articles.philly.com/2013-08-06/news/41096922_1_west-philadelphia-neuroimaging-psychology *Philadelphia Inquirer* (August 6, 2013).

69. Dan Solomon, "Video of a Homeless Austin Man Went Viral Because It Shows

How Crappy Everybody Treats Homeless People," http://www.texasmonthly.com/daily-post/video-homeless-austin-man-went-viral-because-it-shows-how-crappy-everybody-treats *Texas Monthly* (August 13, 2014).
70. Scott Keyes, "State Rep. Smashes Homeless Peoples' Stuff With a Sledgehammer," http://www.alternet.org/state-rep-smashes-homeless-peoples-stuff-sledgegammer *Alternet* (November 19, 2013).
71. Zaid Jilani, "San Francisco Church Installs Watering System to Drench Homeless and Keep Them Away," http://www.alternet.org/news-amp-politics/san-francisco-church-installs-watering-system-drench-homeless-and-keep-them-away *Alternet* (March 18, 2015).
72. Colby Itkowitz, "Rep. Don Young: Wolves would solve homelessness," http://www.washingtonpost.com/blogs/in-the-loop/wp/2015/03/05/rep-don-young-wolves-would-solve-homelessness/ *Washington Post* (March 5, 2015).
73. Leanne Suter, "Homeless Man Set on Fire While Sleeping at Ventura Beach," http://abc7.com/news/homeless-man-set-on-fire-while-sleeping-at-ventura-beach/480692/ (January 18, 2015).
74. Gabe Wildau, "O'Reilly: 'Irresponsible and lazy . . . that's what poverty is'," *Media Matters*, http://mediamatters.org/research/2004/06/16/oreilly-irresponsible-and-lazy-thats-what-pover/131278 (June 16, 2004).
75. Craig Harrington, "Fox's Gasparino Calls Public Pensions 'Ponzi Schemes,' Wishes More 'Stigma' Was Attached To Welfare," http://mediamatters.org/blog/2014/08/21/foxs-gasparino-calls-public-pensions-ponzi-sche/200506, *Media Matters* (August 21, 2014).
76. "National Review's Rich Lowry: It's 'A Disgrace' That Stigma Of 'Being On The Dole' Has Eroded," http://mediamatters.org/video/2013/08/16/national-reviews-rich-lowry-its-a-disgrace-that/195450 *Media Matters* (August 16, 2013).
77. Eric Schroeck, "Fox News' Shame Test For The Poor," http://mediamatters.org/blog/2012/05/21/fox-news-shame-test-for-the-poor/184948 *Media Matters* (May 21, 2012).
78. "Editorial: Food stamps expansion driven by politics," http://usatoday30.usatoday.com/news/opinion/editorials/story/2012-07-04/SNAP-farm-bill-food-stamps/56020262/1 *USA Today* (July 4, 2012).
79. "Forbes On Fox Panelist: 'Why Can't We Make Someone Feel Embarrassed' For Being On Welfare?" http://mediamatters.org/video/2012/08/18/forbes-on-fox-panelist-why-cant-we-make-someone/189430 *Media Matters* (August 18, 2012).
80. Jordan Weissman, "Newt Gingrich Thinks School Children Should Work as Janitors," http://www.theatlantic.com/business/archive/2011/11/newt-gingrich-thinks-school-children-should-work-as-janitors/248837/ *The Atlantic* (November 21, 2011).
81. Reese, Diana. 2013. "West Virginia: Lawmaker wants kids to work for 'free lunch.'" *Washington Post* ("She the People" blog), http://www.washingtonpost.com/blogs/she-the-people/wp/2013/04/24/west-virginia-lawmaker-wants-kids-to-work-for-free-lunch/, April 24.
82. Dave Constantin, "How Today's School Lunch Lines Promote Class Segregation," http://www.alternet.org/education/how-todays-school-lunch-lines-promote-class-segregation *Alternet* (September 21, 2014).
83. David Edwards, "Principal stopped school's shaming free lunch kids with hand stamps, says it got her fired," http://www.rawstory.com/rs/2014/01/principal-

stopped-schools-shaming-free-lunch-kids-with-hand-stamps-says-it-got-her-fired/ *The Raw Story* (January 6, 2014).
84. Progress Ohio, "Tea Partiers Mock And Scorn Apparent Parkinson's Victim," http://youtu.be/6ik4f1dRbP8 *YouTube* (uploaded March 17, 2010).
85. Luke Brinker, " 'Join the club': Rand Paul mocks people on disability," http://www.salon.com/2015/01/14/join_the_club_rand_paul_mocks_people_on_disability/ *Salon* (January 14, 2015).
86. Eric Hananoki, "Fox Host Tells Caller Her Bipolar Disorder Is "Made Up" And "The Latest Fad" For Money," http://mediamatters.org/blog/2015/01/30/fox-host-tells-caller-her-bipolar-disorder-is-m/202349 *Media Matters* (January 30, 2015).
87. Zachary Pleat, "Fox Business Rebukes Poor People For Not Being Ashamed Of Their Poverty," http://mediamatters.org/blog/2011/05/19/fox-business-rebukes-poor-people-for-not-being/159642 *Media Matters* (May 19, 2011).
88. Stephen C. Webster, "Fox News contributor: 'It gets a little comfortable to be in poverty,'" http://www.rawstory.com/rs/2013/03/31/fox-news-contributor-it-gets-a-little-comfortable-to-be-in-poverty/ *The Raw Story* (March 31, 2013).
89. "Fox's Charles Payne Laments Lack Of 'Stigma' Surrounding Food Stamps," http://mediamatters.org/video/2013/03/28/foxs-charles-payne-laments-lack-of-stigma-surro/193311 *Media Matters* (March 28, 2013).
90. "Fox's Charles Payne: 'If You Can't Pass A Test To Become A Bus Driver But You Know You're Still Going To Eat, There's A Problem'," http://mediamatters.org/video/2012/04/06/foxs-charles-payne-if-you-cant-pass-a-test-to-b/185193 *Media Matters* (April 6, 2012).
91. "Payne Downplays U.S. Poverty: 'The Very Poor Suffer From Gout. In The 1920s And '30s That Was Called The Rich Man's Disease'," http://mediamatters.org/video/2012/02/04/payne-downplays-us-poverty-the-very-poor-suffer/184951 *Media Matters* (February 4, 2012).
92. Simon Maloy, "Jim Crow For The Poor," http://mediamatters.org/blog/2012/02/28/jim-crow-for-the-poor/186143 *Media Matters* (February 28, 2012).
93. "Limbaugh 'media tweak': 'If people cannot even feed and clothe themselves, should they be allowed to vote?'" http://mediamatters.org/video/2010/12/03/limbaugh-media-tweak-if-people-cannot-even-feed/174021 *Media Matters* (December 3, 2010).
94. Matthew Vadun, "Registering the Poor to Vote is Un-American," http://www.americanthinker.com/2011/09/registering_the_poor_to_vote_is_un-american.html *The American Thinker* (September 1, 2011).
95. Matt Gertz, "Ted Nugent's Budget Deal: Suspend Vote for Welfare Recipients," http://mediamatters.org/blog/2012/12/04/ted-nugents-budget-deal-suspend-vote-for-welfar/191666 *Media Matters* (December 4, 2012).
96. Zaid Jilani, "Tea Party Nation President Says It 'Makes A Lot Of Sense' To Restrict Voting Only To Property Owners," *ThinkProgress*, http://thinkprogress.org/politics/2010/11/30/132532/tea-party-voting-property/ (November 30, 2010).
97. Kyle Mantyla, "Fischer: Only Property Owners Should Be Eligible To Vote," http://www.rightwingwatch.org/content/fischer-only-property-owners-should-be-eligible-vote *Right Wing Watch* (January 15, 2014).
98. Emily Arrowood, "These Fox Figures' Suggestions For Best Voting Practices Sound Similar To Jim Crow Laws" http://mediamatters.org/blog/2014/10/02/these-

fox-figures-suggestions-for-best-voting-p/200996 *Media Matters* (October 2, 2014).
99. David Edwards, "Fox and Ann Coulter prep for 2016: Bring back 'literacy tests' so voting is 'a little more difficult'," http://www.rawstory.com/2015/04/fox-and-ann-coulter-prep-for-2016-bring-back-literacy-tests-so-voting-is-a-little-more-difficult/, *Raw Story* (April 15, 2015).
100.Matthew Yglesias, "Newt Gingrich Proposes Reviving "Poll Tests" Of The Sort Outlawed In The Civil Rights Era," http://thinkprogress.org/yglesias/2011/05/14/200982/newt-gingrich-proposes-reviving-poll-tests-of-the-sort-outlawed-in-the-civil-rights-era/ *Think Progress* (May 14, 2011).
101.Charles Riley, "Tom Perkins' big idea: The rich should get more votes," http://money.cnn.com/2014/02/14/investing/tom-perkins-vote/index.html *CNN Money* (February 14, 2014).
102.David Badash, "'Small Government' GOP Vice Chair: I Would Sterilize Poor Women On Medicaid," http://www.thenewcivilrightsmovement.com/vice_chair_of_arizona_gop?recruiter_id=2 TheNewCivilRightsMovement.com (September 12, 2014).
103.Lance Hill and Tim Wise, "Report on Louisiana House Bill No. 1584: The Duke Sterilization Plan," in *The Politics and Background of David Duke: A Resource Packet* (New Orleans: Louisiana Coalition Against Racism and Nazism, December, 1991).
104.Karen Tumulty, "Gramm's Politics of Controversy: Plan for Balanced Budget Keeps Capital Off Balance," http://articles.latimes.com/1985-11-13/news/mn-5379_1_balanced-budget-proposal *Los Angeles Times*, (November 13, 1985).
105.Alex Henderson, "McDowell County, USA Has Close to Haiti's Life Expectancy: Welcome to Third World America," http://www.alternet.org/corporate-accountability-and-workplace/mcdowell-county-usa-has-close-haitis-life-expectancy-welcome *Alternet* (October 16, 2013).
106.Catherine Rampell, "The Haves and the Have-Nots," http://economix.blogs.nytimes.com/2011/01/31/the-haves-and-the-have-nots/?_php=true&_type=blogs&_r=0 *New York Times/Economix* (January 31, 2011).
107."Hannity: 'Poor In America Is Not Poor Like Around The Rest Of The World'," http://mediamatters.org/video/2011/12/06/hannity-poor-in-america-is-not-poor-like-around/184720 *Media Matters* (December 6, 2011).
108.Jason Notte, "Charles Koch: $34,000 puts you in the top 1%," http://money.msn.com/now/post--charles-koch-dollar34000-puts-you-in-the-top-1percent *MSN Money* (July 15, 2013).
109.Robert Frank, "Luxury CEO: The Poor Should Stop Wining," http://www.cnbc.com/id/101410955 *CNBC* (February 12, 2014).
110."Limbaugh Claims Unemployed Spend Their Benefits On Lottery Tickets, 'Smirnoff Ice And Chips'," http://mediamatters.org/video/2013/01/11/limbaugh-claims-unemployed-spend-their-benefits/192195 *Media Matters* (January 11, 2013).
111."FOX News' Andrea Tantaros: I Should Live Off Food Stamps As a Dieting Technique (VIDEO)," http://www.huffingtonpost.com/2012/11/21/fox-news-andrea-tantaros-food-stamps-dieting-technique_n_2172496.html *Huffington Post* (November 21, 2012).
112.David Shere, "Fox Cites Ownership Of Appliances To Downplay Hardship Of Poverty In America," http://mediamatters.org/research/2011/07/22/fox-cites-ownership-of-appliances-to-downplay-h/148574 *Media Matters* (July 22, 2011).

113. Robert Rector, "How Poor are America's Poor? Examining the 'Plague' of Poverty in America" www.heritage.org/Research/Reports/2007/08/How-Poor-Are-Americas-Poor-Examining-the-Plague-of-Poverty-in-America (Washington, DC: Heritage Foundation, August 27, 2007), 1
114. Robert Rector and Rachel Sheffield, "Air Conditioning, Cable TV, and an Xbox: What is Poverty in the United States Today?" http://www.heritage.org/research/reports/2011/07/what-is-poverty (Heritage Foundation, Backgrounder #2575), July 19, 2011.
115. "Right-Wing Blogger Hoft Criticizes Summer Heat Relief For The Elderly And Chronically Ill," http://mediamatters.org/blog/2012/07/13/right-wing-blogger-hoft-criticizes-summer-heat/187111 *Media Matters*, (July 13, 2012).
116. The idea that the poor should sell anything of value before going on public assistance is ridiculous for a few reasons that should be obvious, but which apparently conservatives cannot comprehend. First, some of the items in question do not even belong to the poor, but rather to their landlords. Things like refrigerators, microwaves and air conditioning units usually come provided in apartments, so they are not possessions that the poor have the legal right to sell. Second, even if the poor sold every real thing of value that they owned, like televisions, video games, or their own personal microwaves, the amount they would receive would hardly suffice to keep them from needing assistance. Such items as these might fetch them a few hundred dollars, which would not be enough for even one month's rent or groceries, let alone enough to pay medical bills.
117. Darlena Cunha, "This is what happened when I drove my Mercedes to pick up food stamps," http://www.washingtonpost.com/posteverything/wp/2014/07/08/this-is-what-happened-when-i-drove-my-mercedes-to-pick-up-food-stamps/ *Washington Post* (July 8, 2014).
118. Rolf Pendall, Christopher Hayes, Arthur (Taz) George, Zach McDade, Casey Dawkins, Jae Sik Jeon, Eli Knaap, Evelyn Blumenberg, Gregory Pierce, and Michael Smart, *Driving to Opportunity: Understanding the Links among Transportation Access, Residential Outcomes, and Economic Opportunity for Housing Voucher Recipients* (Washington, DC: Urban Institute, March, 2014).
119. Michael Corkery and Jessica Silver-Greenberg, "Miss a Payment? Good Luck Moving That Car," http://dealbook.nytimes.com/2014/09/24/miss-a-payment-good-luck-moving-that-car/?_php=true&_type=blogs&_r=0 *New York Times DealB%k* (September 24, 2014).
120. "The New York Times' 'homeless' hooey," http://nypost.com/2013/12/09/the-new-york-times-homeless-hooey/ *The New York Post* (December 9, 2013).
121. Matt McLaughlin, "Let them eat applesauce: Right-wing media mock the uninsured," http://mediamatters.org/research/2010/02/26/let-them-eat-applesauce-right-wing-media-mock-t/160988 *Media Matters* (February 26, 2010).
122. Eric Dolan, "Gohmert: Cutting food stamps not evil because poor people buy king crab legs," *The Raw Story*, http://www.rawstory.com/rs/2013/06/20/gohmert-cutting-food-stamps-not-evil-because-poor-people-buy-king-crab-legs/ (June 20, 2013); U.S. Department of Agriculture, 2014. "SNAP Average Monthly Benefits Per Person," http://www.fns.usda.gov/pd/18SNAPavg$PP.htm
123. David Badash, "'Small Government' GOP Vice Chair: I Would Sterilize Poor Women On Medicaid," http://www.thenewcivilrightsmovement.com/vice_chair_

of_arizona_gop?recruiter_id=2 TheNewCivilRightsMovement.com (September 12, 2014).
124.James Mabli, Jim Ohls, Lisa Dragoset, Laura Castner, and Betsy Santos, *Measuring the Effect of Supplemental Nutrition Assistance Program (SNAP) Participation on Food Security*, http://www.fns.usda.gov/sites/default/files/Measuring2013.pdf (Prepared by Mathematica Policy Research for the U.S. Department of Agriculture, Food and Nutrition Service, August, 2013): B-14.
125.Tom Philpott, "People on Food Stamps Make Healthier Grocery Decisions Than Most of Us," http://www.alternet.org/news-amp-politics/people-food-stamps-make-healthier-grocery-decisions-most-us *Alternet* (March 10, 2015).
126."Double Value Coupon Program," http://www.wholesomewave.org/our-initiatives/double-value-coupon-program/
127.Jeanine Grant Lister, "The poor are treated like criminals everywhere, even at the grocery store," http://www.washingtonpost.com/posteverything/wp/2015/04/01/the-poor-are-treated-like-criminals-everywhere-even-at-the-grocery-store/?tid=pm_pop *Washington Post* (April 1, 2015).
128.Tim Carpenter, "Senate moves bill containing GOP-backed welfare reforms," http://www.hutchnews.com/news/local_state_news/senate-moves-bill-containing-gop-backed-welfare-reforms/article_830f1a8d-a577-559a-9e44-87e40a638270.html, *Hutchinson Kansas News* (April 1, 2015).
129.Libby Watson, "Fox Leaves Out Important Information In Welfare Study To Hype 'Entitlement Nation'," http://mediamatters.org/blog/2014/10/08/fox-leaves-out-important-information-in-welfare/201087 *Media Matters* (October 8, 2014).
130.Arthur Kane, "Colorado welfare recipients withdraw money in Hawaii, St. Thomas, Vegas," http://watchdog.org/174626/colorado-welfare-recipients-travel-with-taxpayer-money/ *Colorado Watchdog* (October 6, 2014).
131.Arthur Kane, "Despite law, Colorado doesn't block welfare withdrawals at liquor stores, casinos," http://watchdog.org/174023/despite-law-colorado-doesnt-block-welfare-withdrawals-liquor-stores-casinos/?preview=true *Colorado Watchdog* (October 2, 2014).
132.Jillian Kay Melchior, "Welfare Money Goes to Pot In Colorado," http://www.nationalreview.com/article/371814/welfare-money-goes-pot-colorado-jillian-kay-melchior *National Review* (February 24, 2014).
133."O'Reilly Juxtaposes Stats On Poverty And Substance Abuse, Says, 'Maybe Poverty Is Not Exclusively An Economic Problem'," http://mediamatters.org/video/2011/10/11/oreilly-juxtaposes-stats-on-poverty-and-substan/183197 *Media Matters* (October 11, 2011).
134.Substance Abuse and Mental Health Services Administration, *Results from the 2013 National Survey on Drug Use and Health: Summary of National Findings*, NSDUH Series H-48, HHS Publication No. (SMA) 14-4863. Rockville, MD: Substance Abuse and Mental Health Services Administration (2014), 27. http://www.samhsa.gov/data/NSDUH/2013SummNatFindDetTables/NationalFindings/NSDUHresults2013.pdf
135.Maia Szalavitz, "Study: Whites More Likely to Abuse Drugs Than Blacks," http://healthland.time.com/2011/11/07/study-whites-more-likely-to-abuse-drugs-than-blacks/ *TIME* (November 7, 2011).
136.John Celock and Arthur Delaney, "Drug Testing Bills Proliferate In State

Legislatures," http://www.huffingtonpost.com/2013/04/11/drug-testing-welfare_n_3063962.html *Huffington Post* (April 11, 2013).
137. Salvatore Colleluori, "*Columbus Dispatch* Omits Key Facts On Drug Testing For Welfare Recipients," http://mediamatters.org/research/2012/12/07/columbus-dispatch-omits-key-facts-on-drug-testi/191738 *Media Matters* (December 7, 2012).
138. National Institutes of Health, "NIAAA Researchers Estimate Alcohol and Drug Use, Abuse, and Dependence
Among Welfare Recipients," http://www.nih.gov/news/pr/oct96/niaaa-23.htm (October 24, 1996).
139. Bryce Covert, "Why Do Americans Feel Entitled to Tell Poor People What to Eat?" http://www.thenation.com/blog/198369/why-do-americans-feel-entitled-tell-poor-what-eat?utm_source=facebook&utm_medium=socialflow# *The Nation* (February 18, 2015).
140. Craig Harrington, "Food Stamp Program Hits Historic Low For Waste, Fox Attacks It Anyway," http://mediamatters.org/blog/2014/07/24/food-stamp-program-hits-historic-low-for-waste/200203 *Media Matters* (July 24, 2014).
141. U.S. Department of Agriculture, Food and Nutrition Service, Program Accountability and Administration Division, Quality Control Branch, *Supplemental Nutrition Assistance Program, Quality Control, annual Report, Fiscal Year 2012* http://www.fns.usda.gov/sites/default/files/snap/SNAP_QC_2012.pdf (December, 2013).
142. Dottie Rosenbaum, "Setting the Record Straight on SNAP, Part 3: Waving the 'Fraud, Waste, and Abuse' Flag," http://www.offthechartsblog.org/setting-the-record-straight-on-snap-part-3-waiving-the-fraud-waste-and-abuse-flag/?utm_source=feedburner&utm_medium=email&utm_campaign=Feed%3A+OffTheCharts Blog+%28Off+the+Charts+Blog+%7C+Center+on+Budget+and+Policy+Prioriti, *Off the Charts*, (September 11, 2013).
143. U.S. Department of Agriculture, Food and Nutrition Service, Office of Research and Analysis, *Building a Healthy America: A Profile of the Supplemental Nutrition Assistance Program* (Washington, DC: USDA, April, 2012), 29-30.
144. U.S. Department of Health and Human Services, *Welfare Indicators and Risk Factors: Thirteenth Report to Congress* http://aspe.hhs.gov/hsp/14/indicators/rpt_indicators.pdf (2014), A-5.
145. Ife Floyd and Liz Schott, "TANF Cash Benefits Continued to Lose Value in 2013" (Center on Budget and Policy Priorities, October 21, 2013), 1.
146. Kaaryn S. Gustafson, *Cheating Welfare: Public Assistance and the Criminalization of Poverty* (New York: NYU Press, 2011), 57-59.
147. Kaaryn S. Gustafson, *Cheating Welfare: Public Assistance and the Criminalization of Poverty* (New York: NYU Press, 2011), 184-185.
148. Craig Harrington, "Right-Wing Media Think Unemployed Americans Spend Too Little Time Working," http://mediamatters.org/blog/2014/09/11/right-wing-media-think-unemployed-americans-spe/200730 *Media Matters* (September 11, 2014).
149. Ali Meyer, "BLS: Unemployed More Likely to Go Shopping on Average Day Than Look for Job," http://cnsnews.com/news/article/ali-meyer/bls-unemployed-more-likely-go-shopping-average-day-look-job *CNS News* (September 8, 2014).
150. Media Matters (VIDEO), http://mediamatters.org/embed/static/clips/2014/09/10/36714/fnc-hn-20140910-charlespayne_unemploymentinsurance_lazy (September 10, 2014).
151. United States Department of Labor, Bureau of Labor Statistics, "American

Time Use Survey - 2013 Results," http://www.bls.gov/news.release/pdf/atus.pdf (June 18, 2014).
152.Nasrin Dalirazar, "Reasons People Do Not Work: 2004," P70-111, http://www.census.gov/prod/2007pubs/p70-111.pdf (U.S. Census Bureau, Washington, DC: 2007).
153.Zachary Pleat, "Fox Message Testing: Week-Long Series To Label Safety Net Beneficiaries 'Takers'," http://mediamatters.org/research/2011/05/24/fox-message-testing-week-long-series-to-label-s/179984 *Media Matters* (May 24, 2011).
154.Justin Baragona, "Paul Ryan Claims Black Men Are Lazy And The Cause Of Poverty In This Country," *Politics USA*, http://www.politicususa.com/2014/03/12/paul-ryan-claims-black-men-lazy-poverty-country.html (March 12, 2014).
155.Ben Dimiero and Hannah Groch-Begley, "The Worst Part Of Paul Ryan's Poverty Plan Is Based On A Media Myth," http://mediamatters.org/research/2014/07/24/the-worst-part-of-paul-ryans-poverty-plan-is-ba/200200 *Media Matters* (July 24, 2014).
156."Nugent: Cut 'Social Welfare Programs' Because Poverty Is Based On 'Poor Decisions' 'We Need To Punish'," http://mediamatters.org/blog/2011/12/19/nugent-cut-social-welfare-programs-because-pove/185489 *Media Matters* (December 19, 2011).
157.Mark R. Rank, "Poverty in America is Mainstream," http://opinionator.blogs.nytimes.com/2013/11/02/poverty-in-america-is-mainstream/?_php=true&_type=blogs&_php=true&_type=blogs&_r=2 *New York Times* (November 2, 2013).
158.U.S. Department of Health and Human Services, *Welfare Indicators and Risk Factors: Thirteenth Report to Congress* http://aspe.hhs.gov/hsp/14/indicators/rpt_indicators.pdf (2014), III-11
159.U.S. Department of Health and Human Services, *Welfare Indicators and Risk Factors: Thirteenth Report to Congress* http://aspe.hhs.gov/hsp/14/indicators/rpt_indicators.pdf (2014), I-5.
160.U.S. Department of Health and Human Services, *Welfare Indicators and Risk Factors: Thirteenth Report to Congress* http://aspe.hhs.gov/hsp/14/indicators/rpt_indicators.pdf (2014), II-26.
161.U.S. Department of Health and Human Services, Office of Family Assistance, "Characteristics and Financial Circumstances of TANF Recipients, Fiscal Year 2011," Appendix, http://www.acf.hhs.gov/sites/default/files/ofa/appendix_fy2011_final_amend.pdf (October 29, 2013).
162.U.S. Department of Agriculture, Food and Nutrition Service, Office of Research and Analysis, *Building a Healthy America: A Profile of the Supplemental Nutrition Assistance Program* (Washington, DC: USDA, April, 2012), 11.
163.Jeff Bollier, "Grothman adjusting to differences in Washington," http://www.thenorthwestern.com/story/news/politics/2015/02/20/grothman-oshkosh-listening-session/23769335/ *The Oshkosh Northwestern* (February 23, 2015).
164.U.S. Department of Health and Human Services, Office of Family Assistance, "Caseload Data, 2013" (March 11, 2014), http://www.acf.hhs.gov/programs/ofa/resource/caseload-data-2013.
165.U.S. Department of Health and Human Services, Office of Family Assistance, "Characteristics and Financial Circumstances of TANF Recipients, Fiscal Year 2011," Appendix, http://www.acf.hhs.gov/sites/default/files/ofa/appendix_fy2011_final_amend.pdf. (October 29, 2013).

166. U.S. Department of Health and Human Services, *Welfare Indicators and Risk Factors: Thirteenth Report to Congress* http://aspe.hhs.gov/hsp/14/indicators/rpt_indicators.pdf (2014), II-12.
167. U.S. Department of Health and Human Services, *Welfare Indicators and Risk Factors: Thirteenth Report to Congress* http://aspe.hhs.gov/hsp/14/indicators/rpt_indicators.pdf (2014), II-18.
168. U.S. Department of Health and Human Services, Office of Family Assistance, *Temporary Assistance for Needy Families Program (TANF), Tenth Report to Congress.* http://www.acf.hhs.gov/sites/default/files/ofa/10th_tanf_report_congress.pdf (2012), ix.
169. U.S. Department of Health and Human Services, Office of Family Assistance, *Temporary Assistance for Needy Families Program (TANF), Tenth Report to Congress.* http://www.acf.hhs.gov/sites/default/files/ofa/10th_tanf_report_congress.pdf (2012), 88.
170. U.S. Department of Health and Human Services, *Welfare Indicators and Risk Factors: Thirteenth Report to Congress* http://aspe.hhs.gov/hsp/14/indicators/rpt_indicators.pdf (2014), II-9.
171. Shelley K. Irving, 2010. "Using SIPP to Gauge the Behavior of Welfare Recipients: TANF Reauthorization, 2010," *SEHSD Working Paper* #2010-12. (U.S. Census Bureau: Washington DC., for presentation at the 2010 Fall Research Conference of the Association of Public Policy Analysis and Management, November 4-6, 2010, Boston, Massachusetts), 8-10.
172. U.S. Department of Health and Human Services, *Welfare Indicators and Risk Factors: Thirteenth Report to Congress* http://aspe.hhs.gov/hsp/14/indicators/rpt_indicators.pdf (2014), A-12.
173. Ann C. Foster and William R. Hawk, "Spending patterns of families receiving means-tested government assistance," http://www.bls.gov/opub/btn/volume-2/spending-patterns-of-families-receiving-means-tested-government-assistance.htm (U.S. Labor Department, Bureau of Labor Statistics, *Beyond the Numbers*, 2:26, December, 2013).
174. U.S. Department of Health and Human Services, *Welfare Indicators and Risk Factors: Thirteenth Report to Congress* http://aspe.hhs.gov/hsp/14/indicators/rpt_indicators.pdf (2014), A-27
175. U.S. Department of Health and Human Services, Office of Family Assistance, "Characteristics and Financial Circumstances of TANF Recipients, Fiscal Year 2011," Appendix, http://www.acf.hhs.gov/sites/default/files/ofa/appendix_fy2011_final_amend.pdf (October 29, 2013).
176. United States Department of Agriculture, Food and Nutrition Service (FNS), Office of Policy Support, *Characteristics of Supplemental Nutrition Assistance Program Households: Fiscal Year 2013*, www.fns.usda.gov/sites/default/files/ops/Characteristics2013.pdf (December 2014), 59. To clarify, the official calculations in the above document for each racial group are smaller than those provided here, because the official data includes 7.4 million SNAP beneficiaries whose race was unreported in the data. So, of the forty-seven million recipients in 2013, non-Hispanic whites represented forty-five percent of those whose race was known, while blacks were thirty-one percent of recipients whose race was known and Hispanics were nineteen percent of those whose race was known. If we apply these relative racial percentages to those whose race was unknown (a seemingly reasonable proposition), the relative

rates of use for each group will appear as noted herein.
177.Neil Shah, "Food-Stamp Use Starting to Fall," http://www.wsj.com/articles/food-stamps-starting-to-fall-1409606700?mod=capitaljournalrelatedbox *Wall Street Journal* (September 1, 2014).
178.U.S. Department of Agriculture, Food and Nutrition Service, Office of Policy Support, "Supplemental Nutrition Assistance Program," http://www.fns.usda.gov/sites/default/files/pd/34SNAPmonthly.pdf (March 6, 2015).
179.U.S. Department of Agriculture, Food and Nutrition Service, Office of Policy Support, "Supplemental Nutrition Assistance Program," http://www.fns.usda.gov/sites/default/files/pd/34SNAPmonthly.pdf (March 6, 2015).
180."A Quick Guide to SNAP Eligibility and Benefits," http://www.cbpp.org/cms/index.cfm?fa=view&id=1269 (Washington D.C.: Center on Budget and Policy Priorities, September 29, 2014).
181.U.S. Department of Agriculture, Food and Nutrition Service, Office of Policy Support, *Characteristics of Supplemental Nutrition Assistance Program Households: Fiscal Year 2013*, http://www.fns.usda.gov/sites/default/files/ops/Characteristics2013.pdf (December 2014), xv-xvi, 21.
182.United States Department of Agriculture, Food and Nutrition Service, Office of Research and Analysis, *Building a Healthy America: A Profile of the Supplemental Nutrition Assistance Program* (Washington: USDA, April, 2012), 25.
183.U.S. Department of Agriculture, Food and Nutrition Service, Office of Policy Support, *Characteristics of Supplemental Nutrition Assistance Program Households: Fiscal Year 2013*, http://www.fns.usda.gov/sites/default/files/ops/Characteristics2013.pdf (December 2014), 61.
184.Lynda Laughlin, "A Child's Day: Living Arrangements, Nativity, and Family Transitions: 2011," *Current Population Reports*, P70-139, http://www.census.gov/content/dam/Census/library/publications/2014/demo/p70-139.pdf (U.S. Census Bureau, Washington, DC., December 2014).
185."Fox's Stacey Dash: Government Assistance Is 'The Democratic Party's New Version Of Slavery,'" http://mediamatters.org/video/2014/12/19/foxs-stacey-dash-government-assistance-is-the-d/201961 *Media Matters* (December 19, 2014).
186.Lynda Laughlin, "A Child's Day: Living Arrangements, Nativity, and Family Transitions: 2011," *Current Population Reports*, P70-139, http://www.census.gov/content/dam/Census/library/publications/2014/demo/p70-139.pdf (U.S. Census Bureau, Washington, DC., December 2014).
187.Kelsey Farson Gray and Jenny Genser, *Characteristics of Supplemental Nutrition Assistance Program Households: Fiscal Year 2013*, http://www.fns.usda.gov/sites/default/files/ops/Characteristics2013.pdf (Alexandria VA: U.S. Department of Agriculture, Food and Nutrition Service, Office of Policy Support, 2014).
188.National School Lunch Program: Participation and Lunches Served, http://www.fns.usda.gov/sites/default/files/pd/slsummar.pdf (Alexandria VA: U.S. Department of Agriculture, Food and Nutrition Service, Office of Policy Support, 2014).
189.Sharon Parrott and LaDonna Pavetti, *Cato Gets It Very Wrong: The Safety Net Supports, Rather Than Discourages, Work*, http://www.cbpp.org/files/8-21-13pov.pdf (Washington, DC: Center on Budget and Policy Priorities, August 21, 2013).
190.Michael Tanner and Charles Hughes, *The Work Vs. Welfare Trade-Off: 2013* (Washington DC: Cato Institute, 2013).
191.Eslami, Esa, Kai Filion, and Mark Strayer. "Characteristics of Supplemental

Nutrition Assistance Households: Fiscal Year 2010." Report submitted to the U.S. Department of Agriculture, Food and Nutrition Service. (Washington, DC: Mathematica Policy Research, September 2011).
192. U.S. Department of Agriculture, Food and Nutrition Service, Office of Policy Support, *Characteristics of Supplemental Nutrition Assistance Program Households: Fiscal Year 2013*, http://www.fns.usda.gov/sites/default/files/ops/Characteristics2013.pdf (December 2014), 62.
193. Andrew Gothro and Carole Trippe, *Multiple Benefit Receipt Among Individuals Receiving Food Assistance and Other Government Assistance*, http://www.mathematica-mpr.com/Publications/PDFs/nutrition/multiple_benefit.pdf (Washington, DC: Mathematica Policy Research, July 26, 2010),17.
194. Andrew Gothro and Carole Trippe, "Multiple Benefit Receipt Among Individuals Receiving Food Assistance and Other Government Assistance," http://www.mathematica-mpr.com/Publications/PDFs/nutrition/multiple_benefit.pdf (Washington, DC: Mathematica Policy Research, July 26, 2010), 18.
195. U.S. Department of Agriculture, Food and Nutrition Service, Office of Policy Support, *Characteristics of Supplemental Nutrition Assistance Program Households: Fiscal Year 2013*, http://www.fns.usda.gov/sites/default/files/ops/Characteristics2013.pdf (December 2014), 62.
196. Andrew Gothro and Carole Trippe, *Multiple Benefit Receipt Among Individuals Receiving Food Assistance and Other Government Assistance*, http://www.mathematica-mpr.com/Publications/PDFs/nutrition/multiple_benefit.pdf. (Washington, DC: Mathematica Policy Research, July 26, 2010),18.
197. Sharon Parrott and LaDonna Pavetti, *Cato Gets It Very Wrong: The Safety Net Supports, Rather Than Discourages, Work*, http://www.cbpp.org/files/8-21-13pov.pdf (Washington, DC: Center on Budget and Policy Priorities, August 21, 2013), 2.
198. Sharon Parrott and LaDonna Pavetti, *Cato Gets It Very Wrong: The Safety Net Supports, Rather Than Discourages, Work*, http://www.cbpp.org/files/8-21-13pov.pdf (Washington, DC: Center on Budget and Policy Priorities, August 21, 2013), 1.
199. Andrew Gothro and Carole Trippe, *Multiple Benefit Receipt Among Individuals Receiving Food Assistance and Other Government Assistance*, http://www.mathematica-mpr.com/Publications/PDFs/nutrition/multiple_benefit.pdf. (Washington, DC: Mathematica Policy Research, July 26, 2010), 18.
200. Sharon Parrott and LaDonna Pavetti, *Cato Gets It Very Wrong: The Safety Net Supports, Rather Than Discourages, Work*, http://www.cbpp.org/files/8-21-13pov.pdf (Washington, DC: Center on Budget and Policy Priorities, August 21, 2013), 2.
201. Andrew Gothro and Carole Trippe, *Multiple Benefit Receipt Among Individuals Receiving Food Assistance and Other Government Assistance*, http://www.mathematica-mpr.com/Publications/PDFs/nutrition/multiple_benefit.pdf (Washington, DC: Mathematica Policy Research, July 26, 2010), 17.
202. Andrew Gothro and Carole Trippe, *Multiple Benefit Receipt Among Individuals Receiving Food Assistance and Other Government Assistance*, http://www.mathematica-mpr.com/Publications/PDFs/nutrition/multiple_benefit.pdf. (Washington, DC: Mathematica Policy Research, July 26, 2010), 20.
203. Patricia Cohen, "Aid to Needy Often Excludes the Poorest in America," http://www.nytimes.com/2015/02/17/business/economy/aid-to-needy-often-excludes-the-poorest-in-america.html?_r=0 *New York Times* (February 16, 2015).
204. Robert Rector, Katherine Bradley, and Rachel Sheffield, *Obama to Spend 10.3*

Trillion on Welfare: Uncovering the Full Cost of Means-Tested Welfare or Aid to the Poor http://www.heritage.org/research/reports/2009/09/obama-to-spend-103-trillion-on-welfare-uncovering-the-full-cost-of-means-tested-welfare-or-aid-to-the-poor (Washington DC: Heritage Foundation, Heritage Special Report, September 16, 2009)

205. Brittany Rush, "Where the Money Goes," http://healthcarecostmonitor.thehastingscenter.org/brittanyrush/where-the-money-goes/ *Health Care Cost Monitor* (2013).

206. "Medicaid Moving Forward," http://kff.org/medicaid/fact-sheet/the-medicaid-program-at-a-glance-update/ (Kaiser Family Foundation, June 17, 2014).

207. David B. Muhlhausen and Patrick D. Tyrrell, *The 2013 Index of Dependence on Government* http://thf_media.s3.amazonaws.com/2013/pdf/SR142update.pdf (Washington, DC: The Heritage Foundation, November 21, 2013).

208. "To Fox's Stephen Moore, Unemployment Insurance Is 'Like A Paid Vacation For People,' http://mediamatters.org/video/2014/01/08/to-foxs-stephen-moore-unemployment-insurance-is/197491, *Media Matters* (January 8, 2014).

209. Alan Pyke, "Wall Street Journal Revives Conservative Notion That Social Insurance Breeds Laziness," http://mediamatters.org/blog/2013/01/09/wall-street-journal-revives-conservative-notion/192117 *Media Matters* (January 9, 2013).

210. "Ben Stein Asserts That 'A Lot Of' Unemployed 'Would Not Prefer To Go To Work'." http://mediamatters.org/video/2011/04/30/ben-stein-asserts-that-a-lot-of-unemployed-woul/179223 *Media Matters* (April 30, 2011).

211. "Limbaugh: 'Extended unemployment benefits do nothing but incentivize people not to look for work'," http://mediamatters.org/video/2010/06/29/limbaugh-extended-unemployment-benefits-do-noth/166960 *Media Matters* (June 29, 2010).

212. "Limbaugh: Obama is 'in the process of creating and building a permanent underclass' by extending unemployment benefits'," http://mediamatters.org/video/2010/04/12/limbaugh-obama-is-in-the-process-of-creating-an/163060 *Media Matters* (April 12, 2010).

213. U.S. Congress, Joint Economic Committee, *The Case for Maintaining Unemployment Insurance: Supporting Workers and Strengthening the Economy* http://www.jec.senate.gov/public/?a=Files.Serve&File_id=3e1016fc-2ef2-451d-bcee-193c1f08b174 (December, 2011).

214. Congressional Budget Office, "Unemployment Insurance in the Wake of the Recent Recession," http://www.cbo.gov/publication/43734 (November 28, 2012).

215. Will Kimball and Rick McHugh, "How Low Can We Go? State Unemployment Insurance Programs Exclude Record Numbers of Jobless Workers," http://www.epi.org/publication/how-low-can-we-go-state-unemployment-insurance-programs-exclude-record-numbers-of-jobless-workers/ (Washington, DC: Economic Policy Institute, March 9, 2015).

216. Christopher Ingraham, "Wal-Mart has a lower acceptance rate than Harvard," http://www.washingtonpost.com/blogs/wonkblog/wp/2014/03/28/wal-mart-has-a-lower-acceptance-rate-than-harvard/?Post+generic=?tid=sm_twitter_washingtonpost *Washington Post* (March 28, 2014).

217. Scott Paul, "Shocker: Only 6 Out of 100 Applicants Can Get a Job at McDonalds - It's Time for Politicians to Stop Ignoring Our Jobs Crisis," http://www.alternet.org/story/150839/shocker%3A_only_6_out_of_100_applicants_can_get_a_job_at_mcdonald's_--_it's_time_for_politicians_to_stop_ignoring_our_jobs_crisis *Alternet* (May 4, 2011).

218. Isaiah J. Poole, "After 5 Years of 'Recovery,' Still Only Half as Many Jobs as Job Seekers," *OurFuture.org* (Campaign for America's Future), August 12, 2014.
219. Economic Policy Institute, "Ratio of Job Seekers to Job Openings Holds Steady at 2.9-to-1" (press release), http://www.epi.org/press/ratio-job-seekers-job-openings-holds-steady/ (November 22, 2013).
220. Matthew O'Brien, "The Terrifying Reality of Long-Term Unemployment," *The Atlantic*, http://www.theatlantic.com/business/archive/2013/04/the-terrifying-reality-of-long-term-unemployment/274957/ (April 13, 2013).
221. Jonathan Chait, Jonathan, "Obama's Plan to End Discrimination Against the Long-term Unemployed," *New York*, http://nymag.com/daily/intelligencer/2014/01/obama-hire-the-long-term-unemployed.html (January 27, 2014).
222. Matthew O'Brien, "The Terrifying Reality of Long-Term Unemployment," *The Atlantic*, http://www.theatlantic.com/business/archive/2013/04/the-terrifying-reality-of-long-term-unemployment/274957/ (April 13, 2013).
223. Media Matters, "Limbaugh: Obama Is "Punishing Achievers" By Trying To End Discrimination Against Long-Term Unemployed," http://mediamatters.org/video/2014/01/31/limbaugh-obama-is-punishing-achievers-by-trying/197870 (January 31, 2014).
224. Barry Rithotlz, "How McDonalds and Wal-Mart Became Welfare Queens," http://www.bloomberg.com/news/2013-11-13/how-mcdonald-s-and-wal-mart-became-welfare-queens.html *Bloomberg News* (November 13, 2013).
225. Alyssa Figueroa, "Walmart Is Holding Food Drives Again to Urge Workers to Help Feed Their Co-Workers," http://www.alternet.org/labor/walmart-holding-food-drives-again-urge-workers-help-feed-their-co-workers *Alternet* (November 20, 2014).
226. Americans for Tax Fairness, *Walmart on Tax Day: How Taxpayers Subsidize America's Biggest Employer and Richest Family*, http://www.americansfortaxfairness.org/files/Walmart-on-Tax-Day-Americans-for-Tax-Fairness-1.pdf (Washington, D.C., Americans for Tax Fairness, April 2014).
227. Michele Simon, *Walmart's Hunger Games: How America's Largest Employer and Richest Family Worsen the Hunger Crisis http://www.eatdrinkpolitics.com/wp-content/uploads/Walmarts_Hunger_Games_Report.pdf EatDrinkPolitics.com* (November, 2014).
228. Michele Simon, *Walmart's Hunger Games: How America's Largest Employer and Richest Family Worsen the Hunger Crisis http://www.eatdrinkpolitics.com/wp-content/uploads/Walmarts_Hunger_Games_Report.pdf EatDrinkPolitics.com* (November, 2014).
229. Susan Berfield, "Fast-Food Wages Come With a $7 Billion Side of Public Assistance," http://www.businessweek.com/articles/2013-10-15/mcdonalds-low-wages-come-with-a-7-billion-side-of-welfare *Business Week* (October 15, 2013).
230. Susan Berfield, "Fast-Food Wages Come With a $7 Billion Side of Public Assistance," http://www.businessweek.com/articles/2013-10-15/mcdonalds-low-wages-come-with-a-7-billion-side-of-welfare *Business Week* (October 15, 2013).
231. Sylvia A. Allegretto, Ken Jacobs, Dave Graham-Squire and Megan Emiko Scott, "The Public Cost of Low-Wage Jobs in the Banking Industry," http://laborcenter.berkeley.edu/the-public-cost-of-low-wage-jobs-in-the-banking-industry/ (University of California-Berkeley Labor Center, October 27, 2014).
232. Paul Carr, "New San Francisco billboard warns workers they'll be replaced by iPads if they demand a fair wage," http://pando.com/2014/07/17/new-san-francisco-

billboard-warns-workers-theyll-be-replaced-by-ipads-if-they-demand-a-fair-wage/ *Pando Daily* (July 17, 2014).

233. David Edwards, "Fox host: Living wage supporters think workers were born with 'deficiencies'," http://www.rawstory.com/rs/2014/07/28/fox-host-minimum-wage-workers-were-born-with-deficiencies-or-they-would-get-higher-pay/ *The Raw Story* (July 28, 2014).

234. "Martin Luther King Jr. Talks about the Labor Movement," http://www.aft.org/yourwork/tools4teachers/bhm/mlktalks.cfm (American Federation of Teachers).

235. Janet Allon, "8 Colossal Jackasses From the Right-Wing Fringe: Just-Stop-Being-Poor Edition," *Alternet*, http://www.alternet.org/tea-party-and-right/8-colossal-jackasses-right-wing-fringe-just-stop-being-poor-edition?paging=off¤t_page=1#bookmark (March 8, 2014).

236. Michael D. Shear and Michael Barbaro, "In Video Clip, Romney Calls 47% 'Dependent' and Feeling Entitled," *The Caucus (blog)* (New York Times), http://thecaucus.blogs.nytimes.com/2012/09/17/romney-faults-those-dependent-on-government/ (September 17, 2012).

237. Ben Craw and Zach Carter, "Paul Ryan: 60 Percent Of Americans Are 'Takers,' Not 'Makers'," *Huffington Post*, http://www.huffingtonpost.com/2012/10/05/paul-ryan-60-percent-of-a_n_1943073.html (October 5, 2012).

238. Tom Kludt, "Billionaire Sam Zell: Leave The One Percent Alone, We Just 'Work Harder'," http://talkingpointsmemo.com/livewire/sam-zell-one-percent *Talking Points Memo* (February 7, 2014).

239. Harry Binswanger, "Give Back? Yes, It's Time For The 99% To Give Back To The 1%," http://www.forbes.com/sites/harrybinswanger/2013/09/17/give-back-yes-its-time-for-the-99-to-give-back-to-the-1/ *Forbes* (September 17, 2013).

240. Tom Perkins, "Progressive Kristallnacht Coming?" http://online.wsj.com/news/articles/SB10001424052702304549504579316913982034286, *Wall Street Journal* (online) (January 24, 2014).

241. Robert Frank, "I Wanted the Biggest," *Wall Street Journal*, http://blogs.wsj.com/wealth/2007/11/05/i-wanted-the-biggest/, (November 5, 2007).

242. Nick Denton, Nick, "Tom Perkins' manslaughter conviction," *Gawker*, http://gawker.com/269896/tom-perkins-manslaughter-conviction, (June 18, 2007).

243. Ari Levy and Pui-Wing Tam, "Kleiner Perkins Co-Founder's Nazi Comment Draws Criticism," *Bloomberg News*, http://www.bloomberg.com/news/2014-01-26/kleiner-perkins-shocked-by-co-founder-comment-on-nazis.html (January 26, 2014).

244. Mark Gongloff, "Rich Man Doubles Down on Warning That Poor People are Basically Nazis," *Alternet*, http://www.huffingtonpost.com/2014/01/27/thomas-perkins-doubles-down-holocaust_n_4674266.html, (January 27, 2014).

245. Emily Peck, "WSJ Defends Paranoid Rich Guy, Naturally," *Huffington Post*, http://www.huffingtonpost.com/2014/01/30/wsj-defends-kristallnacht_n_4694727.html, (January 30, 2014).

246. Charles Payne, "Sometimes, Paranoids Get it Right," http://finance.townhall.com/columnists/charlespayne/2014/01/29/sometimes-paranoids-get-it-right-n1786234/page/full *TownHall Finance* (January 29, 2014).

247. Ben White and Maggie Haberman, "The rich strike back," *Politico*, http://www.politico.com/story/2014/03/the-rich-strike-back-104753.html?ml=po_r, March 18, 2014.

248. Ezra Klein, "AIG CEO: Anger over AIG bonuses 'just as bad' as lynchings," http://www.washingtonpost.com/blogs/wonkblog/wp/2013/09/24/aig-ceo-anger-over-aig-bonuses-just-as-bad-as-lynchings/ *Washington Post* (September 24, 2013).
249. Erin Anderssen, "You need to be thanking the super-rich, London Mayor Boris Johnson says," *Toronto Globe and Mail*, http://www.theglobeandmail.com/life/the-hot-button/you-need-to-be-thanking-the-super-rich-says-london-mayor-boris-johnson/article15486982/ (November 18, 2013).
250. "Rich Man Calls Rising Income Inequality 'Fantastic'," http://www.huffingtonpost.com/2014/01/22/rich-man-inequality_n_4644678.html?utm_hp_ref=media&ir=Media *Huffington* Post (January 22, 2014).
251. Oxfam Issue Briefing, "Wealth: Having it All and Wanting More," http://policy-practice.oxfam.org.uk/publications/wealth-having-it-all-and-wanting-more-338125 (London: Oxfam International, January 19, 2015).
252. Rick Perlstein, *The Invisible Bridge: The Fall of Nixon and the Rise of Reagan* (New York: Simon & Schuster, 2014, Kindle Edition), Kindle Locations 9118-9123.
253. Chuck Marr and Chye-Ching Huang, *Misconceptions and Realities About Who Pays Taxes* http://www.cbpp.org/files/5-26-11tax.pdf (Washington DC: Center on Budget and Policy Priorities, September 17, 2012), 5.
254. "Fox Host: 'I Envy' Americans Too Poor To Owe Federal Income Taxes," http://mediamatters.org/video/2014/04/15/fox-host-i-envy-americans-too-poor-to-owe-feder/198903 *Media Matters* (April 15, 2014).
255. Chuck Marr and Chye-Ching Huang, *Misconceptions and Realities About Who Pays Taxes* http://www.cbpp.org/files/5-26-11tax.pdf (Washington DC: Center on Budget and Policy Priorities, September 17, 2012)
256. Carl Davis, Kelly Davis, Matthew Gardner, et.al. *Who Pays? A Distributional Analysis of the Tax Systems in All 50 States* http://www.itep.org/pdf/whopaysreport.pdf (Washington D.C.: Institute on Taxation and Economic Policy, January 2015), 3-4.
257. "Who Pays Taxes in America?" http://www.ctj.org/pdf/taxday2014.pdf (Washington, D.C.: Citizens for Tax Justice, April 7, 2014).
258. "Who Pays Taxes in America?" http://www.ctj.org/pdf/taxday2014.pdf (Washington, D.C.: Citizens for Tax Justice, April 7, 2014).
259. SourceWatch, "Total Wall Street Bailout Cost," http://www.sourcewatch.org/index.php?title=Total_Wall_Street_Bailout_Cost (July, 2011).
260. Andrew Zajac and Christie Smythe, "Boies Poised for Possible Upset in AIG $25 Billion Bailout Trial," http://www.bloomberg.com/news/2014-11-03/boies-poised-for-possible-upset-in-aig-25-billion-bailout-trial.html, *Bloomberg.com* (November 3, 2014).
261. Office of the Special Inspector General for the Troubled Asset Relief Program, *Quarterly Report to Congress*, http://www.sigtarp.gov/Quarterly%20Reports/October_29_2014_Report_to_Congress.pdf, (October 29, 2014).
262. Andrew Frye, "Munger Says `Thank God' U.S. Opted for Bailouts Over Handouts," http://www.bloomberg.com/news/2010-09-20/berkshire-s-munger-says-cash-strapped-should-suck-it-in-not-get-bailout.html, *Bloomberg News* (September 20, 2010).
263. Stephen Moore, "A $1.2 Tril Corporate Welfare State Lurks In U.S. Budget," *Investor's Business Daily*, http://news.investors.com/ibd-editorials-brain-trust/031414-693376-corporate-welfare-to-fortune-500-is-exposed.htm (March 14, 2014).
264. David Sirota, "The Real Welfare Queens," http://inthesetimes.com/arti-

cle/16362/the_real_welfare_queens *In These Times* (February 28, 2014).
265. Tax Policy Center, "Tax Facts: Present Value of Selected Tax Expenditures, 2011," http://www.taxpolicycenter.org/taxfacts/displayafact.cfm?Docid=615 (Urban Institute/Brookings Institution, March 15, 2013).
266. Tax Policy Center, "Tax Facts: Historical EITC Receipts—Earned Income Tax Credit: Number of Recipients and Amount of Credit, 1975-2010," http://www.taxpolicycenter.org/taxfacts/displayafact.cfm?Docid=37 (Urban Institute/Brookings Institution, November 20, 2012).
267. Carl Davis, "Tax Incentives: Costly for States, Drag on the Nation," http://www.itep.org/pdf/taxincentiveeffectiveness.pdf (Washington, DC: Institute on Taxation and Economic Policy, August 12, 2013).
268. Alan Peters and Peter Fisher, "The Failures of Economic Development Incentives," http://www.crcworks.org/cfscced/fisher.pdf *Journal of the American Planning Association* (70:1, Winter, 2004), 27-37.
269. Philip Mattera, *Subsidizing the Corporate One Percent: Subsidy Tracker 2.0 Reveals Big-Business Dominance of State and Local Development Incentives* http://www.goodjobsfirst.org/sites/default/files/docs/pdf/subsidizingthecorporateonepercent.pdf (Washington, DC: Good Jobs First, February, 2014).
270. Michelle Alexander, *The New Jim Crow: Mass Incarceration in the Age of Colorblindness* (New York: New Press, 2012).
271. Andrea Nill-Sanchez, "Private Prisons Spend Millions On Lobbying To Put More People In Jail," http://thinkprogress.org/justice/2011/06/23/251363/cca-geogroup-prison-industry/ *Think Progress* (June 23, 2011).
272. *Criminal: How Lockup Quotas and "Low-Crime Taxes" Guarantee Profits for Private Prison Corporations* http://www.inthepublicinterest.org/article/criminal-how-lockup-quotas-and-low-crime-taxes-guarantee-profits-private-prison-corporations (In the Public Interest, 2013).
273. Alex Henderson, "9 Surprising Industries Profiting Handsomely from America's Insane Prison System," http://www.alternet.org/news-amp-politics/9-surprising-industries-profiting-handsomely-americas-insane-prison-system *Alternet* (February 18, 2015).
274. Simon McCormack, "Prison Labor Booms As Unemployment Remains High; Companies Reap Benefits," http://www.huffingtonpost.com/2012/12/10/prison-labor_n_2272036.html?utm_hp_ref=crime *Huffington Post* (December 10, 2012).
275. Beth Schwartzapfel, "Modern-Day Slavery in America's Prison Workforce," http://prospect.org/article/great-american-chain-gang *American Prospect* (May 28, 2014).
276. Jeffrey Sachs, "The Pharma Drug That Is Bankrupting America," http://www.alternet.org/drugs/pharma-drug-bankrupting-america *Alternet* (February 17, 2015).
277. Mark Clayton, "Budget hawks: Does US need to give gas and oil companies $41 billion a year?" http://www.csmonitor.com/USA/Politics/2011/0309/Budget-hawks-Does-US-need-to-give-gas-and-oil-companies-41-billion-a-year *Christian Science Monitor* (March 9, 2011).
278. Lynn Stuart Parramore, "Sh*t CEOs Say: 6 Outrageous Statements from America's Big-Mouthed Overlords," http://www.alternet.org/print/economy/sht-ceos-say-6-outrageous-statements-americas-big-mouthed-overlords *Alternet* (March 3, 2013).
279. Paritosh Bansal, "Goldman's share of AIG bailout money draws fire,"

http://www.reuters.com/article/2009/03/18/us-aig-goldmansachs-sb-idUS-TRE52H0B520090318 *Reuters* (March 18, 2009).
280.George Gilder, *Wealth and Poverty* (New York: Basic Books, 1981), 118.
281.Katy Waldman, "Americans Think They're Smarter Than Average, Especially Rich White Guy Americans," http://www.slate.com/blogs/xx_factor/2014/05/14/americans_think_they_re_smarter_than_the_average_american_rich_white_guys.html *Slate* (May 14, 2014).
282.Herbert G. Gutman and the American Social History Project, *Who Built America: Working People and the Nation's Economy, Politics, Culture and Society - Volume I* (New York, Pantheon, 1989), 286.
283.Herbert G. Gutman and the American Social History Project, *Who Built America: Working People and the Nation's Economy, Politics, Culture and Society - Volume I* (New York, Pantheon, 1989), 365-6.
284.James W. Loewen and Charles Sallis, *Mississippi: Conflict and Change* (New York: Pantheon, 1980), 141.
285.Herbert G. Gutman and the American Social History Project, *Who Built America: Working People and the Nation's Economy, Politics, Culture and Society - Volume I* (New York, Pantheon, 1989), 227-228.
286.Howard Zinn, *A People's History of the United States* (New York: Harper Perennial, 1980), 247-249.
287.Herbert G. Gutman and the American Social History Project, *Who Built America: Working People and the Nation's Economy, Politics, Culture and Society - Volume I* (New York, Pantheon, 1989), 516-7.
288.Philip F. Rubio, *A History of Affirmative Action, 1619-2000* (University Press of Mississippi, 2001).
289.Herbert G. Gutman and the American Social History Project, *Who Built America: Working People and the Nation's Economy, Politics, Culture and Society - Volume I* (New York, Pantheon, 1989), 518.
290.Herbert G. Gutman and the American Social History Project, *Who Built America" Working People and the Nation's Economy, Politics, Culture and Society - Volume I* (New York, Pantheon, 1989), 327-342.
291.James Loewen, *Lies My Teacher Told Me: Everything Your American History Textbook Got Wrong* (New York: The New Press, 1996), 203.
292.G. William Domhoff, "Wealth, Income and Power," http://www2.ucsc.edu/whorulesamerica/power/wealth.html?print *WhoRulesAmerica.net* (retrieved, September 3, 2014).
293.Les Leopold, "4 Secretive Ways Wall Street Extorts You," http://www.alternet.org/corporate-accountability-and-workplace/4-secretive-ways-wall-street-extorts-you *Alternet* (February 5, 2013).
294.Lawrence Mishel and Alyssa Davis, "CEO Pay Continues to Rise as Typical Workers Are Paid Less," http://www.epi.org/publication/ceo-pay-continues-to-rise/ *Economic Policy Institute* (June 12, 2014).
295.Lawrence Mishel and Alyssa Davis, "CEO Pay Continues to Rise as Typical Workers Are Paid Less," http://www.epi.org/publication/ceo-pay-continues-to-rise/ *Economic Policy Institute* (June 12, 2014).
296.Alan Dunn, "Average America vs the One Percent," http://www.forbes.com/sites/moneywisewomen/2012/03/21/average-america-vs-the-one-percent/ *Forbes* (March 21, 2012).

297.John Cassidy, "Forces of Divergence," http://www.newyorker.com/magazine/2014/03/31/forces-of-divergence *New Yorker* (March 31, 2014).
298.Ben Mathis-Lilley, "United States' Highest-Paid CEO Works for Company That's Never Turned a Profit," http://www.slate.com/blogs/the_slatest/2014/08/21/highest_paid_ceo_s_company_has_never_turned_profit_cheniere_energy_and_charif.html?wpsrc=slatest_newsletter *Slate* (August 21, 2014).
299.Reuters, "Billions Of Dollars In Fines Later, Jamie Dimon Gets A Raise," http://www.huffingtonpost.com/2014/01/24/jpmorgan-dimon-pay-raise_n_4656711.html *Huffington Post* (January 24, 2014).
300.Emily Cohn, "Former CEO: Executive Pay Is 'A Fraud'," http://www.huffingtonpost.com/2014/02/13/leo-hindery-ceo-pay_n_4784162.html *Huffington Post* (February 13, 2014).
301.Kim Bhasin, "Why Your Boss Is Afraid To Give You A Raise, According To One CEO," http://www.huffingtonpost.com/2014/11/04/container-store-ceo_n_6096478.html?utm_hp_ref=business *Huffington Post* (November 4, 2014).
302.Michael J. Cooper, Huseyin Gulen, and P. Raghavendra, "Performance for Pay? The Relation Between CEO Incentive Compensation and Future Stock Price Performance," http://papers.ssrn.com/sol3/papers.cfm?abstract_id=1572085 (January 30, 2013).
303.Robert Reich, "Just Imagine if People Were PaidWhat Their Work is Really Worth to Society," *Alternet*, http://www.alternet.org/labor/robert-reich-just-imagine-if-people-were-paid-what-their-work-really-worth-society (August 4, 2014).
304.Matthew Brown and Jesse Westbrook, "Clive Hedge Fund Pays Partner $34 Million After Losing Year," http://www.bloomberg.com/news/2013-05-14/clive-hedge-fund-pays-partner-33-5-million-after-losing-year.html *Bloomberg News* (May 14, 2013).
305.Ilia D. and Gwen Yu, "Higher Risk, Lower Returns: What Hedge Fund Investors Really Earn," http://ssrn.com/abstract=1354070 *Journal of Financial Economics* (July 1, 2009).
306.Robert Reich, "Just Imagine if People Were Paid WhatPaidWhat Their Work is Really Worth to Society," *Alternet*, http://www.alternet.org/labor/robert-reich-just-imagine-if-people-were-paid-what-their-work-really-worth-society (August 4, 2014).
307.Terence Channon, "Top 10: Highest-Paying Jobs in the U.S.," http://www.askmen.com/top_10/entertainment/top-10-highest-paying-jobs-in-the-us.html (accessed, February 3, 2014).
308.http://www.myplan.com/careers/top-ten/highest-paying.php
309.Robert Reich, "The Paid-What-You're-Worth Myth," *Huffington Post*, http://www.huffingtonpost.com/robert-reich/paid-what-youre-worth_b_4964290.html (March 14, 2014).
310.Neil Irwin, "As Walmart Gives Raises, Other Employers May Have to Go Above Minimum Wage," http://www.nytimes.com/2015/02/20/upshot/as-walmart-gives-raises-other-employers-may-have-to-go-above-minimum-wage.html?hp&action=click&pgtype=Homepage&module=second-column-region®ion=top-news&WT.nav=top-news&_r=4&abt=0002&abg=1 *The New York Times* (February 19, 2015).
311.Robert Reich, "The Paid-What-You're-Worth Myth," *Huffington Post*, http://www.huffingtonpost.com/robert-reich/paid-what-youre-worth_b_4964290.html (March 14, 2014).

312. Seth Hanlon, "Tax Expenditure of the Week: The Mortgage Interest Deduction," http://www.americanprogress.org/issues/open-government/news/2011/01/26/8866/tax-expenditure-of-the-week-the-mortgage-interest-deduction/ *Center for American Progress* (January 26, 2011).
313. "New Report Predicts U.S. Wealth Transfer of $59 Trillion, With $6.3 Trillion in Charitable Bequests, from 2007-2061," http://www.bc.edu/content/dam/files/research_sites/cwp/pdf/Wealth%20Press%20Release%205.28-9.pdf (Boston College, Center on Wealth and Philanthropy, May 28, 2014).
Stephen J. McNamee and Robert K. Miller, Jr., *The Meritocracy Myth* (Lanham, MD: Rowman and Littlefield, 2009), 62.
314. Stephen J. McNamee and Robert K. Miller, Jr., *The Meritocracy Myth* (Lanham, MD: Rowman and Littlefield, 2009), 64.
315. Carl Sandburg, *Abraham Lincoln* (New York: Harcourt Brace and World, 1954), 271.
316. Paul Lienert and Marilyn Thompson, "GM Didn't Fix Deadly Ignition Switch Because It Would Have Cost $1 Per Car," http://www.huffingtonpost.com/2014/04/02/gm-ignition-switch-dollar-per-car_n_5075680.html?utm_hp_ref=business, *Huffington Post* (Reuters), April 2, 2014.
317. Matt Taylor, "Wall Street Criminals are Still a Protected Class in America," http://www.vice.com/print/wall- street-criminals-are-still-a-protected-class-in-america-808 *Vice* (September 3, 2014).
318. "Going Rogue: Share Traders More Reckless Than Psychopaths, Study Shows," http://www.spiegel.de/international/zeitgeist/going-rogue-share-traders-more-reckless-than-psychopaths-study-shows-a-788462.html *Der Spiegel* (September 26, 2011).
319. Chris Hedges, "No Arrests Inside Goldman Sachs, Though We Were Arrested Outside," http://www.commondreams.org/views/2011/11/04/no-arrests-inside-goldman-sachs-though-we-were-arrested-outside, *Common Dreams*, November 4, 2011.
320. David Morris, "Sad But True: Corporate Crime Does Pay," http://www.alternet.org/sad-true-corporate-crime-does-pay *Alternet* (August 16, 2012).
321. Heather Perlberg and John Gittelsohn, "Wall Street Unlocks Profits From Distress With Rental Revolution," http://www.bloomberg.com/news/2013-12-20/wall-street-unlocks-profits-from-distress-with-rental-revolution.html *Bloomberg* (December 20, 2013).
322. Paul K. Piff, Daniel M. Stancato, Stéphane Côté, Rodolfo Mendoza-Denton, and Dacher Keltner, "Higher social class predicts increased unethical behavior," *Proceedings of the National Academy of Sciences* http://www.pnas.org/content/109/11/4086.full.pdf+html, 2012 109 (11) 4086-4091.
323. PK Piff, MW Kraus, S. Côté and D. Keltner, "Having less, giving more: the influence of social class on prosocial behavior," http://www.ncbi.nlm.nih.gov/pubmed/20649364, *Journal of Personality and Social Psychology* (November 2010) 99(5):771-84.
324. Daisy Grewal, "How Wealth Reduces Compassion," http://www.scientificamerican.com/article/how-wealth-reduces-compassion/, *Scientific American* (April 10, 2012).
325. Anne Manne, "'The A**hole Effect': What Wealth Does to the Brain," http://www.alternet.org/culture/ahole-effect-what-wealth-does-brain *Alternet* (July 9, 2014)
326. Benjamin I. Page, Larry M. Bartels and Jason Seawright, "Democracy and the Policy Preferences of Wealthy Americans," *Perspectives on Politics* 11:1, http://faculty.

wcas.northwestern.edu/~jnd260/cab/CAB2012%20-%20Page1.pdf (March, 2013).
327.Michael Inzlicht and Sukhvinder Obhi, "Powerful and Coldhearted," http://www.nytimes.com/2014/07/27/opinion/sunday/powerful-and-coldhearted.html?_r=2 *New York Times* (July 25, 2014).
328.Ohio State University, "Winning makes people more aggressive toward the defeated." www.sciencedaily.com/releases/2012/02/120229104746.htm *ScienceDaily* (February 29, 2012).
329.David Callahan, *The Cheating Culture: Why More Americans are Doing Wrong to Get Ahead* (New York: Harcourt, 2004), 20.
330.David Callahan, *The Cheating Culture: Why More Americans are Doing Wrong to Get Ahead* (New York: Harcourt, 2004), 206-210.
331.Sam Polk, "For the Love of Money," www.nytimes.com/2014/01/19/opinion/sunday/for-the-love-of-money.html?_r=1&gwh=CC266D1CAAD89F61EC4B932C3E074ABF&gwt=pay. *New York Times* (January 19, 2014).
332.Sam Polk, "For the Love of Money," www.nytimes.com/2014/01/19/opinion/sunday/for-the-love-of-money.html?_r=1&gwh=CC266D1CAAD89F61EC4B932C3E074ABF&gwt=pay. *New York Times* (January 19, 2014).
333.Bruce E. Levine, "Why do Some Americans Speak so Confidently When They Have no Idea What They're Talking About?" *Alternet*, (January 22, 2014).
334.Reuters, "Quarter Of Wall Street Executives See Wrongdoing As Key To Success: Survey," http://www.huffingtonpost.com/2012/07/10/wall-street-wrongdoing_n_1660871.html?ref=topbar *Huffington Post* (July 10, 2012).
335."Investing in Jim Cramer's Money Madness," CXO Advisory Group, http://www.cxoadvisory.com/2146/individual-gurus/measuring-money-madness/ (CXO Advisory Group, May 15, 2009); and "Jim Cramer Deconstructed," http://www.cxoadvisory.com/2809/individual-gurus/jim-cramer/ (CXO Advisory Group, June 15, 2009).
336.Bruce E. Levine, "Why do Some Americans Speak so Confidently When They Have no Idea What They're Talking About?" *Alternet*, (January 22, 2014)
337.Moshe Adler, *Economics for the Rest of Us: Debunking the Science That Makes Life Dismal* (New York: New Press, 2010),78-9.
338.Brian Miller, *State of the Dream, 2014: Health Care for Whom? Enduring Racial Disparities* (Boston: United for a Fair Economy, January, 2014): 2.
339.Tara Culp-Ressler and Adam Peck, "Without Obamacare, Families Making Under $5,000 Aren't Poor Enough For Medicaid In Some States," http://thinkprogress.org/health/2012/08/15/690761/without-obamacare-families-making-under-5000-arent-poor-enough-for-medicaid-in-some-states/ *Think Progress* (August 15, 2012).
340."Limbaugh: Requiring Coverage Of Pre-Existing Conditions Is 'Welfare,' 'Nonsense'." http://mediamatters.org/video/2013/08/08/limbaugh-requiring-coverage-of-pre-existing-con/195297 *Media Matters* (August 8, 2013).
341.Scott Kaufman, "Private probation company threatens innocent parents of dying child with jail if they don't pay court fees," http://www.rawstory.com/rs/2014/12/private-probation-company-threatens-innocent-parents-of-dying-child-with-jail-if-they-dont-pay-court-fees/ *raw Story* (December 29, 2014).
342."The New Debtor's Prisons," http://www.economist.com/node/21589903/print *The Economist* (November 16, 2013).
343."The New Debtor's Prisons," http://www.economist.com/node/21589903/print

The Economist (November 16, 2013).
344. Alicia Bannon, Mitali Nagrecha and Rebekah Diller, *Criminal Justice Debt: A Barrier to Reentry* (New York University School of Law: Brennan Center for Justice, 2010; *In for a Penny: The Rise of America's New Debtor's Prisons* (American Civil Liberties Union, October 2010);
345. *Pay the Rent or Face Arrest: Abusive Impacts of Arkansas's Draconian Evictions Law* (Human Rights Watch, 2013),1.
346. Matt Taibbi, "The $9 Billion Witness: Meet JPMorgan Chase's Worst Nightmare," http://www.rollingstone.com/politics/news/the-9-billion-witness-20141106 *Rolling Stone* (November 6, 2014).
347. Matt Taibbi, "Why Isn't Wall Street in Jail?" http://www.rollingstone.com/politics/news/why-isnt-wall-street-in-jail-20110216?print=true *Rolling Stone* (February 16, 2011).
348. Ben Protess and Jessica Silver-Greenberg, "HSBC to Pay $1.92 Billion to Settle Charges of Money Laundering," http://dealbook.nytimes.com/2012/12/10/hsbc-said-to-near-1-9-billion-settlement-over-money-laundering/?_php=true&_type=blogs&_r=0 *New York Times* (December 10, 2012).
349. Democracy Now, "Matt Taibbi: The SuperRich in America Have Become 'Untouchables' Who Don't Go to Prison," http://www.alternet.org/books/matt-taibbi-superrich-america-have-become-untouchables-america-who-dont-go-prison?page=0%2C10&paging=off¤t_page=1#bookmark *Alternet* (April 15, 2014).
350. Franklin Delano Roosevelt, "Speech at Madison Square Garden" (October 31, 1936), http://millercenter.org/president/speeches/speech-3307. As a side note, my praise here for FDRs directness in confronting the financial elites of his time—and for that matter my obvious support for the New Deal policies that were so central to the rebuilding of the American economy after the Depression—should not be mistaken for uncritical fandom of the Roosevelt presidency. FDRs decision to intern Japanese Americans was an unforgivable racist crime, which should forever complicate progressive praise for his administration. He also approved many restrictions on free speech and association during the war, more generally, and failed to push as hard on southerners in his own party (when it came to inclusion of blacks in New Deal programs) as he did the rich when it came to economic policy. While there may have been little choice at the time but to settle for what was possible, given the power of southern Senators and Congressmen, the fact that he said so little suggesting his opposition to their racism and pro-segregation stance is also an ethical stain on his presidency.
351. Xander Landen, "More cities across the U.S. consider homelessness a crime," http://www.pbs.org/newshour/rundown/homelessness-now-crime-cities-throughout-u-s/ *PBS Newshour* (July 19, 2014).
352. Dan Solomon, "San Antonio's Plan To Criminalize Giving To Panhandlers Is Drawing Fire," http://www.texasmonthly.com/daily-post/san-antonios-plan-criminalize-giving-panhandlers-drawing-fire *Texas Monthly* (September 9, 2014).
353. Brady Meixell and Ross Eisenbrey, *An Epidemic of Wage Theft Is Costing Workers Hundreds of Millions of Dollars a Year* http://www.epi.org/publication/epidemic-wage-theft-costing-workers-hundreds/ (Washington, DC: Economic Policy Institute, September 11, 2014).
354. Dana Ford, "Judge orders Texas teen Ethan Couch to rehab for driving drunk,

killing 4," http://www.cnn.com/2014/02/05/us/texas-affluenza-teen/ *CNN* (February 6, 2014).
355. Michael Martinez and Dan Simon, "Outcry as businessman gets work-release after 7 DUIs, car crash," http://www.cnn.com/2014/05/21/justice/washington-state-seven-duis-case/ *CNN* (May 22, 2014).
356. David Edwards, "Wealthy fund manager avoids felony charges after running over cyclist because of . . . wealth," http://www.rawstory.com/rs/2010/11/08/wealthy-fund-manager-avoids-felony-charges-running-cyclist/ *The Raw Story* (November 8, 2010).
357. Bruce Vielmetti, "Billionaire Johnson heir gets brief jail term in sex assault case," http://www.jsonline.com/news/crime/johnson07-b99285933z1-262145461.html *Milwaukee Journal Sentinel* (June 6, 2014).
358. David Ferguson, "Du Pont heir never completed court-ordered treatment after conviction for daughter's rape," http://www.rawstory.com/rs/2014/04/10/du-pont-heir-never-completed-court-ordered-treatment-after-conviction-for-daughters-rape/ *The Raw Story* (April 10, 2014).

CHAPTER III

1. Richard Wilkinson and Kate Pickett, *The Spirit Level: Why Greater Equality Makes Societies Stronger* (New York: Bloomsbury, 2009).
2. Stephen J. McNamee and Robert K. Miller, Jr., *The Meritocracy Myth* (Lanham, MD: Rowman and Littlefield, 2009), 67.
3. Ronald Takaki, *A Different Mirror: A History of Multicultural America* (Boston: Back Bay Books/Little, Brown and Co., 1993), 334.
4. Derrick Jensen, *The Culture of Make Believe* (New York: Context Books, 2002), 323-324.
5. "Upper Bound," http://www.economist.com/node/15908469 *The Economist* (April 15, 2010).
6. Pew Research Center, *Beyond Red Vs. Blue: The Political Typology* http://www.people-press.org/files/2014/06/6-26-14-Political-Typology-release1.pdf (June 26, 2014).
7. Imara Jones, "The Great Isolation of the 1%," *Alternet*, http://www.alternet.org/news-amp-politics/great-isolation-1 (February 12, 2014).
8. Carmen Stavrositu,"Does TV Viewing Cultivate Meritocracy?" Paper presented at the annual meeting of the International Communication Association, Sheraton Phoenix Downtown, Phoenix, AZ, May 24, 2012, http://citation.allacademic.com/meta/p_mla_apa_research_citation/5/5/5/7/7/p555778_index.html?phpsessid=e41301c471dbe00f80f2efd512c3e239 *All Academic* (September 13, 2014).
9. Rick Perlstein, *The Invisible Bridge: The Fall of Nixon and the Rise of Reagan* (New York: Simon & Schuster, 2014), Kindle Locations 195-197.
10. "Remarks by the President on Economic Growth and Deficit Reduction," http://www.whitehouse.gov/the-press-office/2011/09/19/remarks-president-economic-growth-and-deficit-reduction (September 19, 2011).
11. Ben Mathis-Lilley and Chris Wade, "Watch Barack Obama Talk About How America Is the Greatest Country on Earth in 13 Different Speeches," http://www.slate.com/blogs/the_slatest/2015/02/20/barack_obama_loves_america_and_thinks_it_s_great_video_evidence_contradicts.html?wpsrc=slatest_newsletter&sid=5388f432dd52b8e41100c960 *Slate* (February 20, 2015).

12. AP/National Opinion Research Center, "The People's Agenda: America's Priorities and Outlook for 2014," http://www.apnorc.org/PDFs/Peoples%20Agenda/AP_NORC_2014_PeoplesAgenda_Poll_Topline_FINAL_FXD.pdf (December, 2013), 6. Since large numbers of people of color would likely consider addressing racism and racial inequity to be a high priority, these numbers are especially startling. They suggest that those believing the government needs to address such matters are disproportionately black and brown, meaning that far fewer than twenty-six percent of whites would think such things to be of crucial importance.
13. Thandeka, "The Whiting of Euro-Americans: A Divide and Conquer Strategy," http://msuweb.montclair.edu/~furrg/spl/thandekawhiting.html *World: The Journal of the Unitarian Universalist Association*. Vol. XII No: 4 (July/August 1998), 14 –20.
14. Theodore Allen, *The Invention of the White Race: Volume I: Racial Oppression and Social Control* (New York, Verso, 2012).
15. Herbert G. Gutman and the American Social History Project, *Who Built America: Working People and the Nation's Economy, Politics, Culture and Society - Volume I* (New York, Pantheon, 1989), 420.
16. Corey Robin, *The Reactionary Mind: Conservatism from Edmund Burke to Sarah Palin* (Oxford University Press, 2011, Kindle Edition), 56.
17. "Letter of S.F. Hale, Commissioner of Alabama to the State of Kentucky, to Gov. Magoffin of Kentucky," (December 26, 1860), http://civilwarcauses.org/hale.htm.
18. Ronald Takaki, *A Different Mirror: A History of Multicultural America* (Boston: Back Bay Books/Little, Brown and Co., 1993), 152.
19. Herbert Hill, "Racism Within Organized Labor: A Report of Five Years of the AFL-CIO, 1955- 1960," *The Journal of Negro Education* (Vol. 30, No. 2, Spring, 1961).
20. Eric Arnesen, " 'Like Banquo's Ghost, It Will Not Down': The Race Question and the American Railroad Brotherhoods, 1880-1920," http://www.jstor.org/stable/2168390 *American Historical Review* 99 (1994), 1629.
21. W.E.B. DuBois, *Black Reconstruction in America, 1860-1880* (New York: The Free Press, 1998), 700.
22. Ronald Takaki, *A Different Mirror: A History of Multicultural America* (Boston: Back Bay Books/Little, Brown and Co., 1993), 204.
23. David R. Roediger, *The Wages of Whiteness: Race and the Making of the American Working Class* (London: Verso, 1991), 12-13.
24. Carter A. Wilson, *Racism: From Slavery to Advanced Capitalism* (Thousand Oaks California, Sage Publishing, 1996), 100-101.
25. Ronald Takaki, *A Different Mirror: A History of Multicultural America* (Boston: Back Bay Books/Little, Brown and Co., 1993), 331.
26. Derrick Bell, "Police Brutality: Portent of Disaster and Discomforting Divergence," in *Police Brutality: An Anthology*, Jill Nelson, ed. (New York: W.W. Norton, 2000), 95.
27. Ronald Takaki, *A Different Mirror: A History of Multicultural America* (Boston: Back Bay Books/Little, Brown and Co., 1993), 350.
28. Philip Perlmutter, *Legacy of Hate* (Armonk, NY: M.E. Sharpe, 1999), 121.
29. Douglas Massey and Nancy Denton, *American Apartheid: Segregation and the Making of the Underclass* (Chicago: University of Chicago Press, 1993).
30. Kenneth J. Neubeck and Noel A. Cazenave, *Welfare Racism: Playing the Race Card*

Against America's Poor (New York: Routledge, 2001).
31. Rudolph Alexander, Jr. *Racism, African Americans and Social Justice* (Lanham, MD: Rowman and Littlefield, 2005), 85.
32. Gerald Grant, *Hope and Despair in the American City: Why There are No Bad Schools in Raleigh* (Cambridge, MA: The President and Fellows of Harvard College, 2009), 17-18.
33. Tax Foundation, "U.S. Federal Individual Income Tax Rates History, 1862-2013 (Nominal and Inflation-Adjusted Brackets)," http://taxfoundation.org/article/us-federal-individual-income-tax-rates-history-1913-2013-nominal-and-inflation-adjusted-brackets (2013).
34. Premilla Nadasen, Jennifer Middelstadt and Marissa Chappel, *Welfare in the United States: A History with Documents, 1935-1996* (New York: Routledge, 2009), Kindle Location 473.
35. Premilla Nadasen, Jennifer Middelstadt and Marissa Chappel, *Welfare in the United States: A History with Documents, 1935-1996* (New York: Routledge, 2009), Kindle Location 503.
36. Kenneth J. Neubeck and Noel A. Cazenave, *Welfare Racism: Playing the Race Card Against America's Poor* (New York: Routledge, 2001).
37. Premilla Nadasen, Jennifer Middelstadt and Marissa Chappel, *Welfare in the United States: A History with Documents, 1935-1996* (New York: Routledge, 2009), Kindle Location 785-790.
38. Peter Edelman, *So Rich, So Poor: Why It's So Hard to End Poverty in America* (New York: The New Press, 2012), 20.
39. Premilla Nadasen, Jennifer Middelstadt and Marissa Chappel, *Welfare in the United States: A History with Documents, 1935-1996* (New York: Routledge, 2009), Kindle Location 1336-1341.
40. Martin Gilens, *Why Americans Hate Welfare* (Chicago: University of Chicago Press, 1999).
41. Rick Perlstein, "Exclusive: Lee Atwater's Infamous 1981 Interview on the Southern Strategy," *The Nation*, http://www.thenation.com/article/170841/exclusive-lee-atwaters-infamous-1981-interview-southern-strategy?_r=hpyr# (November 13, 2012).
42. Corey Robin, *The Reactionary Mind: Conservatism from Edmund Burke to Sarah Palin* (Oxford University Press, 2011, Kindle Edition): 50.
43. David Dante Troutt, "Why America Is Still a Deeply Racist Country," *Alternet*, http://www.alternet.org/books/why-america-still-deeply-racist-country?paging=off¤t_page=1#bookmark (January 31, 2014).
44. David Dante Troutt, "Why America Is Still a Deeply Racist Country," *Alternet*, http://www.alternet.org/books/why-america-still-deeply-racist-country?paging=off¤t_page=1#bookmark (January 31, 2014).
45. Thomas Frank, *What's the Matter With Kansas? How Conservatives Won the Heart of America* (New York: Metropolitan Books, 2010).
46. Centers for Disease Control and Prevention, "Nonmarital childbearing, by detailed race and Hispanic origin of mother, and maternal age: United States, selected years 1970-2010," http://www.cdc.gov/nchs/data/hus/2011/007.pdf (2011).
47. Brady E. Hamilton and Stephanie J. Ventura, "Birth Rates for U.S. Teenagers Reach Historic Lows for All Age and Ethnic Groups," http://www.cdc.gov/nchs/data/databriefs/db89.pdf *NCHS Data Brief, No. 89* (April, 2012).

48. U.S. Department of Health and Human Services, *Indicators of Welfare Dependence Twelfth Report to Congress* http://aspe.hhs.gov/hsp/13/Indicators/rpt.pdf (2010).
49. Algernon Austin, "Should We Be Worried About the Declining Black Marital Birth Rate?" http://www.blacknews.com/news/thora_institute101.shtml#.VBM-h1ZHSLna *Black* news.com
50. "Glenn Beck: Obama agenda driven by 'reparations' and desire to 'settle old racial scores'," http://mediamatters.org/video/2009/07/23/glenn-beck-obama-agenda-driven-by-reparations-a/152403 *Media Matters* (July 23, 2009); "Beck: 'The health care bill is reparations. It's the beginning of reparations'," http://mediamatters.org/video/2009/07/22/beck-the-health-care-bill-is-reparations-its-th/152321 *Media Matters* (July 22, 2010).
51. "Limbaugh criticizes health care reform as 'a civil rights bill' and 'reparations'," http://mediamatters.org/video/2010/02/22/limbaugh-criticizes-health-care-reform-as-a-civ/160735 *Media Matters* (February 22, 2010).
52. "The Right Attacks Health Care as 'Reparations'—Again," http://nomoremister.blogspot.com/2010/02/right-attacks-health-care-reform-as.html *No More Mister Nice Blog* (February, 2010).
53. Michael Tesler, "The Spillover of Racialization into Health Care: How President Obama Polarized Public Opinion by Racial Attitudes and Race," http://mst.michaeltesler.com/uploads/ajps11full.pdf 2010.
54. Binyamin Appelbaum and Robert Gebeloff, "Who Benefits From the Safety Net?" *Economix Blog*, (*New York Times*), http://economix.blogs.nytimes.com/2012/02/13/who-benefits-from-the-safety-net/?_php=true&_type=blogs&_php=true&_type=blogs&_r=1 (February 13, 2012).
55. Richard Myers, "Limbaugh unveils 'Baracka Claus', asserts Democrats bribe Hispanics for votes, mocks w/Feliz Navidad," http://www.dailykos.com/story/2012/11/13/1160965/-Limbaugh-unveils-Baracka-Claus-asserts-Democrats-bribe-Hispanics-for-votes-mocks-w-Feliz-Navidad *Daily Kos* (November 13, 2012).
56. Jerry Markon and Karen Tumulty, "Romney: Obama's gift giving led to loss," http://www.washingtonpost.com/politics/romney-obamas-gift-giving-led-to-loss/2012/11/14/c8d7e744-2eb7-11e2-89d4-040c9330702a_story.html?wpisrc=nl_politics *Washington Post* (November 14, 2012).
57. Ben Leubsdorf, "Sununu: Democrats won election by turning out voters who are dependent on government," http://www.concordmonitor.com/home/3140299-95/sununu-base-government-former *Concord Monitor* (December 4, 2012).
58. "Fox Business Host: Food Stamp Program Is A 'Deliberate' Effort To Buy Votes," http://mediamatters.org/video/2015/02/12/fox-business-host-food-stamp-program-is-a-delib/202508 *Media Matters* (February 12, 2015).
59. Alberto Alesina, Edward Glaeser, and Bruce Sacerdote, *Why Doesn't the U.S. Have a European-Style Welfare State?* http://scholar.harvard.edu/files/glaeser/files/why_doesnt_the_u.s._have_a_european-style_welfare_state.pdf (Harvard Institute of Economic Research, Discussion Paper 1933, November, 2001).
60. Drew Westen, "How Race Turns Up the Volume on Incivility: A Scientifically Informed Post-Mortem to a Controversy," http://www.huffingtonpost.com/drew-westen/how-race-turns-up-the-vol_b_295874.html *Huffington Post* (November 23, 2009).
61. Rick Perlstein, *The Invisible Bridge: The Fall of Nixon and the Rise of Reagan* (NY: Simon & Schuster, 2014), Kindle locations 6772-6776.

62. Suzanne Mettler, "Our Hidden Government Benefits," http://www.nytimes.com/2011/09/20/opinion/our-hidden-government-benefits.html *The New York Times* (September 19, 2011).
63. Suzanne Mettler, "Our Hidden Government Benefits," http://www.nytimes.com/2011/09/20/opinion/our-hidden-government-benefits.html *The New York Times* (September 19, 2011).
64. Malcolm Gladwell, *Outliers: The Story of Success* (New York: Little, Brown, 2008). 28-30. Interestingly, by being held out a year, these students become accelerated relative to the younger kids in their own *grade*, even though relative to other children their own *age* who started school earlier—and who are now a grade ahead of them—they do worse on so-called IQ tests. This is because the extra year of schooling enjoyed by kids whose birthdays made it logical to start them earlier gives those children a bump relative to their same-age peers who started later. In other words, an extra year of age in a given grade pays dividends at each grade level, while an extra year of schooling pays dividends at every age level. Either of these can provide a long-term edge, but given that we tend to be judged relative to others in our particular school classes, rather than age, the kids who were held out longer are the big winners. After all, they will be competing for college slots against people with whom they graduated, not against the larger pool of eighteen year olds. A sixteen year old who started school at the age of five because he or she was born in October—and who is now a junior in high school—would likely have higher IQ (for what that's worth) than another sixteen year old born in July, who was held out of school until shortly after he or she turned six, simply because the extra year of schooling will typically bring about such a result. But the first of these sixteen year olds would be competing in class with other kids, many of whom had been held back a year because they had summer birthdays, and who are now seventeen in that same junior class. Relative to *those* children—the ones against whom our first bright sixteen year old was competing for placement in advanced classes, or against whom he or she would be taking the SAT and hoping for a slot at Harvard—the higher IQ compared to some sixteen year old sophomore wouldn't do much good. In this scenario, the accelerated sixteen year old with the extra year of school will be going up against seventeen year olds who have the same amount of schooling as they, but who also have the added edge of age, maturity, and the possible presumption of greater ability by their teachers.
65. Malcolm Gladwell, *Outliers: The Story of Success* (New York: Little, Brown, 2008), 56-68.
66. Malcolm Gladwell, *Outliers: The Story of Success* (New York: Little, Brown, 2008), 52.
67. Malcolm Gladwell, *Outliers: The Story of Success* (New York: Little, Brown, 2008), 50-55.
68. Malcolm Gladwell, *Outliers: The Story of Success* (New York: Little, Brown, 2008), 55.
69. Stephen Steinberg, *The Ethnic Myth: Race, Ethnicity and Class in America.* (Boston: Beacon, 1989), 95-103.
70. Nick Hanauer, "The Pitchforks Are Coming . . . For Us Plutocrats," http://www.politico.com/magazine/story/2014/06/the-pitchforks-are-coming-for-us-plutocrats-108014.html#.VE_KwJHSJfM *Politico* (July/August 2014).
71. " 'I can't breathe': Eric Garner put in chokehold by NYPD officer – video,"

http://www.theguardian.com/us-news/video/2014/dec/04/i-cant-breathe-eric-garner-chokehold-death-video *The Guardian* (December 4, 2014).
72. Radley Balko, "But for Video: Tamir Rice Edition," http://www.washingtonpost.com/news/the-watch/wp/2014/12/02/but-for-video-tamir-rice-edition/ *Washington Post* (December 2, 2014).
73. "Ohio Walmart CCTV captures John Crawford shooting – video," http://www.theguardian.com/world/video/2014/sep/25/ohio-shooting-walmart-video *The Guardian* (September 24, 2014).
74. "Rekia Boyd Settlement: Family Of Unarmed Chicago Woman Killed By Off-Duty Cop May Get $4.5 Million," http://www.huffingtonpost.com/2013/03/10/rekia-boyd-settlement-fam_n_2849382.html *Huffington Post* (March 10, 2013).
75. David Edwards, "Texas cops go silent after retracting claim woman had gun when officer killed her," http://www.rawstory.com/2014/02/texas-cops-go-silent-after-retracting-claim-woman-had-gun-when-officer-killed-her/ *Raw Story* (February 20, 2014).
76. Travis Gettys, "Walter Scott might still be alive if police had taken another black man's claims about cop seriously," http://www.rawstory.com/2015/04/walter-scott-might-still-be-alive-if-police-had-taken-another-black-mans-claims-about-cop-seriously/ *Raw Story* (April 9, 2015).
77. David A. Graham, "The Mysterious Death of Freddie Gray," http://www.theatlantic.com/politics/archive/2015/04/the-mysterious-death-of-freddie-gray/391119/ *The Atlantic* (April 22, 2015).
78. Joseph Goldstein, "Judge Rejects New York's Stop-and-Frisk Policy," http://www.nytimes.com/2013/08/13/nyregion/stop-and-frisk-practice-violated-rights-judge-rules.html?pagewanted=all *The New York Times* (August 12, 2013).
79. Mark Berman and Wesley Lowery, "The 12 key highlights from the DOJ's scathing Ferguson report," http://www.washingtonpost.com/news/post-nation/wp/2015/03/04/the-12-key-highlights-from-the-dojs-scathing-ferguson-report/ *Washington Post* (March 4, 2015).
80. Diane Ravitch, "The Myth of Charter Schools," http://www.nybooks.com/articles/archives/2010/nov/11/myth-charter-schools/ *New York Review of Books* (November 11, 2010).
81. Mike Klonsky, "KIPP's child abuse for other people's children," http://michaelklonsky.blogspot.com/2013/12/kipps-long-record-of-child-abuse-must.html *Mike Klonsky's SmallTalk Blog* (December 12, 2013).
82. Jeff Bryant, "The Ugly Truth about Charter Schools: Padded Cells, Corruption, Lousy Instruction and Worse Results," http://www.alternet.org/education/truth-about-charter-schools-padded-cells-corruption-lousy-instruction-and-worse-results *Alternet* (January 10, 2014).
83. "James Baldwin on 'The Negro and the American Promise'," http://www.pbs.org/wgbh/americanexperience/features/bonus-video/mlk-james-baldwin/ (1963).
84. Derrick Jensen, *Endgame, Volume I: The Problem of Civilization* (New York: Seven Stories Press, 2006), 330.

RECENT AND FORTHCOMING IN THE OPEN MEDIA SERIES

Writing on the Wall
Selected Prison Writings of Mumia Abu-Jamal
Edited by Johanna Fernández

Because We Say So
By Noam Chomsky

The Violence of Organized Forgetting
By Henry Giroux

Disposable Futures
The Seduction of Violence in the Age of Spectacle
Brad Evans and Henry A. Giroux

Narrative of the Life of Frederick Douglass, an American Slave,
Written by Himself
A New Critical Edition
by Angela Y. Davis

Border Patrol Nation
By Todd Miller

Dying To Live
A Story of U.S. Immigration in an Age of Global Apartheid
By Joseph Nevins, with photography by Mizue Aizeki

Occupy the Economy
Challenging Capitalism
By Richard Wolff and David Barsamian

City Lights Books | www.citylights.com